P9-CQZ-386

The Yellow Kids

ALSO BY JOYCE MILTON

The Rosenberg File: A Search for the Truth (with Ronald Radosh)
Vicki (with Ann Bardach)

The Yellow Kids

★★★

Foreign Correspondents in
the Heyday of Yellow Journalism

Joyce Milton

■■ HarperPerennial
A Division of HarperCollins*Publishers*

Permission has generously been granted to include in this volume quotations from: Brisbane Papers, George Arents Research Library for Special Collections, Syracuse University; Crane Papers, Rare Book and Manuscript Library, Columbia University; John Berryman Papers, Manuscripts Division, University of Minnesota; Joseph Pulitzer Papers, Rare Book and Manuscript Library, Columbia University; Sylvester Scovel Papers, Division of Library and Archives, Missouri Historical Society; World Papers, Rare Book and Manuscript Library, Columbia University.

This book was originally published in hardcover in 1989 by Harper & Row, Publishers, Inc.

THE YELLOW KIDS. Copyright © 1989 by Joyce Milton. All rights reserved. Printed in the United States of America. No part of this book may be used or reproduced in any manner whatsoever without written permission except in the case of brief quotations embodied in critical articles and reviews. For information address HarperCollins Publishers, 10 East 53rd Street, New York, NY 10022.

First HarperPerennial edition published 1990.

The Library of Congress has catalogued the hardcover edition as follows:

Milton, Joyce.
   The yellow kids.

   1. Press—United States—History—19th century. 2. Press—United States—Influence—History—19th century. 3. Foreign correspondents—United States—History—19th century. 4. Journalistic ethics—United States—History—19th century. 5. Press—United States—Objectivity—History—19th century. 6. United States—History—War of 1898. 7. Klondike River Valley (Yukon)—Gold discoveries. 8. Cuba—History—Revolution, 1895–1898.   I. Title.

PN4864.M55   1989   071'.3'09034   88-45898

ISBN 0-06-016115-9

ISBN 0-06-092015-7 (pbk.)

90 91 92 93 94 FG 10 9 8 7 6 5 4 3 2 1

Contents

VIII
****
Regulars Get No Glory

Acknowledgments

EARLY IN MY SEARCH for the papers of Sylvester Scovel and his widow, Frances Scovel Saportas, I contacted scores of individuals named Scovel, Saportas, Cabanné, or Link, all surnames mentioned in Mrs. Saportas's letters to John Berryman. I would like to thank all those, too numerous to mention, who so patiently responded to my inquiries about their family tree, in particular Theodore Link, Jr., whose late father took care to preserve his aunt's papers and donate them to the Missouri Historical Society.

Special thanks are also due to Martha Clevenger of the Missouri Historical Society library, who uncomplainingly searched for and duplicated so many documents from the uncatalogued papers. Also, thanks to the staff of the Brooklyn Public Library, especially Alice James of the interlibrary loan division; Lowell W. Coolidge of the Andrews Library, the College of Wooster, Wooster, Ohio; Ken Craven of the Harry Ransom Center at the University of Texas; Al Lathrop of the University of Minnesota's Wilson Library; Kathleen Mainwaring of the George Arents Research Library, Syracuse University; Abigail Mellen and Arthur Brisbane for information about the Brisbane family; Mrs. Ralph Stallman; Eileen Simpson, whose book *Poets in Their Youth* alerted me to the existence of the Scovel-Saportas papers in the first place; Ray Mendez of New York City for his reminiscences about the Cuban view of the *Maine* disaster; Dr. Eugenie Fribourg and the American Diabetes Association; and staff members of the Cleveland Athletic Association, the Cleveland Public Library, the St. Louis *Post-Dispatch* research department, and the Bentley Historical Library of the University of Michigan.

Finally, I would like to thank my editor Terry Karten, my copy editor Cynthia Merman, and Brad Miner, without whose help and suggestions this book would never have been written.

Introduction

IN THE SUMMER of 1896, "Hogan's Alley" was the most popular cartoon comic in New York, and the most popular character in "Hogan's Alley" was the Yellow Kid. "Hogan's Alley" wasn't a comic strip—the idea of telling a story in a series of panels had yet to catch on. It was a single-frame cartoon featuring a large cast of tenement-district urchins who lampooned a different upper-class fad every week, from motorcars and golfing to the Madison Square Garden dog show. Of all the "Hogan's Alley" gang, the Yellow Kid was definitely the ringleader—impudent, hyperactive and, in the eyes of some, vaguely foreign and sinister looking. He seemed the perfect mascot for the paper he appeared in: Joseph Pulitzer's New York *World.*

Pulitzer was not yet the universally revered figure he later became. Formerly a successful publisher in St. Louis, he had left that city under a cloud of scandal after a prominent Democratic leader was shot dead in the office of his paper's managing editor. Aside from its color comics, the *World* was perhaps best known for sensational headlines like BAPTIZED IN BLOOD, LITTLE LOTTA'S LOVERS and, after 392 children died during a heat wave, the unforgettable HOW BABIES ARE BAKED.

Even Pulitzer's most respectable accomplishment, the raising of the money for the Statue of Liberty's pedestal, was not warmly appreciated by everyone. The *World* campaign had been a little too pointedly directed at the paper's immigrant constituency. At a time when immigrants were pouring into New York at the rate of one thousand a day and many native-born Americans feared that they would soon be politically disenfranchised, Pulitzer's success at organizing the foreign-born, even if only on behalf of a statue, seemed to set a dangerous precedent.

As deplorable as Pulitzer was, the most recent arrival on the New York newspaper scene was even worse. William Randolph Hearst, a Californian who had purchased the New York *Journal* in the fall of 1895, was heir to a fabulous fortune based on silver and gold mines, a rich kid whose politics were even farther to the left than Pulitzer's. Moreover, Pulitzer, however shrill and sensational, had ambitions to be an educator and opinion-maker. No one suspected him of seeking high office on his own behalf. With Hearst there was no such assurance. Hearst's admiration for the founding father of the Golden State, John C. Frémont, was well known, and there were many who suspected him of wanting to become the Frémont of Cuba—and further, of wanting that only as a stepping-stone to the White House.

One story about Hearst that everyone knows, if only from the bowdlerized version presented in the movie *Citizen Kane,* is that he sent reporter Richard Harding Davis and artist Frederic Remington to Cuba in the winter of 1896–97 to report on the rebellion against the Spanish colonial government. Remington supposedly found himself in Havana with nothing much going on. He cabled Hearst: "Everything is quiet. There is no trouble here. There will be no war. I wish to return." Hearst immediately cabled back: "Please remain. You furnish the pictures, and I'll furnish the war."

Hearst always denied sending such a telegram, and there is no proof that he did, even though it accurately reflects his views at the time. The anecdote is misleading, however, in that it conjures up the image of the power-drunk millionaire capitalist sitting in the safety of his New York office and browbeating reluctant staffers to promote a policy they did not believe in.

Few people realize that this story was first told in a spirit of approbation. Correspondent James Creelman, who included the anecdote in his 1901 memoir, *On the Great Highway,* was filled with admiration for Hearst's expansionist politics, which were solidly in the tradition of Thomas Jefferson and Andrew Jackson, and he considered the Spanish-American War one of the great triumphs of yellow journalism.

It was only through "the processes of yellow journalism," wrote Creelman, that "the conscience of the nation found its official voice." He continued:

> The time has not yet come when all the machinery employed by the American press in behalf of Cuba can be laid bare to the public. . . . Things which cannot be referred to even now were attempted.
>   . . . If the war against Spain is justified in the eyes of history [and Creelman clearly thought it would be], then "yellow journalism" deserves its place among the most useful instrumentalities of civilization. It may be guilty of giving the world a lop-sided view of events by exaggerating the importance of a few things and ignoring others, it may offend the eye by typographical violence, it may sometimes proclaim its own deeds too loudly; but it never deserted the cause of the poor and downtrodden.[1]

The heyday of yellow journalism—or, as its admirers called it, "the journalism that acts"—was a period of turmoil, both in the United States and, on a smaller scale, within the newspaper business. New technologies were raising the cost of doing business, forcing owners and publishers to compete for readers by offering a product that was more entertaining, and more simplified in its approach to the news, than ever before. At the top, the competition was exemplified by the bitter feud between Pulitzer, the eccentric idealist who read Schopenhauer, George Eliot, and Shakespeare for entertainment, and Hearst, the all-American whiz kid whose ignorance of history was exceeded only by his genius for public relations.

But the era of yellow journalism was also the beginning of

what Irvin S. Cobb called "the time of the Great Reporter." Previously, editors and publishers had been the stars of the newspaper business, while reporting was considered a grubby dead-end job, suitable mainly for self-educated boys from poor families, black sheep, and alcoholics. By the middle of the 1890s, however, reporting had become glamorous. To a large extent, this development was brought about by the celebrity correspondent Richard Harding Davis. Davis did not consider himself a member of what he called "the new school of yellow kid correspondents." Nevertheless, he created the type, both by example and through books such as his 1893 novella, *Gallegher*, which made a hero of the lowly city room copyboy. But the rising prestige of the reporter was also, in large part, a by-product of the competition for readers, which led to a bidding war for talent. Ambitious young men—and a few young women—who might in other times have gone into the professions, business, or the fine arts, were drawn to try their luck in the newspaper business.

The typical yellow kid reporter was the agnostic son of a Protestant minister, a drop-out from the genteel tradition who put his faith in science, social progress, and the superiority of American know-how, not necessarily in that order. Impetuous, daring, and resourceful, he was seldom content merely to cover the news; he set out to make it, solving murders, cracking burglary rings, going undercover to investigate conditions in prisons and insane asylums, joining the stampede to the Klondike to prospect for gold, or taking part in illegal expeditions to smuggle arms to the anti-Spanish rebels in Cuba.

Richard Harding Davis, whose attitude toward his juniors vacillated between fond admiration and condescension, caricatured the type in Albert Gordon, the protagonist of "The Reporter Who Made Himself King":

He had left Yale when his last living relative died and had taken the morning train for New York, where they had promised him reportorial work on one of the innumerable Greatest New York Dailies. He arrived at the office at noon, and was sent back over the same road on which he had just come, to Spuyten Duyvil, where a train had been wrecked and everyone of consequence to suburban New York killed. One of the old reporters hurried him to the office again with his "copy," and after he had delivered that, he was sent to the tombs to talk French to a man in Murderers' Row . . . at eight, he covered a flower show in Madison Square Garden; and at eleven was sent over the Brooklyn Bridge in a cab to watch a fire and make guesses at the losses to the insurance companies.

He went to bed at one, and dreamed of shattered locomotives, human beings lying still with blankets over them, rows of cells and banks of beautiful flowers nodding their heads to the tunes of the brass band in the gallery. He decided when he awoke the next morning that he had entered upon a picturesque and exciting career, and as one day followed another, he became more and more devoted to it. He was twenty then, and he was now twenty-three, and in that time he had become a great reporter, and had been to Presidential conventions in Hayti, Indian outbreaks on the Plains, and midnight meetings of moonlighters in Tennessee, and had seen what work earthquakes, floods, fire and fever could do in great cities, and had contradicted the President and borrowed matches from burglars. And now he thought he would like to rest a bit, and not to work again unless as a war correspondent. The only obstacle to his becoming a great war correspondent lay in the fact that there was no war.[2]

Davis's satirical portrait captures the drive and frenetic ambition of the yellow kids, who were nothing if not young men in a hurry. But it fails to do justice to their dedication. The best of these reporters were deeply committed on the issues, particularly to the proposition that the United States had a responsibility to help Cuba throw off the yoke of Spanish colonialism. They worked prodigiously—one correspondent single-handedly produced thirty thousand words of copy and took three thousand photographs during a six-week assignment in the Yukon. They did whatever was necessary to get their stories, often with little support from editors back home, who kept the correspondents on a short leash financially and all too frequently ran stories that imperiled their safety, all the while pressuring them for ever more sensational scoops.

The exploits of the yellow kids who spent the bulk of their careers working for Hearst are fairly well known, at least in outline, thanks in large part to the memoirs of such New York *Journal* veterans as James Creelman, Charles Michelson, Willis Abbot, and George Clarke Musgrave. Much less has been written about the New York *World* during this period, and few have attempted to explain why Joseph Pulitzer, a lifelong opponent of imperialism, became one of the leading supporters of the war against Spain.

The New York *World*'s roster of correspondents at one time or another included such unlikely colleagues as Stephen Crane, the self-conscious rebel and literary genius who was a hero to so many of his peers, and the ultraconservative George Rea, later a spokesman for American business interests in China. But the *World*'s most influential and colorful correspondent during this era was Sylvester Henry Scovel, the greatest yellow kid of them all. Although today Scovel's name barely rates a passing reference in journalism textbooks, he dominates this narrative as his example dominated the years 1896–98. Ralph Paine, his sometime bitter rival, called him "the buoyant and irrepressible Sylvester Scovel ... [for whom] life was one superb and compelling gesture after another." Elsewhere, Paine wrote of "Sylvester Scovel the magnificent" whose star blazed across the heavens of journalism "like a detonated meteor."[3]

Famous in his own time, Scovel is best remembered today for the incident that brought his career as a war correspondent to a dramatic finale. It was high noon, July 17, 1898, the day that Spain surrendered to U.S. forces in Cuba. Delegations from both the U.S. and Spanish armies had gathered in the courtyard in front of the governor's palace in Santiago de Cuba to mark the official transfer of power. To a solemn accompaniment of drumrolls, the flag of Spain was lowered for the last time and presented to the ranking Spanish officer, General Juan Toral. An honor guard of three young American officers had assembled on the palace roof, awaiting the signal to raise the Stars and Stripes. The Ninth Infantry regimental band stood ready, poised to play the opening notes of "Hail Columbia."

Suddenly, there was a commotion.

As Ralph Paine describes the scene in his memoir, *Roads of Adventure*:

> Beside the flagpole, there appeared the active, compact figure of the incomparable Sylvester Scovel, Special Commissioner of the New York *World*. His hand grasped the halliards of the flag.

At this spectacular moment in the histories of Spain and the United States, what was more natural and to be expected than that Scovel should be in the center of the stage?

This was journalism as his career had interpreted it. He had a flamboyant audacity which would have made him a dazzling motion-picture hero. There was only one Sylvester Scovel.

Behold him, then, defying martial edict, conspicuous upon the hoary palace roof, ready to assist in hoisting the American flag, while the commanding general and his staff glared in blank amazement. Scovel was told to come down. He paid no attention. The rude hands of soldiers pulled him down. He was tremendously indignant. The affront was unpardonable. To General Shafter himself he rushed to argue the matter, this interference, this insult to the "New York World."

The corpulent General Shafter had suffered much in Cuba and his temper was never amiable nor his language colorless. He told Sylvester Scovel to shut up or be locked up, and brushed him to one side. Sylvester Scovel swung with his good right arm and attempted to knock the head off the major-general commanding the American Army in Cuba.

It was a flurried blow, without much science behind it, and Scovel's fist glanced off the general's double chin, but it left a mark there, a red scratch visible for some days. Then, indeed, was the militant young journalist hustled away and locked up. It was an incident of war without precedent.[4]

The story of Sylvester Scovel's assault on the commanding general of the Fifth Army Corps has often been retold by authors for whom it symbolizes the vulgar, arrogant, and irresponsible conduct of the yellow press.

Some writers, like Gregory Mason, can scarcely conceal their glee over Scovel's disgrace:

Strangely enough for a Spanish town, no jail seemed to be at hand, so a resourceful subaltern conceived a much more fitting punishment for a newspaper man who loved publicity. Scovell [sic] was ordered to mount an empty pedestal and fill the place of a statue of a Spanish patriot, which the Cubans had knocked down. There, in the blazing sun, he was kept by prodding bayonets until the army could find a properly dingy dungeon for his incarceration.[5]

By 1959, when Margaret Leech came to write her popular history, *In the Days of McKinley,* the details of the anecdote had been telescoped. Although Leech, a former *World* staff reporter herself, was married to Ralph Pulitzer and thus might have been expected to recall the name of her father-in-law's star reporter, she did not identify Scovel by name or newspaper. Instead, he appears only as an "obstreperous war correspondent" in a battered derby who took a swing at the commanding general, and it is this version that has often been repeated since.

When I set out to reexamine the role of the yellow kid correspondents in Cuba, the story of how Scovel punched the general seemed a perfect counterpoint to Hearst's boast that he'd provide the war. Between them, the two anecdotes encompassed the saga of the yellow press, from the bumptious jingoism of its heyday in 1896 to its repudiation two years later by a public already disillusioned with the war.

In contrast to the anecdote about Hearst's message to Remington, the Scovel incident was abundantly documented. The confrontation took place before sixteen hundred U.S. troops and nearly one hundred correspondents. It was discussed and debated and moralized upon in hundreds of editorial columns, both in U.S. and foreign newspapers.

Then, in the course of investigating material about Stephen Crane collected in the John Berryman papers at the University of Minnesota, I happened upon a letter written by Scovel's widow, Frances Scovel Saportas. "Poor man," she muses, "that story followed him until, and after, his death. It never happened as it was told, but it was too good a story to be corrected."[6]

Tantalizingly, Mrs. Saportas never said what had really happened. Instead, she rambled on about another controversial incident involving an army general that a friend of hers, an army nurse, had happened to witness—the occasion when General Patton reportedly struck a patient in an army field hospital. *That* story, she complained, was outrageously misrepresented by "that miserable Drew Pearson." And, added the widow of the notorious yellow kid correspondent, "Scovel, Davis, and Crane would not stoop to write the kind of news *these* men dwell on. Sylvester always said he was paid so much because he *knew what not to print.*"[7]

This piqued my curiosity. What if the incident that seemed so perfectly to sum up the role of the yellow press in Cuba was not what it seemed?

Why, really, did the yellow kid punch the general?

Or did he?

When the *World* Was Young

The Go-Ahead Spirit

ON THE MORNING of October 28, 1886, the sun struggled unsuccessfully to break through the blanket of fog that had settled over New York harbor. The air was dank and leaden, and a predawn rainstorm had drenched the red, white, and blue bunting that hung from every lamppost, window ledge, and cornice in the business district, causing the red dyes to bleed a little into the white, so that the city looked as if it had been invaded overnight by an army of energetic but incompetent laundresses. It was an unpromising beginning for a civic holiday, but the people of New York were not about to let a mere act of nature spoil their jubilant mood. By seven A.M., three hours before the festivities were officially slated to begin, the streets from Madison Square south to the Battery were filled. Several thousand more revelers had crowded onto the Brooklyn Bridge, where they jostled for space for themselves and their picnic lunches, undeterred by the fact that the marvel they had come to see, the Statue of Liberty, was only intermittently visible through the heavy mist.

Uptown at Madison Square, twenty thousand people, cheerful in spite of the threatening skies, had turned out to march in the parade that would welcome Lady Liberty to New York. The marching units began with the U.S. Marine band, the Sons of Lafayette, and the New York Seventy-first Regiment National Guard, known as the "Gallant Seventy-first," and continued with the Washington Guard drill team escorting the coach used by President Washington to ride to his inauguration, followed by a delegation of Freemasons, the student body of Columbia University, various Negro bands, a scale model of the *Monitor* escorted by a young boy in a full-dress Navy uniform, volunteer firemen pulling the city's oldest fire engine, wagons carrying invalid veterans of the Grand Army of the Republic, and, finally, representatives of every conceivable organization with a Franco-American membership—among them the Alsace-Lorraine Union and three culinary societies—and marching bands playing the "Marseillaise." The procession took more than three hours to pass the reviewing stand, by which time President Grover Cleveland and the other dignitaries had already departed to catch the boats that would take them to the statue itself for the official dedication.

The ceremony on tiny Bedloe's Island had originally been planned for a small audience, with seats in the reviewing stands allotted to the usual assortment of politicians, committeemen, and business and civic leaders. However, the New York *World*'s announcement that it was hiring a boat so that its employees could watch the festivities from offshore had inspired a rush of imitators. Every seaworthy vessel in New York harbor, and some not so seaworthy, had been pressed into service for the occasion. By midmorning, millionaires' yachts, excursion steamers, fishing vessels, ferryboats, and hundreds of flag-draped rowboats and dinghys, some dangerously overloaded, were anchored in the vicinity.

Charles Bigot, covering the occasion for the Paris Press Association, was amazed at the show of popular enthusiasm: "It looks as if at this moment the entire population of the three cities [New York, Brooklyn, and Jersey City] is on the water," he wrote in his notebook. "When we arrive at Bedloe's, a hundred, two hundred ships are already grouped around us, forming a kind of floating archipelago of crowded islands; and other ships never stop coming from everywhere."[1]

Another reporter, summing up the spirit of the day, said simply, "human joy has rarely been so bright."[2]

As it was impossible to manage a traditional unveiling for a 151-foot-tall statue, the organizers of the event had compromised by having a red, white, and blue tarp—they preferred to call it a veil—draped over Liberty's eyes. This arrangement gave the statue a bizarre aspect; it looked less like a bride than a harem girl, some thought. The tarp also figured in the only major foul-up of the day. During the keynote speech of former secretary of state, Senator William Evarts, a hopeful official misinterpreted one of Evarts's extended rhetorical pauses and prematurely gave the signal for the unveiling. Sculptor Frédéric-Auguste Bartholdi, hiding in the statue's head, unloosed the ropes. The tarp fell. The cannons boomed. The assembled boats offshore tooted their horns. Senator Evarts, meanwhile, continued his remarks, speaking for another half an hour, undeterred by the fact that his audience was no longer paying the slightest attention.

However inadvertently, Evarts had contributed the one moment of the day that would be recalled in every history book. However, it was another orator, the French engineer and promoter Ferdinand de Lesseps, who made the strongest impression on those in attendance. The choice of Lesseps to make the official presentation on behalf of France had caused no little consternation among the event's New York sponsors. A few years earlier, many American investors, including some prominent members of the committee organizing the day's festivities, had purchased stock in the company formed by Lesseps to build a canal across the Isthmus of Panama. The investors had been criticized at the time for supporting a plan that would result in a transoceanic canal operating under foreign ownership. Now the project was in trouble, there were rumors of bankruptcy, and the disgruntled investors resented Lesseps for luring them into the scheme that was not only unpopular, but unprofitable.

According to Cuban journalist José Martí, who was covering the Liberty Day celebration for the New York *Sun* as well as for several Latin American papers, many spectators at the prededication parade, while hugely enjoying the celebration, were cynical not only about the presence of Lesseps but about the motives of the French in general. Circulating among the crowd, Martí heard one man, speaking of the Revolutionary War, observe mockingly that "France only helped us because her king was an enemy of England." Another remarked sarcastically that France was giving us the statue as a bribe, "so that we will let her finish the canal in peace."

Nevertheless, when Lesseps got his chance to speak, he instantly won over his audience. Eighty-one years old but still vigorous and imposing, he seemed larger than life as he stood bareheaded in the drizzle and addressed the crowd in a voice that Martí described as "resonant like bronze." Martí's heart went out to Lesseps because he was the only speaker of the day even to mention the existence of the "other America," expressing the hope that "the thirty-eight stars of North America will soon float at the side of the banners of the independent states of South America, and will form in the New World, for the benefit of all mankind, the peaceful and prolific alliance of the Franco-Latin and the Anglo-Saxon races."[3]

In the meantime, the Frenchman charmed his North American listeners with his definition of the statue's symbolism: "In landing beneath its rays, people will know that they have reached a land where individual initiative is developed in all its power; where progress is a religion....You are right, American citizens, to be proud of your 'go ahead.' You have made great headway in a hundred years thanks to that cry."[4]

Lesseps's speech got top billing in newspaper accounts of the festivities, and the editorial writers were particularly taken with this tribute to our nation's "go ahead" spirit. The phrase seemed to capture perfectly the buoyant mood of the country, the sense that progress was not only a religion, but a peculiarly American religion, inseparable from the promise of democracy.

While Lesseps, Evarts, and the "silver orator" Chauncey Depew dominated the proceedings on that first Liberty Day celebration, the true hero of the occasion sat in silence on the unvarnished pine reviewing stand. In the spring of 1886, the thirty-nine-year-old publisher Joseph Pulitzer had learned that "the big girl," as her creator Bartholdi called her, was sitting in a Rouen warehouse divided up among 210 packing crates, her shipment to the United States delayed because the American Committee for the

Statue of Liberty had been unable to raise the money to pay for the statue's pedestal. In two decades of fund-raising, the committee had received little help from New York's newspapers. James Gordon Bennett, Jr., the owner of the New York *Herald*, had advocated abandoning the Liberty project and substituting in its place a modestly scaled statue of Lafayette. The *New York Times*, in 1876, had asserted that "No true patriot can support such expenditures for a bronze female in the present state of our finances."

Pulitzer had at first pointed out in an editorial that the committee's $100,000 deficit could be eliminated with "the dash of a millionaire's pen." When no benefactor came forward, he took the challenge to his readers in an impassioned editorial:

> There is but one thing that can be done. *We* must raise the money.
> The *World* is the people's paper, and it now appeals to the people to come forward. . . . [The statue] is not a gift from the millionaires of France to the millionaires of America, but a gift of the whole people of France to the whole people of America. Take this appeal to yourself personally. . . . Let us hear from the people.[5]

No one had yet officially suggested that the statue had anything to do with immigration. Although Emma Lazarus's sonnet, "The New Colossus," had been written two years earlier, its sentiments were too controversial for the American Committee, which continued to solicit funds on the basis of the statue's significance as a symbol of Franco-American friendship. Within five months of Pulitzer's appeal, nickel and dime contributions from the *World*'s immigrant readers enabled the campaign to reach its goal. Pulitzer's effort was acknowledged by the committee, which had his name engraved on a gold rivet placed in the statue's toe, an honor he shared only with Bartholdi.

Through his efforts, the "big girl" had been transformed into a people's monument.

Pulitzer's autobiography was the typical immigrant success story in every way but one: He was not born poor. His father,

Philip Politzer, or Pulitzer, was a Jewish grain broker from Mako, Hungary. His mother, Louise (née Berger), was a Roman Catholic whose two brothers were officers in the Austro-Hungarian army. Philip Pulitzer had a heart condition, and in 1853 he sold his business and moved the family to Budapest. Joseph, six years old at the time, was educated along with his two brothers and a sister by a home tutor and in private schools. Louis, the eldest of the brothers, died shortly after the move to Budapest, and Philip Pulitzer passed away a few years later. Joseph was in his early teens when his mother remarried, and tension between him and his stepfather was probably the reason for his impulsive decision, at seventeen, to run away from home to join the army, any army.

Although he was six foot two and an excellent horseman, Pulitzer did not impress recruiters as a good candidate for the soldier's life. Nearsighted and narrow chested, a pale kid with a beak of a nose, a prominent pointy chin, and pink cheeks that flushed at the slightest provocation, he looked exactly like what he was: a middle-class bookworm. Turned down by the Austrians, by the French Foreign Legion, and by recruiters for the British Army of India in London, he eventually made his way to Hamburg, Germany, where he ran into a U.S. agent who was signing up foreign volunteers for the Union Army.

The year was 1864, and the Grand Army of the Republic was desperate for cannon fodder. Arriving in Boston in September, Pulitzer was inducted into the First Lincoln Cavalry, a regiment organized by Carl Schurz, the exiled German revolutionary who was now a Union general. Several companies of the First Lincoln were made up entirely of German-speaking volunteers, many of them career soldiers who had fought in the Revolutions of 1848. Pulitzer was assigned to one of these companies and spent the final months of the Civil War riding cavalry patrols in northern Virginia, under the command of grizzled noncoms who barked out their orders in German and took special delight in thinking up ways to torment the scholarly, high-strung, half-Jewish private.

When the war ended, Pulitzer joined the ranks of rootless, unemployed veterans. Still wearing his tattered uniform, he was pounding the streets of New York looking for work when he ventured into the lobby of French's Hotel on Park Row to get his shoes shined. He was ejected by an officious doorman, an insult to himself and his uniform that he never forgave. In despair, he sold an embroidered silk handkerchief, the last of the personal belongings he had brought with him from home, for seventy-five cents. He spent the money on a supply of food and then hopped a freight car headed for St. Louis, a city with a large German-speaking population.

In St. Louis, he spent three years drifting from one dead-end job to the next. Hired as a mule hostler he lasted only two days—"The man who has not cared for sixteen mules does not know what work and troubles are," he later reminisced.[6] Then came stints as a stevedore, a crewman on a riverboat, a hack driver, a process server and, at the height of a summer cholera epidemic, the warden of an island in the Mississippi where the Department of Health buried unclaimed bodies. He spent every spare moment at the city's Mercantile Library, studying English, reading law, and kibitzing in the chess room.

It was Pulitzer's brilliance at chess that brought him his first real opportunity. Among the intellectual Germans who frequented the Mercantile Library's chess room were Dr. Emil Preetorius and Carl Schurz, the former sponsor of Pulitzer's cavalry regiment. Determined to do something for their bright but impoverished young partner, Preetorius and Schurz found him a job as a bookkeeper in a lumberyard and eventually hired him as a reporter on their small German-language paper, the *Westliche Post.*

Pulitzer had just turned twenty-one and was attempting to disguise his hatchetlike profile with a beard. The first growth to appear was bright red and scraggly and instead of hiding his jutting chin only drew attention to it. A ferociously hard worker, he ran full tilt from one assignment to another, and as soon as he arrived at the scene of a story began firing questions at everyone in sight in rapid, heavily accented English. The reporters from the English-language press immediately nicknamed him "Joey the Jew" and, like his former comrades-in-arms, set to work thinking of ways to make the greenhorn's life miserable. Almost every day one of them would slip him an ersatz "tip," sending him on a wild-goose chase to some distant and unwelcoming corner of the city.

William Fayel, a reporter for the St. Louis *Democrat* during Pulitzer's first years in journalism, recalled that the teasing ended abruptly when the *Democrat*'s city editor, Major Gilson, noticed that his paper was being scooped regularly by a mere ethnic weekly and posted a notice ordering his reporters to spend less time "deluding" the German cub reporter and more time competing with him.

Fifteen years later, the greenhorn reporter had become the publisher of the most innovative, exciting English-language newspaper in the Middle West and a power to reckon with in Missouri politics. Along the way, he had also accumulated a modest but comfortable personal fortune and a wife, the former Washington, D.C., socialite Kate Worthington Davis, who was, of all things, a distant cousin of the former president of the confederacy, Jefferson Davis.

There is a common misconception that Pulitzer was a joyless workaholic. On the contrary, Pulitzer was an enthusiast, a man of boundless intellectual curiosity who, despite poor health, managed to live every day to the utmost. During the fifteen years when he was laying the groundwork of his career, he still found time to ride horseback, manage his own investments, and study Plato and Aristotle in the original Greek. Planning his wedding trip to Europe, and worried about having empty hours to fill, he invited his actor friend John McCullough to travel on the same ship so they could discuss Shakespeare. Surprisingly, considering this beginning, his marriage worked out well, largely thanks to Kate, who possessed a remarkable ability to accommodate her husband's eccentricities without losing either her dignity or her good humor. The Pulitzers entertained regularly and traveled extensively, and during periods when business kept Joseph working long hours at the office, he encouraged his wife to bring the children around for a visit every afternoon.

By 1880, it was becoming apparent that Pulitzer and St. Louis were not suited to each other. When Pulitzer settled in St. Louis, it was the fourth largest metropolitan area in the nation, with ambitions to become the railroad hub of the West and eventually surpass New York as a center of commerce. Fifteen years later, the city had fallen to sixth in population and had clearly lost the race for regional economic leadership to Chicago. Pulitzer never tired of reminding St. Louians that the decline was partly due to their parochial outlook; they, in turn, found his brash style increasingly uncongenial.

Pulitzer subscribed to the journalistic philosophy of his mentor Charles Dana, who once said: "I have always felt that whatever Divine Providence permitted to occur, I was not too proud to report."[7] The *Post-Dispatch* published the details of a Liggett heiress's quarrel with her family over her plans to marry a man they considered unsuitable, discussed the drinking habits of various local Protestant clergymen and, as a matter of policy, refused to pass off suicides as accidental deaths. When an operatic diva had one snort too many before a performance, the *Post-Dispatch* reviewer charged gleefully that she had come on stage FULL AS A TICK. The death of a local businessman in a downtown hotel, meanwhile, made the front page, headlined, A WELL KNOWN CITIZEN STRICKEN DOWN IN THE ARMS OF HIS MISTRESS. St. Louis was too much of a small town in spirit to forgive such candor.

The simmering resentments came to a head in the autumn of 1882 when Colonel Alonzo Slayback, a well-known attorney and Bourbon Democrat, with his friend William Clopton in tow, barged into the office of the *Post-Dispatch*'s managing editor John Cockerill to complain about a "card," or personal announcement, that had insulted his good name. The door slammed shut, there was shouting, and seconds later, reporters working in the city room heard a shot. Rushing into Cockerill's office, they found Colonel Slayback lying dead, a pistol clutched in his right hand. Despite Clopton's testimony that Slayback had been unarmed when he entered Cockerill's office, a grand jury ruled that Cockerill had shot Slayback in self-defense. Rumor had it that the gun had been planted by a loyal city room employee before the police arrived, and this was the version of events that won credence, especially among the prominent families who controlled a large percentage of the paper's advertising accounts.

The scandal left Pulitzer exhausted and depressed. His doctors recommended a long vacation in Europe, and he and Kate arrived in New York with their bags packed for a ten-week stay abroad. While they were at the Fifth Avenue Hotel waiting for their liner to sail, Pulitzer, who was supposedly to be resting in bed on doctor's orders, managed to slip out to buy himself a newspaper.

The New York *World*'s former owner was the railroad magnate Jay Gould, who had acquired the paper absentmindedly as part of a package deal that gave him control of the Texas & Pacific Railroad. Gould happened to have been a client of Alonzo Slayback's law partner, James Broadhead, but loyalty did not prevent him from selling out to Pulitzer for the hefty sum of $346,000, payable in installments over four years. As a result of this transaction, the most notorious of the robber barons became the mortgage holder of the newspaper that would make its reputation by relentless attacks on monopoly capitalism and corruption. But business was business; the contradiction bothered Gould not at all. He obligingly granted an interview for Pulitzer's inaugural edition in which he said of the paper's new look. "I like it first-rate. I think it is going to be a great success... but its new editorial tone is not to my liking. I am afraid it is going to become dangerous."[8]

Tall Enough to Spit on the *Sun*

JOSEPH PULITZER'S name has become so firmly identified with the era of yellow journalism that the modern reader, scanning a typical issue of the *World* for the first time, is likely to wonder what the fuss was about. True, the paper published more than its share of lurid crime news and assaulted its readers with shock headlines—A MOTHER'S FEARFUL DREAD and PIERCED HIS WIFE'S EYES and A CHILD FLAYED ALIVE were typical. Its notion of a science story was the "discovery" of yet another sea monster or a candidate for the title of "the world's fattest boy," a contest endlessly extended as nominees for this dubious honor kept turning up, many suggested by parents eager to see their child's name in print. Nevertheless, unlike today's tabloids, the *World* was a paper for people who read. The stories were long, the type size small, and the editorial page was packed with brief, caustic commentaries intelligible only to those well acquainted with the details of local and national political controversies. Considering that the typical *World* reader was an immigrant from

Germany or eastern Europe, with at best a few years of primary education in a language other than English, the paper assumed a level of literacy that makes today's popular press look dismayingly condescending.

Nor, certainly, can Pulitzer be accused of inventing sensational journalism. Indeed, it might be argued that the history of the free press *is* the history of sensationalism. In an authoritarian society, there can be only two versions of reality: the "official" version and gossip. The first independent papers to appear in prerevolutionary France were political broadsides whose goal was to propagate the views of the publisher and his faction. Similarly, the first American newspaper, Ben Harris's *Publick Occurrences Both Foreign and Domestick*—which appeared in August 1690, promising its readers that it would be published monthly or even more often if the "glut of occurrences" demanded it—featured in its first issue an inflammatory story about atrocities allegedly committed by the Mohawk Indians (excoriated as "miserable Salvages [*sic*]") as well a report that the king of France had been sleeping with his son's wife.

After the Revolution, party mouthpieces like Philip Freneau's *Gazette* and Benjamin Franklin Bache's *Aurora* lambasted President Washington as a would-be dictator who conducted himself "as if he were the omnipotent director of a seraglio," a thief who stole from the public treasury by overreporting his expenses, and a traitor (for making a treaty with England). Federalist papers like the *Porcupine's Gazette* and Alexander Hamilton's *Evening Post* replied in kind, accusing Thomas Jefferson of paying bribes, perjuring himself, and keeping a slave mistress, Sally Hemings. Publishers were prosecuted under the Alien and Sedition Acts, sued for libel, even beaten up by hired gangs on the streets. Ultimately, however, it was economics that forced the press to become more circumspect. By the 1830s, the typical big-city newspaper cost six cents, a price that limited its circulation to a class of readers who demanded a more sedate tone. While the free-swinging tradition was still alive, especially in the Western states, it seemed that the press was at last on the road to respectability.

No sooner had this trend been established, however, than a series of technical innovations, including the invention of the cylinder press, changed the rules of the game. Anyone with a few hundred dollars could launch a penny paper, and a few bold publishers were able to put together papers exciting enough to attract and hold a mass audience. The first to find a winning formula was James Gordon Bennett, a Scottish-born reporter who started the New York *Herald* in 1835 for a total investment of $500. Bennett sent reporters to cover crime and court proceedings, and he regularly published society news, a practice condemned as vulgar. He opened the first Washington bureau and hired a network of special correspondents to send timely reports on events in Europe and the major cities of the Americas. When the Civil War broke out, he sent forty "specials" to report the battlefield news.

Witty, idiosyncratic, and volatile, Bennett took special delight in outraging polite society. He violated the taboo against referring to undergarments by name by printing the word *petticoat,* and was denounced in return as a "pestilential scoundrel." A lapsed Catholic, he editorialized against what he called "the dogmas and driveling of the Catholic Church in the last stage of decrepitude." President Lincoln, at one time or another, was branded by the *Herald* as a "traitor," an "imbecile," and a "smutty joker," and on the eve of the Civil War, Bennett's sarcastic suggestion that the middle states ought to join the South in secession, leaving New England to enjoy its righteousness in solitude, resulted in the *Herald*'s offices nearly being burned down by an outraged mob.

Individuals who became the targets of Bennett's slashing wit sometimes resorted to physical retaliation. In 1836, James Watson Webb, owner of the rival *Courier & Enquirer,* became so outraged over a *Herald* story accusing him of profiting from the stocks he touted in his editorial columns that he attacked Bennett on the street. Striking Bennett from behind with his cane and knocking him to the ground, Webb then held his victim's jaws open and spat down his throat. Bennett, unimpressed, resumed his attacks on Webb as soon as he was well enough to return to the office. In 1850, John Graham, a defeated candidate for district attorney whose election the *Herald* had opposed, accosted Bennett on Broadway, and while Mrs. Bennett looked on, he and his two brothers flailed away at the publisher with horsewhips. In 1852, a black-powder bomb marked "For Mr. Bennett only" was delivered to the *Herald*'s offices. Henrietta Bennett eventually became so unnerved by these episodes that she moved to France, taking her children with her.

In 1867, Bennett retired, turning the *Herald* over to his French-educated son and namesake, James Gordon Bennett, Jr. An avid yachtsman and man-about-town, Jimmy Bennett had a flair for creating news as well as reporting it. He dispatched Henry Stanley to the Congo to "find" Dr. Livingstone (who had no idea that he was lost) and organized a *Herald* expedition to search for the fabled Northwest Passage. In 1877, however, Bennett's career was abruptly cut short when he committed the most notorious faux pas in the annals of New York society. While paying a New Year's Day call at the home of his sweetheart, Caroline May, he overindulged in champagne and relieved himself in the fireplace —or, according to some accounts, in the grand piano. The next day, Miss May's brother accosted Bennett on the steps of the Union Club; there was a fight, followed shortly by a duel, during which Fred May purposely fired into the air but Bennett tried (unsuccessfully) to mortally wound his opponent. Curiously, the May family was willing to forgive and forget; it was Bennett who held a grudge. Abandoning New York forever, he retreated to Paris, where he lived the life of a fabulous eccentric, drinking prodigiously, terrorizing editors from afar, and indulging his obsession with owls by dreaming up owl-related stories that inevitably received prominent coverage on the *Herald*'s front page.

Under its absentee owner, the *Herald* remained the only New York paper with a truly international outlook, unrivaled in its coverage of European events, but its place as New York's most provocative daily was taken over by Charles A. Dana's *Sun*. Dana, who purchased the *Sun* in 1869, broadened the definition of news, encouraging his reporters to dig for the human interest angle behind every story. "Make it interesting!" was Dana's motto, and he applied it to all coverage, from boxing matches to book reviews. By keeping his paper small—the *Sun* was a four-page paper for most of its history—he was able to avoid becoming dependent on advertising revenues, preserving his freedom to use his paper as a soapbox and, occasionally, as a bully pulpit.

Dana prided himself on his inconsistency, boasting that "no citizen in this town can go to bed at night with the certainty that he can foretell the *Sun*'s editorial course on any given topic."[1] He campaigned against capital punishment and in favor of keeping the public libraries open on Sundays so that working people could use them, and he published Jacob Riis's exposés of conditions in the tenements and sweatshops of the Lower East Side. But he was bitterly opposed to labor unions and condemned woman's suffrage on the grounds that it would introduce "a spitefulness that is peculiarly feminine" into political discourse, a charge hard to reconcile with his own gleeful malice. Another Dana motto, the one printed on his paper's masthead, was "The Sun Shines For All"—though not, perhaps, for Horace Greeley, whom Dana accused of being in love with his cow, or for the noted liberal minister Henry Ward Beecher, to whose affair with a parishioner the *Sun* devoted 120 columns of newsprint and 96 editorials.

As Dana became more erratic and vitriolic with age, New York opinion makers began to say, once again, that his style of personal journalism was becoming obsolete. America was growing up, and surely the country deserved a more mature, responsible press. The voice of the new era would be the revived *New York Times*, which in 1896 came under the ownership of Adolph Ochs, whose motto "It Does Not Soil the Breakfast Cloth" was eventually modified to "All the News That's Fit to Print."[2] In the meantime, the chief spokesman for journalistic responsibility was E. L. Godkin, editor of the influential small-circulation magazine, *The Nation*. Godkin's calls for more objective reporting and editorial policies that championed the public interest rather than the personal hobbyhorses of publisher-owners were hard to fault. Unfortunately, as was often overlooked by his admirers, his definition of the "public interest" invariably coincided with the interests of the educated upper middle class. Long an opponent of universal suffrage—he thought that a literacy test or property ownership ought to be a qualification for voting—he was deeply suspicious of democracy.

Pulitzer arrived in New York just as Godkin and his allies were congratulating themselves that the era of no-holds-barred journalism was finally coming to a close. Godkin defined the working class as a special interest. Pulitzer called it the "aristocracy of labor." Moreover, he made no secret of his ambition to use his popularity with immigrant workers to establish himself as a king-maker in New York Democratic politics. During the hard-fought election of 1884, when the Republicans were making an issue of the discovery that the Democrat, Grover Cleveland, had fathered an illegitimate child, Pulitzer hit back by giving front-page coverage to a comment by a member of a delegation welcoming the Republican candidate James Blaine to New York, characterizing the Democrats as the party of "rum, Romanism and rebellion."

That same evening, Blaine was feted at a campaign banquet at Delmonico's hosted by Jay Gould. The guest list read like a who's who of robber barons. The menu featured canvasback duck, terrapin à la Maryland, and the inevitable *huîtres*—no one, it seemed, ever dined at Delmonico's without lining his stomach with at least a dozen oysters. The next morning, the *World* devoted half of its front page to a Walt McDougall cartoon lampooning the banquet as "The Royal feast of Belshazzar Blaine and the Money Kings," depicting the financiers gorging themselves on the fruits and viands of monopoly capitalism.

On November 4, Grover Cleveland carried his home state, New York, by a mere 1,149 votes, giving him the winning edge in one of the closest presidential elections in American history. Pulitzer was credited with providing the margin of victory, and as has often happened in New York before and since, power, or at least the reputation of wielding power, was soon followed by social acceptance. Pulitzer's role in raising money for the Statue of Liberty the next year completed his rise to respectability. The man once known as "Joey the Jew" and "the loudest voice west of the Mississippi" was acknowledged as a civic benefactor and invited to dine at the ultra-Republican Union League Club with such sponsors of the American Committee as William Waldorf Astor and J. Pierpont Morgan, coincidentally, two of the most prominent of the "churlish millionaires" he so often excoriated his editorials.

It was the pattern of Pulitzer's life that every triumph was followed by a plunge to the depths. Within a few months of the Liberty Day festivities, Pulitzer became involved in a bitter feud with Charles Dana, whose New York *Sun* he had once praised as "without exception, the best newspaper in the world."[3] Dana, who could always sense his enemy's point of vulnerability, attacked Pulitzer not so much for being Jewish as for turning his back on his heritage. The son of a Catholic mother, Pulitzer had never considered himself a Jew and had joined the Episcopal Church after his marriage. He had done nothing dishonorable, but Dana had hit a sensitive point, and under the strain of the feud, his health, always fragile, began to deteriorate. The most dramatic warning sign came one afternoon when Pulitzer suddenly discovered that he could no longer read the print in his own newspaper. A physician diagnosed a broken blood vessel in one eye. Pulitzer was a diabetic, a condition for which there was then no treatment, and this was the first of a series of accidents to his sight that would eventually leave him almost blind.

Unfortunately, the complications of diabetes were only the beginning of Pulitzer's problems. For some months, his family and employees had been concerned about his mental state. Patience had never been one of Pulitzer's virtues, but now his moods had become truly fearsome. In the office, he would lash out with bursts of profanity so explosive and so crude that they embarrassed even veteran reporters, a breed not known for being easily shocked.

He was also becoming so abnormally sensitive to noise that everyday sounds—the crackling of paper or carriages passing in the street outside his window—caused him actual physical pain. The problem became so acute that he would spend the remainder of his life in search of a soundproof retreat. Vacationing in Europe on the advice of his doctors, he habitually rented the rooms above, below, and adjacent to the suite he was actually occupying to shield himself from noisy neighbors. In 1895, he purchased Chatwold, the Bar Harbor home he had formerly rented during the summer season, and ordered the construction of an annex, a granite-walled "tower of silence" where he could isolate himself from the domestic noises of his growing family. But despite the tower's foot-thick walls, Pulitzer complained that vibrations from the plumbing and ventilation systems in the basement jarred his nerves. In 1902, when he commissioned the firm of McKim, Mead & White to build him a new in-town residence on East Seventy-third Street, the architects were instructed to have the walls packed with mineral wool, the windows triple insulated, and the floor of Pulitzer's study specially mounted on a foundation of ball bearings, a design intended to insulate the room from external vibrations.

The exact nature of Pulitzer's "nervous affliction," as it was called at the time, remains mysterious. Writing in 1941, biographer James Barrett looked to Freudian psychology for an explanation: Pulitzer, he theorized, had been traumatized by "early hardships and persecutions," such as the abuse he suffered during stints in the cavalry and as a cub reporter. As a result he had developed a "psycho-neurosis" characterized by "a fear complex, associated with noises."[4] A later biographer, W. A. Swanberg, writing in 1967, called his subject an undiagnosed manic-depressive. This sounds more plausible; however, Pulitzer's mood swings did not fit the classic manic-depressive pattern. As one employee noted, he was the nicest man in the world every morning, and a terror by afternoon.

Another suggestion made by Swanberg, in passing, was that Pulitzer may have suffered from Gilles de la Tourette's syndrome, a condition one of whose manifestations is uncontrollable outbursts of profanity. At first glance, this would seem to be the most improbable diagnosis of all, given that the only evidence Swanberg offered was that Pulitzer sometimes interjected curses midword, creating such coinages as "inde-goddam-pendent." Pulitzer's family, secretaries, and employees always denied suggestions that he had mental problems of any sort, insisting that his swearing was nothing more than a bad habit. Nevertheless, it is true that Pulitzer exhibited many of the characteristics of a well-adapted Tourette's sufferer—a hyperactive mind and idiosyncratic sense of humor, a love of music and wordplay, and an attraction to speed and spinning objects. In fact, it is interesting to compare Pulitzer's personality with that of "witty, ticcy Ray," a Tourette's sufferer described by neurologist Oliver Sacks. Ray was a young man of outstanding intelligence and strength of character whose life "was continually in crises of one sort or another, usually caused by his impatience, his pugnacity, and his coarse and brilliant 'chutzpah.' "[5] The characterization fits Pulitzer exactly.

As his nervous symptoms became more troublesome, Pulitzer's multiple-track mind seemed to become more brilliant and acute than ever. Always a voracious consumer of the printed word, he hired secretaries to read to him for hours each day, from his favorite author, George Eliot, German philosophy, popular American, English, and French novels, Latin and Greek classics, and biographies and political memoirs, in addition to dozens of newspapers and magazines. He could recall large chunks of his reading verbatim, and when he was in a communicative mood, his talk poured forth seamlessly, moving with ease from a discourse on philosophy to the merits of a particular piano virtuoso to an analysis of local politics, always interspersed with instructions to his aides regarding his investments and minute details of the *World*'s daily operations. Setting out to compile a list of topics for editorials, he came up with eighty subjects at a single sitting. He was addicted to speed, and during his daily carriage rides he encouraged his drivers to maintain a breathtaking pace. *World* editors, who were sometimes invited along on these outings to discuss business, often found themselves scared speechless, much to Pulitzer's disgust.

Pulitzer's incessant mental activity was the despair of his physicians, one of whom was the celebrated neurologist S. Weir Mitchell, the same specialist who treated many well-known female "hysterics," including Alice James. Mitchell was one of the originators of the rest cure, almost universally recommended during the 1890s for depression and other "nervous ailments." Essentially, his theory was that a human being possessed only so much energy, and if too much were expended on mental and emotional activity, the body would inevitably suffer.

Ordered to give up books, business, and stimulating conversations on politics and the arts, everything, in short, that made his life worth living, Pulitzer understandably resisted. For this he was scolded by his physicians, his wife, and his paid companions, even as they engaged in a well-intentioned conspiracy to keep him from learning that the rest they kept urging on him would do nothing to preserve his doomed eyesight.[6] In 1890, after he suffered a detached retina in his left (formerly his "good") eye, the troublesome patient reluctantly agreed to Dr. Mitchell's advice that he retire from active control of the *World*.

In obedience to his doctors' orders, Pulitzer did not even attend the ground-breaking ceremony for his new corporate headquarters. Twenty stories tall and topped by a gleaming gilded dome, the Pulitzer Building represented a double revenge on Charles Dana and French's, the hotel from which he had been ejected when he was a homeless, hungry veteran. Two years earlier, Pulitzer had purchased the French's property and ordered the hotel demolished; the headquarters that rose in its place dwarfed Dana's plant next door, cutting off its view of the East River and making it possible, so it was said, for *World* editors to lean out their windows and "spit on the *Sun.*" Just a year after the first shovel of dirt was turned over, the Dome, as it was informally called, was complete, its 149 rental suites fully occupied, the printing plant in the basement already functioning. More amazing by today's standards, the $2.5 million project had been financed entirely out of current revenues. Announcing its move to its new headquarters, the *World* described it boastfully as "a People's Palace Without a Cent of Debt or Mortgage."

Only one thing was lacking—the physical presence of the man who had made the paper such a success. The publisher's office on the top floor had been specially designed with three enormous windows to take advantage of the magnificent East River view "stolen" from Dana. But it was a view that Pulitzer could no longer see, and his oversized desk, with its state-of-the-art telephone system with direct links to the newsroom, plant, and business offices below, was destined to remain unoccupied for the next twenty-one years.

A Climax to Recent Victories

Everybody is an artist in his line—
Editors draw salaries and gamblers draw cards.
—Outcault's Yellow Kid, November 22, 1896

ALTHOUGH OFFICIALLY RETIRED, Pulitzer could never quite bring himself to renounce the *World.* Constantly on the move in a vain search for mental peace, he divided his time among his Fifty-fifth Street townhouse (superseded in 1902 by a still-grander house uptown), Chatwold in Bar Harbor, his winter "cottage" on Jekyll Island, Georgia, and various rented homes in Europe. But wherever he went, he could not resist the temptation to keep up daily communication with the office, peppering his editors with queries, suggestions, and criticisms, all the while insisting that he expected the recipients to exercise their best independent judgment, regardless of the wishes of their boss.

Increasingly, these communications were couched in an arcane cable code of Pulitzer's own invention. Pulitzer styled himself ANDES, a name suggestive of lonely grandeur. The *World* was known as GENUINE, the managing editor as GRUESOME. For some unknown reason code words beginning with *g* predominated: Tammany Hall was GREYHOUND; rival publisher James Gordon Bennett, Jr., was GAITER; the Democratic Party was GOSLING; Theodore Roosevelt was GLUTINOUS. A typical message might warn GULCH (assistant business manager Don Seitz) to pay closer attention to the NAPOLEON (expenses) charged by distributors in order to increase the NELSON (net earnings).

With the best of intentions, Pulitzer repeatedly tried to cure himself of his interfering ways. On several occasions he designated a successor, theoretically giving him full power to run the paper, only to discover with the first political or business crisis that came along that his chosen deputy did not handle the situation exactly as he would have done. The fear that as a blind, absentee owner he might be taken advantage of led Pulitzer to divide power at the Dome among several competing fiefs. At any one time, there were two, three, four, or even more individuals who each believed he had a secret understanding with the boss: If he passed certain tests, which usually included reporting on the activities of his colleagues, he would become the heir apparent.

A perennial victim of these tactics was the paper's chief editorial writer, William Henry Merrill, an employee who had served the Boss with unquestioning loyalty for many years. Encouraging Merrill to spy on the managing editor, Pulitzer held out the tantalizing promise that Merrill would be named his successor in his will. "Please assume this hypothetical case (subject to change)," the Boss wrote in one letter, "JP dead . . . old M (Merrill) the only trustee supposed to know anything about newspapers."[1]

Another employee who suffered under the delusion that he would be Pulitzer's designee was Solomon S. Carvalho, a talented reporter and businessman who had been lured away from the New York *Sun.* Not long after arriving at the *World,* Carvalho had secured the lucrative advertising business of the city's major department stores. As a reward, in the summer of 1892, he was summoned across the Atlantic to the rented villa in the Paris suburbs where the Boss was living. An austere man who rather resembled the Russian wolfhounds he raised as a hobby, Carvalho found himself subjected to a week-long interview during which he was relentlessly grilled on his knowledge of the newspaper business, current affairs, literature, and every other topic imaginable. He returned to New York both exhausted and exhilarated. Pulitzer was the most "brilliant" intellect he had ever encountered, he declared. A few days' conversation with him was worth years of formal education. Carvalho had been given reason to believe that he had passed the Boss's test with flying colors. He had been elevated to the post of vice president and chief financial officer, with full responsibility of running the *World.*

No sooner had Carvalho begun to settle in to his role as chief executive and heir apparent, than the Boss announced that he had decided to split control of the paper between two fiefdoms. Carvalho would retain control of the business end of the operation while the editorial side would be managed by Charles H. Jones, formerly in charge of the *Post-Dispatch.* According to Don Seitz, Jones "wore whiskers in a smooth shaven vicinage and his ladylike manners were objectionable."[2] The hapless target of many practical jokes, he managed to keep his sense of humor until the *World* ran a Walt McDougall cartoon satirizing sexual hanky-panky on the Asbury Park boardwalk that featured an extremely unflattering caricature of Jones's wife.

Typically, it was a political crisis that brought an abrupt end to Jones's tenure. Pulitzer prided himself on being the scourge of the corrupt rich and the friend of the workingman. But he also revered the Constitution. No one had ever believed more devoutly in working within the system, and he could not bring himself to condone the increasingly radical tactics of labor. When the Pullman strike broke out in 1894, Jones authorized an editorial suggesting that the strikers would be within their rights to defy an injunction ordering them back to work. Carvalho loyalists were quick to alert the Boss, and Jones was transferred back to St. Louis. Within a year he and Pulitzer were wrangling in court over control of the *Post-Dispatch,* and the thankless task of representing the Boss in the grudge lawsuit fell to Carvalho, who was kept busy shuttling back and forth between New York and St. Louis while his authority at the Dome slowly but surely eroded.

No sooner had the problem of Jones been consigned to the lawyers, than another crisis arose, this one dire enough to bring Pulitzer back to New York from Bar Harbor, where he had just settled into his recently completed granite tower. In the autumn of 1895, the United States suddenly found itself on the brink of war with Great Britain. Public opinion was rabidly anti-British.

The New York *Sun* was gleefully anticipating naval engagements in the English Channel, and even the normally sedate *Tribune* had denounced those who objected to an immediate invasion of the British Isles as "peace-at-any-price cuckoos." Theodore Roosevelt, who at the time was police commissioner of New York City, expressed a popular viewpoint when he wrote to his good friend Henry Cabot Lodge, "I don't care if our seacoast cities are bombarded or not; we would take Canada."[3]

In retrospect, the cause of the fuss seems trivial. Since 1814, British Guiana and Venezuela had been engaged in a dispute over their common border. The territory involved, the Yuruari district, was site of one of the richest veins of gold in the world, not to mention vast petroleum reserves. Nevertheless, control of the Yuruari was not, on its own, an issue that would have caused the average American to call for a naval blockade of the Thames.

The disagreement loomed large because it was perceived to be part of a pattern. American politicians and economists had been saying for years that the only way out of the economic doldrums was for America to find new markets abroad. Unfortunately, other industrial nations had exactly the same idea. The decade of the 1890s saw a ferocious scramble for territory, trade concessions, and all varieties of political and economic influence in Asia, Africa, and Latin America. The untapped markets of the globe were being divvied up, and industrial countries who missed their chance now to carve out spheres of influence would be doomed to a generation of economic stagnation, even decline. In Latin America, where the real interest was control of the unbuilt trans-isthmian canal, Germany, France, and Britain, not to mention the United States, all had interests, but it was Britain that seemed most often to step on Uncle Sam's toes. In 1894, for example, the British had landed troops in Nicaragua in support of a rebellion by the Mosquito Indians, outraging the United States, which at the time was allied with the government in Managua.

Pulitzer was no isolationist, but he did subscribe to the idealistic view that the United States had a special mission in world affairs to shun the imperialistic power politics of the Old World and promote democracy among our sister states in the New. He wrote a series of editorials condemning the Cleveland administration for meddling in a dispute that was "none of our business" and warning that it was playing a dangerous game in manipulating public opinion. "Let the war idea once dominate the minds of the American people," he wrote, "and war will come whether there is cause for it or not."[4]

Not content with writing editorials, Pulitzer also sent hundreds of cables to well-known Britons, inviting the recipients to contribute messages of friendship to the *World*'s special Christmas issue. When the issue appeared it featured portraits of the Prince of Wales and Lord Salisbury under the headline PEACE AND GOOD WILL, along with pages of friendly messages responding to Pulitzer's peace sentiments.

The impact of the Christmas issue in dampening the war spirit was so great that Secretary of State Richard Olney threatened to have Pulitzer prosecuted for violating an old law against conducting "intercourse with any foreign government, with the intent to influence the conduct of any foreign government in relation to any controversy with the United States." Commissioner Roosevelt, agreeing that the Christmas issue was tantamount to treason, wrote his friend Lodge that in the event that war did break out, he was looking forward to arresting the editors of the *World:* "it would give me great pleasure to have them put in prison the minute hostilities began."[5]

In the excitement of putting together the Christmas issue, no one at the city room had wasted much time worrying about the arrival in town of William Randolph Hearst, a young California millionaire who had purchased a nearly defunct "chambermaid's paper," the *Journal,* and was editing it from a rented office on the eleventh floor of the Dome.

Earlier that fall, *World* reporters on their way to work found themselves sharing the elevators with workmen staggering under armloads of California redwood paneling intended for the renovation of the office that had formerly housed the Associated Press cable facility of the Hearst's *San Francisco Examiner.* For a few weeks the renovation job had been an office joke. The *Journal* was not a profitable paper and bets were exchanged over which would come first, bankruptcy or the hammering of the last carpenter's nail.

By December, however, the *Journal* was still on the streets, achieving a healthy circulation with a format that was a virtual copy of the _World_'s, and Hearst himself was very much in evidence, appearing for work in a plaid flannel suit, a costume that marked him forever in the eyes of the office wags as a rube.

Shortly after Christmas, Hearst's business cards began appearing mysteriously on the desks of certain key _World_ staff members, bearing a handwritten message: "Call me."

Among the first to receive a summons was Morrill Goddard, the thirtyish editor of the enormously profitable Sunday edition. The creator of the Sunday magazine, Goddard had a flair for innovative illustrated layouts and was the acknowledged master of the "crime, underwear and pseudo-science" school of journalism, a tradition still faithfully upheld by the supermarket tabloids. Goddard's idea of a science feature was a half-page article on the anatomy of the human leg, illustrated with drawings of the provocative stocking-and-garter-clad limbs of an assortment of popular actresses and showgirls. For a feature on conditions in the slums, he hired an Episcopal minister to live in a Hell's Kitchen tenement for a month. Goddard also promoted the career of the _World_'s first woman star, Nellie Bly, whose first assignment was to feign insanity to get herself committed to the asylum for poor women on Blackwell's Island. Bly's exposé was so successful that she then went incognito to investigate conditions in a sweatshop and a woman's prison, exposed the trickery of a popular mesmerist, and traveled with Buffalo Bill's Wild West Show.

Under Goddard's leadership, the Sunday _World_ had achieved a circulation of 600,000—an accomplishment for which he was being generously rewarded. Nevertheless, out of curiosity, he accepted Hearst's invitation to meet for a drink in the saloon bar of the Hoffman House, a lavishly furnished fin de siècle room complete with authentic Bouguereau nudes hung over the bar. Hearst opened the conversation, Goddard later confided to colleagues, by pulling a thick wad of bills out of his pants pocket (if these were the same plaid flannels that had caused so much mirth in the city room, they no longer looked quite so foolish) and offering a spot bonus of fifteen thousand dollars if Goddard would agree to come over to the _Journal._

Goddard nearly choked on his drink. "But I need my writers and artists," he sputtered.

"All right," agreed Hearst affably. "Let's take the whole staff."[6]

Goddard pocketed the cash, walked out of the bar, and spent the rest of the afternoon opening bank accounts all over town, convinced that he had better get the money safely salted away before Hearst came to his senses and demanded its return. But Hearst was as good as his word. A few days later, the entire Sunday staff except for one secretary decamped en masse to the *Journal*'s temporary quarters in the *Tribune* building down the street.

Flamboyant as it was, Hearst's raid on the *World*'s staff was in step with established business practice. There was no such thing as job security on a nineteenth-century newspaper. Publishers hired and fired on a whim—Pulitzer was said to have gotten rid of employees because he could not stand the way they ate soup, and James Gordon Bennett, Jr., was widely believed to promote only those editors favored by his beloved Pekingese lapdogs, a foible that led one (successful) candidate to prepare for his job interview by rubbing his face and hands with chopped liver. Editors and reporters frequently changed jobs for equally frivolous reasons. Top employees worked on the contract system and a one-year agreement was inevitably referred to as a "long-term" contract.

If Goddard's defection shocked those he left behind at the Dome, it was because the *World* was considered an exception to the rule. Despite his eccentric and often nakedly manipulative treatment of his employees, Pulitzer inspired almost fanatical loyalty. He was not merely respected, he was *venerated*, as a genius and as a man of principle.

Solomon Carvalho was so determined to hold onto Goddard and the Sunday staff that he immediately topped Hearst's offer. The prodigals returned and went to work, only to disappear again a day later when Hearst upped the ante by another 25 percent.

At this point, Pulitzer, who seemed to have a better perspective on the defection than anyone at the Dome, called a halt to the bidding war. He ordered Hearst evicted from the eleventh floor, quipping, "I will not have my building used for purposes of seduction!"[7]

Pulitzer's immediate concern was financial. The *World* had recently invested in a new technology, the benday tint-laying process, and was preparing to publish New York's first full-color Sunday comics supplement. Now it had no staff to produce its flagship edition. Moreover, the daily *Journal*, which sold for a penny, half the newsstand price of the *World*, had in a mere two months moved within thirty-five thousand copies of the *World*'s circulation. If the pattern continued with the Sunday edition, which brought in the bulk of the paper's advertising revenues, the *World* faced certain ruin.

The question was whether the *World* should allow itself to be drawn into a price war, or simply sit tight, hoping that Hearst would either run out of money or weary of publishing at a loss and raise his price. Carvalho favored the price cut. His competitive instincts had been aroused and he was willing to spend the Boss's last penny, if necessary, to beat Hearst. According to Don Seitz, business manager John Norris also strongly favored a cut. If the two-cent *World* sold an average of 185,000 copies a day, he argued, then a one-cent *World* would sell twice that. It might even sell half a million! Seitz, whose understanding of market economics was more sophisticated, wrote Norris a memo arguing that things wouldn't necessarily work out that way, but Norris refused to believe him.

On February 7, Pulitzer invited Norris and Carvalho to travel down to his Jekyll Island cottage to discuss the situation. The three men left New York in a private railroad car and by Philadelphia their argument had become so heated that Pulitzer cut short the journey and ordered the car returned to New York. Carvalho and Norris had prevailed, however, and on February 8, 1896, the *World* announced its new pricing policy, bravely calling it "a climax to recent victories."

★★★

A Young Man Who Can Scan
Every Ode of Horace

WHEN THAT FRENZIED weekend was over, the real beneficiary of Goddard's departure was Arthur Brisbane, who was named by Pulitzer to reorganize the Sunday staff. A Carvalho protégé, Brisbane was the paper's pet radical, the kid who ended every political argument by promising his colleagues that, "Come the revolution, I will take care to see that your rope is padded."

Blond and pale, with penetrating blue eyes and finely chiseled features, Brisbane seemed younger than his thirty years. His unique upbringing had infused him with a bright-eyed self-assurance and abundant confidence that whatever fate held in store for him, he could never be ordinary. As a result, he was one of those individuals destined to pass directly from the status of prodigy to middle-aged disappointment.

He was the son of Albert Brisbane, one of the founders of Brook Farm and, during the many years he lived abroad, a friend of Karl Marx. Unlike Marx, however, the Fourier socialist Brisbane

31

believed that the triumph of the working classes would come about gradually, without violent upheavals. Since he also happened to be the owner of large real estate holdings in the Genesee Valley and in downtown Buffalo, New York, he was able to experiment with various schemes for promoting scientific agriculture and cooperative food distribution.

In 1867, Albert's wife Sara died after giving birth to a son, Fowell, and Albert decided to sell his Sixty-ninth Street Manhattan townhouse and move to a farm in Plainfield, New Jersey, where he could test his ideas on health and education on his own sons. An older girl and boy, Alice and Hugo, whom Albert judged to be too spoiled by civilization to make good experimental subjects, were shipped off to their Aunt Hannah in Ohio. Arthur, age two and already nicknamed by his father "the little philosopher," and Fowell, then just four months old, were installed at Fanwood Farm with their father, where they were encouraged to grow up free and unfettered, "like young colts."

The boys never saw a barber or a doctor. For that matter, they seldom saw other children, and when they did, their long blond tresses and eccentric ways made it hard for them to fit in. They were fed according to their father's very particular ideas of nutrition, on a diet consisting solely of yogurt, salads, a little red wine diluted with water. They were given no spending money. Above all, they were forbidden to learn to read, on the ground that reading would inhibit their developing powers of independent thought. Mostly they roamed the farm, climbing trees and riding bareback on the plow horse.

Fowell, despite all his father's theories, was a frail child and a slow learner, most likely mildly retarded as the result of brain damage suffered at birth. He idolized his older brother and the two of them communicated in a private language that consisted of a series of monosyllabic code words. "When someone was talking bombastically or at all insincerely or eccentrically," Arthur later explained by way of example, "we always said, 'Zark,' in a very low, deep tone, and it seemed to express everything we meant it to mean."[1]

Arthur, who was active and outgoing, begged his father for spending money. When he was seven, he was told that he could earn his allowance by raising rabbits to sell to a wholesale meat market in the city. Albert insisted, however, that the boy come along when the rabbits were delivered to the butcher so that he could witness the result of the project. Apparently Arthur did not find this disturbing, but he staged a rebellion of sorts by using his weekly trips to the city to teach himself to read, studying the billboards and road signs he saw out the train window.

A year later, Albert married Redelia Bates, a petite, devoutly religious brunette. By now, Arthur was a secret, compulsive reader, and Redelia, not very enthusiastic about her husband's theory of child rearing, soon grew tired of snatching books out of her stepson's hands. Finally she negotiated a compromise. Arthur could read, but only if he read aloud so that Fowell would not be left out. Arthur obeyed but, he later confessed, he took out his resentment on Fowell by deliberately mispronouncing words, confusing the poor boy, who idolized his brother and imitated everything he said or did.

Redelia Brisbane also subverted her husband's system by taking the boys to church and Sunday school, the first time they had ever attended any public gathering. Arthur recalled that he and Fowell had been so isolated from their peers that they were not even conscious of being different. As far as they were concerned, the only embarrassing member of the family was their stepgrandmother, who sang in church in a loud, tremulous voice, "Al-a-a-a-s, and did my Saviour-r-r ble-e-e-d, and did my Saviour-r-r die-ya," while the boys did their best to stifle their giggles. Arthur had no idea that children were supposed to be deferential in the presence of adults, and on his first day in Sunday school, when the minister asked for hymn requests, he jumped up boldly, his hair curling down his back, and loudly demanded his favorite hymn, "Dare to be a Daniel, Dare to Stand Alone."

After this episode, Redelia presented her husband with an ultimatum: The experiment had gone on long enough; she wanted the boys put in school, where they could mix with children their own age. Albert gave in reluctantly, but only on the condition that they be sent to boarding school in France, where they would not be exposed to the materialistic values and vices of American society. Arthur and Fowell were understandably frightened at the prospect of being sent so far away, but Redelia, determined to save the children from growing up freaks, promised them that they wouldn't have to go alone. Hugo and Alice were summoned back from their aunt's and Redelia set out for Europe with all four children in tow. Fowell became ill on shipboard, and in Paris Redelia broke another of her husband's rules by taking him to a doctor.

Hugo and Alice remained in France for only a short time before returning to New York State, where Hugo died a few years later in a freak accident on the site of one of his father's construction projects. Fowell and Arthur stayed at the school for ten years. The curriculum was strong in every subject except English, which was taught by an instructor with such a shaky grasp of the fundamentals that he insisted that his students pronounce the word knife as "can' i fee." After years of such instruction, Arthur found that he could no longer speak his native tongue with any confidence; he knew the correct pronunciations in theory, but he was never sure when he might revert to his schoolboy habits.

At the age of nineteen, Arthur Brisbane returned to the United States, where he planned to enter Harvard. While passing through New York, he looked up Charles Dana, a former Brook Farm communard and an old friend of his father's. A great believer in liberal education, Dana had often declared that the ideal cub reporter was "a young fellow who knows the Ajax of Sophocles, and had read Tacitus, and can scan every ode of Horace."[2] In Brisbane he had found his ideal in the flesh, and he promptly offered him a job on the *Sun.* Brisbane accepted, on the theory that if journalism did not work out, Harvard would always be there.

In his first months at the *Sun,* Brisbane put Dana's faith in the value of classical studies to severe test. "I did not know a thing about New York," he recalled many years later. "I did not know where the Brooklyn Bridge was. And then, too, I had never written in English. For some months, I had to write first in French and then translate into English. Besides, I did not know what to say."[3]

The stilted quality of Brisbane's prose puzzled copy editors, who never caught on that he was using a pocket dictionary to translate his notes. Still, for all his liabilities, he was a fast learner. His prose had a quality of wide-eyed innocence, as if he were seeing everything for the first time—which he was—and because he asked so many obvious questions, he often got scoops that his jaded colleagues missed. Solomon Carvalho, who was a *Sun* editor at the time, took him under his wing and taught him the rudiments of the news story. Winning the confidence of his peers was more difficult. With his foreign education and odd manner of speech, Brisbane was considered if not exactly effeminate, certainly effete, and no doubt his position as Dana's golden boy did not endear him to colleagues. He decided literally to fight for acceptance, by taking boxing lessons with the New York Athletic Club pro Mike Donovan. Growing up wild "like a colt" had made Brisbane surprisingly strong and quick, and he was soon adept enough to do a little light sparring with Gentleman Jim Corbett, a feat that impressed his colleagues far more than his knowledge of Latin and French literature.

In 1888, at the age of twenty-three, Brisbane became the *Sun*'s European correspondent. Shortly after he arrived, the Jack the Ripper murders became the talk of London, and Brisbane, who was still considered rather too intellectual for the pursuit of daily journalism, surprised his editors back home by covering the crimes in all their gory particulars.

During his stay abroad he went to Chantilly, France, to report the heavyweight title match between John L. Sullivan and Charlie Mitchell. According to *Herald* correspondent James Creelman, he and Brisbane visited Mitchell in his dressing room before the fight and Brisbane inadvertently said something that prompted Mitchell to take a swing at him. Brisbane punched back, and by the time the two men were separated Mitchell had sustained a blow that left him somewhat befogged. At any rate, Sullivan soon had Mitchell on the ropes, and Brisbane's account of the match set a new standard for emotionalism in sports reporting with its bathetic description of Mitchell's manager urging his battered fighter to stay on his feet for the sake of his family, who badly needed the purse money: "Think of the kids, Charlie. Think of the dear little kids a-callin' for you at home, and a-countin' on you for bread. Think of the kids, 'n knock his ear off him and knock it off him again."[4]

Having successfully disproved the canard that he was too intellectual for the *Sun*, Brisbane was summoned home, and shortly before his twenty-fifth birthday he was appointed editor in chief of the evening edition. This was considered a remarkable vote of confidence in one so young, a signal that Dana was grooming him to take over the paper.

While establishing himself at the *Sun*, Brisbane had remained loyal to his brother, who would never be capable of taking care of himself. During Brisbane's stint in London, Fowell lived in his brother's rented home in the Seagate section of Brooklyn. Later, Brisbane purchased a farm in Hempstead, Long Island, where he lived with Fowell and his paid companion. Many weeknights, however, he stayed at his club in town. He was part of a smart social set in Manhattan that included Charles Dana Gibson, Augustus St. Gaudens, and the correspondents Stephen "Stenie" Bonsal and David Graham Phillips. The friends met several evenings a week for dinner and the theater, after which they gathered at the home of the *Sun*'s art critic, Mrs. Schuyler Van Rensselaer, to discuss painting, philosophy, and literature, sessions that often lasted until dawn.

In less serious moments, the friends enjoyed elaborate private games, including one invented by Brisbane, which was based on cats. Players got so many points for spotting a cat crossing a street, more for seeing a cat in a window, and so on. The fun, in those days when telegrams were still delivered by hand, lay in keeping one another informed of changes in their running scores. One of the friends would be at a banquet, speaking engagement, or some other stuffy event when suddenly a messenger would arrive bearing an "urgent" telegram from Brisbane: TWO CATS IN A WINDOW. TWO. UNSIGNED.

Bright, athletic, and given to extravagant gestures, Brisbane was considered one of New York's most eligible bachelors. When he decided to give a girl "a rush," he sent her not just a bouquet but a crate of American Beauty roses, never a box of candy but ten pounds of the finest Maillard chocolates. His energy seemed boundless, and he never allowed his social life to interfere with his performance at the *Sun;* after an hour or two of sleep at his club, he showed up at his office fresh and rested.

On weekends and holidays, he often visited his family's country estate in the Genesee Valley, where he went fox hunting with his three cousins, the Cary brothers, who referred to him, teasingly, as "the Enemy of Private Property." David Gray, who was a member of the Genesee Valley Hunt Club at the time, recalled

Brisbane's arrival at a dinner party given by Mrs. Samuel Howland, August Belmont's daughter, who "lived simply in the country with a butler and three or four footmen and a stable with forty horses." Brisbane, "the precursor of the parlor Bolsheviks," arrived for the evening wearing "a pink evening coat, white waistcoat and…a white tie, somewhat sketchily arranged."

The other dinner guests, remembered Gray, were "only a little more reactionary than the Grand Dukes. After the ladies left, Sam Howland had out several bottles of old Lafite, and Brisbane made the best guesses as to the years…. Everything was peaceful for a time and then, how it started I never knew, but Brisbane began telling the Club Boys what he thought of Wall Street, and how the People ought to own the gas company and the street car lines. When he stopped for a swallow of claret someone would say, 'But that isn't so.'

" 'Oh isn't it?' said Brisbane, and then would come out with a torrent of facts and figures that would bury anybody….

"Finally someone said, 'Mr. Brisbane, don't you realize that this kind of talk will bring on another French Revolution?'

" 'Whether I talk about it or not,' said Brisbane, 'it is coming. Where you want to be when it comes is a matter for each of you to decide. I have no hesitation in telling you that for myself, when the mob goes down Wall Street, I want to be marching with it— well to the rear.' "[5]

Successful, loyal to his family, and still an outspoken advocate of socialism, Brisbane, one might think, had turned out rather well by his father's criteria. But Albert Brisbane was not an easy man to please.

In 1889, when Albert accidentally learned that another *Sun* correspondent, a much older man, was getting eighty dollars a week, five dollars more than Arthur, he wrote instructing his son to go immediately to Dana and demand a raise to at least a hundred a week. At the same time, he urged Arthur to redouble his efforts to use the paper as a forum to "enlighten the American public on the real nature of the great economic movement in Europe…. The economic revolution which is coming will destroy the rotten reign of a capitalist oligarchy which lives on monopoly, privilege, spoilation, robbery and legislative suborning of corruption."[6]

Guilt and greed were the twin weapons wielded by the elder Brisbane in a correspondence that sets a standard for parental nagging. Although the family had the resources to pay for more than a few evenings on the town and oversize boxes of chocolates, Arthur was continually urged to cut his expenses. He was advised to give up dining out, worry more about his digestion, drink fourteen glasses of water a day, and consume more roughage. At the same time, his father counseled him to take on a second career to augment his income: Perhaps, Albert suggested, Arthur could write a potboiler and "RETAIN THE COPYRIGHT." Or take over the marketing of a version of the pneumatic tube, which Albert had invented but so far had been unable to sell to investors. Or improve the productivity of some farming property in New Jersey that was not earning as expected. In the meantime, he reminded his son, journalism was all very well as an educational experience but could be regarded only as a prelude to the "real work" of adult life.

No one could have pleased such a father, so it is not surprising that Brisbane spent his life searching for a mentor who could offer the approval he craved. Dana, aging and personally remote, did not offer the assurances about his future that Brisbane hoped for, and by 1890 the *Sun* was so burdened by debt that its very survival was in doubt. Brisbane decided to follow his friend Carvalho across the street to the *World*, where he found in Pulitzer a more worthy hero.

Pulitzer, in turn, took a fatherly interest in Brisbane. Pulitzer always appreciated a skillful raconteur. "Tell me a story" was his first demand of any new visitor, but it was not easy to tell him something he had not already heard. Brisbane was one of the few who could manage consistently to amuse the Boss. He knew French literature and Parisian gutter slang, society gossip and boxing lore; from his father he had acquired a repertoire of anecdotes about Brook Farm and the leaders of the Paris Commune.

Brisbane had the ability to draw Pulitzer out of his worst depressions, and on Pulitzer's part, there seems to have been a certain satisfaction in having stolen away the protégé of his bitter enemy, Dana. He gave Brisbane the code name HORACE, an allusion to Dana's characterization of the ideal reporter. Soon after joining the *World*, Brisbane convinced Pulitzer that despite his near blindness he could still enjoy his favorite exercise of horseback riding. "Once a cavalryman, always a cavalryman," he assured the Boss, and from then on, whenever Pulitzer was in town, he and Brisbane met for a morning trot around the bridle paths of Central Park.

Considering that there were employees who joined the *World* in 1890 or later who had never so much as *seen* Pulitzer, Brisbane's almost daily meetings with the Boss were bound to be interpreted as a sign that he had become virtually a surrogate son. Brisbane himself was slow to realize that Pulitzer's enjoyment of his company did not necessarily mean that the Boss was grooming him as his successor. During his first five years at the *World*, he held a number of responsible posts—political reporter, editor of the Sunday edition in pre–Morrill Goddard days, and assistant business manager, during which time he secured the important Straus department store account. But none of these assignments lasted very long, and when his friend Carvalho became tied down handling the Jones/*Post-Dispatch* case, Brisbane began to realize that his own career was going nowhere. It had become evident that what Pulitzer really wanted was for Brisbane to become his personal secretary, a tiresome, dead-end job. Brisbane refused more than once, but he could not afford to ignore the Boss's summonses to Paris, Wiesbaden, Jekyll Island, Bar Harbor, or wherever to deliver briefings on the latest happenings at the Dome.

Morrill Goddard's resignation came just in time to save Brisbane from remaining a glorified errand boy. Everyone else at the *World* had accepted the premise that Goddard's genius for schlock was unique. Brisbane alone was convinced that "crime, underwear and pseudoscience" would be easy to imitate. He accepted the challenge of saving the *World*, putting together a Sunday edition, with no staff, in one week.

Pulitzer's gratitude was less than Brisbane had hoped for. The Boss had never been entirely comfortable with Goddard's brand of sensationalism, and no sooner had Brisbane's first issue gone to press than Pulitzer began bombarding him with suggestions to tone down the Sunday magazine supplement. For the forthcoming week's edition, he urged Brisbane to run a "nice interview" with General O. O. Howard, the Civil War hero and founder of Howard University, with "a nice picture" of the general on the cover. How Brisbane was to manage this without compromising circulation was his problem.

Although ignoring a direct suggestion from the Boss was simply not done, Brisbane thought his readers would be far more interested in the fate of a convicted murderess who was scheduled to become the first woman executed in New York's electric chair. He sent Kate Swan, one of the *World*'s very resourceful women reporters, up to Ossining, where she managed to ingratiate herself with the executioner, who allowed her to be photographed sitting in the electric chair wearing a Redfern gown. An etching based on this photograph ran the next week, along with an exclusive interview in which the executioner vowed, I WILL KILL NO WOMAN, a promise which, in the event, was not kept.

The same issue featured actress Pearl Etynge's confession of her "slavery to morphia" and a full-page drawing of "The Missing Head of Pearl Bryan" whose mutilated, decapitated body had been found earlier in the week. There was also a column of letters from readers who had been invited to contribute their thoughts on the topic "Why I Failed in the Battle of Life."

Brisbane had managed to out-Goddard Goddard. Newsstand circulation that week jumped by fifteen thousand and Pulitzer sent a three-word message of concession: "You were right."[7]

Fortunately for Brisbane, Richard Felton Outcault was a freelancer and had not followed the exodus to the *Journal.* Outcault's cartoon "Hogan's Alley" was the toast of New York that winter, and inaugurating the Sunday *World*'s new color comics without it would have been unthinkable.

Outcault had once aspired to be a serious painter, and when he was still in his teens Thomas Alva Edison had seen some of his work and was so impressed that he financed a year's study in Paris. When Outcault returned to New York, however, he found the artist's life hard going, and within a few years he had married and drifted into newspaper work to support his family. "Hogan's Alley" had no pretensions to seriousness; it aimed to evoke "a wild bust a'lafter," entertaining the *World*'s working-class readers by poking fun at the pretensions of the bourgeoisie.

Desperate to fill up space in his first Sunday edition, Brisbane had asked for two "Hogan's Alleys," and Outcault decided to use his second cartoon to introduce a new character, a snaggletoothed urchin in a shapeless ankle-length gown who came to be called the Yellow Kid.

The kid's gown was yellow for the simple reason that the pressroom supervisor Charles W. Saalburgh was having problems finding a nonsmear yellow ink and wanted a good test area to try out his latest formula. Outcault made the kid bald, with vaguely Asian features, no doubt intending to lampoon the yellow peril hysteria that had erupted the previous year in the wake of the Sino-Japanese war, when Kaiser Wilhelm had warned that Western civilization was about to be swallowed up by *die gelbe Gefahr.* This topical allusion was lost on the great majority of *World* readers, however. They loved the Kid for the manic gleam in his eye and the sense that wherever he appeared, mayhem could be expected to erupt at any moment.

The Yellow Kid had no greater fan than William Randolph Hearst. Unlike Pulitzer, on whom the humor of the comics was completely lost, Hearst was an avid follower of "Hogan's Alley." And he immediately fell in love with the Kid. He coveted him. His only regret was that the *Journal* as yet had no full-color presses and so was unable to publish the strip.

Unable to steal the Kid away from the *World,* Hearst did the next best thing—he mounted a campaign to publicize a *Journal* mascot he called the Yeller Feller. By the summer of 1896, America was in the midst of a bicycle craze and Hearst took advantage of the mania by organizing a coast-to-coast "Yeller Feller" relay race. The race began in San Francisco, where a cyclist dressed head to toe in yellow departed from the *Examiner* offices carrying letters from the city postmaster and, for reasons clear to no one at the time, from an obscure regular army colonel named William Rufus Shafter. The letters were passed on to other members of the relay team, who pedalled hell-bent along the right-of-way of the Southern Pacific Railroad, over the Sierras, and across the sweltering desert. The race almost came to a tragic end on the Great Plains when one participant was nearly swept away by a summer storm powerful enough to knock out a railroad bridge, but on September 7, the thirteenth day of the event, the anchorman of the team left Kingsbridge in the Bronx, headed for the *Journal*'s new headquarters on Park Row. Racing down Broadway, the cyclist attracted the attention of a squadron of bicycle police who gave chase, pursuing their quarry all the way to the reviewing stand, a Keystone Cops finish that delighted the crowds.

An event in itself, the relay race was just the opening salvo of a week-long bicycle carnival sponsored by the *Journal.* There followed a series of competitions among members of local cycling clubs culminating in a grand bicycle parade down Central Park West on September 12. Cyclists dressed as Uncle Sam, Lady Liberty, and William Jennings Bryan accompanied a procession of unwieldy, homemade floats and Hearst's own musical entry—the first, and presumably last, New York appearance of Professor Bimberg's Bicycle Mounted Band. Later, the *Journal* rented Madison Square Garden for an awards ceremony, where prizes were distributed by the beautiful if ubiquitous Anna Held, whose instinct for publicity had made her Morrill Goddard's favorite Broadway personality.

The genius of the campaign, or the idiocy of it, depending on one's point of view, was that it was a promotion without a product: There was no Yeller Feller cartoon. At least not yet.

Never had a cartoonist been so elaborately wooed, and no one was surprised when the *Journal* finally acquired its own benday machines in October and Outcault promptly defected to Hearst. Outcault made his debut with the *Journal* on the morning following a rally for William Jennings Bryan in Madison Square Garden and the paper proudly announced its kidnapping of the Kid by publishing his picture on the front page, boasting, "Look who we found wandering around Madison Square!"

But Brisbane was not about to give up the comics' trademark character so easily. The *World* had a staff artist named George Luks whose job was to draw renderings of news photographs, which the paper did not yet have the technical ability to print directly, and in an office with no shortage of practical jokers, Luks was famous for his wicked sense of humor and his ability to parody the work of his colleagues. His favorite amusement was to submit illustrations containing various disgusting and/or obscene details, always signed with someone else's name, in the hope that someday one of them would find its way into print and one of his colleagues would take the blame. Brisbane asked Luks to try his hand at imitating Outcault's work, and the result was so successful that it took a trained eye to distinguish whose work was whose.

So for a time there were two Yellow Kids. Both papers hired gangs of kids to distribute Kid posters, and soon their gap-toothed look-alike smiles stared out at New Yorkers from billboards, lamp-posts, newsstands, and even the sides of trolley cars and milk trucks. The street gangs got into the spirit of the war: Defacing the competition's posters was considered part of the job, and when rival gangs ran into each other on the street they sometimes ended up exchanging volleys of rotten tomatoes, eggs, or whatever missiles happened to be handy. Pulitzer and Hearst, meanwhile, had taken their custody battle to the courts, where both claimed copyright to the name "Hogan's Alley."

To editors of more conservative newspapers, the war of the yellow twins seemed to symbolize everything that was wrong with American journalism: New technologies had brought with them rising costs, forcing papers to compete for circulation with ever more eye-catching headlines and strident promotion campaigns. Ervin Wardman of the New York *Press* may have been the first to use the phrase, but by the end of 1896, "yellow journalism"—also called "yellow kid journalism"—had become a part of the language. Although in hindsight, historians of journalism have identified roughly half of the newspapers published in the United States as "yellow" to some degree, only Hearst and, at the *World*, Arthur Brisbane, actually embraced the label.

Even Outcault came to loathe the Yellow Kid so deeply that he pleaded, "When I die don't wear yellow crepe, don't let them put the Yellow Kid on my tombstone."[8] Outcault dropped the Kid as soon as his contract was up and a few years later, after moving on to the *Herald*, he began drawing a strip called "Buster Brown," based on the adventures of his son and the family's pet bulldog.

At the Dome, Brisbane did his best to keep the Yellow Kid furor alive by encouraging Luks to insert references to the feud in his cartoons—jokes about twins, doubles, and ringers abounded. An eternal adolescent at heart, Brisbane enjoyed running the magazine so much that his pleasure in his work was almost indecent. Charles Edward Russell, Brisbane's assistant on the Sunday edition, later recalled that Brisbane took special delight in dreaming up pseudoscience features. He subscribed to hundreds of publications from all over the world and spent every Monday morning browsing through them, searching for tales of sea monsters, wild boys raised by wolves, or lost pygmy tribes. "Ain't science wonderful!" he would snort, before dispatching a reporter to investigate yet another report of a two-headed calf or "*World*'s fattest boy." Brisbane's enthusiasm was so great that Outcault, when he was still at the *World*, took to spoofing it in his cartoons, once announcing the discovery in Hogan's Alley of a "geographical goat" whose "port side has a map of the eastern & western hemispheres," whose "starboard side [is] covered wit de map of Ireland" and whose tail "is a living image of de nort' pole." [9]

Of course, all this was far from the "real work" of attacking monopoly capitalism that Albert Brisbane had enjoined his son to pursue. Although Brisbane senior had passed away in 1890, his son still felt as keenly as ever the burden of his father's ambitions for him. To anyone who would listen, he insisted that he really disdained his job and was just marking time at the *World* while accumulating a nest egg that would eventually enable him to found a publication in which he would promote his socialist ideals.

"We were a couple of radicals in those days," reminisced Russell some years later, "and after the paper had gone to press, we would sit and talk for hours about sociological matters. Brisbane at this time was at least as radical as I was. I heard him say on many occasions that he was more than willing to sacrifice himself for the common people. In fact he declared himself willing to go to jail for them. Of course, he also wanted his job and to make as much money as possible.... Arthur radiated optimism and believed that basic social reform would soon be established." [10]

II

Filibuster Thrills

The Peanut Club

THE VENEZUELAN CRISIS dominated the headlines for a few weeks, then was abruptly forgotten. A foreign news story with far more staying power was the uprising against Spanish colonial rule that had begun in Cuba in February 1895. Among Democrats, and New York Democrats especially, Cuba was second only to Ireland as a touchstone issue. For a ward boss to be indifferent on the question of who ruled Havana was like being indifferent to the question of who ruled Dublin—unthinkable. Democratic newspaper publishers were equally passionate on the subject of Cuba Libre. Unfortunately, virtually the only source of information about the rebellion was the daily press briefing held in the law offices of Horatio Rubens, Esq., in the old New York Life Building at 66 Broadway.

Rubens was not Cuban. For that matter, he had never even visited Cuba. His connection with the island went back only to 1893 when, fresh out of Columbia Law School, he was asked by his roommate, a Cuban exile named Gonzalo de Quesada, to go to

Key West to defend a group of cigar makers who had been arrested for protesting an attempt by American factory owners to
import nonunion labor from Cuba.

Rubens's companion on this trip was the organizer, journalist,
and poet, José Martí. Jailed and banished from his homeland at
the age of sixteen for writing a letter remonstrating with a school
friend who had joined the Spanish army, Martí had been living in
exile in New York since 1881, supporting himself and his family
by working as a free-lance journalist and children's book writer
and by doing translations, among them the Spanish version of
Helen Hunt Jackson's best-selling novel *Ramona*. A slight man
with soulful eyes, a prematurely receding hairline, and a weak chin
camouflaged by an incongruously bushy mustache, Martí did not
look like a revolutionary. Too young to participate in the unsuccessful revolution that had been fought in Cuba from 1869 to
1879, he had never been under fire. Nevertheless, he was one of
those rare individuals capable of expressing a single ideal with
such utter clarity and conviction that they become its living embodiment. In his mind, the Republic of Cuba already existed fully
formed and free of the racism, class divisions, and economic stagnation that had plagued the island for so many decades. Liberation
from Spanish rule, he once wrote, would bring about "the spiritual
union of the Cuban people" and lead to the establishment of what
he called, touchingly, "sincere democracy."[1]

Arriving in Key West, Rubens and Martí found themselves
surrounded by a delegation of angry Conchs, who resented the
interference of a fancy New York lawyer in their affairs. Rubens
was mightily impressed with the quiet courage displayed by Martí
in facing down the factory owners and by the firm but tactful way
he managed to calm tempers on both sides. And on the train back
to New York, listening to the poet-organizer talk with passionate
longing of his beloved homeland Rubens experienced an epiphany. It struck him that his life so far had been petty and pointless:
"I not only sympathised with Cuba, I was aroused to an enthusiasm of potential activity which suddenly gave my life new meaning."[2]

Rubens became legal counsel to the Cuban Revolutionary
Party, which meant that he did free legal work for them. After the
outbreak of fighting in Cuba, however, he began to assume a more

prominent role. Martí, who had returned to the island to fight side by side with the Dominican-born leader of the 1869 Cuban rebellion, Máximo Gómez, was shot in a skirmish a few weeks after the fighting began. Rubens's friend, Gonzalo de Quesada, had become the party's lobbyist in Washington, and most other experienced leaders had either joined Gómez's rebels in Oriente Province or were on their way there. This left the party's affairs in New York in the hands of sixty-year-old Tomás Estrada Palma, a Quaker convert who had supported himself after arriving in the United States by running a school for Cuban-American children in Orange County, New York. "Don Thomas" was an impressive figure, a large, vigorous man whose mane of white hair made him instantly recognizable. But, as more than one reporter noted, every time he told a lie, even a small lie, he compulsively cleared his throat—a fatal flaw in a press spokesman.

Shortly after the rebellion began, Rubens became the Cubans' official spokesman, volunteering the use of his law offices as the headquarters of the provisional government in exile. Reporters who attended Rubens's daily press briefings tended not to take seriously Estrada Palma's claim to be minister plenipotentiary of the Cuban Republic. They continued to refer to the Cuban leadership by its old name, the Junta, or, jokingly, as the Peanut Club, after Rubens's habit of keeping the office well supplied with peanuts.

According to Rubens's memoirs, the reporters were not alone in thinking that there was something faintly humorous about the efforts of the Cuban conspirators. Most of the Junta officials left in New York were in their fifties or older. In their youth, they had taken potshots at Spanish soldiers. Now they were shopkeepers and small businessmen, law-abiding by habit. Typical of the group was the Brooklyn club president, Juan Fraga, an elderly cigar store owner. When a sympathetic customer who was in the construction business gave Fraga six sticks of dynamite, he packed them in a valise and set out to deliver them to Rubens's office. But on the East River ferry, a notorious haunt of sneak thieves and pickpockets, the valise was stolen. Fraga was terrified that the dynamite would be recovered by the police and somehow traced to him, and even more terrified that it wouldn't. Haunted by the fear that the explosives might blow up the wrong people, Fraga hurried to

66 Broadway and announced that he had decided to turn himself in. It took Rubens all afternoon to talk him out of it.

For a time during the summer of 1895, the Cubans had success smuggling arms by filibuster boat, but by autumn the federal authorities had identified most of the boats and individuals involved with the trade and were squeezing the network dry. On October 15, treasury agents boarded a Cuban-chartered boat carrying 12 volunteers, 100 Remington long rifles, 25 Winchesters, and 50,000 cartridges—$9,000 worth of guns and ammunition all lost to the rebels. On November 9, another boat was seized, resulting in the arrest of an experienced rebel officer and 35 volunteers, as well as the confiscation of a Hopkins cannon with 220 rounds of ammunition and another 100 Remingtons. Out of 71 officially approved filibusters launched between 1895 and early 1898, only 27 reached their destinations; 33 were intercepted by U.S. authorities and the rest were lost due to bad weather, accidents at sea, or attacks by Spanish patrol boats.

In Washington, Quesada was doing his best to persuade the Cleveland administration to recognize officially that a state of belligerency existed on the island of Cuba. It would then be legal under the Neutrality Act for Americans to sell arms to the insurgents, and the loss of expensive shipments to seizure, at least, would no longer be a problem. Quesada had an ally in Senator Wilkinson Call of Florida, where filibustering ranked as a major industry. But despite Call's help and overwhelming support in Congress, the White House had so far refused to hear Quesada's case.

In the meantime, the rebels needed to expand their base of donors to pay for the lost shipments. Fund-raising became another of Rubens's responsibilities, and he turned first of all to August Belmont, Jr., a Tammany Democrat whose father had played a role in pre–Civil War attempts to purchase Cuba from Spain. Belmont himself placed no strings on his contributions, but a few wealthy sympathizers were not so easy to please. One of them, Willie Astor Chanler, a socially prominent dilettante explorer and later a Democratic congressman from New York, "wanted a filibuster thrill," and Rubens arranged for him to leave New York disguised as a steward on board a schooner that was sailing for Bermuda, where it would rendezvous with the filibuster boat *Lauriston.* In Bermuda, Chanler was seen dining with the schooner's captain and smoking custom-rolled Cuban cigarettes, and British consular officials received a tip mistakenly identifying him as the insurgent general, Carlos Roloff. When a delegation arrived to investigate the possibility that the schooner might be engaged in gunrunning, the captain ordered Chanler to start behaving like a steward and sweep the decks. The captain had nearly succeeded in bluffing his way through the interview, when one of the officials happened to notice Chanler energetically sweeping *into* the wind.

A failure as a smuggler, Chanler returned to New York and redeemed himself by giving Rubens a letter of introduction to Tammany boss Richard Croker. Croker listened sympathetically to Rubens's appeal for a contribution, then explained apologetically that Tammany could not give very much because it had just been through a difficult election and its treasury was "depleted."

"That's fine," said Rubens, for whom the word *depleted* meant a balance of several hundred dollars at most. "We'll be happy with whatever you've got left."

Croker blanched and said he'd have to think about that.

Some days later, Rubens got a message from Croker asking him to bring a delegation from the Junta to call at Tammany headquarters. The summons touched off a minor crisis as the impoverished exiles scoured their closets and their friends' closets for something suitable to wear. On the appointed day, they showed up dressed to a man in ill-fitting black broadcloth coats. Estrada Palma's cuffs were so badly frayed that Rubens warned him to keep his hands in his pockets throughout the interview.

Whatever Croker had been expecting a group of revolutionaries to be like, this was not it. "They look like a lot of undertakers," he complained in a loud aside to a member of his office staff.[3] But Rubens had inadvertently discovered the first rule of fundraising: Never ask for too little. After more grumbling about Tammany's poverty-stricken condition, Croker sat down and wrote a check for thirty thousand dollars.

If Rubens had any qualms about what he was doing—and there is no indication that he did—he was no doubt reassured that public opinion was on his side. The conviction that there was a special relationship between the United States and Cuba went back to Thomas Jefferson, who had considered acquiring the island during the Napoleonic Wars. Nevertheless, American interest in Cuba was always motivated by a volatile combination of idealism, greed, and apprehension. For one thing, by the 1840s the cause of annexation had become intertwined with the politics of slavery. Cuba had over 400,000 black slaves as early as the census of 1841 and it was a land, moreover, where the slave trade still flourished, despite a nominal policy to the contrary. At one time or another, Southern congressmen and their Northern allies in the Democratic Party put forth various schemes to annex Cuba and immediately bring it into the Union as a slave state, or better yet, two slave states.

Cuba was also a favorite destination of the filibusters, freelance arms smugglers, and adventurers like William Walker, who had launched a private invasion of Nicaragua in 1855 and succeeded in establishing himself as dictator. The best-known Cuban filibuster was W. F. Crittenden, a West Point graduate from Kentucky, who joined with the Venezuelan Narciso López in a plot to foment an uprising in Cuba. With financial help and encouragement from Charles Dana of the New York *Sun*, López and Crittenden put together an army of about 450 men, mostly veterns of the Mexican-American War. In 1851, their expedition landed in Playitas, west of Havana. Contrary to López's predictions, there were no cheering crowds on the beach to welcome them, and no spontaneous uprisings were sparked by their example. Most of the volunteers simply wandered off into the countryside. Crittenden, who had remained behind with a party of volunteers to unload their ship, never made it off the beach.

American filibusters' activity in supplying the Cuban rebels during the rebellion of 1869–79, known as the Ten Years War, led to a number of incidents that brought the United States and Spain to the brink of war. During the last two decades of the nineteenth century, every American high school student knew of the fate of the gunrunning ship *Virginius:* Captured by the Spanish while in international waters, it was seized and its crew and passengers— 156 men, many of them American citizens—were executed by a firing squad.

As a result of the negotiations that brought an end to the Ten Years War, Spain had reluctantly agreed to emancipate Cuba's slaves, and in the United States the cause of Cuba Libre began to outgrow its base as the pet cause of Southern white supremacists. While many Southerners continued to support the Cubans for sentimental reasons, they were now joined by former abolitionists and American blacks, who idolized the mulatto insurgent general Antonio Maceo, a daring cavalryman and a self-educated scholar who was said to carry volumes of philosophy and French literature in his saddlebags. Organized labor was also strongly behind the Cuban cause, led by AFL president Samuel Gompers, who had started his career as president of the cigar-makers' union. Union Army veterans, many of whom recalled being shot at during the Civil War with Spanish-made bullets, also favored selling guns to the rebels, on the simple grounds that the time had come to return the favor.

Perhaps the strongest center of pro-Cuban activity was the business community of the industrial Midwest. The National Association of Manufacturers and trade journals such as *Age of Steel*, published in St. Louis, had been working hard to develop markets for American goods in Latin America. In contrast to the sugar magnates back East, who saw Cuba primarily as a source of cheap commodities, the Midwestern businessmen believed that the end of Spanish rule would be followed by rapid economic development, to the benefit of both Cuba and the United States.

During the fall of 1895, the Cuban-American Liberty League, a support group founded by businessman William O. McDowell, held a series of rallies in Chicago, Kansas City, Akron, Cleveland, and Philadelphia to raise money for the Junta. The Chicago rally drew two thousand supporters, and its list of sponsors reads like a roll call of patriotic, fraternal, and veterans' associations: the Union League of Chicago, the Grand Army of the Republic, the Sons of Colonial Wars, the Civil Service Reform Association, the German-American Committee, and several National Guard drill units.

A more ambitious Liberty League project, the great Cuban-American Fair, opened in Madison Square Garden in New York on May 26, 1896. For two weeks the entire floor of the Garden was filled with booths selling tropical produce, potted plants, specialty food items, Havana cigars and smoking accessories, and Cuban handicrafts. The concessions were managed by society matrons like Mrs. Barrett van Aiken, who, according to the New York

World, recruited "bevvies" of debutantes to stroll among the crowds, selling bouquets of roses. Another concessionaire was Mrs. W. H. Jennys, who presented a living tableau on the subject "Gypsy Camp in a Rocky Grotto," featuring herself as the gypsy queen attended by a half dozen Broadway showgirls. That the equation of Cubans with gypsies existed only in Mrs. Jennys's mind did not prevent the tableau from becoming one of the fair's best money-makers. For the more serious-minded, there was also an evening of lectures sponsored by the league's Women's Congress: The program featured Mrs. Ellen Miles, who described her recent trip to Nicaragua, and Miss M. E. Ford, whose address was entitled, "Mexico, Land of Mañana."

For the rally held on the opening night of the fair, the keynote speaker was General Daniel Sickles. Forty-three years earlier, during the administration of Franklin Pierce, Sickles had been the guiding spirit behind the Ostend Manifesto, one of the best-known efforts to acquire Cuba for the United States. Sickles was a flamboyant character who had lost a leg at the Battle of Gettysburg and later served as minister to Spain, though he was perhaps best known for having shot and killed his wife's lover, Philip Key, son of Francis Scott Key, on a Washington, D.C., street. Always one to speak his mind, Sickles came out strongly in favor of the eventual annexation of Cuba.

This was not the official position of the Junta, although most of the Americans in the audience probably did not realize it. Gómez and the Maceo brothers were Hispanic nationalists who considered themselves heirs of Simón Bólivar. Highly suspicious of U.S. motives, they would have preferred not to accept any help at all from the North American colossus. Ironically, however, their brothers in Latin America had proved indifferent to the Cuban cause. This left the job of paying for the war to Cubans in the United States who, not surprisingly, tended to be strongly pro-American. As a group of naturalized Cubans explained in a joint letter to the New York *Herald,* "Thousands of Cubans have joined or helped on the revolution, only because they thought and still think that independence would pave the way to annexation. If there are some who oppose it, it is because they lack a full knowledge of the American constitution and of the spirit of American institutions, and have been led to believe that annexation would mean only a change of masters."[4] Even Estrada Palma, though he did not say so publicly, secretly hoped that after the war the Cuban people, after taking a "holiday" to savor their victory over Spain, would petition the United States to take over the island.

The truth of the adage that politics makes strange bedfellows had never been more aptly demonstrated. The nationalist generals mistrusted their own minister plenipotentiary in New York, loathing the very title. American labor leaders and socialists were appalled to learn that Andrew Carnegie had become a sponsor of the Liberty League. The New York *Tribune*, meanwhile, taunted Southerners like Senator Call and Fitzhugh Lee of Virginia for supporting self-determination for black Cubans while blacks in their own states were denied the right to vote. How was it, asked the *Tribune* rhetorically, that men who never protested "the lynching of the 'nigger' in the South" were so intent on "loving the 'nigger' in Cuba. Can it be that they regard 'niggers' in Cuba more favorably than in Georgia or Mississippi?"

With the Insurgents

AMONG THE VISITORS to the Liberty League rally held in Pittsburgh in September of 1895 was a twenty-six-year-old Ohioan, Sylvester "Harry" Scovel. Until three months earlier, he had been the immensely popular general manager of the Cleveland Athletic Club, earning a more than comfortable salary promoting amateur theatricals and sports events. But he had given up the job he loved at his father's urging to go into the insurance business, only to discover that he couldn't work up any enthusiasm for what he called "the most distasteful occupation of roping all my friends into the benefits corrall of Life Insurance."[1]

Scovel had the not terribly original idea that it would be more interesting to be a writer than an insurance salesman. For several years he had been a free-lance drama critic for newspapers in Cleveland and Pittsburgh, and given his choice, he would have liked to become a playwright or a humorist in the style of Finley Peter Dunne, the creator of the Irish bartender-philosopher, Mr.

Dooley. Realistically, however, he knew that he had a better chance of breaking into the newspaper world as a foreign correspondent. The era that Irvin S. Cobb would describe as "the time of the Great Reporter"[2] was just beginning, and foreign correspondents or, as some papers preferred to call them, "traveling commissioners," were the greatest reporters of all, highly paid specialists and celebrities in their own right.

While attending the Liberty League rally it had occurred to him that there was tremendous interest in the Cuban situation but a dearth of accurate reporting. Under Spanish military law it was a crime for anyone, even a journalist, to consort with the rebels, and the handful of correspondents active in Cuba had been intimidated by the recent arrest of the New York *World*'s Manuel Fuentes, who had been jailed for attempting to obtain an interview from a local insurgent commander.

Scovel saw a chance to score a coup that would establish his reputation, but only if he moved quickly. With a stake of two hundred dollars, he arrived in New York on October 4 and presented himself at the headquarters of the New York *Herald*, the paper best known for coverage of international affairs, where an editor named Taylor listened to his plans and told him that if he were able to smuggle news dispatches out of Cuba the *Herald* would certainly be interested in publishing them at the rate of twenty-four dollars per column. This was good enough for Scovel: He turned up later that afternoon at Horatio Rubens's office to ask for advice on reaching the rebels.

Rubens took the aspiring correspondent out to dinner and outlined the reasons why going to Cuba was a foolish idea. Aside from the fact that Scovel spoke no Spanish, even if he managed to evade arrest there was no guarantee that the insurgent commander Máximo Gómez would welcome the arrival of an American reporter.

Quite possibly, Rubens may also have suspected Scovel of being a spy. As he well knew, the Spanish Mission in Washington had hired Pinkerton detectives to infiltrate the filibuster network, and Scovel's lack of experience as a reporter raised doubts about his true intentions. At any rate, Rubens did not suggest putting Scovel on board a Junta mission to Cuba, but by the end of dinner he was sufficiently convinced to go back to the residential hotel overlooking Gramercy Park where he lived and write a letter of introduction to Gómez on Junta stationery.

A week later, Rubens recalled in his memoirs, Scovel again showed up in his office. Upon arriving in Havana by passenger steamer, he had been challenged by Customs officials who detained him for questioning. Scovel laughingly described how he had managed to shred Rubens's letter and swallow the pieces before the police arrived to interrogate him.

Far from being discouraged, Scovel insisted that he planned to try again. But this time, he joked, he wanted no part of a letter of introduction, "even if it was written on bond paper. I'd rather rely on my wits than risk choking to death."[3]

Rubens suggested that Scovel try taking the steamer *Niagara* to Cienfuegos on the southern coast, where the authorities were likely to be less rigorous about checking the credentials of American visitors, and he offered the name and address of a Cuban contact who was in secret communication with the insurgents. He wished Scovel luck and shook his hand—and that was the last he heard of him for three months. Scovel never got in touch with the Junta's network in Cienfuegos and neither the *Herald* nor his family ever reported him missing, all of which must have led Rubens to wonder whether the talkative volunteer had been a Pinkerton spy after all.

Like so many others who went to Cuba in the years 1895–97, Scovel was a minister's son, a background so frequent that one is tempted to think that a fairy godmother appeared uninvited at the christenings of preachers' sons born in the late 1860s and early 1870s and whispered the words "Cuba Libre" over the cradles.

The middle child in a family of five, Scovel was born in July 1869 in Pittsburgh, where his father, the Reverend Sylvester Fithian Scovel was minister of the historic First Presbyterian Church. The Scovels (or Scovills; the name was spelled both ways) were prominent members of the Ohio branch of an old Connecticut Yankee family and distant connections of the Cleveland banker and philanthropist Philo Scovill, who had been one of the founders of the Cleveland-Pittsburgh Railroad. Mrs. Scovel, the former Caroline Woodruff, was one of the organizers and first president of the Presbyterian Board of Missions. Rev. Scovel was a well-respected scholar. Fluent in French and German, a translator of Latin and Greek texts, he liked to say that he "studied Hebrew to exercise his mind, and piano to rest his mind."[4] A teacher of moral philosophy as well as a minister, he was especially interested in youth work, and his lecture on "Popular Corruption," first delivered to the student body of Washington and Jefferson College in southwestern Pennsylvania, was widely reprinted in religious periodicals.

However successful Sylvester Scovel's warnings about the dangers of popular corruption may have been with undergraduate audiences, they only succeeded in making a rebel out of his second son. Baptized Sylvester Henry, he had been given his middle name in honor of his mother's brother, but by the time he started first grade he was so thoroughly sick of hearing the question, "Why can't you be more like your Uncle Henry?" that he vowed that when he learned to write he would never use his hated middle name. He kept his promise, always signing himself simply "Sylvester Scovel," but his childhood nickname of Harry stuck with him and only strangers ever addressed him as Sylvester.

Harry's earliest memory was of watching his elder brother, Minor, build a tower out of blocks, pausing just long enough to announce to his mildly shocked parents that he intended to keep on until his creation was "tall enough to smoke out the Heavenly Father."[5] Minor fulfilled this early promise by growing up to become a civil engineer, employed by a firm that specialized in designing and constructing blast furnaces. Harry, who never quite forgave himself for not thinking of the line first, did his best to live up to it on other ways. A bright, mischievous boy, he got into one scrape after another and was usually, though not always, able to charm his way out of trouble. Harry's teachers would remember him as high-spirited and cheeky. His father branded him insolent.

Sylvester Scovel did not believe in striking a child in anger. His method was to wait until he had composed himself and then go to his son's room where he would, as Harry's wife later put it, "pray and lick him, lick him and pray."[6] He also forced Harry to attend funerals, on the theory that this would encourage him to "contemplate mortality."

Two previous generations of Sylvester Scovels—Harry's

grandfather and greatgrandfather—had been college presidents as well as ministers, and in 1883, Sylvester became the third when he was appointed president of the University of Wooster (since renamed the College of Wooster). Harry, age fourteen, entered the university's college preparatory division where, the family hoped, he would finally settle down and demonstrate an inclination to study theology. Harry, however, took an instant dislike to Wooster, which he described as "a city set on a hill . . . in an atmosphere of rarefied piety."[7] Constantly urged by both parents "to be a model of good conduct to all the young men around him" and, less understandably, to "curb his fondness for athletics,"[8] he divided his energies between sports and organizing elaborate practical jokes. The specifics of these pranks are not recorded, but many years later the alumni notes section of *The Wooster Quarterly* would recall, tactfully, that "His vivacity and versatility and his generous impulsiveness impressed all. Always liking the spice of danger, he seemed to bear a charmed life. Several times before his majority he passed through dangers where his life seemed sure to be forfeited."[9]

On his sixteenth birthday he announced that he had indeed been contemplating mortality and had concluded that there was no God. Since this ruled out a career in the ministry, he wanted to leave school and become an engineer, a profession that, at the time, did not necessarily require a college degree.

The Scovels thought that a few weeks of hard labor would change their son's mind, and Minor, who was by now a junior engineer with the firm of Babcock and Wilcox, arranged for him to be taken on as part of a crew that was constructing a blast furnace in the Tennessee hills. Harry arrived at the site expecting to be made timekeeper, but the foreman, who had a grudge against Minor, no doubt resented being forced to supervise a problem teenager fresh out of prep school. Harry was assigned instead to a crew that was hauling bricks up a mountainside to the construction site. It was the hardest and dirtiest job the project had to offer, and Harry was the youngest and smallest member of the crew, as well as the only white. He stuck it out for three days until he collapsed of heat stroke. When he recovered he was transferred to the only slightly less challenging task of chopping up several acres of felled trees with a handsaw.

To his parents' dismay, Harry refused to beg to come home. He was eventually promoted to operating a locomotive on the narrow-gauge railway that carried lumber from a nearby sawmill. His sixteenth year, he later wrote, was "the most profitable one I ... ever spent." Among the lessons he had learned, and surely not one his father had intended to teach, was to see life from the point of view of what he called the "horny palmed fraternity of toil."[10] His experience as the butt of the sadistic crew boss had taught him what tyranny was, and he shocked his family by arguing in favor of the right of workers to strike.

During the latter part of his stint in Tennessee, a more sympathetic supervisor, a former army officer, urged him to prepare for a career in the navy, where young officers with engineering backgrounds were in demand. Harry took a competitive examination for an appointment to Annapolis from the district of his parents' congressman, William McKinley, but was passed over in favor of a boy from McKinley's hometown of Canton.

Sylvester, eager to see his son back in school, offered to send him instead to the Michigan Military Academy, a private, highly regarded preparatory school. Harry entered the academy as the oldest member of the junior class. After more than a year of hauling bricks and sawing lumber, his five-foot-eight-inch frame had filled out to about 180 pounds, most of which appeared to be concentrated in his neck and shoulders. He quickly became the best equestrian in his class, learning to mount a horse from a running start and ride bareback with spurs. Having worked on a blasting crew, he had no trouble mastering the essentials of firing mortars and artillery pieces. Other habits he had acquired in Tennessee were less suitable in a military cadet: He chain-smoked hand-rolled cigarettes and commanded a colorful vocabulary, a mixture of universally recognized swearwords and picturesque colloquialisms he had picked up from the blacks on his crew. Caught smoking three times in his first three weeks at school, he was confined to quarters every evening for the rest of the semester. The punishment turned out to have its positive aspects. For the first time in his life he had nothing better to do than study, and he made such quick progress that after his midyear exams he was promoted into the senior class.

By the end of his second semester he had made friends with

one of his roommates, Walter Jones, a pink-cheeked, spit-and-polish cadet who was first lieutenant of the corps as well as president of the senior class. "Jonesey" was rarely known to break a rule, but one night a week before graduation he and Harry managed to cadge a single cigarette, which they were determined to enjoy after lights-out. They were puffing furtively near an open window when the officer of the day appeared at the end of the hall. The cigarette butt went out the window and Harry and Jonesey dove for their beds, but the unmistakable smell lingered. Since it was impossible to single out the guilty party, everyone in the room—an entire squad—was put on report.

The next morning, Jonesey and Harry reviewed their situation. Jonesey, if he confessed, would still graduate, but he would be stripped of the honors he had worked so hard to earn. Harry, as a fourth offender, would face certain expulsion. Schoolboy ethics dictated a coin toss, with the loser to take the blame for both of them. Jonesey called tails. The coin came up heads.

"I felt a thrill when I saw that Goddess of Liberty," Scovel later confessed. But though he graduated with his class, seeing Jonesey disgraced while he escaped free and clear had soured his taste for military life. That summer, he accepted a temporary appointment as aide to the commander of the Ohio National Guard, but when his term was up, he decided not to enlist in the regular army. Instead, he entered the University of Michigan where, during his freshman year, he was elected president of the three-thousand-member Association of Independents, an organization that was challenging fraternities' domination of class politics. He was the best athlete in his class, a rising star in student politics, a better-than-average engineering student, and ... bored. In the middle of the first semester of his sophomore year he dropped out and embarked on a series of jobs—supervisor of a waterworks in Lebanon, Kentucky; apprentice to a mechanical draftsman in Pittsburgh; Cleveland sales manager for the Babcock & Wilcox Water Tube & Boiler Company; and insurance agent with the Equitable Life Society in Pittsburgh, a job he loathed but was extremely good at. When a Pittsburgh construction company offered to put him in charge of a major project in Central America if he would return to Michigan for an additional semester of engineering studies, he jumped at the chance to get out of the insurance business. He completed the courses at company expense, but the firm filed for bankruptcy just as he was making arrangements to sail.

Temporarily at loose ends, he went into business with some college friends who ran an engineering firm in Chicago and who claimed to have developed a process for recovering fuel from industrial slag. Within two weeks he managed to raise over thirty thousand dollars from investors in Cleveland, many of them, he recalled, "the best people." Unfortunately, the process, which had looked "exceptionally feasible" on paper, did not work. The engineering firm folded and the investors lost their money.

Far from bearing a grudge, several of the disappointed investors recommended Scovel for the post of general manager and chief fund-raiser of the Cleveland Athletic Club. His first project was a production of an operetta, *Moses Cleaveland Up To Date*. The libretto, written by Scovel and set to music from the public domain, was set in 1796, when the first representatives of the Connecticut Land Company arrived in the Cuyahoga Valley and began purchasing real estate from the Indians. The subject was one Scovel knew well—his forebear Philo Scovill had made the leap from itinerant carpenter to railroad magnate in one generation thanks to his purchase of a tract of woodland in the path of the development of downtown Cleveland. In Scovel's version of this episode of local history, however, the Connecticut Yankees were rubes, hopelessly overmatched in their dealings with the Indians, who nevertheless were tagged with ridiculous names like "Laughing Water" and "Sloppy Weather." As performed by an all-male cast, with Scovel both directing and singing one of the male leads, this was undergraduate-level humor at best. But the Cleveland critics were unanimously enthusiastic and one reviewer called the show "the best all-round amateur performance ever given in this city."[11]

The show was a great success financially. Scovel was a member of the First Cleveland Troop, an equestrian drill team that performed widely throughout the Midwest, and he had the foresight to cast several popular troopers in featured roles. Thanks to advance sales to the troop and other National Guard units in the area, *Moses Cleaveland Up To Date* played to standing room only houses and cleared a two-thousand-dollar profit after three performances. As a result of this success, Scovel was given a contract that guaranteed him a percentage of the gross of all future fund-raisers.

A socially exclusive club with more than a thousand active members, Cleveland Athletic was lodged in a luxurious downtown mansion. Besides fielding a number of amateur sports teams, the club sponsored a poetry society, a drama group, several card circles, and a drinking-and-chowder society, known, inevitably, as The Lotos Club. Scovel was given a suite of rooms off the 100-square-foot main lobby, free board, and a generous salary in addition to his commissions. For a twenty-four-year-old, he was leading an enviable existence. His work took up only an hour or two a day, leaving him time for an afternoon routine consisting of workouts with the fencing, boxing, and wrestling masters, followed by a three-quarter-mile run on the indoor track.

Soon after he became general manager, the club gained national publicity by adopting a policy of accepting members "from all stations in life." Reading between the lines, it would seem that the chief beneficiaries of this democratic-sounding bylaw were certain working-class Irish boxers who represented the club in amateur matches. Nevertheless, the policy created an aura of egalitarianism which, paradoxically, increased the club's social cachet. In most American cities, in-town men's clubs were shunned by the younger generation, who regarded them as stuffy, elitist, and dull. Cleveland Athletic was such a notable exception that it was written up in the prestigious *Century* magazine.

A natural promoter, Scovel soon branched out from organizing drama productions and boxing matches to other events, including a regional billiards tournament. These projects were so profitable that his commissions were running to more than a thousand dollars a month, an enormous sum in 1894 for a bachelor with no living expenses. Even so, he managed to spend his entire income and more on what he later referred to vaguely as "a good deal of riotous living." By July of 1895, he was in deeply in debt and drinking heavily. His father offered to settle his obligations, provided he agreed to return to Pittsburgh, where his brother and a married sister were living, and go back to selling insurance. This was to be Scovel's last chance; if he failed again, his family would not bail him out.

Three months later, when Scovel bolted for Cuba, he kept his plans a secret from his parents, promising himself that he would either return home to Wooster a success, or not return at all.

When he reached Cienfuegos in mid-October, Scovel called at the home of the Cuban contact who was supposed to put him on the underground railroad to the insurgents' headquarters. He was told that the man was out of town "indefinitely." Having already spent more than half of his stake on boat fare and hotel expenses, he decided that rather than wait around until his cash ran out, he might as well try to sneak through the Spanish military lines. Once he got into the countryside, someone was bound to be able to direct him to a rebel camp.

A few blocks from the edge of town, he was stopped by a Spanish patrol. "The night was dark, I was much excited," Scovel recalled, and "I pretended to be an officer of the steamship *Niagara* ashore on a toot." The ruse worked so well that the soldiers escorted him back to the entrance to his hotel, relieving him of his wristwatch and cash along the way.

Two days later, he tried again, abandoning his luggage along with his unpaid hotel bill. This time he was able to slip past the military sentry post on the highway out of town, and he spent the next two weeks wandering in the countryside, hiding by day and emerging at night to beg for food. Finally he ran into a sympathetic stranger who spoke enough English to understand who he was and what he wanted, and who trusted him enough to give him directions to the insurgents' hideout in the mountains.

Ragged, footsore, and half starved, Scovel blundered into the camp of Máximo Gómez on November 1, just in time to hear the insurgent commander announce his plan for an invasion of the western provinces. It was common knowledge that the Ten Years War had failed because the Spanish were able to contain the rebels in Oriente, bottling them up behind a fortified trench that ran the width of the island, the Júcaro-Morón *trocha*. Gómez had no intention of allowing this to happen a second time. For two months bands of rebels had been sneaking across the *trocha* from eastern Cuba, and on November 6, Gómez inspected his regrouped army and issued his orders for carrying the war into the west.

"The chains of Cuba have been forged by its own wealth,"

Gómez declared.[12] Sugar was the basis of Cuba's prosperity, but also the reason for its subjection. Therefore, the immediate goal of the Liberation Army was to destroy the winter cane crop. Gómez's order outlined his strategy for the coming three months: (1) All plantations were to be destroyed, their cane and outbuildings burned. Railroad connections were also to be destroyed. (2) All laborers who aided the sugar factories would be considered traitors to their country. Article three of the order provided that anyone found in violation of article two was to be sentenced to death.

Twenty-five thousand Spanish soldiers had landed in Cuba over the summer, and most of them were stationed in the central provinces, waiting to confront the rebels the moment they came down from their mountain stronghold. Scovel took one look at Gómez's "army"—a few hundred peasant volunteers, "untrained, undisciplined and naturally timid"—and concluded that they would all be slaughtered before long. But he had no money and nowhere to go, and since Gómez was willing to tolerate his presence, he decided to tag along.

The rebels' first encounter with Spanish regulars came on November 30, 1895. Gómez and his followers were camped near Sancti Spíritus in southern Santa Clara Province when the local commander, General Saurez Valdés, rode out of the city to hunt them down. The ensuing fight was described by a twenty-one-year-old English correspondent named Winston Churchill, who had taken a leave from his first commissioned post in the British Army to cover the Cuban rebellion for the London *Daily Graphic.* Churchill was not impressed by his first sight of the Liberation Army. The insurgents, he reported, "neither fight bravely nor do they use their weapons effectively. They can neither win a single battle or hold a single town. Their army, consisting to a large extent of colored men, is an undisciplined rabble." Nevertheless, the skirmish ended with the Spanish column fleeing back to Sancti Spíritus, leaving behind a twenty-mule supply train. Ten Spanish soldiers had been killed and, Churchill admitted, the general and his staff considered themselves lucky not to have lost many more men.

Churchill's dispatch was picked up by the New York *World,* which followed it with an editorial expressing skepticism over the

British correspondent's account of a "sham battle" ineptly fought on both sides. "At any rate," the editorial commented, "a battle in which nobody is killed is not the kind of battle by which Cuban independence can be won."[13]

Scovel would not have disagreed with Churchill's estimate of the rebels' fighting ability, but he was in a position to understand, as Churchill did not, that the point of guerrilla warfare is not the conquest of territory but the demoralization of the enemy. Scovel correctly described the rebel advance as "a march of intimidation and propagandism," and as a former student of military science, he was fascinated by Gómez's ability to accomplish so much with so little.

Throughout December the insurgents plundered Matanzas Province in central Cuba, resting by day and marching by night, torching thousands of acres of cane as they advanced. By all accounts, Gómez's threat of summary executions was not carried out. Most landowners had already fled with their families to the safety of the cities. A few who stayed behind to defend their property were held hostage and in some cases were condemned in mock trials before being "pardoned." Thousands of peasants, realizing there would be no winter crop and seeing that for once rebellion against Spain might actually have a chance of success, joined the insurgents.

On December 23, an army led by the Spanish military governor, Captain-General Arsenio Martínez de Campos, nearly bottled up the insurgents near Coliseo, but Gómez anticipated the trap and led his followers to safety. Martínez Campos promptly marched his army back to Havana, where he began to prepare for the arrival of the rebels at the gates of the capital.

But Gómez's apparent triumph contained the seeds of diplomatic disaster. In applying his scorched earth policy, Gómez had not spared the property of American citizens. A number of the wealthiest Cubans had taken U.S. citizenship, or in some cases even sold out to American consortiums, precisely in the hope of sheltering their property in the event of revolution. To Gómez and his advisers it hardly seemed fair that the property of exiles should be spared, while landowners who had remained in Cuba, many of them rebel sympathizers, were impoverished. Moreover, Gómez seems to have had the idea that American property owners would react to the loss of their investments by pressuring Spain for reparations.

This was a fateful miscalculation. Secretary of State Olney had close connections with Boston sugar magnate Edwin Atkins and other major American investors in Cuba, and even American politicians who had no personal stake in the matter felt that since the Cubans wanted a favor from Washington in the form of a resolution that would make arms sales legal, they ought to be prepared to treat American citizens favorably in return.

Tómas Estrada Palma had been in Washington for a month, waiting for Olney to find time to see him. When the first news of the burning of American-owned sugar mills in Matanzas reached the United States, Olney's calendar suddenly cleared, and the Cuban delegation got its appointment. Coughing compulsively, as he always did when forced to lie for the sake of expediency, Estrada Palma did his best to defend Gómez's policy as a necessary evil. "Well, gentlemen," replied Olney. "There is only one term for such action. *We* call it arson." [14]

Havana, meanwhile, was in turmoil. Over the years, the population of Havana had been inured to a certain level of civil disorder in the provinces, but the ability of the army to protect the capital had never been in doubt until now. On January 6, the insurgents reached Hoyo Colorado, a Havana suburb. Their arrival coincided with the Feast of the Epiphany, and a rumor circulated that Spanish troops stationed along the highways in the city had been caught off guard while celebrating the holiday. All that day the city waited to be overrun. That same afternoon, the Associated Press actually reported the fall of Havana. According to the AP story, which was attributed to a source in Boston, the last cable message from the capital had been, "Morro Castle alone holds out," after which the wire abruptly went dead.

This, of course, was a hoax; Gómez had never intended to march into the city. But he had won a psychological victory. Martínez Campos was already writing his resignation, which was forwarded to Madrid the next day. Gómez, meanwhile, had divided his army in half. One force, under his command, would spend the next few weeks conducting raids in Havana Province. A second, led by Antonio Maceo, departed on a lighting sweep through the far western province of Pinar del Río.

By now Scovel was feeling "mentally desperate." For three months he had been busily writing dispatches and sending them by courier to Junta agents in the towns, who had promised to see that they were smuggled onto boats bound for New York. He had no idea whether any of his reports had actually reached the *Herald*, and after riding with Maceo's army as far as the border of Pinar del Río, he decided to turn back and attempt to enter Havana, where American newspapers were sold regularly in the hotel district. He was carrying a borrowed military credential made out in the name of a twenty-year-old journalist, Alejandro de Quesada, but it was doubtful whether he had learned enough Spanish in three months to make the impersonation plausible. Arrested as he tried to bluff his way past a sentry post, he spent the night of January 12 in a dank cell in Morro Castle.

Unfortunately for Scovel, he had been mistaken for "El Inglesito," an English-speaking mercenary whose legendary exploits were probably a composite of the careers of several foreigners attached to the insurgent movement. A group of prisoners was scheduled to face the firing squad in four days and Scovel's jailers warned him that he would be included.

Coincidentally, another American, Charles Salomon of New York, had been arrested the same day as Scovel, picked up by Customs agents who discovered in his luggage a letter on Junta stationery, no doubt similar to the one Rubens had originally given Scovel. Salomon claimed to be working for the New York *Journal*, and whether or not this was actually the case, he was quickly vouched for by the *Journal*'s Havana correspondent, Charles Michelson. Less than twenty-four hours after his arrest, Salomon was out of jail and aboard a steamer bound for New York.

The *Herald*'s man in Havana, George Bronson Rea, was less helpful. On hearing that "El Inglesito" was in Morro Castle and claiming to be employed by his newspaper, Rea hurried to the governor's palace and indignantly denied any connection between the *Herald* and this Scovel character. An appeal from the American consul to the *Herald*'s New York office produced the same result. Spain was not about to provoke the United States by executing a legitimate journalist, but a mercenary was another story.

On his fourth day in Morro Castle, Scovel was visited by the New York *World*'s Havana correspondent, Dr. William Shaw

Bowen. An experienced political reporter, Bowen was sympathetic to Spain's problems in Cuba and a personal friend of Martínez Campos. He went to see Scovel expecting to meet one of the American drifters who occasionally turned up in Havana, a merchant seaman separated from his ship, perhaps, or an army deserter lured to the island by the insurgents' promise of high pay for sharpshooters and artillerymen. To his surprise, he discovered a young man who was not only articulate and sincere in his claim to be a journalist, but a college president's son, in short, an individual whose death at the hands the Spanish was unlikely to pass unnoticed.

"What are your ends?" Bowen asked.

"To make a reputation as a war correspondent," Scovel insisted.

This was good enough for Bowen, who cabled *World*'s managing editor Bradford Merrill and obtained permission to hire Scovel. Governor Sabas Marín, Martínez Campos's temporary replacement, ordered Scovel released and deported, but this was merely a gesture to placate Loyalist sentiment. Grateful to Bowen for averting an international incident, Marín told him that, personally, he didn't care whether Scovel left the island or not.

While he was waiting for a military court to process his papers, Scovel had another visitor, an embarrassed and effusively contrite George Rea. Rea explained that Taylor, the *Herald* editor who hired Scovel, had been fired from the paper not long after. When Scovel's dispatches arrived in the mail, and a number of them had indeed arrived, they were either destroyed or forwarded unopened to Taylor. The only exception was one early report, which had been published without a byline in accordance with the *Herald's* usual policy. The New York office, having realized its mistake, had authorized Rea to pay Scovel twenty-seven dollars, more than twice its usual half-column rate, a sum they considered sufficient to settle the paper's debt to him in full.

Though privately he wondered what sort of man would go out of his way to denounce a fellow American in trouble, Scovel saw the humor of the situation and accepted Rea's apology. But he never forgave the *Herald,* a grudge eventually reciprocated by the *Herald's* New York editors.

In fairness to Rea, he was an inexperienced journalist who

only days earlier had almost been thrown into Morro Castle himself, on suspicion that *he* was the elusive "El Inglesito." A lanky redhead in his mid-twenties, the Brooklyn-born Rea was an electrical engineering graduate of Stevens Institute of Technology who had come to Cuba five years earlier to work for the O. B. Stillman Company, the second largest American sugar producer on the island. He had joined the *Herald* just two weeks earlier, after insurgent raids in Havana Province had shut down the Stillman refinery.

Like Scovel, Rea was an avid student of military history, and he was fascinated to hear Máximo Gómez extolled as a military genius. Scovel told Rea that he and Gómez had become great friends, and now that he had a commitment from the *World*, he intended to obtain an exclusive statement from the general for his paper. Furthermore, while he was not about to do the *Herald* a favor by guiding their representative to Gómez, if Rea managed to locate the insurgent leader on his own, he would personally arrange an interview. Finding the insurgents was the easiest thing in the world, he added. At any given time, 80 percent of the peasants left in the countryside knew precisely where the rebels were and would be happy to tell you "if you knew what to ask."

Rea must have listened to all this with a good deal of skepticism. He had been in Cuba for five years and here was Scovel, after three months, a buddy of the famously enigmatic Gómez, the beneficiary of a secret arrangement with the interim governor, and now an expert on how to talk to peasants. On January 18, when Rea left the capital determined to get to Gómez first, Scovel was sitting in a café drinking whiskey. He cheerfully wished Rea luck, promising again that when Rea reached the insurgent headquarters, "I'll introduce you to the Old Man."

After a week of what he described as "variable and exciting adventures"[15] in strife-torn Havana Province, George Rea wandered into the camp of a Liberation Army officer, Colonel Pedro Díaz. Díaz and his men were on their way to join Gómez, who was about to set up temporary headquarters at an abandoned sugar plantation in the southwestern part of the province, and they invited him to come along.

The next morning, January 25, Rea was waiting at the plantation with Díaz and his three hundred followers when Gómez's army arrived. The column of mounted men, several thousand strong, was an impressive sight, Rea thought. But his first glimpse of the general himself was a resounding disappointment. Instead of the military genius and elder statesman so glowingly described by Scovel, he saw only a "chocolate-colored old man, who gave one the idea of a resurrected Egyptian mummy." Even more disconcerting, riding directly behind Gómez at the head of the general's personal entourage was Harry Scovel.

Over the next several days, Rea's disappointment with the insurgent general hardened into contempt. He was shocked to see the old man lose his temper and lash out with his sword at a teenage porter accused of killing a packhorse, and he was infuriated when Gómez, pontificating on military history at the dinner table, announced, "You Americans don't know how to fight. You never did. You have been thrashed in every war since gaining your independence."

Gómez was a controversial character, even among Cubans who had fought side by side with him for decades. His correspondence reveals a professional military man of courtly instincts and deep loyalties, perhaps not unlike George Washington, with whom he has sometimes been compared. But Gómez was also famous for his volatile temper, a quality all the more troublesome now that the elderly commander had taken rather too enthusiastically to a doctor's advice that he take a little brandy to relieve the arthritis pain in his legs. Moreover, Gómez was a Santo Domingan, and thus suspected by some Cubans—not to mention Americans—of wanting to become dictator of a pan-Caribbean empire.

Nevertheless, reading between the lines of Rea's account of his problems with Gómez, one can see all too plainly how the nervous, rather self-important young *Herald* correspondent managed, quite unwittingly, to get the general completely riled—arguing with him at his own table and later that night barging into the general's bedroom to ask about provisions for his horse, a matter that could easily have been handled by an orderly.

The misunderstandings continued the next morning. At eight A.M., the insurgents marched out to the nearest railway line, tore up a section of track, and settled down to await the arrival of the Havana-Guanajay troop train. Unfortunately, their timing was off and the train that fell into their trap turned out to be the regularly scheduled Havana express. While the rest of the insurgents set about looting the freight cards, a dozen or so men swarmed over the locomotive, trying to figure out a way to put the engine out of commission.

"Scovel and myself laughed heartily at their antics," wrote Rea in his description of the incident. But Scovel was laughing at Rea, not with him. Determined to get back at Rea for denouncing him in Havana, he had confided to Gómez, out of Rea's hearing, that the *Herald* correspondent was an "expert engineer" who "knew more about railroads than any man on the island." Gómez then approached Rea, demanding that he supervise the job of disabling the engine.

Rea knew nothing about trains and he was terrified of doing anything that might endanger his claim to noncombatant status. Nevertheless, it seemed unwise to annoy Gómez any further. Examining the boiler, he discovered that the engineer had already lowered the pressure to about twenty pounds. Satisfied that no real harm would be done, he instructed the insurgents to destroy the blow-off valve, releasing an impressive billow of steam.

Gómez, wrote Rea, was so impressed by this feat that he offered to make Rea his chief of engineers, with a command of 150 men and a large cash reward—payable after the insurgents' victory, of course—if he could figure out a way to permanently disrupt traffic on the Batanabao rail line.

For Rea, this was one more proof that Gómez was ignorant as well as "insolent." It never seemed to occur to him that he had been had.

Despite their difference of opinion where Gómez was concerned, Rea and Scovel developed a close, if always somewhat tense, friendship. Scovel wasted no time in discovering the aristocratic Rea's secret: His wealthy banker father was the son of potato famine refugees, and Rea himself had dropped an *h* from his surname, originally Rhea, because he considered the streamlined spelling "less Irish." Scovel immediately nicknamed his colleague "the son of Brian Boru."

A sense of humor was a requirement for a yellow-journal correspondent, even a war correspondent, and both Scovel and Rea portrayed themselves in their dispatches as Yankee innocents abroad, bumbling their way across the Cuban countryside, seldom more than one step ahead of the coldly efficient Spanish Army. On one occasion, when they attempted to reach the cable office in the town of Quivicán to file their dispatches, they ran into a Spanish ambush and narrowly escaped capture. Rea recalled the inglorious incident: "Like the good soldiers that they were, [the Spanish] formed an ambuscade to capture us 'vivita' on entering the town. A fight was the result. On second thought, I think the letter 'l' inserted in the word 'fight' would probably express our conduct more clearly. Scovel was unhorsed, and narrowly escaped capture, and my own 'genuine Cuban plug' was killed. By a miracle, we gained the canefields and escaped." Scovel, describing the same close call, remembered the sensation of running after his panicky horse, knowing that his only chance of escape was to catch up with the animal and leap onto its back. He had performed the same stunt with the First Cleveland Troop, but never with bullets whizzing all around. Worse, he happened to be wearing an ankle-length mackintosh that flapped around his calves as he ran and made jumping all but impossible. How he managed to get into the saddle and pull Rea up behind him he never knew.

Ironically, Rea's chief complaint about the insurgents was not that they made war on civilians. Indeed, he later wrote that he had never seen a dead civilian during the entire time he traveled with the insurgents. On the contrary, what outraged him was that Gómez seemed determined to avoid bloodshed at all costs. At the end of his second week with the insurgents, Rea was at the Santa Lucía ranch in Hoyo Colorado when a Spanish column two thousand strong was sighted approaching on the main road. Gómez remained in the living room of the main house, calmly perusing a stack of American newspapers, until the whine of an artillery shell passing overhead dislodged him from his easy chair. Almost offhandedly, he gave the order to scatter, and within minutes only the occasional rippling of the distant cane fields gave any indication that nearly one thousand rebels and several hundred horses were concealed there. This was the sort of performance that Scovel considered the essence of Gómez's genius, but to Rea, who compared the wholesale flight to the "Coney Island handicap," it was shameful. He had been brought up to believe that war was a gentleman's pastime, and no gentleman would run from a fair fight, even if hopelessly outnumbered.

Some of the younger officers, impatient for glory, shared Rea's views. One group of junior officers, well connected with the civilian president of the provisional replublic, Salvador Cisneros Betancourt, had begun to discuss the possibility of overthrowing Gómez.

Gómez, too, was frustrated at times. During the retreat witnessed by Rea, Gómez's horse had been shot in the rump, a humiliating mishap for a veteran cavalry officer, and as a result, the old man was even more moody than usual. According to Rea, one night not long after the retreat, the headquarters staff was eating dinner when Gómez stopped picking at his rice and watery stew and glared at Rea, who was sitting next to Scovel at the far end of the table.

"Mr. Rea," he rasped. "By what right do you sit at my table and eat? How do I know you are not a Spanish spy in disguise?"

For Rea, this ridiculous accusation was proof that Gómez was irrational. Nevertheless, it did provide a pretext for the insurgent commander to rid himself of a visitor he considered a bad influence on his young staff officers. In fact, Gómez was so eager to get rid of Rea that he offered him ten gold pieces in travel money if only he would transfer his reporting activities to the other wing of the insurgency, Antonio Maceo's army in Pinar del Río.

The morning after the scene at the dinner table, Rea noted, Harry Scovel departed for Havana on one of his mysterious "important missions." While he was gone, Antonio Maceo arrived in camp to confer with Gómez, and when the conference ended, Rea decided to take Gómez up on his suggestion.

Antonio Maceo, the "Bronze Titan," was the stuff that romantic legends were made of—though, as Scovel noted in his journal, not necessarily the stuff of victory. Twelve times wounded during the Ten Years War, Maceo was the self-educated son of peasant parents, a fearless philosopher-soldier with a reputation for never refusing a fight. During the two and half months Rea remained with Maceo he saw more than thirty-five "hard skirmishes and guerrilla fights," every one led personally by Maceo.

"As day after day I witnessed him at the head of his men, directing the fray from the front ranks of the firing line," Rea later wrote, "I could not but feel a certain admiration for the man who, despite his color, was so far the superior of the many 'opera bouffe' generals in the Cuban Army of Liberation.... Maceo devoted himself strictly to the campaign; he never refused a fight, and often when the enemy did not bother him for a few days, he went out looking for them to remind them he was still alive."[16]

Cuba's Bloodless Battles

WHILE SCOVEL AND REA were riding with the insurgents, sleeping on the bare ground and eating horse meat (when they could get it), most American newsmen in Cuba were reporting the progress of the revolution from their curbside tables at the outdoor café of the Inglaterra Hotel. It has been said that every war has its hotel, the inevitable meeting ground of correspondents, diplomats, and spies, but few wartime hotels have ever been as seductive as the Inglaterra, ironically, owned and staffed by the very middle-class Spanish Loyalists whom the journalists regularly excoriated in their copy.

Perhaps the best description of the Inglaterra's charms was penned by Murat Halstead, the veteran correspondent and political commentator who came to Cuba as the New York *Journal*'s special commissioner in the winter of 1895–96. Halstead occupied one of the hotel's choice rooms, so large that the glass doors opening onto his private marble balcony were eight feet wide.

His four-poster bed had a headboard inlaid with mother of pearl, a red velvet canopy, gauzy curtains pinned back by crimson ribbons, and a lace-trimmed "pantaloons" disguising its metal legs. But it was the service at the hotel that sent Halstead into raptures. Every morning at seven he rang the buzzer above the headboard of his bed, confident that his signal would be answered by the hall porter in *exactly* 150 seconds. He then gave his order to the porter and *exactly* five minutes later a servant arrived with a silver tray—solid silver, not plate—holding two solid silver pitchers, the one with the right-handed handle containing hot coffee and the left-handed pitcher containing hot milk, a crusty roll still warm from the oven, and two peeled oranges. "The remarkable thing about the oranges," Halstead wrote, "next to that they are good, is that they are usually of the same size; but if one is larger than average the other is that much smaller, and this is as invariable as if the oranges were weighed on scales that accounted for the hundredth part of an ounce." [1]

For the day's main meals, served at eleven A.M. and seven P.M., Halstead repaired to the hotel café where, he rhapsodized, "they cook chicken almost as well as in Paris," and the steaks were "as tender as Delmonico ever served." The cucumber and tomato salads were the freshest, the olives the tastiest, and the omelets, though unpromisingly listed on the menu as "grumbled egss [*sic*] with onions," were at once light and satisfying, an entreé that "prepares the stomach for serious enjoyment." Halstead could find fault only with the Cuban habit of preparing fish in a thick tomato sauce, but this was more than compensated for by the island's abundance of fresh fruits—pineapple sweet as honey, juicy mangoes, or his favorite, the *mamey*, "a fruity apotheosis" served as is, or in nonalcoholic cocktails or, occasionally, in the form of a sorbet, "a cup of blooming snow, that is as vanilla ice cream might be if it were translated and frozen in heaven."

Between meals, one could always relax in the bar, where the supply of crushed ice was inexhaustible even on the hottest days and bartenders had elevated the mixing of cocktails into a performance art: Using a pair of delicate crystal glasses instead of a cocktail shaker, the bartender would swoosh the ingredients energetically from one glass to the other, "clinking the crystal in a way that would delight a German's sense of sound." Next, he would "fling" the drink through a strainer, catching it in the smaller of the two glasses, which was invariably filled to the rim without a drop left over, after which the large glass would be returned to the counter with a triumphant *thwack.*

Almost more admirable than its bartenders were Havana's barbers, artists who conveyed the impression that "the state of one's hair is highly esteemed. My barber here is almost the barber of my soul," wrote Halstead.

Finally, the sublime service was made all the more enjoyable by certain peculiarities of the currency exchange rates. American gold and silver pieces were valued at a 20 percent premium over their Spanish equivalents, and Spanish gold pieces at a premium over Spanish silver. Thus, an American who treated three friends to drinks at the bar might pay the bill with a U.S. five-dollar gold piece and receive a Spanish five-peso gold piece and forty cents as change. Ordering a second round of drinks and paying with the Spanish gold piece, he would receive as change five Spanish silver pieces and forty cents. Many Americans were quick to learn the obvious lesson. "It seems that there is money to be made from taking to drink," Halstead heard one delighted Yankee comment. "The more liquor I buy, the more money I've got. This must be the double standard."

An island of private elegance amid public shabbiness, the Inglaterra was a metaphor for Cuba itself. The neighborhood outside was hot, often smelly, and always noisy, the granite paving stones echoing at all hours with the clatter of horses' hooves. Many of the streets in the business district were so narrow that two carriages stopped abreast of each other could create a traffic jam that stretched for blocks, and the sidewalks were so inadequate that it was constantly necessary to step into the gutter to pass approaching pedestrians. In the cathedral, the Columbus monument stood perpetually unfinished. The university, once the pride of the New World, taught such an outmoded curriculum that wealthy Cubans sent their children abroad to school as a matter of course.

Summing up the legacy of four hundred years of colonial rule, Halstead commented that if only Spain had invested half as much during that time building roads as it was now spending on constructing *trochas,* the history of the island would have been completely different—a statement hard to fault. His prescription for Cuba's future, however, was controversial. The island, he wrote, was "almost as plainly ours as Long Island" and the time had now come for it to "yield to the drift of manifest destiny." Halstead readily admitted that this was a prescription for imperialism, but imperialism, he mused, had brought California into the Union, a move that turned out rather well.

As long as he was in Cuba, Halstead kept his annexationist views to himself, and he was able to do his job without interference. But all that changed with the arrival on February 10 of the new military governor, Captain-General Valeriano Weyler y Nicolau. It was common knowledge that Martínez Campos's replacement would have a mandate from Madrid to use whatever means necessary to put down the rebellion, and even before Weyler's appointment had been made official, Junta sources had begun planting items about atrocities he had allegedly committed during the Ten Years War, many of them based on an incident known as "the dance of Guáimaro." According to Junta lobbyist Gonzalo de Quesada, who claimed to be quoting a history of the war written by the late Manuel de la Cruz:

> The Dance of Guáimaro is famous in Puerto Príncipe. He [Weyler] captured a number of ladies of the best society of this province. They were taken to the village of Guáimaro. Around a large bonfire in the public square he placed the defenseless women. The ferocious hordes of negros who comprised the fourth company of his command were ordered to violently undress the prisoners. Then they played an African dance, and the unfortunate Cubans who refused to participate were whipped by Weyler himself![2]

It was the Spanish who normally resorted to racist scare tactics, but this shows that they were not alone. In a letter to the editor of the *New York Post*, Quesada insisted that there were survivors of the "dance" still living in Puerto Príncipe Province. Curiously, none ever came forward, even though an affidavit from a victim of Weyler's cruel whims would have been a tremendous propaganda coup.

A blue-eyed Spaniard of German ancestry, Weyler was a tough professional soldier but by no means the monster he was portrayed as being, as even the *Journal* admitted on occasion. One of the few American correspondents able to get close enough to the captain-general to learn anything of his private life was the *Journal*'s premier sob sister, the resourceful Kate Masterson. During a brief tour of Cuba shortly after Weyler's appointment, Masterson managed to ingratiate herself so thoroughly that Weyler invited her to his suite in the governor's palace where he showed her photographs of his children back in Spain and then revealed his secret indulgence—a well-appointed bathroom, complete with a large tub and a shower operated by a brass pull chain. In her account of the meeting, Masterson pretended to be scandalized—all those Turkish towels, all that hot water, when the Cuban people were suffering so!—but even she could not manage any sustained outrage over a penchant for soft towels, and the picture that emerges is one of a lonely, rather monkish, old man.

Nevertheless, Weyler has the dubious distinction of being the inventor of the concentration camp. Under his edict, the rural population was to be uprooted from the land and resettled in *zonas de reconcentración*, pacified areas near the island's fortified cities and towns. In preparation, Weyler immediately began recruiting Cuban-born irregulars, known as *guerrilleros*, who would do most of the dirty work of evicting the peasants from their land. Additionally, he set out to confine Maceo's army in Pinar del Río by constructing a second *trocha*, a twenty-three-mile barrier of barbed wire and earthwork fortifications stretching from Mariel in the north to Majana in the south, equipped with electric lights and artillery pieces and manned by an estimated fifteen thousand troops.

Máximo Gómez, whose historical allusions were often on the mark, called Weyler "our Philip II" and the insurgent leader admitted that he secretly rejoiced when he heard of his appointment. Similarly, Martínez Campos confided to friends his conviction that Weylerism would be the beginning of the end for Spanish rule, adding that "even the dead will rise out of their graves to fight Weyler."[3]

Another aspect of Weyler's policy was unremitting hostility to the American press. Censorship became so strict that even routine dispatches had to be smuggled out of the country by boat and filed from Florida. Worse yet, the edict making communication with the rebels a crime, never actually applied against legitimate journalists by Martínez Campos, was now enforced. Expulsions would become commonplace. A few suffered jail—or worse.

The first victim of the Weyler's war on the press was New York *World* correspondent Honoré Lainé. Described by the paper as "an educated Frenchman," Lainé was a former sugar planter who had turned up in the capital on January 9 with the story of how his plantation in Navajas had been overrun by insurgents who held him hostage for eight days before allowing him to escape with nothing but the clothes on his back. William Shaw Bowen was planning to leave Havana when Martínez Campos's permanent replacement took office, and just a few days before he hired Scovel he also recruited Lainé, on the understanding that he would report news from Havana. Lainé filed a few dispatches and then, while on his way to tour the site of a rebel raid in the southern part of the province, he dropped out of sight, reportedly picked up by the Spanish.

The *World*, for a reason never explained, made no fuss over Lainé's disappearance. Perhaps it felt that since he was not an American citizen, publicity would only hurt his case. And perhaps, Bowen having recently left Havana, there was simply no one on hand to investigate.

The next target of Weyler's antipress campaign was Murat Halstead's junior partner, Charles Michelson, an athletic Westerner who was a personal favorite of Hearst.

Michelson was a native of Virginia City, Nevada, site of the Comstock Lode and the Ophir Mine, the foundation of the Hearst family fortune. Hearst saw Michelson as the rugged adventurous type, the sort of young man he might have become if only he had grown up working his father's claim instead of studying with tutors in the Hearsts' San Francisco mansion or trailing his mother around Europe, imbibing culture. In reality, the closest Michelson had ever come to mining was the hours he spent as a child in the Miner's Union Library, poring over volumes of Dickens and Victor Hugo. His German-born parents were prosperous storekeepers who made sure their sons spent their free time studying, a strategy that paid off with Charles's elder brother Albert, who won an appointment to Annapolis and later became a physics professor at Cleveland's Case School of Applied Science. Albert Michelson devoted himself to a series of complex experiments designed to prove the existence of ether, the invisible fluid believed to permeate the universe. Albert's experiments eventually led to the first accurate measurement of the speed of light, and in 1907, he became the first American to win the Nobel prize in physics. During the 1880s, however, when the much younger Charlie was growing up, Michelson was deeply depressed over his inability to find ether; he considered himself a failure and his example did little to nudge Charles in the direction of a scholarly career.

After finishing high school, Michelson clerked in company stores in various mining towns, then drifted into journalism. He idolized Hearst and left a better job on the San Franciso *Call* to go to work for the *Examiner*. But Hearst took no particular notice of Michelson until one day when he and veteran reporter Allen Kelly, an avid outdoorsman, happened to get into an argument on the subject of the California grizzly bear. The *Examiner*'s logo included a picture of a bear and the slogan "Monarch of the Dailies," and Hearst wondered, in passing, whether this was an appropriate symbol for the paper, considering that the California grizzly was extinct. Kelly argued that this wasn't so; there were still grizzlies roaming free in the mountains. Hearst challenged him to prove it by capturing one alive, and he insisted that Kelly take the much younger Michelson along for protection.

Michelson accompanied Kelly into the Tehachapi Mountains where, to his immense relief, he discovered that Kelly did not intend for them to go unaided after grizzlies. With the help of a small army of professional trappers, a live grizzly was eventually captured and shipped back to San Francisco. Christened Monarch, it became the *Examiner* mascot and was displayed in a cage in Golden Gate Park.

By 1895, Michelson had become assistant editor of the *Examiner*'s Sunday edition. When Hearst moved to New York, taking the editor in chief with him, he hired a replacement from another paper instead of promoting Michelson, who quit in disgust, rejoining the *Call*. Hearst didn't miss him until three months later when he decided to send an adventurous young correspondent to Cuba to make contact with the insurgents and thought of Michelson the bear hunter. Hearst offered an advance of five thousand dollars plus, Michelson recalled later, the chance to become a "full fledged war correspondent...." " "This," he wrote, "was bait I could not resist."[4]

Michelson turned out to be an excellent correspondent, much too good to suit Weyler. One of his first articles, entitled "Cuba's Bloodless Battles," concluded bluntly that the only reason the rebellion had not been wiped out was that "Spanish soldiers do not fight." In late February 1896, a month after this report appeared, Michelson and his interpreter, Laurence Betancourt, were arrested as they tried to cross military lines to visit the site of a reported massacre of unarmed villagers near Marianao, west of Havana. Betancourt was released. Michelson, after being interrogated all night in his hotel room while soldiers searched his belongings, landed in a dank, narrow cell in Morro Castle.

Having been kept up by his interrogators all the previous night, Michelson had no trouble falling asleep when dark fell. He awoke several hours later with the refreshing feeling that a cool, delicate hand was gently caressing his face. Opening his eyes, he discovered that the fingers he was feeling were actually the cool feet of a good-size rat that was straddling his face, the better to sniff at his hair.

The *Journal* did not at first publicize Michelson's arrest. The problems of reporters were not considered news, and Halstead believed that quiet negotiations would be the most effective way to handle Weyler. It was the *World*, whose editors were already having second thoughts about their handling of the Honoré Lainé incident, that broke the news in a major story by Gus Roeder, the New York staffer who had recently replaced William Shaw Bowen. Perhaps inadvertently, the *World* had discovered the ideal tactic for handling Weyler. The persecution of American journalists was an easy story to report, a lot easier than the ambiguous progress of the guerrilla war in the interior. Politicians in Madrid were flabbergasted to see how agitated American public opinion became over the treatment of a few newspapermen, and since war with the United States was not in their plans, they made it clear to Weyler that his mandate did not extend to executing American correspondents.

On the tenth day of his incarceration, Michelson was roughly rousted from his cell by a pair of guards. "Where am I being taken?" he demanded.

"*Afuera,*" came the answer. "Outside."

Knowing that the courtyard adjacent to the jail was occasionally used for executions, Michelson assumed the worst and hung back, forcing the guards to grab him by the elbows and hustle him along. The next thing he knew he was all but propelled out the main gate of the fortress. Only when he heard the massive iron grate clang shut behind him did it dawn on him that he had been resisting his own release.

James Creelman's
Midnight Journey

DISGUSTED over being forced to release Michelson, Weyler retaliated by ordering both him and Murat Halstead deported. The *Journal* replaced them with the notoriously lazy Frederick W. Lawrence, a former police court reporter well known when he worked for the *San Francisco Examiner* for his arrangement with a representative from a rival paper, by which they attended court on alternate days, writing each other's stories. In no mood to play the hero, Lawrence rarely left the Inglaterra, which did not prevent him from producing some of the most colorful tales to come out of the war.

Lawrence's tour de force was his vivid reportage of an imaginary campaign. In a saga that lasted nearly six weeks, Maceo and his army of twenty-five thousand (!) were said to have crossed and recrossed the Mariel *trocha*, been rescued from a siege by Gómez, and, finally, captured and burned the cities of Pinar del Río and Santa Cruz in a single night—a neat trick considering that the two are more than three hundred miles apart.[1]

Another Lawrence scoop was his report on the existence of "Amazons" who supposedly rode with the insurgent army. According to Lawrence, Gómez had appointed one woman, Colonel Adele Pilotro, to command a regiment even though her husband, also a colonel but with the Spanish Army, was active in the same district. *Journal* readers were invited to speculate on the exquisitely agonizing dilemma that would arise should husband and wife ever find themselves face-to-face on the field of battle.

Because the Hearst press was known in later years for its lackadaisical coverage of foreign news, it is often assumed that the *Journal* never made any serious effort to do a good job of covering the Cuban rebellion. Nothing is farther from the truth. Hearst himself was intensely interested in the events unfolding in Cuba, but after Michelson's arrest he concluded that it was pointless to waste a serious correspondent on Havana. Instead, he focused his efforts on recruiting a correspondent who would operate outside Spanish lines, becoming the *Journal*'s answer to Scovel.

Hearst's handpicked choice for this role was Grover Flint. Flint was a most unusual war correspondent—he had actual combat experience, having served with the First Cavalry during the Indian wars; he was also fluent in Spanish. After arriving in Cuba in late March of 1896, he quickly caught on to the insurgents' use of embroidered religious badges, of a type sewn by girls for their sweethearts and brothers, as a sort of secret code. After traveling by train to Cárdenas in Matanzas Province, Flint simply wandered past the military guard at the train station and struck off into the countryside wearing a badge bearing the motto, *El corazón de Jesús está con migo* ("the heart of Jesus is with me").

Flint spent about two months with Gómez. His saddlebags containing his writing supplies were soon lost or stolen, so he was forced to scribble his dispatches with borrowed pencil stubs. His mackintosh was no match for the Cuban rains, and his clothing became infested by an unfamiliar parasite "larger than a bedbug," which the insurgents solemnly assured him was not native to Cuba but had been imported to the island by Spanish troops. He also witnessed one of the few pitched battles fought during the rebellion—based on official Spanish reports, he estimated that it took about 5,545 bullets to kill one insurgent, "making obsolete the old Franco-Prussian War ration of 1,000 to one man."[2]

Interestingly, considering its implications for the future of U.S.-Cuban relations, Flint considered the fuss over Gómez's violent temper and authoritarian personality much ado about nothing. Gómez, he pointed out, had to maintain his authority over several thousand undisciplined and often underfed volunteers. Flint suspected that Gómez purposely cultivated a reputation for ferocity, a strategy, Flint thought, that in the long run actually reduced the need for harsh discipline.

Flint eventually published a popular book about his adventures, *Marching with Gómez,* but as far as the *Journal* was concerned, he was a great disappointment. Flint's descriptions of combat were thrilling, but much of his writing belongs to the gullible-tourist-of-the-revolution genre. For example, his book included glowing descriptions of "communal workshops" in Oriente, where patriotic Cubans practiced a form of primitive communism, producing shoes, saddlery, and other necessities for the insurgents—a story Scovel dismissed as fantasy. Far worse, from Hearst's point of view, Flint was not very successful when it came to getting his copy out of the countryside. He had entrusted his dispatches to couriers provided by the insurgents, and since he suspected that they would be none too reliable he had tried to hedge his bets by dividing each dispatch in two sections, sending even-numbered pages with one messenger and odd-numbered pages with another. Only four and a half articles ever reached Florida, and these were cabled without explanation to New York in the order that they arrived. The disjointed copy nearly drove *Journal* editors mad with frustration until, at last, two matching halves showed up and they were able to piece together a single publishable story.

Although the *Journal*'s Frederick Lawrence was unexcelled as a writer of fantasy, he had stiff competition. The *World* also picked up rumors of Amazons with the insurgents, printing a version that claimed that an entire regiment of women was riding with Maceo in Pinar del Río. "Nothing more dreadful has ever been conceived by mortal men than the behavior of the women who fight in Cuba," the paper warned. "In battle they show no mercy; they hack, hew with their machetes, and shout in such a way as to alarm any opponent, and yet, when the fight is over, they are as tender to their foes as to their friends."[3]

The illiterate peasants who had joined the insurgents, meanwhile, were reported to be capable of amazing technical feats. According to a pre-Lawrence story in the *Journal*, the Cubans had discovered a way to fashion cannons out of tree trunks, "the strangest artillery of modern times."[4] Still another story reported that these same peasant soldiers destroyed a cane field in Havana Province by dousing black snakes with kerosene and then setting them alight. The snakes obligingly slithered up and down the rows of cane, setting fire to many acres before they expired.

Editors who ran such stories, it should be emphasized, did not necessarily expect anyone to believe them. The world was a much larger and more mysterious place in the 1890s than today, and the popular press, not just in New York but across the country, tended to view news from exotic locales as a form of entertainment, a good source of fantasy and horror stories. Alert readers could usually spot frauds because they were ascribed to Cuban sources, usually anonymous, in Key West, Tampa, Boston, or Chicago. The *World*, in particular, became adept at running such items as straight news and then indignantly denouncing them, sometimes the same day they appeared.

Furthermore, while the yellow press printed a good deal of nonsense about Cuba, it was also the source of most of the serious news about the island. In most cases, the nonyellow papers did not attempt to challenge Weyler's censorship restrictions. Instead of posting their own correspondents to Havana, they tended to rely on the Associated Press whose record for accuracy was scarcely better than Lawrence's. Conservative papers that did attempt independent coverage of the Cuban situation often committed gaffes as bad as anything found in the yellow press. For example, Stanhope Sams of the *New York Times* was responsible for the myth that the rebels had their capital at the (nonexistent) city of Cubitas in Puerto Príncipe, and even the *Herald*, which took foreign news seriously, could not resist the occasional Amazon story.

Without excusing such fabrications, most of them were published during the first year of the war, when the Cuban rebellion was seen as colorful rather than tragic or even significant in terms of its implications for the United States. By April of 1896, Joseph Pulitzer was already concerned about the backlash caused by such news fakes, and his response was to send to Havana the *World*'s—for that matter, with the possible exception of Richard Harding Davis, the world's—top foreign correspondent, the formidable James Creelman. Creelman was recently returned from the Far East, where he had been covering the Sino-Japanese War. Originally pro-Japan, he had demonstrated his objectivity by his description of the massacre of unarmed civilians by Japanese troops at Port Arthur.

A short, stocky man with a black goatee who spoke in rapid-fire, staccato bursts, the Canadian-born Creelman specialized in interviewing the greatest men and women of the day. And since he considered himself the conscience of the fourth estate, he normally did as much talking as listening. Creelman had traveled to Yasnaya Polyana to interrogate Count Leo Tolstoy on his views of modern marriage. He had lectured Pope Leo XIII on Protestant-Catholic relations and exchanged views on the brotherhood of mankind with Chief Sitting Bull. To his way of thinking, the press was one wheel on the great juggernaut of industrial society, which was moving inexorably forward, rolling over the outworn value systems that got in its way, sometimes regrettably, sometimes not.[5] "The beauty about Creelman," William Randolph Hearst once observed, "is the fact that whatever you give him to do instantly becomes in his mind the most important assignment ever given any writer.... He thinks that the very fact of the job being given him means that it's a task of surpassing importance, else it would not have been given to so great a man as he."[6]

Creelman arrived in Havana in late March, shortly after a *Harper's Weekly* photographer, Thomas Dawley, was arrested for crossing the Mariel *trocha* to photograph and interview Antonio Maceo. *Harper's Weekly* had consistently opposed American involvement in Cuba, but this did not make matters easier for Dawley, who was brought back to Havana chained to another prisoner in an unventilated boxcar with a sheet-metal roof. He reached Havana half-cooked and was paraded through the streets, interrogated, and then held for five days in Morro Castle before being released as a gesture of welcome, Weyler said, to the newly appointed American consul, Fitzhugh Lee.

No doubt this incident was on Creelman's mind when he visited the governor's palace to present his credentials. He listened skeptically as Weyler complained that if not for the encouragement of the American newspapers, the revolution would die out within a matter of months. Half of the American journalists on the island were Junta agents and the others were plain liars, Weyler screeched. "They poison everything with falsehood! They ought to be suppressed!"

This was too much for Creelman. "But the American newspapers did not stir up Mexico and Peru and the other Spanish-American colonies to rebellion," he reminded the captain-general. "The American newspapers were not in existence when the Netherlands fought against the Spanish crown for independence."[7]

At this point in the argument, Creelman noticed that one of Weyler's civilian secretaries had entered the room with some documents that required his signature. Standing just out of Weyler's line of sight, the aide rolled his eyes in an expression of disgust, and Creelman realized that he had met this secretary before; he had been introduced to him by another correspondent as a rebel sympathizer and regular informant of the Junta.

At that moment, Creelman later wrote, he knew that Spain was finished in Cuba.

Leaving the palace, Creelman retired to the Café Inglaterra to calm his nerves with a drink. The evening was an unusually pleasant one and the café happened to be filled with Spanish officers in full-dress uniform, conversing noisily among themselves but, so far, ignoring the solitary American in their midst.

At that moment another American, wearing a baggy, ill-cut business suit and a battered derby, strolled in off the street and sat down at Creelman's table. "Nice evening," the stranger remarked.

Creelman belatedly recognized his *World* colleague, Harry Scovel.

" 'Great God,' I whispered. 'Don't you know they're looking for you!' "

" 'Yes, I know,' he answered quickly. 'They're looking for me, but this is the last place they will expect to find me. Don't whisper;

it will excite suspicion. I've dropped my identity for the present. I'm Mr. Brown—Mr. Brown of New York—traveling about in search of a chance to make good investments.'"[8]

Scovel's recent dispatches—notably an exclusive interview and personal message from Gómez, published in the *World* on February 23, 1896—had prompted Weyler to offer a five-thousand-dollar reward for Scovel's capture, dead or alive. And like everyone else in Cuba, Creelman had been under the impression that Scovel was hiding in some rebel stronghold in the hills.

To Creelman's astonishment, Scovel cheerfully explained that he had spent most of the previous six weeks in New York, returning to Havana on the regularly scheduled Ward Line steamer.

On February 4, Scovel continued, he had been shot in the leg while observing a skirmish between Maceo's bodyguard and a Spanish patrol. When the leg became infected, his interpreter had arranged for him to be smuggled into Havana, where, with the connivance of a consular official attached to the U.S. health service, he was put on board a tramp steamer, disguised as an American businessman who had come down with tropical fever and was being sent home for medical treatment.

In New York Scovel had met his employers, Bradford Merrill and Pulitzer, for the first time. Merrill immediately offered Scovel a contract at a salary of sixty dollars a week plus four hundred dollars in expense money. This moderately generous offer seemed a fortune to Scovel, who went on a shopping spree, purchasing a good saddle, a camera, a mess kit equipped with a combination knife, spoon, and fork, and a "typewriting machine," the last by no means standard equipment for a correspondent in the field. Scovel was soon well enough to consider returning to Havana, but his plans were delayed by Pulitzer, who was having an attack of conscience. Pulitzer had grave doubts about the morality of sending reporters into dangerous situations merely for the sake of a story. Lainé was already missing, presumably dead, and he did not want to be responsible for another fatality. "Mr. Scovel must not go to Cuba if he puts his life at risk," he wrote Merrill.[9] For more than a week, memos on the subject flew between the Dome and Pulitzer's town house, until the Boss was finally cajoled into approving the assignment.

Merrill had another concern. Scovel's friendship with Horatio Rubens, not to mention with General Gómez himself, invited charges that he was an agent of the Junta. "You will conduct yourself carefully as a non-combatant—as a news correspondent solely," he warned in his letter formally notifying Scovel of his new contract.[10]

Whether or not Scovel observed these guidelines is a matter of interpretation. Unlike many correspondents of the time who wore sidearms as a matter of course, Scovel never carried a weapon. However, he did have a special relationship with the insurgents. Scovel had acted as a courier, delivering a packet of letters from Gómez to Estrada Palma in New York, and in any event, Scovel's friendship with Gómez guaranteed him special treatment, so special that one can well understand why Weyler regarded him as a Junta agent. By late March, Scovel was in Florida, where he had been promised passage aboard the filibuster schooner *Martha*, and on April 1, 1896, the Junta's Key West agent, José Dolores Poyo, wrote Estrada Palma: "Last night, eleven of the expeditionaries who were here embarked for Cuba, armed, equipped with 100 cartridges each, [and] serving as the escort of my good friend, the *World* correspondent Sylvester Scovel, who is once again marching to the front of the revolution." Poyo nervously reported that on his own initiative he had spent $240, about half the budget allotted for the entire expedition, on equipment for Scovel's eleven-man bodyguard. The arrangement had been made between him and Scovel, he promised Estrada Palma, "so that no one will suspect a thing."[11]

The *Martha*, however, ran into bad luck. When it approached its prearranged landing point, there were Spanish gunboats patrolling in the vicinity and the schooner was forced back to its home port of Bahia Honda. After being informed that the *Martha* might not sail again for several weeks, Scovel decided to make his own arrangements for getting into Cuba, borrowing the clothes and identification papers of Harry Brown, a veteran *World* reporter, who happened to be in Key West.

During his meeting with Creelman in the Inglaterra café, Scovel stressed that Pulitzer's priority at the moment was for well-documented investigations into reports that Spanish troops were committing atrocities against civilians. No doubt with Scovel's help, Greelman arranged to cross the military cordon around Havana to visit the village of Campo Florida where, a few days earlier, unarmed villagers had allegedly been massacred by Spanish troops. Riding with two Cuban guides, Creelman left Havana after nightfall, evading the sentry posts on the major road out of the city. In a field just outside the village, his guides pointed out a mound of fresh earth. As Creelman stood by holding a lantern, the guides began disinterring the evidence. "The hands of the slain Cubans were tied behind their backs," Creelman wrote later. "The sight . . . would have moved the hardest heart. I made a vow at that moment that I would help to extinguish Spanish sovereignty in Cuba, if I had to shed my blood for it." [12]

Creelman's account of his journey, complete with a list of the names of thirty-three victims, was sent out of Havana by steamer and appeared in the *World* on May 1. That same day Creelman personally delivered a copy of his story to Weyler. If the captain-general cared to know "the real cause of the war," he announced, he ought to conduct an investigation of the "crimes against civilization" committed at Campo Florida.[13] Weyler's response was to order Creelman off the island. And for good measure, when the captain-general signed the deportation order, he added the name of the troublesome Frederick Lawrence as well.

Scovel's armed bodyguard finally caught up with him on May 18, at Hoyo Colorado, near Havana. Scovel was determined to produce a report on civilian deaths so well documented that it could not possibly be dismissed. In the first installment of his series, published on May 27 to coincide with the opening of the Great Cuban-American Fair in Madison Square Garden, Scovel described riding with his escort in the gray light before dawn through a ghostly countryside of abandoned farmhouses and empty barns. Many farmers had slaughtered their livestock rather than let the Spanish confiscate them, and the fields were dotted with carcasses in varying stages of decay; the entire countryside smelled of death. The rainy season had begun, and in San Pedro, the first village on his itinerary, Scovel found a flock of about fifty vultures gathered in the village square, their wet feathers gleaming with coppery highlights, picking away at a pile of carrion that proved to be human remains. "I came here with the conviction that the reports of these slayings of unarmed men were very much exaggerated," Scovel wrote. But now, he said, he was convinced that James Creelman had "hit the nail on the head."[14]

Early in June, he and his escort slipped through the Mariel *trocha* into Pinar del Río Province. Over the next six weeks, they collected 196 affidavits testifying to incidents of brutality that resulted in a total of 212 deaths. Aside from two incidents of multiple murder, one in Mariel and the one near Marianao, most of the testimony described random killings and disappearances, the sort of banal horrors all too familiar in countries torn by partisan warfare.

Doroteo Delgado, a middle-aged woman who lived near Mariel, testified: "Yesterday in the morning at the approach of the column of Colonel Frances from Mariel to the place called 'La Merced' they spoke to my son, 18 years old, asking for the insurgents, and as he answered that he did not know, one of the soldiers, in the presence of his chief, stuck him five or six times with the barrel of his carbine, leaving him much injured...." The irregulars went from house to house asking for the location of a rebel "hospital." "Then they came back to my house.... I said I knew there was one in Mariel and one in Guanajay and they beat me with a cane."[15]

Florinda Espinosa said: "My two nephews were killed by the troops for no reason whatsoever. They went to visit some friends, and when they arrived at La Vigia near Cabañas, they were caught by the irregulars [attached to] a column of infantry. Francisco Espinosa tried to run and the irregulars killed him with a shot to the head. They then took Pelaya Espinosa to San Sebastian, where they hacked him to pieces with an infantry bayonet. Neither of my nephews were *insurrectos* and they had nothing to do with the war. One was twenty years old, the other nineteen."

Although Scovel's articles were admittedly highly emotional, they differed from earlier atrocity reports in that they cited specific locales, the names and ages of witnesses, even in many cases the names of the leaders of the *guerrillero* death squads. Only the names of the witnesses who gave the depositions were withheld from the published articles, for fear of reprisals.

Concurrently with these reports, the *World* published four long interviews Scovel had conducted with General Maceo. Repeatedly invited by Scovel to characterize Weylerism as a "war of extermination," Maceo demurred. It would be going too far, he insisted, to say that the Spanish had embarked on a "general slaughter of children." The cases Scovel was uncovering, though tragic in themselves, were no more than "occasional horrible examples."[16]

Maceo, the "Bronze Titan," was the idol of the ex-slaves who made up most of the insurgent army and was by far the most charismatic hero of the revolution, both at home and abroad. For that very reason, unfortunately he was suspect in the eyes of the upper-class Creoles who dominated the civilian wing of the revolution. White Cubans were haunted by the example of Haiti, where Toussaint L'Ouverture's rebellion against France had been followed by the massacre of white slaveholders and the establishment of a black republic. As a result, Maceo and his army in Pinar del Río had been quietly abandoned, while filibuster ships continued to carry goods to resupply rebel commanders in central and eastern Cuba.

In his conversations with Scovel, a weary-sounding Maceo insisted that he had no political ambitions and was looking forward to a quiet retirement as soon as the war was over. At the same time, he stressed the blow to Cuban morale that would result if his fast-dwindling "army" were actually exterminated. These comments were obviously intended to send a message to Junta officials in the United States, and apparently they succeeded. In September 1896, two months after the interview appeared, Maceo was resupplied by a filibuster expedition led by Colonel Leyte Vidal. Among the volunteers in Vidal's party was Máximo Gómez's son Panchito, his presence a signal that Gómez had sided with Maceo against the civilian leaders.

The survival of Maceo's army was still very much in doubt when Scovel finished his tour of Pinar del Río in early August. Scovel was counting on leaving the island via Havana, but in Mariel he and his escort discovered that the fortified *trocha*, which a few months earlier had consisted of little more than a simple barbed-wire fence guarded by regular patrols, was now all but impassable. The *trocha* had been reinforced by a double barrier of tree trunks, brushwood, and barbed wire, enclosing and protecting the railroad right-of-way, the installation of electric lights had been completed, and the jungle trails on both sides had been booby-trapped with trip-wire mines. Searching for a way around this formidable obstacle, Scovel and his companions pressed southward until they reached the bayous of the Majana swamp. Crossing the swamp took three days and two nights, with nothing to eat or drink but "green water." The gunshot wound that Scovel had received the previous February had never completely healed, and after three days of soaking in polluted swamp water it became dangerously infected. Once again, by the time he reached Havana Scovel was too ill to walk under his own power, and once again, friends connected with the American Consulate contrived to have him shipped home in disguise.

Scovel's condition must have been alarming, because when he reached New York, Brad Merrill offered him a four-month furlough to recuperate. He headed for Cleveland where the local society pages duly took note of "the prodigal's return." As the result of his series on Spanish atrocities, which had been nationally syndicated, Scovel had become a minor celebrity—a hero to some, a dangerous agitator to others—and he soon found that his notoriety did not mix well with his leadership of the local "fast" set.

Before he had been in town two weeks, the local papers reported that he and his companions had been ejected from a Cleveland theater, allegedly for making "insulting remarks" during a performance by the actress Dorothy Drew. The scandal was widely reported by Republican newspapers, and one editorial writer for a newspaper in Elmira, New York, gleefully noted that the self-appointed "managing editor of the Cuban war" had proven himself to be a "little boy in need of a paddling."[17]

In a letter published in the Cleveland papers, Scovel gave a different version of the unpleasant episode. A group of rowdies in adjoining seats had been whistling and shouting insults at Miss Drew, and when an usher asked the troublemakers to leave, they loudly refused. At this point, Scovel and his friends intervened on the usher's side. In the meantime, however, the intermission curtain had come down and Miss Drew, unnerved, retreated to her dressing room in tears, refusing to return until the entire section had been cleared. Rather than cause Miss Drew "further distress," Scovel said, his party left the theater voluntarily after helping the manager eject the rowdies.

Scovel's account was supported by the theater manager, and a local reporter assigned to investigate the matter concluded that most of the blame lay with Miss Drew for overreacting, an interesting commentary on Cleveland theater manners in the 1890s. Whatever the facts, Scovel drew the obvious conclusion that he had to choose between his Cleveland friends and his reputation. He immediately left for an extended visit with his brother's family in Pittsburgh, and within a matter of days he was assiduously courting a twenty-five-year-old St. Louis socialite whom he met at the home of mutual friends.

Frances Cabanné was a stylish brunette with a heart-shaped face and ebullient personality. She was also an accomplished horsewoman and athlete.

"I beg you not to love me," she told Harry, a request that he believed, no doubt rightly, was not meant to be taken literally.

However, the obstacles to marriage seemed insurmountable. The Cabannés were Roman Catholics and one of St. Louis's oldest families. In fact they were *the* oldest family, direct descendants of a French trader who established his homestead on land that later became St. Louis's Forest Park. Frances's father, the improbably named Sarpy Carr Cabanné, was a prosperous grain broker and Bourbon Democrat, a member of the faction that had still not forgiven the shooting of Colonel Slayback in the offices of Pulitzer's *Post-Dispatch*. Julia Cabanné was a housebound invalid, and the family assumed that Frances, as the eldest daughter, would choose a husband from St. Louis so that she would be available to nurse her ailing mother. The chances of the Cabannés consenting to their daughter's betrothal to a Joseph Pulitzer protégé and a Protestant (they didn't know he was an atheist, which was of course even worse) seemed remote, but Frances was at least as headstrong as Harry, and by the end of October the couple was so serious that her family was thoroughly alarmed.

Fortunately, at least from the family's point of view, Scovel was urgently summoned back to New York. The Cuban rainy season was over, and General Weyler was expected to launch his first major campaign in the countryside sometime before the beginning of 1897. Brad Merrill wanted Scovel to head for Florida, where the *World* would have a boat ready to ferry him to Cuba.

Before leaving New York, Scovel completed a long four-part essay on the Cuban situation, which dominated the front pages of the *World* during November. Attacking the romanticized tales of Amazons and "communal workshops" circulated by his rivals, Scovel noted that Spain still held a decisive advantage in the conflict, with some 200,000 men in the field as opposed to 50,000 "sturdy patriots" on the republican side. Nevertheless, he predicted, the rebellion would never be put down so long as "the Spanish military brain is held captive by the *trocha* idea." As for Weyler, Scovel added, the captain-general "has never been credited with military genius. *But* he handles his columns better than Martínez Campos." The stage, therefore, was set for a decisive campaign, at nearly even odds. "The struggle to free Cuba will soon be worthy of the bloody name and fame of war," he concluded hopefully.[18]

III

Our Intrepid
Special Commissioners

Shrapnel, Chivalry,
and Sauce Mousseline

DURING the autumn of 1896, when not reading Scovel's accounts of the war in Cuba, purchasers of the New York *World* were following the misadventures of that indefatigable self-promoter, Anna Held, who was being sued by her milkman for nonpayment. Miss Held had a standing order for forty quarts of milk a day, which she supposedly used for her much publicized beauty baths, but she was refusing to pay her bill, complaining that the milkman persisted in delivering Jersey milk, so rich it "looked like butter" and completely unsuitable for her beauty routine. In other major news, Brooklynites were getting used to the new Atlantic Avenue trolley, "De only Fast ting in Brooklyn," according to the Yellow Kid; Lillie Langtry had sued her husband for divorce, the better to pursue her liaison with the Prince of Wales; and the mugging of a Mrs. Thompson, in broad daylight on a crowded street in Passaic, New Jersey, was deemed unusual enough to rate a full twelve column inches.

Journal readers were being kept up-to-date on the activities of the American-born Duchess of Marlborough, the former Consuelo Vanderbilt, who was attempting to introduce the new sport of bicycle hockey to British society. They could also follow the saga of "The Shocking Depravity and Dare Devil Exploits of Beautiful Martha White—A Typical Female Degenerate Who Lives Among the Moonshiners in the Mountain Fastnesses in Georgia." And the Sunday magazine, under the editorship of Morrill Goddard, continued to churn out features guaranteed to keep husbands and wives bickering well into midweek. One such article posed the question "Are Women Really Only Big Children?" and answered it with a resounding "Yes," citing as evidence the theories of phrenologist Cesare Lambroso.

The feud of the yellow kids was at its height. The *World* was spending two hundred dollars a week to pay boys to distribute posters. The *Journal* allocated three times that amount. Destroying the posters of the competition was part of the game, and George Luks burlesqued the street fights in a cartoon depicting his yellow kid as "Maceo de Cuben" presiding over a fracas at the Hogan's Alley *trocha.*

Although the two papers were often accused of being as indistinguishable as the silly grins of the twins' faces, this could not be said of their positions on the big story of the fall, the presidential election.

Much to the horror of Joseph Pulitzer, his beloved Democratic Party had adopted a platform that called for rampant inflation as the solution to the country's problems. Although personally sympathetic to his party's nominee, the thirty-six-year-old Congressman William Jennings Bryan, Pulitzer could not bring himself to support free silver, which he denounced as "a species of hysteria," an intentional pun. When Hearst came out for Bryan, practically the only major publisher east of the Mississippi to do so, Pulitzer was convinced that the California mining heir was backing the Democratic candidate only because he expected to profit from the speculation in precious metals that would inevitably be touched off by a Bryan victory. *World* editorials denounced Hearst for practicing "Anaconda politics" and accused him of having a "double stake" in the election, allusions to the Anaconda and Homestake mines, the basis of the Hearst family fortune.

In fact, Hearst had his doubts about the merits of free silver, but he allowed himself to be swept along by the enthusiasm of his employees. Charlie Michelson, for example, had once worked as a clerk in a mining company store where he and all the miners were paid in Mexican pesos, exchangeable only at rates set by the company. It was hard to convince Westerners like him that sound money was essential to anyone apart from New York bankers and Wall Street.

The *Journal* pulled out all the stops for Bryan, promising its readers that a Democratic victory would lead to a doubling of the workingman's wages. Admittedly, this was only because the price of *everything* would double, but the *Journal* took the position that inflation was good for the country. "Go back to the times when we had rising prices and you will find that all kinds of people, including laborers, were prosperous."[1]

Hearst had become Bryan's major financial backer in the East. Although he could not stave off the inevitable Democratic defeat, his paper's attacks on the Republican candidate did serious damage. *Journal* cartoonists had a field day portraying William McKinley as a hollow man, a nonentity in the thrall of what they called "the syndicate," the circle of Midwestern businessmen who were his chief financial backers. Cartoonist Homer Davenport caricatured McKinley as a befuddled would-be Napoleon wondering, "Is my hat on straight?" and, in another full-page cartoon, as "The only man in America *not* talking politics." Mark Hanna, the most prominent member of the "syndicate," was invariably drawn by Davenport as an overstuffed, bilious capitalist wearing a suit decorated with dollar signs.

Pulitzer's inability to commit himself to the Democratic candidate had a terrible effect on his nerves. He had assigned James Creelman to follow Bryan around the country, and at his home in Bar Harbor, he pored over Creelman's daily reports, bombarding the correspondent with lists of questions and demands for additional information, but allowing almost nothing Creelman wrote to be printed. The situation was so frustrating that Creelman accepted a job offer from Hearst leaving the *World* without a senior political correspondent.

On election night, November 7, 1896, the *World* staged a somewhat subdued rally in City Hall Park. Vote tallies and portraits of the candidates were projected onto the side of the Pulitzer Building, which had been transformed for the occasion into "the largest magic lantern screen ever made."[2] As the returns trickled in it was soon evident that McKinley had won a resounding victory, amassing 236 electoral votes to Bryan's 177. "Thousands cheered," reported the *World*, whose tepid account made it clear that the paper's editors were not necessarily among them.

The *Journal*, meanwhile, had rented Madison Square Garden for the Bryanites' last hurrah, and although its candidate lost, the paper's editors had cause for satisfaction. Despite the defection of major advertisers in retaliation for supporting a candidate anathema to the business community, the paper's circulation had risen and it was now securely established as New York's second largest newspaper: The November 8 morning *Journal*, the issue that carried the previous day's election returns, sold 956,921 copies. More important, many smaller Democratic papers that had previously picked up syndicated news and features from the *World* were switching to Hearst, the party loyalist. For the first time since he had arrived in New York, Pulitzer's position as the regional voice of the Democratic party was threatened.

Hearst wasted no time capitalizing on his success. On November 24, the *Journal* inaugurated a new phase in its coverage of the war in Cuba by announcing that it had chartered its own filibuster boat, the 112-foot-long steam yacht *Vamoose*—"the fastest craft that ever left a trail of foam upon the waters of New York."

During a speed trial in New York Harbor the *Vamoose* had been clocked at twenty-six miles per hour, a speed at which, the *Journal* boasted, it would be able to cover the distance between Havana and Key West in well under four hours. What the *Journal* didn't bother to mention was that the *Vamoose* was also a white elephant, leased to the paper by Hearst himself.

When he had lived in San Francisco, Hearst's pride and joy was his fifty-foot speedboat *Aquila*, which he used to race across the bay to Sausalito to pay midday visits to his mistress, Tessie Powers. On moving to New York, he had left the *Aquila* in the care of his mother, but on her first day trip, the yacht ran into choppy seas. Wet, seasick and shaken, Mrs. Hearst decided that she required a larger boat, one broad in the beam so that it would be more stable, yet also very fast, since to her mind a successful trip by water was one that was over as quickly as possible.

At Mrs. Hearst's request, her son ordered the *Vamoose* from a New York shipyard, specifying the largest boat that could possibly be shipped by rail to California. The plan was to sail the finished yacht down to Panama and then bring it across the isthmus on a custom-built crib mounted on three flatbed railroad cars. Two low-clearance bridges would have to be dismantled to allow the boat to pass, but Hearst agreed to pay the costs of having them taken down and speedily reconstructed.

Unfortunately, the president of the Panama Railway Company was a certain Colonel Rives, whose daughter Amélie was the author of a novel, *The Quick and the Dead*, which had received an unappreciative review in the San Francisco *Examiner.* Seldom has the victim of a bad review had such an ideal opportunity for revenge. Amélie Rives waited until the *Vamoose* was already in Panama, then talked her father into canceling the shipping arrangements.[3]

During the sail to Panama, meanwhile, the *Vamoose* had turned out to be unwieldy in bad weather, exactly the quality that Mrs. Hearst could not tolerate. Hearst's income was not boundless, as the world thought, and he hoped to take advantage of a clause in the boat builders' contract specifying that the entire purchase price (variously given as sixty thousand or eighty thousand dollars) would be refundable if the *Vamoose* failed to attain a maximum speed of twenty-six miles per hour. But when the test run was held in New York Harbor, the *Vamoose* passed easily, and the frustrated Hearst decided to cut his losses by leasing the boat to his own newspaper.

So the *Journal* had itself a filibuster boat. The question in many people's minds was why.

Since cable traffic out of Cuba was now strictly censored, Hearst presumably intended to have his *Vamoose* carry dispatches back and forth between Havana and Key West, giving the *Journal* a decisive edge over its competitors. Nevertheless, word that the yacht had been outfitted with a one-pound cannon aroused suspicions that Hearst was planning to launch his own privately financed invasion of Cuba, a notion that Hearst's loose talk did nothing to dispel.

Hearst during this period was given to fantasizing out loud about his ambition to become the successor to Sam Houston and John C. Frémont. Stephen Crane, who happened to be working for the *Journal* that autumn, caricatured Hearst in his novel *Active Service* as "Sturgeon," the filibuster-mad publisher of the "New York *Eclipse.*" In one scene of the novel, Sturgeon tries to talk his correspondent Rufus Coleman into going to Cuba for his newspaper. Seated on the edge of a table in his office, "dangling one leg dreamily," Sturgeon outlines his "great scheme":

> Now listen. This is immense. The *Eclipse* enlists a battalion of men to go to Cuba and fight the Spaniards under its own flag— The *Eclipse* flag. Collect trained officers from here and there— enlist every young devil we see—drill 'em—best rifles—loads of ammunition—provisions—staff of doctors and nurses—a couple of dynamite guns—everything complete, best in the world. Now, isn't that great. What's the matter with that now? Eh? Eh? Isn't that great? It's great, isn't it? Eh?[4]

Nevertheless, Hearst did not dare openly defy the Neutrality Act. For its maiden voyage, the *Vamoose* was to be limited to a cargo of medical supplies and other nonmilitary aid. To make the most of the publicity value of the expedition, Hearst hired as his special correspondent the dazzling Richard Harding Davis, man about town, star reporter, and best-selling author.

Richard Harding Davis's celebrity far exceeded his accomplishments. He had posed for his friend, the artist Charles Dana Gibson, who used him as a model for the male counterpart of the Gibson girl, and his square-jawed, pink-cheeked good looks were considered the ultimate in male appeal, his character the epitome of what used to be called "muscular Christianity." His immensely popular novella, *Gallegher,* about a newspaper copyboy turned detective, had convinced thousands of youthful readers that working for one of the great dailies was the height of glamour. Davis's own life seemed to bear out this fantasy. As one contemporary noted, a typical day for Richard Harding Davis could be summed up as "shrapnel, chivalry and sauce Mousseline, and so to work the next morning on an article."[5]

Davis was given to referring to himself in the third person, by his monogram RHD and, though brought up in Philadelphia, he pronounced his surname Dī'vus. Despite his famous snobbery, those who came to know him well found something admirable and oddly touching about his character. Augustus Thomas, a fellow writer who met him at the Lamb's Club in 1889, observed of Davis that "at his very best he was in heart and mind a boy grown tall."[6]

Davis's mother, the novelist Rebecca Harding Davis, had married late and sacrificed her considerable talent to the need to produce commercial books that would help support her family. Over the years, she had rechanneled her creative energies into the upbringing of her adored eldest son, so much the apple of her eye that she described the birth of his younger brother Charles two years later as "a sequel to the story—an afterpiece."[7] Extending the analogy, her third child, a girl named Nora born in 1872, hardly rated an et cetera.

As an undergraduate at Lehigh University in Bethlehem, Pennsylvania, Davis attracted attention immediately by showing up for classes dressed in impeccably tailored English-cut suits and kid gloves and carrying a cane. He was already writing free-lance pieces for various newspapers, and whenever he did anything even mildly noteworthy on campus, from delivering a speech to participating in a tennis tournament, he sent publicity releases to the national press. Thanks to his own promotional efforts, Davis became the country's best-known undergraduate, a success that did not prevent him from being thrown out of Lehigh for scholastic failure.

In 1889, after a brief apprenticeship at the Philadelphia *Record*, Davis joined the New York *Sun*, where he quickly became the protégé and close friend of Arthur Brisbane. He scored his first major scoop only two weeks after he was hired. Returning on the Hudson River ferry from an assignment in Jersey City, Davis was approached by a professional con artist known as "Sheeny Mike." Mistaking the overdressed young reporter for a wealthy and quite stupid British tourist, Mike offered him an opportunity to invest in an Old Master painting that had suddenly become "available" at a fraction of its value. Davis played the sucker's role to perfection, and when the ferry landed managed to lure Sheeny Mike to the vicinity of police headquarters on lower Broadway where he made a citizen's arrest on the street, turned his culprit over to the law in front of a cheering crowd, and then rushed back to the office to write up the story.

The arrest of Sheeny Mike made Davis the town's hottest journalistic star overnight. Already, colleagues were beginning to talk about "the luck of Richard Harding Davis," though of course luck had nothing to do with it. "Reporters," as a character in one of Davis's short stories observes, "become star reporters because they observe things other people miss and because they don't let it appear that they have observed them."[8]

Many authors draw on their own life experiences as subject matter. Davis was unusual in that he tended to model himself after the characters he created in his fiction. Soon after joining the *Sun*, he began producing a popular series of sketches about a bachelor-about-town named Courtlandt Van Bibber, a sort of upper-class Robin Hood in a top hat and Inverness cape. Before long, Davis had all but become Van Bibber, a celebrity socialite famous for his impeccable manners and boyish gallantry—as one critic said of Van Bibber himself, a sort of "office boy's idea of a gentleman."[9]

To his credit, Davis saw that his beau ideal image could become a trap and gave up his comfortable existence to become an international correspondent for *Harper's Weekly*, traveling to the Middle East and Central America. As a political analyst, he was conservative, often arrogant, but never boring. In a piece written from North Africa, he remarked how tedious the natives must find the English. The Englishman, he observed, constantly says that a man's home is his castle, yet he invades other people's countries and promptly settles in to make a nuisance of himself. He "asks for bitter ale, and complains because he cannot get his bath, and all the rest of it, quite as if he had been invited to come."[10] Yet Davis was no cultural relativist. He had no doubt that the Anglo-Saxon race was superior when it came to managing the world, and after witnessing an 1895 coup attempt in Honduras, he wrote: "The Central American cannot understand that when a bad man is elected to office legally it is better in the long run that he should serve out his full term than that a better man should drive him out and defy the Constitution. . . . What he needs is to have a protectorate established over him, either by the United States or by another power; it does not matter which, so long as it leaves the Nicaragua canal in our hands."[11]

By 1894, Davis's travels were being interrupted by periods when he was bedridden with what he called "nervous storms." Apparently his chief complaint was sciatica, but it was complicated by feelings of depression and worthlessness. The doctors diagnosed "shattered nerves" and Davis complained of bouts of "morbidness" when "all I want to do is turn my face to the wall."[12]

No doubt part of the problem was that Davis, at age thirty the heartthrob of American girlhood, was still a virgin. His name had been linked with a succession of women, notably heiress Helen Benedict, actress Maude Adams, and teenage ingenue Ethel Barrymore, but all these relationships were strictly platonic. His shyness when it came to demonstrations of affection was legendary; when he was an usher at the wedding of his good friend Charles Dana Gibson he was teased by all the guests because he couldn't bring himself to kiss the bride. On another occasion, when asked by an interviewer "what he looked for in a woman" he quipped, "clean gloves." The remark was much quoted. Unfortunately, he meant it. Few women were ever fastidious enough for him to feel entirely comfortable in their presence.

There was one woman who met Davis's impossible standards —Princess Alex of Hesse. The princess happened to be touring the Acropolis in Athens on a day when Davis was there in 1893. He had been too shy to ask for an introduction, but in his fantasies she became his ideal mate, and while bedridden with his "nerve storms," he was working hard on a novel about a young American artist traveling in Europe who falls in love with an exquisite princess whom he knows only from her photograph.

In the novel, the hero, Morton Carlton, follows Aline, his dream princess, around Europe, mooning over her from a distance and confiding his troubles to another American tourist, Edith Morris. On one occasion, Morton tells Edith about his worst nightmare: He is at his own wedding, the vows have just been completed, and as he turns away from the altar his eyes meet those of one of the bridesmaids and he realizes that she, not his bride, is the one he should have married after all. "I care too much to make Platonic friendship possible," frets Morton, "and not enough to marry any particular woman.... In my free state, I can continue to search without any sense of responsibility."[13]

Morton Carlton resolves his problem by realizing that it is Edith he really loves. For Davis, there was no such happy ending, at least not yet. In the fall of 1895, a few months after *The Princess Aline* was published, he began a well-publicized affair with the chanteuse Yvette Guilbert who, according to the New York *World*, possessed the "loveliest neck in New York." Davis made a point of informing his brother that he was "breakfasting and supping with Yvette Guilbert every day."[14] But those in the know understood that Guilbert, though she rarely missed a chance to have her name linked with a celebrity, had a long-standing relationship with her business manager, Teddy Marks.

At the time she met Davis, Guilbert was hoping to crown her extended American tour with a gala recital at the Metropolitan Opera House. Her request to rent the house for one night was opposed by some of the Met's regular patrons, who objected that Guilbert's repertoire of songs such as "Les Ingenues," which even the New York *Journal* called "rather risqué," did not belong in an auditorium dedicated to grand opera. Thanks to Davis's friendship with the likes of music critic Reginald de Koven, the objections of the Met patrons were swept aside. Guilbert sang her recital before a sold-out house and received favorable reviews. Nothing more was heard of Guilbert's great romance with RHD, and a week later she and Teddy Marks announced their engagement.

In May of 1896, a few months after Yvette Guilbert passed out of Davis's life, Hearst offered him a chance to go to Moscow to attend the wedding of Alex of Hesse to Tsar Nicholas II. In many respects, the trip was a disaster. The *Journal* was slow about forwarding expense money and, worse, Hearst failed to make good on his promise to get Davis an invitation to the religious ceremony, forcing him to finagle one for himself by flattering and cajoling the Russian minister of protocol, Count Dashcoff. "I would not do it again for ten thousand dollars," Davis wrote his brother of the assignment. "And if I told you of the way Hearst acted and [*Journal* European correspondent Julian] Ralph interfered with impertinent cables, you would wonder I am sane." Despite his disgust with Hearst, Davis described the event as "the wedding of the century." As for Alex, he found her "much more beautiful and sad looking than ever before."[15]

Six months later, when Hearst came to Davis with another bright idea for a story, the memory of Hearst's broken promises had faded and the chance to go to Cuba on the *Vamoose* seemed too good to pass up. Davis was already completing the final chapters of his next novel, *Soldiers of Fortune,* about a young American civil engineer who single-handedly foils a military coup in the mythical Latin American country of Olancho. As the chief passenger of the *Vamoose,* Davis could play soldier of fortune in earnest. After delivering his one-million-dollar cargo to Gómez, he and his illustrator partner Fred Remington would spend a month with the insurgents in Santa Clara Province. Charlie Michelson would be on board the yacht, waiting offshore to pick up Davis's copy, which would be delivered to the coast by a special unit of Cubans, hand-picked by the Florida Junta.

The *Vamoose* departed from New York in style, racing past the shipping traffic in the harbor as members of its white-jacketed crew stood at attention along the rails. But once again, the *Journal*'s plans went awry almost immediately. The yacht's crew had been hired in Newport on the understanding that the *Vamoose* was a pleasure craft. No one had told them that they were going to be dodging Spanish gunboats off the coast of Cuba, and after taking the yacht as far as Florida, they went on strike. While Michelson tried to negotiate a settlement, Davis was left with nothing to do but sit on the porch of the Key West Hotel twirling the fifty-dollar field glasses he had bought on the *Journal*'s expense account or hang out at Pendleton's newsstand rereading old copies of the *Police Gazette* "for the hundredth time," all the while cursing his bad judgment for being seduced by Hearst's promises yet again.[16]

The *Vamoose* had been gone just a few days when a young Yale graduate named Ralph Delahaye Paine showed up at the offices of the *Journal.* Paine was another minister's son. A muscular six-footer with jug ears and a pleasant but slightly goofy smile, he had grown up in Jacksonville, Florida, where his father preached at the Green Street Presbyterian Church. After graduating from high school he spent a year reporting local news for his hometown paper at a salary of twelve dollars a week. His savings from this job, plus some help from his parents, enabled him to go to Yale, where he rowed crew, played a little football, and wrote poetry that was published in the Yale literary magazine. Graduating with the class of 1894, he went to work at the Philadelphia *Press*. But after two years, his career was going nowhere.

Paine's luck changed when he happened to learn the name of the Junta's chief organizer back home in Jacksonville, a certain Señor Huau. "Wow! This is easy!" was the punning thought that leapt to Paine's mind. José Huau was none other than the owner of the corner cigar store and soda fountain where he had bought ice cream as a child.

Although Paine's editor at the Philadelphia *Press* was not impressed by this discovery, Hearst was. He had just learned of the *Vamoose*'s labor problems and Paine offered him an opportunity to hedge his expensive gamble on the Davis-Remington expedition. As Paine recalled it, Hearst rummaged around his office until he found a long mahogany case, which he opened to display an ornate dress sword with a gold-plated, diamond-encrusted hilt and an elaborately chased scabbard. Hearst explained that at the Cuban-American fair of the previous May the *Journal* had auctioned off chances to vote for the "world's greatest living soldier." The winner of the contest, to no one's surprise, had been Máximo Gómez, and the ceremonial sword, valued at two thousand dollars, was to be his trophy.

Pulling the sword from its scabbard, Hearst showed Paine the inscriptions on the blade: "Viva Cuba Libre" and "To Máximo Gómez, Commander-in-Chief of the Army of the Republic of Cuba."

"These inscriptions would be devilish hard to explain to the Spanish army, if you happen to be caught, wouldn't they?" Hearst mused. "I swear, I don't know what else to do with the confounded thing. Of course, if you are nabbed at sea, you can probably shuck it overboard in time."

"And if I get surrounded on land, perhaps I can swallow it?" Paine suggested sarcastically.

But the errand did have a certain lunatic appeal. "Never mind," he told Hearst. "I am the damn fool you are looking for."[17]

10

****

A Tale of the Tenderloin

I N ADDITION to challenging Pulitzer for primacy on the Cuba story, Hearst had set out to make the New York *Journal* the spokesman for the city's underclass. If the *World* championed the worthy poor, the *Journal* became the first paper to see the news value of the not-so-worthy, and in September of 1896 the paper hired twenty-four-year-old Stephen Crane, already famous as the author of *The Red Badge of Courage*, to write a series of articles that would capture the earthy dramas of the city's night-session police courts.

Crane was still researching the first article in the series when he inadvertently became the protagonist of his own police court drama. On the night of September 15, he visited the Turkish Smoking Parlor—an opium den on Twenty-ninth Street near Sixth Avenue—where he met a twenty-one-year-old auburn-haired beauty named Dora Clark, who confided that she had been the victim of police harassment. Later that night, after interviewing Clark at a nearby tavern, Crane was walking a woman friend of hers to the trolley stand when a policeman approached Clark, who was waiting on the corner minding her own business, and arrested her for soliciting two passers-by.

The arrest created a dilemma for Crane. For all he knew, Clark was a streetwalker, but she certainly hadn't been working that night. "If I have ever had a conviction in my life," he wrote, "I am convinced she did not solicit those two men." What's more, the arresting officer, Detective Charles Becker, was a corrupt cop, "as picturesque as a wolf," and a buddy of a patrolman who had been harassing Clark ever since she refused to go to bed with him.[1]

The next day, despite warnings from the night court desk sergeant, Crane showed up in court to testify on Clark's behalf. At the price of publicly admitting that he had been a patron of an opium den, and in the company of three women politely identified as "chorus girls," he was able to convince the judge to drop the prostitution charge against Clark.

The press was delighted. The Dora Clark case was the perfect 1890s scandal, combining salacious background with plenty of opportunity for self-righteous moralizing. Hearst, to his credit, backed Crane all the way. Editorial writers from Boston to Buffalo also agreed that young Mr. Crane had done the right thing in sacrificing his reputation on the altar of chivalry; however, few could resist winking at Crane's claim that he had been interviewing Clark for the purposes of researching a story. "The chances are that the youthful literary prodigy was on a genuine 'lark,'" opined the Boston *Traveler.* "That is the way it looks to a cold and unprejudiced world."[2]

Unfortunately for Crane, the Dora Clark affair was far from over. Detective Becker was not only corrupt, he had powerful friends. His immediate supervisor was a certain Captain Chapman, who in turn had the confidence of Police Commissioner Theodore Roosevelt. Becker and Chapman were collecting protection money from half the nightspot owners in the Tenderloin, and they were not about to let a mere reporter interfere with their scam.

Stephen Crane was yet another preacher's kid, and one who felt the burdens of the role far more than most. His father, the Reverend Jonathan Townley Crane, was a prolific author of religious tracts and pamphlets urging abstention from drink, tobacco, dancing, card-playing, theater, baseball, and novels. Of this last pursuit, he wrote that it was a dangerous pastime because it tended to generate a "morbid love of excitement." Christians who could not forgo the pleasures of fiction entirely were admonished to proceed with caution and "if any harm results, Stop at once."[3]

When not pamphleteering in favor of abstinence, Jonathan Crane found time to sire fourteen children. Four of the last five babies died in infancy. Stephen, a sickly child born when his mother was forty-five years old, managed to survive.

Jonathan Crane died suddenly of a heart attack when Stephen was seven, and his widow moved the family to Asbury Park, New Jersey, where she eked out a small inherited income by writing articles for various Methodist publications. Mrs. Crane specialized in covering news of the Methodist summer resort of Ocean Grove, a community so straitlaced that even today it bans not only alcoholic beverages but the sale of Sunday newspapers.

By the time he was seventeen, Stephen was fed up with what he called "the Methodist Holy Side Show." Arriving at Syracuse University in fall of 1891, he set out to educate himself in all the vices he had been warned against. He drank, he chain-smoked, he swore colorfully, and he shunned the library, instead spending his time hanging around the town's eighteen whorehouses and scribbling away at a manuscript that may or may not have been the first draft of his novel, *Maggie.* "Crane, you'll never amount to anything," one of his professors lectured him. "Why don't you let up on writing and pay a little more attention to conic sections?"[4]

Syracuse and Crane parted company after one semester and he gravitated to New York where he shared a squalid room on Eastern Avenue (now Avenue A) with a former fraternity brother who was attending medical school. One block away was the Bowery, for Crane the source of endless inspiration. He cultivated the friendship of streetwalkers, con men, alcoholics and—venturing to the West Side of Manhattan—the habitués of Minetta Lane in Greenwich Village, at the time the home turf of a gang of armed robbers who sported such nicknames as "No Toes Charley" and "Bloodthirsty."

Crane had little in common with such chroniclers of slum life as Jacob Riis and Lincoln Steffens. To him, the denizens of the Bowery were not so much victims of a bad environment as fascinating sinners. Although he strove to sound hard-boiled, in reality his view of the criminal underclass was highly romanticized. He preferred to believe that these people had made a moral choice, if the wrong one. Even if damned, they were more alive than the Methodist strivers who were pious from habit.

A familiar figure in New York newspaper offices where he hung around looking for assignments, Crane wore the same shabby sweater for months on end. His fingers were stained yellow with nicotine, his eyes bleary from lack of sleep. He and his friends survived on breakfasts of day-old potato salad (a risky diet in prerefrigeration days) purchased from a Sixth Avenue delicatessen called Boeuf à la Mode, which Crane thought would be more aptly called "The Buffalo Mud."

No one had ever seemed less destined for commercial success. Crane's first novel, *Maggie, Girl of the Streets*, was considered so shocking that even after he paid to have it privately printed, no bookstore would agree to stock it. He was fired from his job as a stringer for the *Herald* because the city editor complained that he couldn't write. His copy was inaccurate, occasionally ungrammatical, and loaded with purple prose—literally. Sent to report a fire, he devoted several paragraphs to a lyrical description of the colorful flames, but got the address of the burning building wrong. And in a story that tried the editor's patience beyond endurance, he concluded a description of a street cleaner knocked down by a horse by writing that the poor wretch, as he fell, erupted in "a jet of violet, fastidious curses."

By 1894, however, Crane had begun to carve out a niche as a chronicler of the underclass. Then came the publication of *The Red Badge of Courage*. Written in much the same ungrammatical, simile-laden style that the *Herald* had rejected as amateurish, the short novel was hailed by *The Atlantic* as "great enough to start a new fashion in literature." Some early reviewers found Crane's descriptions of the private soldier's experience so vivid that they assumed that he must be a grizzled veteran of the Civil War. When it became generally known that Crane had not even been born until six years after the war ended—and, what's more, that he was the author of "blasphemous" verse and a novel whose heroine was a common streetwalker—the pages of the literary monthly *The*

Dial were filled with letters complaining that the novel was vulgar, full of split infinitives, and so lacking in "respect for our own people" that it should never have been published.

At first, Crane encouraged the snipers, cheerfully telling *Book Buyer* magazine that he had never been anywhere near a shooting war and that his only personal experience of the "rage of conflict" had been gained playing intramural football in prep school. By the time he went to work for Hearst, however, he was thoroughly sick of all the fuss. The literary lion William Dean Howells had predicted that Crane's *next* work would be a true masterpiece, a well-meaning comment that was tantamount to a curse. Other reviewers, meanwhile, were sharpening their fangs in anticipation of pronouncing his career a nine-day wonder. "Everybody sits down and calmly waits to see me be a chump," Crane complained.[5]

Theodore Roosevelt was one early fan of Crane's work. They had met at the Lantern Club, an informal supper club frequented chiefly by young newspapermen with literary ambition, and when Crane, who had been on a brief tour of the Southwest in 1894, wrote a story with a wild West setting he sent a copy to Roosevelt for a critique. The story, "A Man and Some Others," won Roosevelt's approval, though, he wrote Crane, he would have preferred that Crane had not allowed the "Mexican Greaser" character to get the better of a frontiersman. Perhaps some day, he suggested, Crane would consider writing another story in which the frontiersman came out the winner—"It is more normal that way!"[6]

Roosevelt was thirty-seven and, as one of New York's three police commissioners, a highly visible and controversial figure. Jacob Riis of the *Sun* wrote admiringly of how the commissioner, disguised in a cape and a slouch hat, made midnight forays into the city's worst neighborhoods in search of policemen who might be spending their shifts in saloons instead of on the beat. Joseph Pulitzer, who viewed Roosevelt's enforcement of the blue laws as an attempt to force middle-class Anglo-Saxon values on German saloon owners and their working-class patrons, was less charmed. In January 1896, a Pulitzer editorial warned darkly that, "Roosevelt, cowboy, bear-fighter, historian, declarer of foreign wars, advocate of blue laws, police mogul, is an able and most loquacious megalomaniac."

When Dora Clark was arrested, Crane's impulse was to fire

off a telegram to his friend Roosevelt. Other *Journal* reporters backed him up by doing investigative stories on Becker's and Chapman's pasts. Among other charges, Chapman had been observed in the company of the proprietor of a house of homosexual prostitutes. But as Crane ought to have realized, Roosevelt saw Crane's role in the controversy as ridiculous, and out of misplaced loyalty to his subordinate, or sheer stubbornness, he refused to investigate the *Journal*'s charges.

Crane himself was ready to admit defeat, but Dora Clark insisted on filing formal charges of misconduct against Becker. Over the next several weeks, Crane, as the most important potential witness in the case, became the target of police harassment. His room was searched without a warrant and when he complained, he was threatened with an arrest on drug charges. Despite advice from friends that this would be a good time to visit his brother upstate in Sullivan County, Crane appeared at Becker's disciplinary hearing, only to find that the proceedings had been turned into an inquest into his own character. The Police Department lawyer, Louis Grant, began by producing an opium pipe that had been seized during the search of his rooms.

"Do you smoke opium?" Grant asked.

"No," said Crane. But when Grant followed up by charging specifically that Crane had used opium at a certain house on West Twenty-seventh Street, he refused to answer.

"On what grounds?" asked Grant.

"Because it would tend to degrade me," replied Crane.

"Isn't it true that you live off income given you by women of the street?"

"No!"

Grant then called the janitor of the Twenty-seventh Street house, who testified that the house was a brothel where male clients were frequently robbed of their money and watches, and that Crane had lived there off and on over a six-month period with a pair of sisters, Amy and Sadie Huntington. Grant also produced a series of witnesses who had seen Crane on the night of Dora Clark's arrest and who claimed that he had appeared "dopey."[7]

Once again, the newspaper world rallied to Crane's defense. The Brooklyn *Daily Eagle* chided the Police Department for putting the reputation of an honest citizen on trial while ignoring the real issue of police corruption. The ever-loyal *Journal* caricatured Becker as "Officer Nightstick" and ran a vigorous editorial charging that Crane was the victim of "a despicable scheme of police intimidation." The editorial further maintained that the opium pipe had been in Crane's room only because "it was part of the bric-a-brac there."

Crane was neither a drug addict nor a pimp, but he did dabble in the vices he so often wrote about. Over the years Crane's friends and biographers have tried to protect him from scandal— one well-known photograph of Crane was found to have been heavily retouched by its owner to change the hookah Crane was smoking into an ordinary tobacco pipe. But the attitude of Crane's newspaper colleagues, who admired his courage in standing up to Becker, did not extend to the editors of the genteel quarterlies. Richard Watson Gilder of the ultrarespectable *Century*, who had previously objected to Crane's use of the oath *B'Gawd* in a story, abruptly canceled his plans to publish "A Man and Some Others."

Worse, Crane had made a dangerous enemy in Charles Becker. Promoted to the vice squad, Becker later became the silent partner of the notorious gangster Herman Rosenthal, whom he conspired to have murdered when Rosenthal threatened to testify against him in court. He ended his life in the electric chair in Sing Sing in 1915, the first New York City policeman ever convicted of murder. Becker's career was still in its early days in 1896, but his reputation was such that when he put out the word that it would no longer be healthy for Stephen Crane to live in New York, the terrified Crane wasted no time in getting out of town.

Crane went up to Harvard. Ivy League football games were major sports stories in the 1890s, and Crane was paid five hundred dollars by the *Journal* for covering Harvard's confrontation with the varsity eleven of the Carlisle Indian School. It was Crane's fantasy that the game would be a symbolic rematch of Custer versus the Sioux, but if the Carlisle team also saw it that way, they were too prudent to say so. Interviewed by Crane in their rooms before the game, the team members seemed merely bewildered by Crane's pointed suggestions that the contest might shape up into a sort of grudge match.

Crane wrote the story his way anyway, comparing the red jerseys of the Carlisle team to the flames of the Indian campfires before Little Bighorn. But even on this level of whimsy, football reporting could not sustain his interest for long. How Crane managed to avoid getting recruited for one of Hearst's Cuban adventures is a mystery. But by early November, he had accepted the offer of his friend Irving Bacheller, a fellow Lantern Club member, to go to Cuba as the correspondent for Bacheller's small news syndicate.

The Sins That March to Music

Unenthusiastic natures, how much they miss!

—Cora Taylor Crane

BY THE WINTER of 1896–97, Jacksonville, Florida, a resort town of some twenty-eight thousand permanent residents, had become the unofficial captial of the Cuban arms trade. Carrying seven hundred dollars in gold, his expense money from Bacheller, Crane checked into Jacksonville's best hotel, the St. James, in mid-November and immediately hooked up with "Cap" Morton, a retired skipper and sometime smuggler who ran a newsstand concession in the hotel lobby. Morton took Crane on a tour of "the Line," as Jacksonville's redlight district was called, ending up at the Hotel de Dream, the town's most elegant "nightclub," where Morton had a special woman friend.

The Hotel de Dream, so-called because it had once belonged to a woman named Ethel Dreme, was a weathered frame building decorated by only a semicircular design that proclaimed the establishment's name in large gilt letters. Inside, the parlor floor consisted of a series of rooms where customers could play cards or roulette, order a late supper, or drink beer or champagne (but not hard spirits) at a dollar a glass while being entertained by the house piano player and the amusing conversation of the owner and manager, Cora Taylor, known as "Miss Cora." The upstairs rooms were reserved for assignations between male customers and a dozen-odd ladies "of unusual comeliness and youth." [1]

Although Taylor's biographer, Lillian Gilkes, would insist that Taylor was not "technically" a madam because the women who worked for her did not actually live on the premises, this distinction was certainly lost on the Hotel de Dream's patrons. Nevertheless, Miss Cora's occupation did not prevent her from being one of the most exceptional and fascinating women of her time. At thirty-one, she had already lost the svelte figure she possessed as a teenager, and her square jaw was a bit too pronounced for her ever to have been considered pretty, but she made up for these shortcomings with her lush mane of blonde hair, her elegant if sometimes fussy clothes and, yes, her brilliant mind. Taylor was at once a genuine intellectual and an unpretentious woman who enjoyed taking over the kitchen to cook up several dozen of her special crullers or even a full-course turkey dinner for her "girls" and a few favored customers. "If she had any false notes, I was all too unskilled in recognizing authentic 'class,' or lack of it, to detect any," wrote Ernest McCready, a correspondent for the New York *Herald* who was a regular at the Hotel de Dream that same winter. "She was a cut above us in several ways." [2]

She was also a poet of the night. "Whatever is too precious, too tender, too good, too evil, too bashful for the day happens in the night," she wrote in her diary. "Night is the bath of life, the anodyne of heartaches, the silencer of passions, the breeder of them too, the teacher of those who would learn, the cloak that sets a man in with his soul." [3]

That November, Cora Taylor happened to be reading Crane's recently issued and not very successful novel, *George's Mother*. Crane himself was traveling "thinly incog.," using an alias to avoid attracting the attention of Pinkertons and treasury agents, but when he showed up at the Hotel de Dream it was inevitable that someone would point out to Miss Cora that the thin, dissolute figure standing next to the roulette wheel was the famous Stephen Crane, author of the book she kept on a shelf behind the bar.

Cora approached in a swirl of stiff taffeta, black lace, and faux pearls to ask for an autograph. Stephen inscribed her book, "To an unnamed sweetheart," adding a note: "Brevity is an element that enters importantly into all pleasures of life, and this is what makes pleasure sad: and so there is no pleasure but only sadness."

Surely this was one of the less prescient inscriptions of all time. Cora had her own ideas about brevity, and about the ties that bound men and women together. "Even when love is so base as to be only a thirst for pleasure it rarely dies in the first embrace," she wrote that same winter. "And who can say he possessed the entire woman in one night of love?"

Unlike Stephen, who could reasonably expect the scandal he had been involved with in New York to be forgotten in time, Cora had rejected middle-class morality with heroic finality. Born in Boston, she was the granddaughter of George Howorth, a well-to-do art dealer and one of the world's leading experts on the restoration of fine paintings. Her father, the painter John Howorth, died when she was six years old. Her mother soon remarried, but Cora did not get along with her stepfather (she never discussed why) and when still a teenager left home to live in New York with an aunt. After a brief first marriage, of which almost nothing is known, she appeared in London, where she took a second husband, twenty-eight-year-old Captain Donald Stewart, whose father was a field marshal and the former commander of Her Majesty's forces in India. A few years later, to use the then popular expression, she bolted from this marriage as well, although she never obtained a divorce.

Cora next turned up in Jacksonville in March 1895. According to local legend, she arrived on a millionaire's yacht—gossip variously named William B. Astor and Pierre Lorillard as the yachtsman—and was left behind after a quarrel with her host. At any rate, within a few months, she had found financial backing to purchase and refurbish the run-down Hotel de Dream.

Cora had hit the high spots, the low, and a good many in between, and she was given to discourses on the role of the "new woman" and denunciations of social hypocrisy. "Sin is easy if only because it meets with such very general encouragement," was one of her remarks. Another observation, typical of the ornate style she affected at times, was, "Zeus had unquestioned right to Io; but

woe betide when she suns her heart in smiles that belong to Hera!"
She defended her occupation as necessary as long as society refused to allow men and women to exercise their normal desires
any other way:

> We do many things in the excitement of companionship which
> our consciences fail to ratify in the secrecy of self-communion.
> We thus tacitly admit that we are irresistibly moved by the vibra-
> tion of a common chord of humanity. If we are piped unto, it
> seems reasonable to dance; and yet no one dances to his own
> solitary piping. If more allowances were made for the innocent
> impulses common to men, as gregarious animals, there might
> be less of the dangerous sense of the pleasure of forbidden fruit
> in their enjoyment.

Despite her identification with the "new woman," Cora had
enough self-knowledge to realize that she would be an outsider
under any social system. "Sometimes I like to sit at home and read
good books," she wrote, "at others I must drink absinthe and hang
the night hours with scarlet embroideries. I must have music and
the sins that march to music. These are moments when I desire
squalor."

Within a week of his arrival in Florida, Stephen Crane was
spending every night at the Hotel de Dream. He had found his
soul mate.

Sometime during the Thanksgiving weekend, Harry Scovel
checked into the St. James. He had come down from New York
with Horatio Rubens, who was in town for a conference of the
Florida representatives of the Junta, but he expected to stay in
Jacksonville just long enough to hire a skipper with knowledge of
the Cuban coast.

In blatant imitation of the *Journal*, the *World* had chartered
its own filibuster boat, a speedy yacht named the *Scooter* that was
being hurriedly refitted in New York Harbor. The plan was for the
yacht to depart from New York simultaneously with the *Vamoose*,
racing it south as far as Jacksonville, where Scovel would be waiting with a skipper and handpicked crew to take the boat to Cuba.

Unfortunately, Pulitzer's economical instincts put him at a

disadvantage when it came to matching Hearst stunt for stunt. The *Scooter* was a bargain charter and the team of "experts" hired by the *World* to take the boat on a shakedown cruise warned that it was unfit for an ocean voyage.

As a result, while the *Vamoose* left New York on schedule on Saturday December 5, the *Scooter*'s departure was postponed two days, then three days more. Scovel impatiently wired Brad Merrill suggesting that they give up on the yacht altogether and charter a well-known filibuster ship, the *Commodore,* which had the reputation of being both reliable and lucky. Merrill was inclined to agree. "I distrust seaworthiness of small boat," he cabled, referring to the *Scooter.*[4] But by the time his answer reached Scovel, the *Commodore* was no longer available.

Stuck in Jacksonville until a boat could be found, Scovel passed the time with Stephen Crane and Cora Taylor at the Hotel de Dream. Scovel and Crane may have met earlier in New York. Certainly, within days of Scovel's arrival in Florida they had become fast friends. Both were slightly obsessive about being the "bad boy" sons of preachers, especially Crane, who liked to joke that "everybody in my family became a Methodist minister as soon as he could walk,"[5] and both were devoted to roulette and horseback riding. Scovel, who could never stand to be physically inactive for long, decided to make it his mission to get Crane in shape for his Cuban adventure, and the two began riding together every afternoon.

No doubt a crucial factor in cementing their friendship was Harry's admiration for Cora. He had never met anyone quite like her (but then, who had?), and since he was in the process of sorting out his own feelings about marriage, he was fascinated by her unconventional views on relations between the sexes. Although he worried that the affair would "be the ruin" of his friend, he soon changed his mind. Cora was "just the woman" for Stevie, he decided.

By December 8 the *Scooter* was still not ready. Merrill warned Scovel that Ralph Paine was on his way to Jacksonville and that he was to have nothing to do with him. "Keep your plans secret." Merrill counseled.

Paine was, coincidentally, an old friend of Stephen Crane; they had covered news of the Jersey shore together when Paine was a junior reporter with the Philadelphia *Press* and Crane was working for his brother Townley's newspaper in Asbury Park. On reaching Jacksonville, Paine inevitably found his way to the Hotel de Dream, where he was surprised and no doubt a little miffed to find that Crane and his new friend Scovel wanted nothing to do with him. Brad Merrill's warning may have been the initial reason for the chilly reception Paine received, but it can hardly have been the only one. Whatever editors in New York might think, competition over stories rarely prevented field correspondents from drinking together in their off-hours. Paine was a great raconteur and generally popular with his colleagues, but he was not the unassuming bumpkin he liked to portray himself as being in his stories, and Crane, who loathed poseurs, may never have liked Paine as much as Paine liked him.

As for Scovel, he failed to see the humor in Paine's story of the two-thousand-dollar sword he was hoping to deliver to Gómez. Two thousand dollars would have saved a Cuban village from starvation, he told Paine, or put shirts on the backs of Gómez's entire army, or for that matter, guns in their hands. "I hope for your sake you never do get to deliver that sword," he warned, "because the Old Man will know where to stick it."[6]

Paine knew his mission was ridiculous, though it perhaps hadn't occurred to him that the sword might actually be offensive to Gómez, but he didn't appreciate being lectured on the subject. Nevertheless, he had the satisfaction of thinking that he had an edge in the race to get to Cuba. He had dropped in at Señor Huau's cigar store, where he found that the chief of the Jacksonville Junta remembered him very well, so well that he agreed to put him and Paine's buddy, *Herald* correspondent Ernest McCready, on the very next filibuster boat out of Jacksonville. The *Three Friends* was already in port, being loaded with munitions packed in cases innocuously labeled "prime lard," "condensed milk," and "salted codfish." Paine went on board on the evening of December 13, feeling quite pleased with himself. A novice at the game, he was going to get to Cuba before RHD, Crane, and even the *World's* number one "special," Scovel.

Scovel, still waiting for the arrival of the *Scooter,* was preoccupied with the latest rumors from Cuba. On the evening of December 8, Spanish authorities in Havana reported that the insurgent general Antonio Maceo had been killed in action. Maceo's death had been "confirmed" at least five times before, most recently the previous May, so the Spanish spokesman's claims met with skepticism. William Shaw Bowen happened to be in Havana on a brief visit, and he and George Eugene Bryson, an old Cuba hand currently working for the *World*, visited the governor's palace where they were shown a gold ring and a small diary said to have been taken from Maceo's corpse. Even so, the *World* at first refused to confirm the report, and in lieu of an obituary it printed a long adulatory essay by Scovel, obviously written months earlier when he was still in Pinar del Río. The essay praised Maceo as "a man without fear, a man of intellect, an honest man and a genuine patriot," and it went on to emphasize Maceo's role as a leader of Cuba's black population, closing with the prediction, "as long as Antonio Maceo lives there will be no race war in Cuba, he loves his country too much to allow it."

On December 10, Bryson received confirmation of the general's death from impeccable insurgent sources. Moreover, Maceo's personal physician, Dr. Zertucha, had arrived in Havana where, announcing that he no longer had the heart to keep up the fight, he accepted an offer of amnesty from Weyler.

Zertucha's decision to quit the fight triggered a wave of rumors that he was responsible for betraying Maceo to the Spanish. According to one story, which appeared in U.S. newspapers, Zertucha had lured Maceo and his bodyguard to a banquet, where Maceo was fed poisoned quail.

"Please telegraph tonight, for publication, your view of probability of truth of report...," Merrill cabled Scovel that evening. "What do you know of character of Zertucha...? Did Gómez ever warn Maceo against him? Your opinion, even if speculation, will be interesting."

Scovel's speculations, whatever they were, did not see print. But he was determined to get to Pinar del Río to conduct his own investigation into Maceo's death, and the delays with the *Scooter* were now more annoying than ever. The yacht's departure had been "belated" once again, Merrill telegraphed, this time because of an "accident to machinery." Finally, on December 13, Cap Morton and his chief engineer were ordered to take the next train to Baltimore, where they could pick up the *Scooter*'s papers from the *World*'s representative, a Mr. Golding, at the Carrolton Hotel and then sail the boat back to Jacksonville. Morton, on reaching Baltimore, pronounced the boat unfit for a dangerous mission in Cuban waters. In fact, he had all he could do to bring the yacht back to Jacksonville.

While Morton was bringing the *Scooter* south, the *Three Friends*, the most notorious filibuster boat in Jacksonville, had set out for Cuba with forty-odd passengers on board, including Ralph Paine, Ernest McCready, a detachment of Cuban volunteers under the command of Colonel Pérez Calvo, and a motley assortment of mercenaries. There were also two American deserters. One, a sharpshooter, bragged to Paine that he had been promised a hundred-dollar bounty for every Spanish officer he killed and he had hopes of returning to the United States with a hundred thousand dollars. The other, a navy gunner named Mike Walsh, explained how he had gone AWOL from the battleship *Maine* at Key West and hijacked a banana boat, forcing its captain to take him to Tampa, where Junta recruiters had promised him an artillery commission in the insurgent army. He was quite proud of his efforts to better himself.

As had been happening to filibuster ships all that winter, the *Three Friends* was followed down the St. James River from Jacksonville by a U.S. revenue cutter. Hoping to shake the feds, the skipper, "Dynamite Johnny" O'Brien, spent four days meandering down the coast, dodging in and out of secluded inlets and coastal swamps. When the passengers complained of boredom, O'Brien allowed Mike Walsh to unpack a Hotchkiss gun, a twelve-pound field piece, and set it up on deck so that he could demonstrate its operation to the eager but inexperienced Cuban volunteers. Paine and McCready felt uneasy about this, particularly as the gun's barrel was not high enough to clear the side of the tug and Walsh had propped up the gun on a makeshift platform consisting of several cartons of live cartridges.

Worse yet, at one of its last stops before finally shaking the revenue cutter, the *Three Friends* gained another passenger— Harry Scovel had rushed south from Jacksonville to catch up with the tug after learning of the *Scooter*'s latest mechanical breakdown.[7] Scovel spent the voyage socializing with the Cubans and

O'Brien, while Paine and McCready were reduced to hanging out with the crew.

On the evening of December 19, the *Three Friends* finally reached the mouth of the San Juan River on the southern coast of Puerto Principe Province. A spotter stationed on the top deck near the wheelhouse reported a suspicious shadow lurking in the shallows, but Dynamite Johnny insisted on trying to land anyway. He did take the precaution of backing into shore, however, the better to make a quick getaway in case of trouble.

Ralph Paine was lined up with the Cubans on deck, clutching Gómez's inscribed sword under his arm, when he noticed that the shadow had begun to move toward them. Seconds later, a rocket fired from the shadow's general direction lit up the night, revealing the unmistakable outline of a gunboat flying the Spanish colors.

The reaction on board was instantaneous. The Cuban volunteers, delighted to be seeing action at last, ran around on deck, firing their brand-new mauser rifles in all directions. The American sharpshooter grabbed his Army bugle and sounded the call to assembly. Mike Walsh enlisted a couple of the mercenaries to help him transfer the Hotchkiss to the stern. Paine and McCready prudently volunteered to go belowdecks for more ammunition. Down in the cargo hold, they found one of the Cubans, a former volunteer fireman from Havana, hacking open packing cases with a hatchet. McCready tackled him just as he was about to lam into a crate filled with nitroglycerin.

Topside, Walsh answered a salvo from the gunboat with the Hotchkiss gun, scoring a clean hit. To everyone's amazement, the sky erupted in a blaze of distress rockets and the gunboat signaled that it was disabled and prepared to surrender.

The *Three Friends* was flying no flag at all. As far as international law was concerned, that made it a pirate ship. Fortunately, perhaps, the appearance of a second gunboat prevented the Cubans from boarding their prize. Instead, O'Brien resorted to the old trick of launching a lantern on a makeshift raft, and the decoy fooled their pursuers long enough to permit the *Three Friends'* escape.

Rather than take his cargo back to Jacksonville where it

would surely be seized by treasury agents, O'Brien decided to stash his passengers and payload temporarily on No Name Key, a tiny island off Florida, while he and the crew returned to their home port to find another boat. Much to their disgust, Paine and McCready learned that they were to be left behind on the key while Scovel returned to Florida with the tug. Just how Scovel managed to rate this favored treatment is not clear, but judging from the telegrams that passed back and forth between Merrill and Scovel, it seems that Pulitzer may have underwritten part of the voyage's cost. Either way, Paine had learned a hard lesson: The most difficult part of a Cuba correspondent's mission was not covering the story but getting his dispatches filed, and when it came to this phase of the job any and all tactics were considered fair.

Nine days later, a small schooner reached No Name Key, bearing some supplies and a message from Captain O'Brien saying that he had chartered another well-known filibuster tug, the *Dauntless*, and was planning to make another try at landing his cargo in Cuba. Paine and McCready, desperate to file their stories, prevailed on the schooner's captain to take them to Key West. To their amazement, there was a welcoming committee waiting for them on the dock. Scovel's dramatic account of their adventure had been featured in the *World* on Christmas Day, under a banner headline that called the encounter THE FIRST NAVAL BATTLE OF THE CUBAN WAR. Paine and McCready, as the first veterans of the "battle" to reach Key West, were treated to a banquet at Palacho's Café, where they broke their nine-day fast with sirloin steak, followed by pompano, followed by turtle stew, all washed down with quantities of red wine. Then came the guava paste, the cheeses, the Cuban coffee, and endless brandy toasts offered in their honor.

The adulation of the Cubans was small consolation for having lost out on a major scoop. In addition, scanning recent editions of the *Journal* at Pendleton's, Paine was dismayed to see that his own paper was cheerfully predicting that the "pirates" of the Río San Juan would be hanged: THREE FRIENDS FILIBUSTERS IN FEAR FOR THEIR LIVES, IF CONVICTED OF THE CRIME THEY WILL BE SENTENCED TO DEATH, THE HOTCHKISS GUN PLAYS AN IMPORTANT PART IN CHARGES, ADMINISTRATION WILL PROSECUTE.

Paine and McCready went ahead and filed their stories, then stumbled into the nearest barbershop for their first shave in nine days. There they ran into RHD himself, looking more pink-cheeked and glowing than usual after a shave, haircut, and a hot towel facial. Davis was in an expansive mood and kindly offered to "lend" the *Vamoose* to get Paine and McCready back to No Name Key in time to catch up with the *Dauntless* and continue on to Cuba.

The *Vamoose* raced to No Name Key, appearing on the horizon just as the Cubans were in the process of ferrying their cargo of guns and ammunition out to the *Dauntless*. The gleaming white yacht approaching at full speed was mistaken for a revenue cutter. In the ensuing panic the small boats scattered and a number of packing crates were dumped into the sea. The Cuban general, Emilio Nuñez, who had arrived on the *Dauntless* to supervise the transfer, was furious. He finally calmed down and agreed to let Paine and McCready come aboard, but when the *Dauntless* made a safe landing at Corrientes Bay on the western tip of Cuba, he abruptly changed his mind and refused to allow them to disembark. American newspapermen, he complained, had already caused him more than enough trouble for one voyage.

Bitterly disappointed, Paine and McCready returned with the *Dauntless* to Jacksonville, where they learned that various members of the *Three Friends* expedition had been indicted for piracy, a capital crime. Among those named by the federal grand jury were Captain Johnny O'Brien, Mike Walsh (in absentia), the tug's engineers and...Ralph Paine. Scovel and McCready were spared because their stories had been published anonymously, but the *Journal* had done Paine the dubious honor of giving him a byline.

Paine hid out for a while at a fleabag in Jacksonville, then swallowed his pride and called his father. Much to his surprise, his father was understanding and if anything rather proud that his son had been enterprising enough to get himself charged with piracy. He helped to set up a false identity and then arranged a series of hideouts, including one with the family of a respected Presbyterian elder.

The *Three Friends* piracy case never came to trial. Napoleon Broward, who owned the tug along with two silent partners, happened to be the local sheriff, and to no one's surprise, the grand jury was unable to find any witnesses willing to identify participants in the affair. Paine stayed in hiding for a month, then got in touch with his former boss at the Philadelphia *Press*, who graciously offered to take him back at his old salary. This left the problem of what to do with Gómez's two-thousand-dollar sword. After consulting with Charlie Michelson, Paine delivered the sword to José Huau at his cigar store. Señor Huau was puzzled. The sword was useless, but it seemed disrespectful to have the thing melted down. Eventually, he arranged for it to be delivered to Gómez's wife at her home in Santo Domingo.

While Paine was hiding out—and Dick Davis and Fred Remington were still twiddling their thumbs in Key West—Scovel and Crane left for Cuba on New Year's Day 1897. Scovel, who had lost faith in both Brad Merrill's schemes and the Junta's filibuster operation, made a safe voyage to Pinar del Río in a small boat piloted by Cap Morton. Crane, meanwhile, departed as one of forty-odd passengers on the "good luck" filibuster boat *Commodore*.

But the *Commodore*'s luck had run out. The boat damaged its keel when it grounded on a sandbar in the St. James River, and when a storm blew up a few hours later, the overtaxed pumps could not keep up. The Cuban volunteers on board and some of the crew escaped in lifeboats, but Crane, who was with the captain and two others in a dinghy, saw seven crew members die before his eyes, including one sailor who was deliberately cut adrift as he desperately tried to haul himself aboard the already overcrowded boat.

Rowing and bailing for all they were worth, Crane and his companions in the dinghy spent the better part of a day fighting strong currents and winds off Daytona Beach, while strollers on shore watched idly. "Sure we saw them, an octogenarian Daytona resident named Fred Silver told an interviewer in 1961, "but we didn't know they were in trouble."[8]

In New York, some newspapers had already announced Crane's death, and Lantern Club colleague Elbert Hubbard penned a bathetic obituary for inclusion in the February edition of his literary magazine, the too-aptly-named *Philistine:* "So here's to you, Steve Crane, wherever you may be! You were not so very good, but you were as good as I am—and better, in many ways—our faults were different, that's all.... When I die I hope I will face Death as manfully as you did; and I hope, too, that I shall go where you are now."[9]

Crane, at the moment this was written, was still madly rowing, cursing the oblivious population of Daytona. On Sunday morning, with still no help in sight, the exhausted survivors tried to pull through the heavy surf on their own. The waterlogged dinghy overturned in the attempt. One crewman was killed, but Crane, the ship's captain, and the cook were tossed up onto the beach, dehydrated and exhausted but still breathing.

Once again, Crane the reporter had become a news maker. Besides his first-person account written for Bacheller's New York *Press*, the ordeal of the *Commodore* survivors became the basis for one of Crane's best short stories. "The Open Boat"—with its famous first line "They never knew the color of the sky"—was immediately recognized as a classic. The story did little to solve Crane's immediate career problem, however. His reputation was still clouded and *Scribner's Magazine* paid only seven hundred dollars for first rights to the story, about a quarter of the fee paid to such first-rank writers as William Dean Howells.

Furthermore, as a result of the failure of the *Commodore* and *Three Friends* expeditions, the Junta decided to suspend all filibuster operations for several months, so Crane's chances of getting to Cuba in the near future were slim. He still did not dare try to return to New York for fear of detective Becker's revenge and, to add to his difficulties, he had been accused of theft by a former actress named Amy Leslie with whom he had had some tangled financial dealings a few months earlier.

As for Cora Taylor, Crane saw no future in his relationship with her. He could scarcely support himself, and an affair with a notorious madam was hardly the way to restore himself to the good graces of the literary establishment. A note he wrote her on January 26 expresses his fatalistic mood: "Love comes like the tall swift shadow of a ship at night. There is for a moment the music of water's turmoil, a bell, perhaps, a man's shout, a row of gleaming yellow lights. Then the slow sinking of this mystic shape. Then silence and a bitter silence—the silence of the sea at night."[10]

This was all very well, except that he did not follow up the sentiment by leaving Jacksonville. Cora herself had once written in her diary, "I am not one of those fools who thinks that souls created for each other must needs come together.... I know the world too well to believe in nonsense like that." But the sea had given Stephen back to her, and two months later, long after any rationale for his presence in Jacksonville had evaporated, he was still at her side, and she was beginning to change her mind.

His Luck Had Run Out

WHILE THE COMPETITION was in Jacksonville scheming to get to Cuba, George Bronson Rea spent a quiet winter at home at his family's brownstone on Third Street in Brooklyn where he celebrated New Year's Day 1897 by marrying his childhood sweetheart, Harriet Carter. Less than a week after the wedding he received an urgent summons from the *Herald*, asking him to cut short his honeymoon to return immediately to Cuba.

The *World-Journal* feud was having a rejuvenating effect on New York's number-three paper, the *Herald*. Still making money at its usual newsstand price of two cents, the paper was also picking up major advertisers scared away from the *Journal* and the *World* by their increasing sensationalism. Encouraged by this development, the *Herald*'s editors began to get into the spirit of the fight, and in January they announced that George Rea had joined the race to get to Gómez. The *World*, which refused even to acknowledge the existence of the *Journal* effort by mentioning it in print, took up the *Herald* challenge. Rea and Sylvester Scovel, the *World* announced, were in a two-man competition to see who would be the first to get Gómez's reaction to the Cleveland administration's latest peace plan, calling for American arbitration to give Cuba an elected home-rule government.

The *Herald* was one of the few American papers to remain in Weyler's good graces, thanks to its moderately pro-Spanish editorial policies, so Rea had no need to sneak into Cuba via the filibuster route. He simply took the next regularly scheduled passenger steamer to Havana, arriving on January 13. A few days later he was in Cárdenas where he ran into Richard Harding Davis, who was staying at the same hotel.

For Davis and Remington, their Cuban adventure had turned out to be a colossal disappointment. After striking a deal with the rebellious crew of the *Vamoose*, they and Charlie Michelson had discovered that Hearst's marvelous yacht was unreliable in heavy seas. The captain made three attempts to reach Cuba, turning back each time because of engine problems. On the last of these voyages, the *Vamoose* was actually within sight of the Cuban coast when the captain announced that he dared not risk a landing. "We had nothing to do with the failure," a frustrated Davis wrote his mother. "I lay on the deck and cried when he refused to go ahead, we had waited so long. The Cubans and Remington and Michelson had put on their riding things but fortunately I had not and so was spared that humiliation. What I don't know about the Fine Art of Filibustering now is unnecessary." [1]

Six weeks after leaving New York, Davis gave up on the yacht altogether, and he and Remington sailed to Havana on the regularly scheduled Plant Line steamer. Remington was dealing with the boredom and frustration by drinking heavily, and he soon sent Hearst his famous cable message—or, at any rate, some similar message—begging to come home. Davis encouraged his departure. "I am so relieved at getting old Remington to go [that I feel] as though I had won $5000," he confessed in another letter to his mother. "He was a splendid fellow but a perfect kid and had to be humored and petted all the time." [2]

With Remington gone, Davis accepted Weyler's offer of a military pass. Seeing Cuba from inside Spanish military lines was not likely to produce any scoops, however, and Davis complained of the humiliating contrast between "the way I was invited to see Cuba and expected to see it and…now the way I am seeing it from [railway] car windows with a *valet.* What would the new school of yellow kid journalists say if they knew that?"[3]

When he met George Rea in Cárdenas, Davis's hopes of making something of the trip revived. Rea obligingly offered to guide him to Gómez's camp in the mountains if they could give the slip to the police spies who were keeping a close watch on their hotel. Unfortunately, on the morning they planned to leave, a recent issue of the *Journal* appeared on the newsstands featuring a front-page picture of RHD, mounted on an imposing stallion the likes of which hadn't been seen in Cuba in years and wearing a sidearm, with a caption announcing that the *Journal*'s star correspondent had *already* joined the rebels! With his picture in the hands of every Spanish officer in town, Davis's chances of getting through military lines were nil. As Rea left him that morning, he later recalled, the last thing he saw was one of Davis's size twelve shoes, kicking out the panel of his hotel room door.

Davis considered much of the proinsurgent reporting coming out of Cuba naive: "They show me the pueblo huddled together around the fortified towns, living in palm huts but I know that they have always lived in palm huts," he complained. "The yellow kid reporters don't know that or consider it."[4] Nevertheless, he did not care at all for the Spanish officers he met, finding them arrogant and callous in the extreme. Invited to witness the execution of a captured insurgent, he was shocked to find that the condemned man was a terrified peasant, barely in his teens. Spanish colonialism, he concluded, was "against history." Like James Creelman, Davis was a firm believer in the juggernaut of progress.

As irritated as he was with Hearst, Davis still felt that he owed the *Journal* one big exclusive, and the opportunity finally came his way as he was leaving Cuba on the American flag steamer *Olivette.* Before the *Olivette* sailed from Havana, customs officials had come on board to search three passengers, a certain Señorita Arango and her two companions, whom they suspected of smuggling letters for the Junta. In a dispatch to the *Journal*, Davis indignantly complained that the officials "demanded that a cabin should be furnished them to which the girls might be taken, and they were then undressed and searched."[5]

Back in New York, Remington was asked to illustrate Davis's dispatch and he contributed a drawing showing a young woman standing naked on deck surrounded by leering Spanish officials. This was not quite what Davis's story had said, and the *World*, recognizing the discrepancy, sent a reporter in Tampa to interview the mortified Señorita Arango, who explained that the strip search had been conducted privately by a matron. Davis himself was so embarrassed by the drawing that he took the unusual step of writing a letter to the editor of the *World* disassociating himself from the *Journal*'s handling of the story.

The Arango incident is often cited as typical of yellow journalism's blatant inaccuracies, but the truth was more complicated. Davis had not said that Señorita Arango was stripped naked on deck, but he had worded his account in such a way as to permit the salacious interpretation that the search had been conducted by male officials. As Davis well knew, verbal descriptions allowed for certain ambiguities. He simply had not counted on Remington raising the ante by taking his insinuations literally. Davis might have been more willing to accept his share of the blame if he weren't already furious with the *Journal* for the way it had mismanaged his assignment. As it was, he vowed publicly that he'd never work for Hearst again.

In the meantime, unknown to George Rea and the *Herald*, Sylvester Scovel had landed surreptitiously on the coast of Pinar del Río on January 2. Over the winter Scovel had become famous. Thanks in large part to Weyler, who had posted a ten-thousand-dollar reward for his capture, Scovel had become a folk hero and tales of his remarkable escapes from the Spanish—some true, many fantastical—were circulating throughout the island. Since the only thing anyone knew for sure about Scovel was that he could ride, the gossip tended to portray him as a sort of Wild-West-show cowboy, very tall and very blond—*muy alto y muy rubio*—who wore a beaded buckskin shirt and a white ten-gallon hat, or, as one version had it, a Mexican sombrero. None of this was true—Scovel had so much disdain for Western-style riding that he had gone to considerable trouble to bring his own English saddle with him when he returned to the island—but the legend made it that much easier for him to get away with his impersonation of a Midwestern businessman.

The disguise Scovel had used the previous year had been subtly altered. Since the real Harry Brown had served briefly as the *World*'s Havana correspondent, Scovel now called himself Harry Williams. Also, he had changed his appearance by growing a pencil-thin mustache and plucking his thick eyebrows—this last concession to the demands of his job shocked RHD, prompting him to boast that at least *he* did not have to shave his eyebrows to get a story.

Scovel spent nearly two weeks in the vicinity of Mariel, investigating the rumors surrounding Maceo's death and satisfying himself that there was no basis to the claims that the general had been betrayed by enemies within the revolutionary movement. From there, he surreptitiously entered Havana for a secret conference with the American consul general, Fitzhugh Lee, who asked him to sound out Gómez on an unofficial American peace plan: If the rebels would accept an armistice based on the promise of home rule, the United States would undertake to guarantee Spanish compliance by means of a treaty, "secret or otherwise."[6]

Scovel's quasi-official errand was one of the worst kept secrets in diplomatic history. The *World* cited "reports" that Scovel was on a secret mission for the State Department, then indignantly if unconvincingly denied that there was any truth to them. In Cuba, the nature of Scovel's errand was so well known that when he rode into Gómez's mountain hideaway, the general's first words to him were, "And now you have come to demand my surrender!"[7]

Gómez reiterated the official Cuban position that this time they would never consider an armistice based on anything short of outright independence. Nevertheless, something the general said in private convinced Scovel that the deaths of Maceo and the general's own son, not to mention the sufferings of the civilian population under Weyler's reconcentration policy, had shaken Gómez's resolve. Scovel came away from their talk with the impression that if the United States were to negotiate separately with Spain, and then send an official delegation to the Cuban leadership "recommending" a settlement, Gómez might accede without a fight.

Scovel carried his report back to Havana, but this time his entry into the city did not go unnoticed. On Wednesday evening, January 13, the *World*'s accredited Havana correspondent, Thomas Alvord, Jr., received a tip from an Associated Press reporter: The Havana police knew Scovel was in the city, and a group of off-duty officers, hoping to collect Weyler's reward, was plotting to ambush him outside the city limits where he would be shot and his body dumped in a cane field. Alvord set out for the house where Scovel was hiding, changing carriages three times along the way to make sure he was not being followed. He failed to convince Scovel to get out of Cuba, but they agreed that it would be too dangerous for him to try to return to Havana to deliver any further dispatches. Instead, Alvord would go to Trinidad de Cuba on the southern coast, where Scovel would meet him at the train station, posing as Alvord's youthful assistant.

Alvord reached Trinidad on schedule, but Scovel failed to show up at the station. Distressed, Alvord cabled "young Lee" (Fitzhugh Lee, Jr.), who had been one of those in on the secret of Scovel's Havana hideout, wanting to know if their "friend" had showed up there. When he received no answer, he assumed that the cable had been stopped by the Spanish. Sure that the authorities were aware that Scovel was in Trinidad, Alvord appealed for aid from an American planter named Stillman, a member of the powerful refinery-owning family, who had been helpful to American correspondents in the past. Stillman, as Alvord reported to Brad Merrill, was "a little hot.... He resented the danger of compromise through my being here and Harry coming."[8]

Nevertheless, Stillman went into Trinidad, where he somehow managed to find Scovel and deliver a message. For good measure, he planted the rumor that Alvord, who was staying at his house, was actually the elusive Scovel.

By the time Stillman returned home, Scovel had managed to escape from Trinidad. As Alvord reported to Merrill: "the English cable operator told me that Scovel stole two boats to get away. The operator says he sailed past the fort under the guns and put his fingers to his nose, disappearing in the dark. I paid $25 dollars for the boats to quiet the owners, for Harry may have to come out that way. I paid $25 for the horse he got also. Gen. Lee remarked last night that Scovel was a born scout. Both Lee and Stillman have the highest admiration for him. He is the coolest, most daring fellow I ever knew."[9]

The next day, three hundred Spanish soldiers descended on the Stillman plantation and began searching the house and out-buildings. As Alvord further reported to Merrill, "officers [were] filling the house when a letter was handed to me from Harry who was hiding in a house close by. I could not go to him, of course, for the lieutenant follows me everywhere. Friends went. They got him clothes, a guide, [and] gave him $25 dollars to buy a horse."[10]

With the help of this Cuban guide, Scovel made another flying visit to the insurgents' camp in the hills. By the morning of February 2, the two of them were on their way back south, where Scovel planned to rendezvous with Cap Morton on the east bank of the Tallabacoa River. The Spanish dragnet was tightening, and Morton had sent word through Alvord that it was too dangerous for him to remain in Cuban waters. If Scovel did not show up that evening, he would have to find some other way to get out of Cuba.

Scovel and his guide got as far as Zaza, a fortified town about six miles north of the port of Tunas, when they discovered that the area was swarming with the troops of the elite Guardia Civil. Scovel was looking much the worse for wear after days of sleeping in the bush. He had exchanged his battered derby for a jipijapa hat, a style popular in the interior and inevitably known to American correspondents as a "hippy-happy" hat, but his thin-soled shoes were falling apart and the clothes he had obtained from Alvord's friends a few days earlier were filthy.

He needed a cover story, and after consulting with his guide, he knocked on the front door of one Francisco Thomé, an elderly landowner of impeccable reputation, well known for his pro-Spanish sympathies. Reverting to his identity as Harry Williams, Scovel explained that he was an American dealer who had come to Cuba to buy scrap metal, delivery to be arranged after the cessation of the hostilities. Scovel's description of the huge profits to be made in scrap metal after the war must have been compelling because Don Francisco practically begged to be allowed to accompany "Señor Williams" into Tunas, where he could introduce him to friends who also had ruined refinery equipment to sell.

Cleaned up and traveling with a prominent citizen who was above suspicion, Scovel felt confident as he boarded the train for the coast. But to his dismay, the Guardia Civil officer inspecting the cars almost immediately clamped a hand on his shoulder and demanded to see his military pass. Too late, Scovel realized his mistake. He had been betrayed by his hippy-happy hat, a style not commonly worn on the southern coast.

Scovel was hustled off to the baggage car, where he spent the rest of the journey under the watchful eyes of a half-dozen soldiers who conducted an animated debate in Spanish, trying to decide whether it would be better to deliver their valuable prisoner alive or shoot him on the spot. The door of the car was wide open, and Scovel considered making a break for it. "I have been a suburbanite, and can jump on and off cars easily," he wrote in his account of the capture. However, the dispute among the soldiers seemed to be resolving itself in favor of letting the "f---ing Yankee" stay alive a while longer, and he was in no hurry to give them an excuse to change their minds.

Reluctantly, he resigned himself: "The pitcher was broken; my luck had run out."[11]

Announcing the capture of its star correspondent, the *World* was at first guardedly hopeful: "WEYLER FEARED AND HATED HIM— Will Not Dare to Shoot Him. . . . But May Try to Keep Him in Prison as Long as Possible" predicted the front-page headlines.

But on February 14, there was SAD NEWS FOR SCOVEL: Thomas Alvord reported that his efforts to find a Havana lawyer willing to represent the *World*'s jailed correspondent had been unsuccessful. Four days later, Scovel was transferred to the provincial center of Sancti Spíritus, where he was arraigned on a variety of capital charges, including consorting with the rebels.

The *World* by now was reporting these developments in oversize banner headlines and double boldface type: SCOVEL MAY DIE, BUT HIS DEATH WILL FREE CUBA, it warned. All other news was pushed to the back pages as the paper printed letters of support from dignitaries and politicians. Eighty-seven newspaper editors from across the country and a number of correspondents—including Richard Harding Davis and Frederic Remington—contributed statements on Scovel's behalf. Resolutions calling for Scovel's release were passed by seventeen state legislatures, the territory of Oklahoma, the city council of Columbus, Ohio, and the Alumni Association of the University of Michigan. The arrest was even denounced on the floor of Congress, and the Senate unanimously approved a resolution calling on the State Department to inform Spain of the "imperative necessity" of transferring Scovel to Havana, where his treatment could be monitored by the U.S. Consulate.

With the exception of Hearst's New York *Journal* and *San Francisco Examiner,* which made it a policy never to mention Scovel's name in print, the story of his imprisonment was treated as major news in prointervention papers across the country. The conservative press, on the other hand, dismissed the whole flap as just one more bout of yellow-journal hysteria. As everyone knew, Spain did not want war with the United States, and it was highly unlikely that it would risk provoking one by executing an American newspaperman.

As Cap Morton reported in a letter, eventually forwarded to Scovel in jail by Fitzhugh Lee, "the St. James gang" in Jacksonville was keeping close watch on this hostile press coverage:

A lady has just brought me a copy of the *Detroit Journal* to read a story of "Cute Sylvester's" exploits and among other things it says: "Scovil boarded the boat off the South East coast of Florida, and he and Crane were among the few passengers saved from the wrecked *Commodore*." That was Crane's first experience of a "Good time" in Cuba with the "Dude Scovil" and a whole lot of balderdash that has about as much truth in it as there is in the statement that I can sing.

Crane is still with us, and is just about the same old Steve. He lives down "Home" as usual, but keeps a room here. . . . Gussie [Morton's woman friend] would give a dollar and a half to see you, and I am not sure [*sic*] that I can say the same for a certain young lady, who has been making all kinds of efforts to learn all about your arrest, and whom you met and danced with just before your departure, would do about the same thing.[12]

It did seem that the critics of the *World*'s coverage had a point. As the *World* itself made clear, Scovel was getting VIP treatment. His prison cell, prominently labeled *calabasa numero uno*, was furnished with a carpet, a comfortable bed, a nightstand, a desk, and even a rocking chair—all provided courtesy of Señora Madrigal, the wife of U.S. consular official, Rafael Madrigal. Within days of his incarceration it was also piled high with small gifts handcrafted by fellow prisoners—leather bridles and belts, straw sculptures, paper flowers, even "decorated toothpicks." Thomas Alvord, who had arrived in Sancti Spíritus on Feburary 26, found his attempts to confer with Scovel constantly interrupted by delegations of young ladies who "fairly overwhelmed" the prisoner with their attentions. As for Scovel himself, he seemed in high spirits. His first comment to Alvord was that his trip had not been a complete failure since "I now hold an option on all the old copper in Pojabo."[13]

World readers were able to follow the saga of Scovel's incarceration through daily letters, datelined "Calaboose #1" and smuggled out of prison by Señora Madrigal. In one letter, Scovel cheerfully reported that he had been allowed a visit from a dentist: "What would the civilized world do without its 'American dentists'? This one hadn't practiced in eight or twenty years and was not familiar with the dentist's delight—the dear old buzzing, nerve twanging boring machine." Nevertheless, Scovel wrote, two chunks of wood propped under the runners had converted his rocking chair into an improvised dentist's station, and he had puffed on a Henry Clay cigar while the dentist extracted a troublesome tooth without benefit of anesthetic. Immediately after the operation, the dentist, his patient, and Rafael Madrigal sat down to a breakfast of buckwheat cakes provided by Madrigal's wife. The quality and quantity of the meals Señora Madrigal provided, added Scovel, explained why her young husband was already so enormous that he had to travel to Havana to get weighed on a factory scale.[14]

In a more serious vein, another of Scovel's prison letters took issue with charges made by the Spanish minister to Washington, Enrique Dupuy de Lôme, who had publicly accused him of being at once an American spy and a commissioned colonel in the insurgent army. "I have never been a Cuban courier. I have never come to Cuba on a filibuster," Scovel wrote, tongue heavily in cheek.[15] The *World* backed up this assertion with a lengthy affidavit from Colonel Federico Pérez Carbo, a member of the late General Maceo's staff.

However, as Scovel later conceded, de Lôme's charges were not without substance, and his role in trying to set up discussions between Consul General Lee and Gómez would surely come out if his case ever came to trial. This possibility had already occurred to officials in the State Department, who were quietly putting pressure on the Spanish Foreign Ministry to get Scovel released.

Scovel's friends in Cuba, however, were afraid that the State Department was moving too slowly. Two days after Scovel's arraignment, the mutilated body of his Cuban guide had been discovered on a road near Tunas, and Scovel himself had been given so many opportunities to escape that he felt sure he was being set up. Rafael Madrigal agreed, warning Alvord that the faction of officers loyal to Weyler was incensed over Madrid's eagerness to appease the United States and might well be tempted to arrange an "accidental death" for the prisoner who had come to symbolize the American public's financial support of the rebels.

On February 28, Captain-General Weyler himself arrived in town and took a look at his troublesome prisoner. Weyler appeared at the door of Calaboose #1, surveyed the heaps of gifts, the flowers, and the comfortable furnishings, and turned on his heel and departed without a word. The warden was demoted the same afternoon and the visits from the admiring young ladies ceased immediately. Scovel, who still found ways to smuggle his correspondence out of jail, described the encounter in his next letter to the *World,* observing that Weyler possessed "as fierce a face and as sloppy a form as ever bore such high titles."[16] For once, the *World* exercised tact, withholding the letter from publication pending Scovel's release.

According to George Rea, who was with the rebels in the mountains, Máximo Gómez was "very blue" over the arrest of Scovel, so much so that he retaliated by taking a hostage of his own, Luis Morote, the correspondent of the Madrid paper *El Liberal.* Morote was captured near the Júcaro-Morón *trocha* and was being held hostage in a cabin in the jungle. To the horror of some of his younger officers, Gómez had let it be known that if Scovel died, Morote would die too.

As for Rea, his "race" with Scovel was forgotten. His first concern was for his friend Harry's safety, and he and Gómez's American bodyguard, Major William D. Smith, begged Gómez to provide them with an escort so that they could get to Sancti Spíritus to offer their assistance.

A friend of Scovel's since they had sailed together on the abortive voyage of the schooner *Martha*, Smith was a colorful character. Born on leap year day, February 29, 1854, he served in the U.S. Army in the Arizona territory, then resigned to attend Harvard Law School. At the age of forty-one, he had abandoned a successful legal practice in Ohio to become a soldier of fortune in Cuba. Smith had ideas of organizing a jailbreak to free Scovel, exactly the sort of harebrained scheme that Rafael Madrigal was warning Scovel's friends in Sancti Spíritus against.

Perhaps Gómez didn't think much of Smith's plan either. The escort he provided consisted of two unarmed men who proposed a meandering tour of overgrown jungle trails that would get the travelers to the provincial capital in "about a week." Recognizing that they were being led on a wild-goose chase, Smith and Rea decided to forge ahead on their own, only to find that the main roads were swarming with Spanish patrols. After four frustrating days, they found refuge in a jungle cabin inhabited by insurgent officer Lieutenant Felix Pérez and his family. Rea managed to procure two bottles of high-proof rum, and he and Smith set out to drown their disappointment. While they drank, they began writing letters, which Pérez promised to have smuggled to Scovel in jail.

"My *Dear Friend*," wrote Smith, "... Rea is here with me and we have plenty of the *Oh Be Joyfull*, but we lack the presence of *one* to make the company complete.... Harry, what the D---- possessed you to get captured, was it necessary for you to enter the place you did? ... I am not upbraiding you, but to the contrary I am here to serve you in *any* manner you *see fit*, even to trying to free you.... Harry, I *am yours to command* and I think Rea is of the same mind."[17]

Rea began his letter by reminding Scovel that he had predicted that he would be arrested: "You will remember my parting words to you. But old man, don't think that I am in any way elated over your mishap." After describing Gómez's threat to execute the Spanish correspondent, Rea went on to pour out his grievances. "I am not treating the old man and his cause as generous as I did before. I have tired of being made a damn fool of by him. I know he thinks the world of you & will do all he can to push you along, but I do not think he should withhold from me any information he might have. Of course I do not hold anything against you as a fair and honorable competition is a good thing." Rea further complained that he had always done his best to ingratiate himself with the Cuban people, bringing them food and other scarce commodities to repay their hospitality. "But," he went on, "I have the impression that the Cubans do not like me, and I am positive they have not treated me fair since your arrival with Gómez. I am determined to tell the truth about this war, and let them go to hell." [18]

The first bottle of rum disappeared. The second was opened. Rea and Smith began reading over each other's shoulders and scribbling comments on each other's letters, debating the question of just who was getting whom drunk. Rea asked about Smith: "Say, was he always the same with you—he don't seem to have any bottom to his copper-lined iron tank." And Smith wrote in the margin of Rea's letter: "By the way, this Rea is a *holy terror*. How long have you *known him?* He is even now standing on the table and telling *me* (or trying to) the length of time this war has been going on." As for Rea's list of complaints, Smith added, "*Some* of it is all right, especially the part about the Spanish reporter.... The rest of his letter are the words of a man who had just asked the lady of this house whether she has any oysters on the half-shell."

Stymied by the insurgents' refusal to cooperate with their scheme to rescue Scovel, Rea and Smith returned to the mountains, where Rea promptly got involved in a shouting match with Gómez. Rea had sent a dispatch to the *Herald* describing how some civilian officials of the provisional republic were using their positions to enrich themselves by seizing abandoned property, and Gómez, when he heard the story, demanded to know why he should offer hospitality to a reporter who wrote things that "hurt the Cuban cause." For Rea, who already believed that the Cubans were getting a free ride from the American press, this was the last straw. He left the rebel's camp that same day, vowing never to return. Back in New York, he resigned from the *Herald* and set out to write a book that would expose what he called "the unscrupulous attempts of other correspondents to embroil the country into a war with Spain, based on issues created only in their imaginative brains." [19]

A week later, the State Department's quiet pressure finally paid off. Weyler was ordered by Madrid to release Scovel and see that he got safely out of the country. The *World* trumpeted Scovel's safe return home as ANOTHER TRIUMPH FOR PUBLICITY!! But in fact, Scovel's arrest had thoroughly intimidated the American press. For the next six months those American correspondents remaining in Havana were circumspect. Cuba faded from the headlines and the new administration of President McKinley enjoyed a brief honeymoon, spared intense pressure from Congress and the public for an immediate solution.

IV

Interlude, Summer 1897

The Greco-Turkish War

N THE POCKET NOTEBOOK that Harry Scovel was carrying at the time of his arrest, among the pages of neatly penciled notes and daily expense totals, he had jotted down a single phrase of personal significance: "Are you still in love, if so why do you travel alone."[1]

This was a question he had plenty of leisure to consider during his weeks in Calaboose #1, and by the time he was released he had come to a decision that would greatly displease Bradford Merrill and Pulitzer. At the very moment when they were trying to figure out how to exploit the newfound celebrity of their "intrepid" special commissioner, Scovel had decided that he was never going to travel alone again. When he arrived in New York on the steamer *Seneca* on March 13, his plans were to head directly for St. Louis, marry Frances Cabanné, and return with her to New York, where they would catch the first boat to Europe. Greece and Turkey were expected to declare war any day, and Scovel, guessing that he would be asked to cover the hostilities from the Greek side, hoped to take his bride with him as far as Athens.

Immediately, a complication arose. President McKinley, who had been inaugurated a week earlier on March 4, 1897, had telegraphed the Dome expressing a desire to meet privately with Scovel. The appointment could not be scheduled immediately as McKinley was still busy organizing his cabinet, and since a summons from the president could not be ignored, Scovel was forced to cool his heels in New York until McKinley found time for him on his calendar.

Waiting for his call to the White House, Scovel had his first real taste of the life of the star "special." Correspondents in the 90s received fan mail, and Pulitzer's office boy, Theodore, had accumulated a thick stack of letters, most of them from women. Scovel was inundated with invitations, but after several run-ins with hostesses who too clearly regarded him as a challenge to their matchmaking skills, he retreated to Arthur Brisbane's farm on Long Island. There he endeared himself to Brisbane forever by befriending Fowell, whom other guests so often slighted.

One invitation Scovel did accept was to a banquet in his honor organized by the Hammer Club, a dinner club composed mainly of Sunday *World* staff including George Luks, Walt McDougall, T. E. Powers, and Alex Kenealy. There was also at least one long meeting with the Boss at his Fifty-fifth Street townhouse, where Scovel regaled his employer with anecdotes about his family, whose Anglo-Presbyterian mores Pulitzer found fascinating. The Reverend Sylvester Scovel had written his son expressing the sentiment that his incarceration in Cuba might have one saving grace. Now that he was expelled from Cuba for good, he could give up journalism and "settle down to some earnest and *good* work,"[2] a sentiment that caused much amusement at the Dome.

Pulitzer had other ideas for Scovel's future. First, of course, he would go to Greece to cover the fight against the Turks. After that there was the possibility of his becoming the *World*'s London —and therefore chief European—correspondent. Now that Creelman had resigned, the promotion would have been a logical next step, but word that the Boss was considering it was to cause no end of trouble for Scovel. The emergence of a new Pulitzer favorite—yet another potential heir to the position of publisher—was an invitation to the factions at the Dome to begin sniping away.

On April 3, Scovel finally received his summons to the White House, where he had a private meeting with McKinley. An hour after leaving the president, he boarded a transcontinental express train for St. Louis. Arriving the next evening, he and Frances kept her parents up until after midnight, cajoling them into giving their approval for an immediate wedding. The ceremony was performed the next morning by the bishop of St. Louis, the Reverend Father McGlynn, a family friend, and the newlyweds departed immediately on the 1 P.M. train to New York. The hastily arranged ceremony was bound to inspire gossip, and Carr and Julia Cabanné released a defensively worded announcement saying that the wedding "had been contemplated for some time" (even if not by them) but had been moved forward "to accommodate Mr. Scovel's professional responsibilities."[3]

On reaching New York, the newlyweds were stunned to discover that Pulitzer was adamantly opposed to Frances's going to Europe. The issue was not so much Pulitzer's fears for her safety —a subject scarcely mentioned in his correspondence on the subject—but his pique over the discovery that his star reporter had another love besides the *World*. In a telegram to Brad Merrill dictated on April 13, Pulitzer defended his refusal to let Frances travel with Harry:

> Answering Scovel's letter. Give him my kind regards and say I hesitate about sending him to Greece because I do not wish to disturb [his] honeymoon or interfere with his domestic relations yet feel convinced a war correspondent exactly like a soldier must be entirely free from trammels or distracting thoughts, perhaps even more than a soldier because [a] soldier is bound by discipline and *compelled* to move like a screw while a war correspondent is left to his individual freedom of action. The state of mind is everything. I cannot ask him to leave Mrs. S. behind and positively do not ask him, but he must assume for his own good that he positively cannot go without leaving his bride on this side of the Atlantic.

Despite his disclaimer, Pulitzer was determined that Scovel *would* go to Greece, and he repeatedly reminded Merrill that in making his decision Scovel should be urged "to bear in mind the possibility of a London place." The London job, as well as an increase in salary that Scovel had been counting on, were to be made contingent on his doing a good job in Athens.[4]

If Frances had been willing to write for the *World*, Brad Merrill might have argued more strenuously on her behalf. He sounded Harry out on this possibility, but Frances—who had some interest in writing and later contributed articles to the St. Louis *Post-Dispatch*—had promised her mother, as a condition of obtaining her blessing for the marriage, that her name, much less her byline, would never appear in Pulitzer's despised rag. As Harry explained to Merrill, "Mrs. Scovel's one condition upon agreeing to become my wife was that, in the pages of the New York *World*, Mr. Scovel is to be treated as a bachelor."[5]

Faced with Pulitzer's intransigence, Harry and Frances agreed that the London assignment was a prize well worth a temporary separation, so just sixteen days after the wedding Frances returned to her family in St. Louis and Harry sailed for Europe on board the USMS *New York*. During the crossing, he did his best to distract himself by helping to organize a "grand concert" to raise money for charity. Among the passengers who performed were the Misses Park, who played duets for two coronets, and a Miss Martin, who sang a song entitled "The Amorous Goldfish." Harry's contribution to the program was a dramatic monologue, "My First Kiss."[6]

Stephen Crane and Cora Taylor, once again calling herself Mrs. Stewart, were already in Greece when Scovel arrived. Cora, for unknown reasons, had found it necessary to sell her business and get out of Jacksonville—possibly, she had been getting financial backing from a local man who was jealous of her affair with Crane. She and Stephen had resolved their dilemma, more or less, by accepting an offer from the *Journal*'s managing editor, Samuel Chamberlain, for both of them to cover the Greek war as correspondents.

However, Stephen was so nervous about the effect gossip could have on his career that he and Cora sailed on the same ship but in separate cabins, pretending not to know each other when they met on deck. In London, Cora stayed out of sight while Stephen was entertained at a series of luncheons attended by such popular authors as Anthony Hope and James Barrie, the sort of events, he remarked, that always left him feeling like a clam floating in the chowder of literature. Stephen then went on to Greece via a steamer out of Marseilles while Cora and her traveling companion, a middle-aged friend named Mathilde Reudy, made a grand tour of the museums and castles of central Europe, finally proceeding to Greece via the Orient Express to Varna, a Black Sea steamer, and another boat that took them from Constantinople to Piraeus.

This elaborate pretense fooled no one. Richard Harding Davis, who had hosted one of the not very successful lunches held in Crane's honor in London, ran into Cora in the railroad station waiting for the boat-train to Calais and sized up the situation at once. In a letter home, he dismissed Mrs. Stewart, whom he certainly knew by reputation, as "a bi-roxide blonde ... whom I did not meet," meaning he cut her dead.[7]

Despite the humiliating and pointless charade, Cora was in high spirits. The *Journal* had promised her that it was going to make her the first woman war correspondent, and she intended to make the most of the opportunity. In Athens, however, she encountered one difficulty after another. To begin with, she discovered that the *Journal,* as was its habit, had hired two people for the same job. John Bass, who was in charge of the *Journal's* contingent in Greece, was apparently unaware of Chamberlain's promise to Cora and had taken on a Smith College graduate named Harriet Boyd, who would be competing with her for by-lines. Worse yet, Dick Davis, who had arrived in Athens via Monte Carlo, showed up as a passenger on the boat that was to take the *Journal* reporters north to the Thessalonian front. Davis was offended at the thought of a woman, *any* woman, aspiring to write about war. This attitude was shared by many Greeks. Determined to win an interview with the crown prince, Cora left Stephen, Dick Davis, and the others to spend an extra day near the Greek army headquarters in Pharsala. There being no hotel, she slept fully dressed on a pool table in the local coffeehouse, only to learn the next morning that Crown Prince Constantine, who had talked to everyone else, would not see her.

But perhaps Cora's greatest problem was that she had been

asked to report the war "as seen through a woman's eyes." In her first dispatch, writing under the pseudonym Imogene Carter, she summed up the female perspective, "To a woman, war is a thing that hits at the hearts and at the places around a table. It does not always exist in her mind as a stirring panorama."[8] But having once said the obvious, she did not find the female perspective on war a very promising angle.

Although no one expected the Greeks to hold out very long against the much larger Turkish Army, the *Journal*, as usual, had spared no expense in covering the conflict. Besides having two female correspondents—who were simultaneously billed by the weekday and Sunday editions as the "only" women at the front—the *Journal* team was supported by a contingent of Greek couriers, translators, and orderlies. The parsimonious New York *World* had only Scovel, who nevertheless expected that covering the war as a regularly credentialed correspondent would be "a bed of roses" compared with Cuba. Arriving in Athens on May 1, 1897, three days after the *Journal* boat had left for the front, Scovel immediately set out to sabotage the competition by bribing a certain Mr. Parren, whom he described as the "Athens cable scoundrel," to make sure that all *World* copy sent via Athens would be put on the wires immediately while *Journal* copy was to be withheld for at least twenty-four hours.

On reaching Lamía, Scovel's next challenge was to find himself a fast horse, a necessity since he would have to deliver personally his dispatches to the seacoast resort of Stilís, where the boat he hired in the *World*'s name would be waiting to take his copy to Athens. Local horse traders, taking advantage of the demand caused by the war, were getting up to nine hundred drachmas for what Scovel described as "miserable brutes" that at best fit "the little girl's definition of the horse: an animal with four legs —one on each corner." He was about to give in and purchase one of these "quadrupeds," when he happened to run into a "big fat red-faced and scared English correspondent" riding a magnificent bay stallion. The correspondent had fled the front in a panic and was happy to sell his mount for a mere six hundred drachmas.[9]

Scovel rode the horse for less than two days. Returning from his first trip to Stilís, he ran into the U.S. military attaché, Captain Dorst, riding a swaybacked plow horse. Scovel's Yankee pride was offended by the sight of an American officer looking so ridiculous, and he impulsively offered to sell Dorst the bay for what he had paid for it. Fortunately, the wonderful horse was easily replaced by another almost as good, which he bought from a Greek cavalry captain whose judgment was temporarily clouded by the effects of two bottles of whiskey Scovel had just shared with him.

No sooner were his arrangements set than the charter boat captain, Cosmides, returned from his first trip to Athens to report that the agreement with "the cable scoundrel" had fallen through because the promised deposit of two hundred pounds sterling had not arrived from New York. Scovel had no choice but to go to Athens himself to try to straighten out the mess. He was still there, furiously cabling Merrill for an explanation of the delay, when ten thousand Turkish troops under Edhem Pasha surprised the Greeks at Velestínon in the only important battle of the war.

By happenstance—or perhaps in yet another demonstration of his fabled good luck—Dick Davis was one of only two journalists on the scene when fighting broke out unexpectedly at Velestínon. He and John Bass of the *Journal* had wandered into the town the previous evening. Finding it abandoned, they broke into the mayor's house where they had a wonderful time, raiding the larder for coffee and other treats and trying on the mayor's "petticoats." The next morning when the shooting started just outside of town, they hurried to the trenches. Davis was on the front line for thirteen hours straight, and while under fire he completed a ten-thousand-word story for the London *Times*, a tour de force in which he compared the noise of the bullets to rustling silk.

Most of the rest of the press corps arrived by train from Volo that afternoon, but Stephen Crane and Cora Stewart did not show up until the second day of the fighting, arriving just in time to see the Greek Army begin its retreat. Crane had the best of excuses —he had been confined to his hotel room with dysentery. Ironically, considering his dislike of Victorian prissiness, Crane had been embarrassed to admit the nature of his malady. Instead, he claimed to have a toothache, a story that caused some of his colleagues to suspect him of shirking. When he did reach the trenches, the journalists on the scene had filed their stories for the day, and Crane immediately became the center of attention. Both John Bass and the reporter for the New York *Tribune* wrote short pieces describing how the famous novelist sat on a box of live ammunition, languidly smoking a cigarette while shells burst all around him. Irked, Davis wrote home that Crane "appears to be a genius with no responsibilities of any sort to anyone....[He] came up for fifteen minutes and wrote a 1300 word story on that. ...He was never near the battlefield, but don't say I said so."[10]

This was hyperbole. Crane and Stewart spent several hours in the Greek Army's number-two battery, were as close to the fighting as Davis had been, and stayed so long that they nearly missed the last train out of Velestínon and got captured by the Turks. Scovel, who had the story from eyewitnesses, wrote admiringly of Stewart that she was the last correspondent to leave the battlefield; while running for the train, she had stopped to rescue a terrified sheepdog puppy left behind by one of the Greek units in its flight.

Crane agreed with Davis that the brave Greek soldiers had been ill served by their officers. (Davis summed up the day's work with a football metaphor: "The Greeks had possession of the ball, and they rushed it into Turkish territory, where they lost it almost immediately on a fumble.") Crane's account was less flippant, but he had trouble focusing on the big picture. Much of his dispatch was taken up by a long anecdote about a courier who had been sent to the rear for field glasses but, through some bizarre misunderstanding, returned carrying a bottle of wine. Cora, meanwhile, obeying her orders to focus on the woman's angle, contributed a description of her near decapitation by an incoming artillery shell.[11]

But the *Journal* at least had a story. Scovel did not reach Velestínon until the battle was over, and after piecing together a secondhand account of the action, he raced back to Athens, where he had to borrow money from the American minister, Eben Alexander, to get his copy on the wire. The expense payment from New York didn't reach Athens until May 17, twelve days after the battle, and then the business office sent only two hundred dollars American, not two hundred pounds sterling. After repaying Alexander, Scovel did not even have enough cash left over to get back north, where he hoped to interview General Smolenski, the Macedonian commander of the Greek Army, and cover the final days of the war.

In response to Scovel's urgent cables, Merrill offered no explanation for the foul-up. Instead, he replied: "Public interest languid in battles. Interview King, Smolenski. Then try Edhem Pacha." [12]

"Honestly, I don't know what's the matter with them at the office," Harry wrote to Frances. The request that he interview the Turkish commander Edhem Pasha was particularly infuriating. Crossing military lines was a necessity in Cuba. On the Thessalonian front it would be a pointless stunt. The Turks had been very reasonable in their dealings with the foreign press, and if the *World* wished to print an interview with the pasha all it had to do was send a properly accredited correspondent via Constantinople.

Knowing the byzantine office politics of the Dome, Scovel suspected that he was the target of deliberate sabotage and began sending his cables directly to Pulitzer's Manhattan townhouse, where Brad Merrill kept an office. "Effectidness simply paralyzed," he wrote. And again: "Desperate for money. Send 40 pounds today." Still, he heard nothing. "I wonder how Mr. Pulitzer is satisfied . . . ," he wrote Frances. "It is too bad that I should come out here expressly to see a battle and miss the only one likely to happen. But it was distinctly not my fault. 'It wuz jus' like dis.' " [13]

He still hoped to redeem himself by getting an exclusive interview with King George, but the palace secretary kept postponing the appointment. The king was said to be suffering from "cardiac spasms," which Scovel blamed on his majesty's recent encounter with James Creelman. Creelman, Scovel wrote Merrill, had "so riled" the king that the poor man had vowed never to meet another American journalist.

Despite the frustration of a wasted journey, Scovel was managing to enjoy himself in Athens. Crane and Stewart had returned from the front and were staying at the same hotel, the Angleterre on Constitution Square, and with Eben Alexander as their guide they spent several days sightseeing. Stephen, still undecided about his future with Cora, was reading *Anna Karenina*, whose plot can hardly have eased his mind, much less Cora's. Nevertheless, speaking in his usual drawl, he managed to keep everyone amused by outlining how he would rewrite Tolstoy's "bully" novel to make it shorter, and thus, in his opinion, better.

Crane was also writing a sketch he called "The Dogs of War" about the adventures of the puppy Cora had rescued from the battlefield. Velestino's interest, wrote Crane, was always in "the thing directly under his nose," and it was this quality that made him the ideal *Journal* mascot. Both Stephen and Cora were slightly potty about dogs (which, unlike human beings, could never betray them). Unfortunately, the pampered pet only added another element of turmoil to their domestic arrangements, which were already carried on in a spirit of barely controlled chaos. The need to have someone to look after Velestino when Stephen and Cora returned to the front became the justification for hiring two teenage servants, the Ptolemy twins, who themselves required more looking after than the dog. And even with two full-time baby-sitters, the puppy kept getting lost until Scovel bought it a collar and leash, a practical solution that does not seem to have occurred to Cora or Stephen.

One is tempted to imagine that if only Pulitzer had been more reasonable, Frances Scovel would at least have had the opportunity to share this sojourn in Athens with her husband and his best friends. But this was not the case. As much as he admired Cora, Harry would not have dared ask his Catholic bride to associate with a former madam, and the implications of this were much on his mind. "Stephen Crane is here with Mrs. Stewart," he wrote her in mid-May. "He is true steel . . . [but] I don't know that I shall see them again. If you were here it would be embarrassing if they were here too."

Adding to his doubts, Harry had some disturbing news from St. Louis. On May 19, he received a letter from Frances mentioning that the rumor was circulating around town that she had been abandoned. Frances insisted that she was "game" enough to hold her head high despite the gossip, but the fact that she mentioned the subject suggests that she was not entirely sure the rumor was unfounded. "Begad!" Harry wrote back. "If our kind calumniator could have seen me kiss your letters in front of the combined consular and diplomatic functionaries of Athens, they would turn tail and slink back into their holes! . . . Do you care to know that I have kept my promise, or rather my prophecy, about being able to stand temptation. . . . Words can't say how I want you."

* * *

The Greek Army was by now in complete disarray, and on May 20, Smolenski asked for a truce. Although Greece had never had any realistic chance of winning the war without outside help, the army's humiliating performance had threatened the survival of the monarchy. Stephen and Cora were back in Athens, having drinks with Harry on their hotel room balcony, when they happened to witness a feature of Balkan politics of the day known as a "café revolution." An angry crowd had gathered in Constitution Square, apparently spontaneously, and an elderly politician named Gennadius wearing an old-fashioned white cockaded bicorne leaped onto one of the wrought-iron café tables and began a harangue, urging the mob to storm the palace across the square and overthrow the king.

At length, Gennadius wound up his oration and mounted the steps of the palace, the surging crowd close behind him. While a lone sentry bravely tried to keep the rioters at bay by pelting them with pebbles, Gennadius pounded on the front door, demanding of the functionary who answered, "I wish to see the king."

"The King does not receive today," said the servant.

And that, to the Americans' amazement, was that. Gennadius drove off in his carriage, while, noted Crane, the crowd "cheered clamorously" as if he had won a great victory.[14]

More interesting than anything any of the Yankee correspondents had to say about the Greco-Turkish confrontation was their collective sense of superiority to Europe's petty quarrels. Even Richard Harding Davis, who came closest to being a true internationalist in outlook, treated the war as an amusing interlude. "After that slaughter-yard and pest place of Cuba, which is more terrible to me now than what it was when I was there, or before I saw that war can be conducted like any other evil of civilization, this opera bouffe warfare is like a duel between two gentlemen in the Bois."[15]

And no one was less internationalist than Stephen Crane, who was bad at languages and already distraught over being so far away from the Bowery, which he often called the academy where he had received his artistic education. Nevertheless, Cora was urging him to settle with her in England, where his works were even more popular than in the United States and literary society was disposed to overlook unconventional relationships such as theirs.

Scovel could see no way out: "I was afraid she would ruin him," he wrote his wife, "but really her influence so far has been the reverse. He has done such good work since that his publishers and others are increasing their offers for future work.... But, poor woman, how will it end? She urges him along, but even if he wished to, he can't marry her, as her husband, Sir Donald Stewart, son of the British Commander-in-Chief of India, will not divorce her." [16]

The couple's plans were still unsettled when Cora and Mrs. Ruedy left for England a few days after the armistice. Scovel had promised to look after Crane, who was still weak from dysentery, but a day or so later, he got orders from New York informing him that his next post would not be London, as he had been promised, but Madrid. He and Crane left Greece together the next morning on the Brindisi steamer.

On board, they were recognized by a fellow passenger who, assuming that foreign correspondents must be multilingual, began questioning them about how many languages they spoke. This was an extremely sensitive subject with Crane, and Scovel broke the tension by launching into an animated conversation in pig latin. Their interrogator failed to catch on, and for the rest of the trip, Scovel and Crane amused themselves by making up languages and practicing them in front of their fellow passengers.

At Brindisi, Scovel changed his plans and decided to accompany Crane as far as Marseilles, where they got involved in some sort of run-in with the authorities. The difficulty seems to have had something to do with the Ptolemy twins, whom Crane had decided to bring with him to England. Possibly Crane's interest in the twins was innocent, although his subsequent talk of writing a novel about the experiences of a boy prostitute suggests otherwise. Anyway, four days passed before Crane and the twins were safely on their way to England. Scovel did not reach Madrid until June 7, where an irate cable from Brad Merrill was waiting for him at the Consulate, demanding to know what he had been doing in Marseilles and why it had taken him so long to get to Spain.

Whether or not the delay was unavoidable—as Scovel not

very convincingly claimed—it was the home office that was being unreasonable. Pulitzer expected Scovel to secure an interview with Spanish prime minister Cánovas, not a very realistic plan since, as Scovel pointed out, the Spanish considered him an agent of the Cuban insurrectionists. Moreover, Scovel added, "what I must truthfully tell him is just what he wishes not to hear."[17]

Within a matter of days the conservative papers had broken the story of Scovel's presence in Madrid and were running editorials raking up the charges made by Dupuy de Lôme a few months earlier. At the invitation of Luis Morote, the correspondent who had been held hostage by Gómez the previous spring, Scovel published a rebuttal in *El Liberal*, expressing his view that the fighting in Cuba had become a stalemate that could be resolved only by U.S.-sponsored negotiations. "That there may be no doubt about my position," he added, "I must in fairness state that I sympathize strongly with the abstract idea of freedom of government, [and] that I have many warm friends among the insurgents, the warmest being Máximo Gómez. . . . [Nevertheless,] I realize that [the Cubans] are not yet ready for absolute independence." The letter went on to advocate a negotiated peace based on home rule, "to be openly or secretly guaranteed by Spain to the U.S."[18]

This was a more candid statement of Scovel's views than was ever likely to be presented to the readers of the *World*. However, it did nothing to change the fact it would be political suicide for any member of the Cánovas government to meet with him. His value as a Madrid correspondent was nil, but Merrill refused to see the obvious and kept sending him irrelevant inspirational messages: "You have a chance to do brilliant work!" and "Exert yourself!"[19]

Perhaps Merrill hoped that given enough time, Scovel's presence in Madrid would somehow provoke a diplomatic incident. On the other hand, he may simply have been reluctant to tell Scovel the bad news: Pulitzer had changed his mind about giving him the London appointment. There were no major stories breaking in Europe at the moment, and Scovel was too valuable to waste on a desk job. Guessing the truth, on June 15 Scovel sent Merrill an ultimatum: either order him to London or summon him home.

That same week, in a private letter to Pulitzer, Scovel wrote that the Spanish peasants were about at the end of their "pathetic but patriotic patience." His sense of the situation was that "Spain would quietly rejoice" if the United States were to take the Cuban problem out of its hands. "Of course [there would be a] thunderous amount of clamor. There might be some stones thrown at Minister Taylor's office here and perhaps some Americans killed in Havana if ships [did not get] there in time. But there would be no war, for the United States, in attempting [to] persuade Cubans [to accept] home rule under [the] Spanish Flag might succeed in doing what Spain . . . really wishes but is ashamed to ask for."[20]

Finally, during the third week of June, Merrill informed Scovel that he was being recalled to New York, and Scovel arranged to return via England so that he could see Stephen and Cora one last time. He found them comfortably settled in a rented country house, Ravensbrook, at Oxted in Surrey. Stephen and Cora were now calling themselves Mr. and Mrs. Crane, and Stephen had given out various versions of the wedding—sometimes he said they had been married in Paris, sometimes in Greece, and one acquaintance was told that the ceremony had taken place in England, with H. G. Wells as a witness.

Cora was thriving. Photographs show a woman who was at least fifty pounds lighter than she had been in Greece, and years younger looking. Her homecooked food and bright conversation that had served her so well at the Hotel de Dream were just as successful with her English circle of friends, which soon came to include the Joseph Conrads and the Moreton Frewens. (Mrs. Frewen was the former Clara Jerome, the sister of Lady Randolph Churchill.) Even the straitlaced Henry James, who pretended to find Cora's Greek sandals and homemade wraparound chitons too eccentric for his taste, was in the habit of bringing guests for lunch to sample her famous crullers.

Stephen was busily planning the big, romantic, commercial blockbuster that his friends kept urging him to undertake. *Active Service* would be the story of Rufus Coleman, correspondent of the New York *Eclipse* (the *Journal*), who is pursued through the Balkans by the "azure-eyed tigress," Nora Black, a more glamorous and predatory version of Cora, who wears erotic black silk stockings and a perfume concocted of orris root and violets and earns more than Coleman as the first woman "special" of the New York *Daylight* (the *World*). The character of Coleman, who fancies himself a writer of history even though his journalism is really only "a cheap telescope for the people at home," was to be Crane's revenge on Dick Davis. Rejecting the "superb" Nora, the repressed newspaperman falls in love with the insipid Marjory Wainwright, based on Cora's competitor in Greece, Harriet Boyd. (Marjory's father, a professor of Greek at a citadel of Protestant righteousness called Washurst College, was based on the Reverend Sylvester Scovel.)

Unfortunately, Crane underestimated the degree of self-knowledge necessary to write a successful novel of manners, and *Active Service*, not completed until 1899, turned out to be less fun to read than it must have been to plan. But the difficulties Crane would face with the book were in the future. He seemed reasonably content with his decision to remain in England, and over the next six months he would write some of his best stories, including "The Bride Comes to Yellow Sky" and "The Blue Hotel." Scovel left England convinced that his friends had found the solution to their problem and were happily settled in their first real home, which was more than he could say for himself and Frances.

Klondike Adventures

Get out your pick, your pan, your pack,
Go to the Klondike, don't come back—
Ho for the Klondike! Ho!
— "Ode to the Klondike," Anonymous, 1897

WITH BOTH Greece and Cuba peaceful for the moment, the big story of the summer of 1897 promised to be the coal miners' strike that was brewing in West Virginia, and Harry Scovel, when his boat docked in New York, was told by E. O. Chamberlin, Brad Merrill's summer replacement, that Pulitzer wanted him to proceed immediately to the coalfields.

Chamberlin's instructions seemingly promised Scovel free rein:

> If . . . you find a class of densely ignorant, and brutal men, getting for their work bigger wages than they ever dreamed of in their own countries, enjoying a coarse abundance that would have been luxury in their previous conditions, say so plainly. If their leaders are demagogues, working upon ignorant and vicious minds for their own benefit, tell the truth about it. . . . If they are men of heroic mould, leading a forlorn type in the cause of humanity, tell the story of it. . . . Breathe the breath of truth into every line you write.

171

But for all these windy exhortations, the truth was that the West Virginia assignment was another test. Pulitzer still had visions of turning Scovel into a political analyst but was concerned about his reputation as an enthusiast for radical causes. Chamberlin got down to business in the final paragraph of his instructions, warning Scovel that this was to be his opportunity to prove once and for all his devotion to "the World's idea of public service." And, he added sternly, "I hope you will appreciate it."[1]

Harry accepted the challenge with enthusiasm. He had been interested in the union movement ever since working on the labor gang in Tennessee, and not incidentally, he was relieved that his new assignment was reasonably convenient to Wooster, where Frances was on a peacemaking visit to his family. He cabled her to take the next train to Pittsburgh and check into the McClure House hotel, where they could spend a few nights together before he left for the coalfields.

Eugene Victor Debs, on his way to a strategy conference with the leaders of the United Mine Workers in Wheeling, was also in Pittsburgh and happened to be staying at the same hotel. The Scovels ran into him in the lobby soon after they checked in, and Harry immediately secured an "exclusive statement" for the *World* in which Debs predicted that the strike would not be over soon, a veiled indication that he intended to counsel the union to ignore court injunctions. Debs also invited Scovel to accompany him to the conference in Wheeling.

Scovel thought that he had scored quite a coup. Having never actually worked at the Dome, he had no way of knowing that Pulitzer had turned against Debs during the Pullman strike of 1894, when the *World*, in a much-quoted editorial, had written off Debs's conversion to socialism as the product of a mind weakened by alcoholism. The problem of how to wean Scovel away from Debs without provoking his resignation was left to Chamberlin, who immediately fired off a barrage of telegrams urging Scovel to forget about attending conferences and get out into the coalfields where the "real" story was to be found.

Genuinely puzzled, Scovel informed Chamberlin that Debs's arrival in Wheeling *was* the big story of the strike so far. Furthermore, he, Scovel, *had* been out in the coal towns, accompanying

Debs and a delegation of union officials as they tried to rally the discouraged and intimidated miners.

At this point, an obviously desperate Chamberlin wrote back that, as no major outbreaks of violence had occurred, the strike was not really so newsworthy after all. He suggested that Scovel give the story one more day, then return to Pittsburgh for a short vacation with his wife while awaiting further developments.

Harry had been separated from Frances almost constantly since their wedding and, as he wrote her, the method he had resorted to in Calaboose #1 to "distract my mind" was no longer working. So he was happy to agree to Chamberlin's suggestion.

On the first day of their promised long weekend together, the Scovels were dressing for a dinner dance that was being held in their honor at the home of one of their Pittsburgh friends when another cable from Chamberlin arrived, ordering Scovel to forget about the coal strike altogether and head immediately for the Klondike.

The great Klondike gold rush had begun a week earlier on July 15, 1897, when the steamer *Excelsior* arrived in San Francisco. A group of lucky prospectors staggered down the gangplank carrying bulging suitcases, carpet valises, leather saddlebags, even cartons of jelly jars—all full of gold. A curious crowd followed the prospectors as they hired a wagon and, the U.S. Mint being closed, headed for the offices of Selby Smelting, where one cache of nuggets after another was dumped out into the assayer's scales, piled high like so much "yellow hulled corn." Within a matter of days, Klondike fever had conquered the West Coast and was beginning to infect the Eastern Seaboard. Thousands of would-be prospectors were heading for San Francisco, Seattle, Portland, and Victoria, British Columbia, where they vied for deck space aboard any vessel that could float, not to mention a few whose qualifications in that regard were extremely doubtful.

Preoccupied with each other and with the coal strike, the Scovels had taken little notice of the sensational news. Frances recalled that their first reaction to the telegram's mention of the Klondike was "very vague...it seemed so far away, it seemed like a dream."[2] She stayed in Pittsburgh while Harry took the midnight train to New York to confer with Chamberlin. He was back by

Sunday morning, having spent just three hours in the city, long enough, as it turned out, for Chamberlin to convince him that the gold rush was a once-in-a-lifetime story.

The *Journal* had already organized its own Klondike expedition, to be led by Californian Joaquin Miller, a former explorer and cowboy now in his midsixties who was known as "the poet of the Sierras." Chamberlin, however, promised that Scovel would not be expected to race Miller to Dawson City and the goldfields. The *World* was not interested in gold, but in the saga of ordinary people from all walks of life driven by hope and by greed to seek their fortunes in one of the most inhospitable places on earth. He instructed Scovel to take his time and "follow the crowds"—to share their hardships and triumphs, do a little prospecting of his own, and possibly even winter over in Dawson City.

Frances, taken aback to learn that she might not see her husband again until the following spring, insisted on accompanying him on the train as far as Chicago, where Harry had relatives. In Chicago she changed her mind and decided to go all the way to Seattle. On this leg of the journey, she met a tiny, demure, somewhat frail-looking woman who was planning to cross the mountains and raft down the Yukon River with her husband.

"If she goes, I can go too," Fran announced. When Harry objected, she reminded him that she had seven hundred dollars of her own money with her, enough to get to Dawson City on her own if her husband wouldn't take her with him.

At the outfitters in Seattle, the fashion-conscious Fran was horrified to learn that women prospectors typically dressed in men's overalls and work boots. After a conference with the storekeeper, she managed to assemble a costume that met her standards of chic—a sweater, worn with knickerbockers, covered by a short, full skirt. Harry, deciding that he might as well live up to his reputation as a cowboy, purchased a fringed buckskin jacket, and when their steamer docked in Vancouver he made a flying trip ashore to buy a guitar. Romantic visions of singing Irish songs around the campfire after a day of invigorating hiking were dispelled by the couple's first sight of Skagway, Alaska, the coastal terminus of the notorious White Pass. It was raining, and the majestic mountains that ringed the town were hidden behind sheets of mist. Skagway's main street, grandly named Broadway, was a river of mud, and the town itself consisted primarily of crude canvas-sided pavilions. Nevertheless, real estate speculators had already divvied up every square foot of flat ground into minuscule building lots and were renting them as campsites for the fantastic price of ten dollars a week. The homemade wooden lot markers made the campground look like nothing so much as an enormous graveyard. They felt as if they had reached the end of the earth.

The Scovels chose a campsite on the corner of Broadway and Fifth Avenue (another mud trough) and struggled to get their tent pitched while contending with gusts of wind that ripped the canvas out of their hands and knocked down the poles. Harry managed to purchase some reasonably dry firewood and Fran set about preparing a meal. She had never cooked before, and the conditions for her first attempt were far from ideal. Trying to boil potatoes in a tin coffeepot over an open fire, she spilled scalding water on her clothes and would have set the tent on fire if the canvas hadn't been too wet to burn.

Nevertheless, she was pleasantly surprised to discover that their fellow prospectors were not at all the rough characters she had expected, but "nature's noblemen, kind and good." In fact, many, under their two weeks' growth of beard and filthy mackinaws, were "gentlemen...people who knew people that we knew."[3] One of these gentleman prospectors, a New York "swell" named Billy Saportas, had already decided to give up looking for gold and instead make his fortune running a combination saloon and hotel, the Holly House. Harry immediately offered to make Saportas the Skagway agent of the New York *World*, responsible for seeing that his dispatches got on board the boat to Seattle. The Holly House saloon was proclaimed the *World*'s "Alaska headquarters" and Scovel conducted interviews there with a number of patrons, including one of the few single women to have made the round-trip to Dawson City, the wonderfully named Gussie Lamore. According to Scovel's story in the *World*, Miss Lamore had been deluged with marriage proposals but was determined to maintain her independence: "She [has] refused every single man in Dawson City, and they have knelt before her with uplifted hands full of gold. Being refused, they tell her that she doesn't know a good thing when she sees it. She wears short skirts, carries an umbrella, and wants to vote."[4]

Scovel's orders were to "follow the crowd," but as he soon learned, the crowd in Skagway was not going anywhere. Of the two trails across the mountains, only the White Pass was at all suitable for pack trains, and unseasonable rains and heavy traffic had left portions of the route impassable. Several thousand would-be prospectors were stranded in Skagway, being fleeced of their money by speculators. Complicating the situation, Dawson City itself was low on food and hundreds of "stampeders" who had packed in earlier in the season were now making their way back along the trail toward Skagway.

Scovel and Saportas made a quick reconnaissance and discovered that the worst bottleneck was several miles outside of Skagway in a place where the trail cut through a narrow gap between two mountains. The cut was partially filled with boulders, some of them ten feet high, so that in places the dirt trail was barely wide enough for a loaded pack animal to squeeze through. Earlier in the year, an attempt had been made to ease the bottleneck by constructing a corduroy road, reinforcing the steeper grades in this section of the trail with logs. But after months of unusually heavy rainfall, some of the logs had worked loose and washed down the cut so that trekkers and pack animals alike had to pick their way over the debris. More recently, there had been several attempts to raise money to dynamite the cut and repair the log road, but since virtually the entire population of Skagway consisted of transients the project never got organized.

Scovel saw a tremendous opportunity for a "*World* stroke." On his own initiative, since there was no telegraph in Skagway, he decided to commit seven hundred dollars of the *World*'s money to purchase dynamite and have the trail through the cut widened. In a letter forwarded to Seattle by boat he informed Chamberlin that if Pulitzer should disapprove the expense he was prepared to make it up out of his own pocket. Saportas organized a public meeting at the Holly House, and by a majority vote it was agreed to stop traffic on the trail so that a crew of volunteers could go to work. The handful of correspondents in Skagway at the time gave the *World*'s enterprise overwhelmingly favorable publicity, and

the Associated Press carried a column-and-a-half interview lion-
izing Scovel as the savior of the stampeders.

With traffic again moving on the trail, Harry and Frances were
ready to make their own dash across the mountains to Lake Bennett, where they would transfer to a boat for the journey down
the Yukon River to Dawson City. Harry found two burly ex-sailors
—one of whom had arrived in Skagway with a library of books
that included *Paradise Lost* and the complete works of Karl Marx
—who agreed to pack in about a third of their 2,700 pounds of
supplies; he and Frances would have to manage the rest of the
gear themselves. Since their horses also had to carry all their own
feed over the pass, it would take twelve animals to do the job.
Fortunately, at the last minute they struck a deal with another
stampeder, an artist named Buell who agreed to help with the
pack train and draw sketches of the trail for the *World*, all in
exchange for twenty dollars and free food.

At dawn on September 1, they left Skagway and started up
the forty-mile switchback trail. Just beyond the spot where the
cut had been dynamited, they discovered a recent mud slide. In
some places the mud was knee-deep. Two of their horses slid off
the trail and were suffocated before they could be pulled free.

Next came the slate mountain called Devil's Hill, where the
trail was bordered by a slope covered in loose slabs of slate, ending precipitously in a five-hundred-foot drop. They had nearly
reached the top when a pair of horses lost their footing and began
sliding toward the lip of the chasm. Instinctively, Frances jumped
between them, hanging onto their bridles, calming them and urging them back toward the trail. Just when it seemed that the
animals had gained so much momentum that they would slide
over the edge, taking her with them, they managed to regain their
footing.

Scovel, immensely proud, would later describe his wife's feat
of "quickness and nerve" in a letter to Joseph Pulitzer, boasting:
"Mrs. Scovel should not be judged by ordinary rules. She is no
ordinary woman."[5]

From Devil's Hill, the Scovels and Buell pushed on, walking
up to fifteen hours a day. There were few level campsites along
the route, and one night the three of them pitched their tents in a

defile so narrow that Fran had to stand on the trail to cook dinner, jumping out of the way every time a pack train came through. Another night she and Harry camped on ground so steep and slick with mud that they kept sliding out of their tent. Still, they managed to reach Lake Bennett in six and a half days, just three days over the record set by experienced mountain guides.

On the shores of the lake, a few enterprising handymen were constructing crude boats and auctioning them off for up to $1,000 each. Harry managed to buy a fairly decent boat for $450, but this left him and Fran almost out of funds. The *World* had set its budget for the expedition based on advice from their Seattle correspondent, Portus Baxter, whose estimates, low by normal standards, did not begin to take into account the runaway inflation in Skagway. Moreover, Scovel still wasn't sure whether the *World* wanted him to winter over in Dawson City. As usual, Chamberlin's most recent instructions had been long in exhortation but short on specifics.

Scovel calculated that the ideal time to leave Lake Bennett would be the end of September, "just the last safe moment for departure ... when the rush down the river would be at its height and ... the scenes at the rapids would be really thrilling." In the meantime, he decided to return down the Dyea Pass, an alternate route to Skagway, and take a ship to the nearest cable office in Comax, Alaska, where money and further instructions from Chamberlin should be waiting for him. Traveling light, he expected to be able to make the round-trip in a week.

He reached Skagway on September 10. No messages from the paper had arrived, but there was an agent of the joint U.S.-Canadian mail service in town who told Scovel that the latest news from Dawson City was not good. Supply ships from the States had been expected to bring provisions via the much longer sea route around the western tip of the Aleutians and via the mouth of the Yukon River at Norton Sound on the Bering Sea. However, when the long-awaited ships reached Dawson City they were found loaded with whiskey and hardware, not the staples that were so desperately needed. Additionally, the private contractors who were supposed to deliver supplies to the Klondike by dogsled during the winter months had bid too low and were on the point of default. This left only the mail service, and it expected to run at most three sled expeditions into Dawson City between freeze-up and the first thaw, which in that part of the world meant sometime around the end of April at the earliest.

Scovel doubted that Pulitzer would be pleased about his spending eight months in the Yukon if he were able to send out at most three dispatches. He suggested to the agent that perhaps it might be worthwhile for the *World* to organize its own dogsled expeditions. The paper could print copies of its thrice-weekly national edition on thin paper and deliver them to Dawson City, eking out the payload with supplies of sugar, flour, and other staples. Although conceived in an alcoholic haze, the dogsled project was actually not a bad idea. The stranded prospectors in Dawson City had plenty of money, and the situation was ripe for an entrepreneur with the capital and daring to supply their needs. The *World* already had agents in Skagway, Seattle, and Victoria, so was in a position to organize the journeys cheaply, and the publicity for the paper would be tremendous.

The steamer *Rosalie* was in port. Scovel calculated that he had eighteen days to get to Seattle and look into the costs of provisioning the sled teams, confer by telegraph with New York, and get back to Lake Bennett before the river froze—ample time, he thought. He landed in Seattle on the morning of September 19 and had his messages on the wire by seven A.M., begging for a quick decision.

But Pulitzer could not make up his mind about the dog train idea. On the one hand, it was a great opportunity for the *World*'s brand of activist journalism; on the other hand, the paper was already operating at a loss and Brad Merrill, who had returned from his summer furlough, warned that "interest in the Klondyke was waning in the East."[6] Scovel was kept waiting for a decision until just before the telegraph office closed on the evening of September 21, and then the message from the Dome was enigmatic: TOO LATE NOW FOR YOU TO DO ANYTHING IN KLONDIKE BEFORE SPRING. REGRET EXTREMELY. PLEASE RETURN NEW YORK, ARRIVING SOON AS POSSIBLE.[7]

Since Harry had specifically explained that it was not too late, he had no idea how to interpret the first part of this message. But the second half was all too clear. Merrill and "Mr. P" had learned from their Seattle stringer that Frances was with him in Alaska and were none too pleased. He surmised that the order calling him back to New York was another test of his loyalty, and this time he felt sure that they meant business. It was a choice between his two loves, his career and his wife. But if his career were cut short, how would he be able to support his wife, who was used to a standard of luxury well beyond the means of a college president's black sheep son?

The Canadian Pacific's transcontinental express was leaving that evening, and Harry had forty-five minutes to make his connection to Vancouver. His mind in turmoil, he grasped at the hope that Fran—a wife "more eager for me to do my best than I am myself"[8]—would understand the necessity of his returning to New York.

There was just time enough to dash off a note to Billy Saportas: "My dear old man—Have just received peremptory orders return immediately New York. It's Havana for sure. Cannot delay and must throw myself upon your friendship to get the madame back from Bennett and aboard ship for Seattle. . . . I'm half crazy to abandon her. I am very sorry to thus thrust my burden upon your shoulders, but I can't do anything else."[9]

No sooner had Scovel boarded the train for New York than he was seized by regret. He decided to get off at the first station, but the express skipped its scheduled stop and by the time he had a chance to disembark it was too late to catch the *Rosalie* on its return trip. He spent the rest of his journey writing love letters, lengthy, guilt-ridden, and passionate.

On the first night of the journey:

> Every minute I picture you waiting at Bennett. Every minute I find out how much I love you, how dear you have become to me since we left Pittsburgh that early morning in August. Before that you were my wife—I admired you, I was proud of you. I had a deep affection for you, but now—now I love you—not "more than I thought I could love any woman"—but more than *any* man has ever loved any woman. . . .
>
> An hour ago I had gone from the smoking room to my (not our) berth and . . . I had decided to stop at the next station, go back to Victoria and take the first steamer to Skagway. I thought I might catch you there and *then* I might be with you, just we two

alone, for two weeks of each other. You would not have tired of me, would you, dear!

But I stopped and sat down again. I had a fight with myself. The reason . . . is something that I couldn't telegraph you. I am afraid the *World* is not entirely satisfied with my Alaskan work. . . . I fancy they think I ought to have gone right in —and yet I may be wrong and it may be the Eastern coal strikes or Havana. (You know 21 strikers were killed the other day in Pa.) However, I thought it over and I *couldn't* see anything to do for us both, but to obey. . . . I am certain that my implicit obedience at great cost to myself (they knew you were at Bennett) will make our position absolutely secure. I think of the future, now, dear. I want to make a big success—for you. I want to make such a reputation that after another year of this work I can go to moneyed men and say, "Here's a good thing—let me have a hundred thousand" and get it—for you darling.

I want to see you shop in your own carriage, charm people by your exquisite dress as well as by your exquisite self and give dinners and receptions. . . .

I can see you as plainly as though you were here—and I always see you in your little skirt and golf stockings and I remember every time I spoke shortly to you and every time that I didn't notice things—and every time that your tenderness made me ashamed of myself. Do you know that I shall never forgive myself for that night at Bennett—when you made yourself so sweet and I scolded you and then (I don't think you knew this) when you suffered with cold and I didn't just take you in my arms and hold you tight all night—every minute of it! I am glad at least that I shall have a whole lifetime in which to atone for it. It has come upon me in a storm. I mean that I love you—that you are my life and my heaven. Darling, I would have come to it anyhow, but our present (short in time, but oh so long!) separation has merely caused you to lose the husband to find the lover—and it will be to the end of the chapter.[10]

A day later, from somewhere between Moose Jaw and St. Paul, he promised:

In New York, darling, if I am not hurried at once to the strikes or to Havana (or if I am) I am going to limit myself to four drinks a day and I will keep from eating and will use the buctus (?) so vigorously that when I meet you at the train you will not recognize your new "trained down" husband, clear-eyed and clear-skinned —and not the puffy object who courted you against your protestations and married you "by force of circumstance."

. . . I love you, ah! so much. I feel a bit afraid of it sometimes. It has taken possession of me. I am no longer my own master.

There was a woman on board the train who had recognized Scovel and had bribed the porter to get the Pullman compartment next door to his, where, he wrote, "not content with hanging around all day, she even whispers my name through the partition every night, probably under the pretext of having such an absorbing passion that she dreams aloud over it—

"Well, I don't even know her name!"

This incident, however, reminded him that he might not be the only one presented with temptations. "Don't flirt too much with any nice young man," he begged, "for you see you have flirted outrageously with *me* dear."

The "storm" of love had swept everything before it. It is difficult to imagine that this was the same man who had detested his parents' friends' middle-class notions of marriage as a partnership in which the wife's job was to "set a moral tone" while spurring the husband on to higher and higher earnings:

Do you realize the power you have? I do and am glad of it. It will land us high up somewhere . . . and your gentle support will keep me "at it" like a toothed coal cutting machine driven by strenuous electricity. I hope this does not sound silly to you. . . . If I am kept in N.Y. a few days, I shall at once find Mark Hanna and set him onto a scheme for a cheap railroad up the Skagway River *at once* and *under Congressional franchise.* You see? This may be a "starter" for us. The scheme is small in outlay and will be big in results.

In Chicago, while waiting for his connection to New York, Scovel took advantage of the layover to visit his relatives, who were aghast to learn that he had left his wife on the shores of Lake Bennett. "I had to talk earnestly and fast for half an hour

before my various middle-aged aunts relaxed their severe inter-
rogatory expressions," he wrote Frances. And even this did not
satisfy his Aunt "Puddin" Belle. "I've a good mind to box your
ears," she told him. And she did.

Aunt Belle's reaction prompted another anguished letter, the
sixth in five days and filling six closely spaced pages: "I am suffering because I can't be with you! And yet I can't say with Frances
Wilson of 'Ermine'—'Ah! If things wazznt as they iz!' For I am
deeply glad that 'they iz as they iz.' "

To his dismay and astonishment, when Scovel arrived in New
York he discovered that his loyalty was unappreciated. The errand
in Havana that had prompted his recall was suddenly no longer
urgent, and Pulitzer was distraught, complaining that the money
spent on outfitting the Klondike trip had been wasted.

Scovel had filed more than thirty thousand words from Skagway, most of which the *World* had used, featuring his reports in a
heavily publicized front-page series that the paper also sold for
national syndication through its own service. Scovel strongly suspected that the message recalling him had been a mistake. There
had been some foul-up over the Havana "emergency," and Merrill,
he wrote to Frances, "doesn't wish to shoulder the blame and
naturally (if I don't explain matters thoroughly) I am the scape-
goat. However, don't worry dear, it will all come out right. We have
done our duty, so let things come hard as they may we 'are men
enough' to stand them, aren't we dear?"

It particularly infuriated him that Merrill and Pulitzer blamed
Frances for slowing down his progress and adding to the cost of
the expedition. In a lengthy letter to Pulitzer, he meticulously, not
to say compulsively, accounted for every penny of his expenses,
pointing out that his wife's seven-hundred-dollar contribution had
more than covered her share of the expedition and part of the
cost of dynamiting the trail besides.

Pulitzer was on the point of relenting when the issue was
clouded by a report published in the *Alaska Mining Record* and
picked up by the New York *Sun* intimating that Scovel—"a man
who from Key West can faithfully describe the details of a battle
in Cuba"—had never crossed the White Pass at all. The *Sun*
described Scovel as a dude who had lolled around town in his
buckskin jacket playing the guitar (as no doubt he had), but went

on to say, inaccurately, that the dynamiting of the trail had been done over the objections of the locals, after which the *World* correspondent had been "invited to get out" of Skagway.

The reporter from the *Mining Record* had talked to Scovel's contact from the mail service in Juneau, and, inevitably, waxed sarcastic about the plan "to start dog-teams to Dawson City with tons of the Sunday *World* for the famishing miners there, so that each might be regaled on the Yellow Kid at $1 per gale." But what really riled him was the *World*'s failure to pay Scovel's bills: "This is the kind of journalism which has gilded with Dutch metal the dome of the *World* building.... The *World* always means "beesness.' " [11]

The *Journal*, meanwhile, was attacking from the opposite perspective, charging that the *World*'s star correspondent, whom it carefully refrained from naming, was guilty of sensationalism, seeing dangers where none existed. Joaquin Miller had reached Dawson City in mid-September and on the day of his arrival he sent out a dispatch vigorously denouncing rumors of a food shortage: "No, there will be no starvation. The men who doubt supplies will get here, where gold is waiting by the ton, miscalculate American energy." [12]

On reading this, Brad Merrill called Scovel into his office and demanded an explanation of why a man forty years his senior was treating the gold rush as a virtual pleasure trip while his dispatches had stressed the hardships of the trail.

While lambasting Scovel in its columns, the *Journal* was doing its best to hire him. He had already received a generous job offer from Sam Chamberlain, and this was followed up by a dinner invitation from James and Alice Creelman who entertained him in their newly redecorated Murray Hill apartment and spent the evening doing their best to convince him that he could be happy working for Hearst. The Creelmans were "charming," Scovel wrote his wife, and he had left the door open to further negotiations. But "I should hate to leave Mr. Pulitzer's service.... He has always treated me well and of course 'The World' practically made me. Still I must be man enough to insist on justice."

Pulitzer's crises of confidence seldom lasted long, and within a matter of days Scovel was back in his good graces. Other correspondents who had been at Skagway during the dynamiting of the White Pass were beginning to come forward with articles and letters defending Scovel's actions, and Pulitzer decided to honor the bills he had run up in Alaska.

There was also a supportive letter from Cora. She and Stephen were mourning the death of their beloved dog Velestino, but in a more cheerful vein Cora assured Harry, "Stephen thinks your idea of the dog newspaper teams is great." Cora, always practical, assumed that Scovel would have managed to earn a commission on the proceeds, as may well have been part of his plan. "Try to get enough gold out of it for a trip to England and come and camp with us," she advised, adding, "Your wife must be a sweet woman and a good one and I am glad Harry. Good women who are not narrow Methodists are few. You are a lucky man altogether."[13]

As for the nettlesome Joaquin Miller, Scovel had run into him and his party in the mountains as he was headed to Dawson City on September 6. The *Journal* correspondent had laughed at Scovel for packing in so much gear, boasting that the key to his success was traveling light, with only a few days' food supply. Scovel predicted to Merrill that Miller was headed for trouble, and time proved him right. Miller reached Dawson City with no provisions except for a single onion in his coat pocket, and he soon had cause to regret sending off reports to the outside world that no emergency shipments to the Klondike were necessary. Finding no food for sale in Dawson City, Miller tried to make his way back to Skagway. En route, he was caught in a snowstorm on one of the high mountain passes and suffered such severe frostbite that an ear fell off and one side of his face was paralyzed. He eventually turned back to Dawson City, where he spent a very hungry winter.

Of the thousands of stampeders who had streamed across the mountains, only a handful struck gold, and many of these were quickly fleeced by profiteers, cardsharps, and con artists. In the event, there was little actual starvation in Dawson City, although by the end of the winter food was literally worth its weight in gold. In the Indian camps and trappers' huts of the Yukon Territory it was a different story. For the territory's permanent residents, unable to afford the inflated prices being charged for the cooking oil and flour that they counted on to eke out their diet of wild game,

Klondike fever proved fatal. But they died out of sight, their sufferings unrecorded. By April, when the dimensions of the problem became known, the Klondike was stale news.

Harry Scovel remained in New York until the beginning of October, when Merrill changed his mind again and decided to send him on to Havana after all. Cuba was once again becoming a hot story, partly in response to the appearance that season of two books by former New York *Herald* correspondents: Stephen Bonsal's *The Real Condition of Cuba Today* and George Rea's *Facts and Fakes About Cuba*.

Thirty-two years old, Stephen Bonsal was an experienced correspondent, best known for a series of articles defending the Turks against accusations that they were responsible for widespread atrocities in Macedonia. Bonsal's reputation for skepticism gave great credibility to his stark conclusions about the state of affairs in Cuba. Based on a tour of *reconcentrado* camps made earlier in the year, he predicted that as many as 400,000 Cubans had been driven from their homes by Weyler's policies and that the island was on the brink of mass starvation on a scale that "would not find a parallel in the history of human suffering."[14]

Rea's book, written in the white heat of indignation after his quarrel with Gómez in March, contradicted Bonsal on nearly every point. Rea excoriated Gómez as an ignoramus and an "opéra bouffe" general. As for Bonsal's estimates of the impact of reconcentration, they were wildly exaggerated, argued Rea, and in any case, it was the insurgents' cut-and-burn policy that was primarily responsible for the devastation of the countryside.

Rea went on to catalog some of the sillier moments of American press coverage of the rebellion, such as the *Journal*'s account of an attempt to assassinate Weyler by lacing his morning cup of hot chocolate with dynamite. (The plan was said to have been foiled when Weyler noticed wires trailing over the side of the cup!) Rea's most attention-getting charge, however, was his attack on Scovel's highly regarded investigation into Spanish atrocities. According to Rea, Scovel, though personally honest, had been duped by his bodyguards. The *World* correspondent had visited only 20 out of the 120 sites in Pinar del Río described in his articles. Moreover, it was more than a little suspicious that the same witnesses' signatures appeared repeatedly on the affidavits collected by his bodyguard. Approximately half of the affidavits collected by Scovel in 1896 survive, and they show no evidence of the sort of obvious fakery Rea complained about. Nevertheless, there must have been at least some truth to Rea's claims since Scovel, normally the last man to ignore an attack on his reputation, conspicuously refrained from rebutting the charges.

Instead, Scovel and Merrill were working on a plan to get Scovel back into Cuba. Once again he would be traveling incognito, using a new disguise concocted with the help of Fitzhugh Lee.

Frances, meanwhile, had waited at Lake Bennett for more than a month for word from Harry. "During this time it rained incessantly," she recalled later. "Dozens of people would start down the lake in their boats to the Yukon, every minute you would hear a cheer of good-bye, some man starting off. I had nothing to read, nothing to do, and no one to talk to but a lot of men who were as kind as they could be, and I got at such a stage that my brain refused to work and I could hardly sleep."

At last, "one day Mr. Supporters came into my tent and told me that he had come up from Skagway in a blizzard to sell out [the equipment] and take me back to the States." [15]

Billy Saportas was none too enthusiastic about his errand. Following a summer of unusually heavy rain the mountain streams were swollen almost to the point of impassibility and the heavily eroded trails were slick with mud. On the way down from Bennett, he and Frances lost their balance trying to ford an engorged stream and were nearly swept away.

The bravery, high spirits, and beauty of his companion made a profound impression on Billy. He was inspired to try his hand at poetry:

> Look at pretty little Frances
> As down the Skagway trail she prances

On the rocks she fairly dances
And has wings, one almost fancies.

Far away in Cuba's isle
Many and many a thousand mile
See a dead and dying pile
Of poor Cuban rank and file.

There her Harry dear was sent,
On a warlike mission bent,
And he never really meant
To leave her living in a tent.[16]

Fran wasn't prancing by the time she reached Skagway. While scrambling over some icy boulders, she twisted her knee, which became stiff and swollen. In excruciating pain, she limped the last eighteen miles to town.

To Frances's surprise, the miserable tent camp she had left a month earlier had been transformed into a prosperous looking village. Ironically, gold had been discovered within easy walking distance of town, so although the heroic souls who had hauled their tons of gear over the passes were lucky if they had boat fare back to Seattle, many of the slackers who had remained on the coast were now rich. The Holly House had acquired a restaurant that served homecooked meals, and among the town's other new amenities was a public bathhouse with facilities for men and women. Fran spent a restful three days there soaking her knee in a tub of hot water. When the steamer *Rosalie* arrived, Billy, by now thoroughly infatuated, insisted on accompanying her all the way back to the States.

Amazingly, nothing that had happened had shaken her faith in her husband. She had written her mother from the shores of Lake Bennett, "Any place is good enough where Harry is but as I have said it is awful—*awful* without him—and in this hole—it is death. I have had several good cries between these lines....*Don't* believe anything except what Harry writes."[17]

In Seattle, when Frances and Billy arrived on October 22, there was a thick packet of letters from Harry waiting at the hotel where she had stored her trunk. Perhaps there had been moments when she had been tempted to lose faith, but no one could have doubted the love of the man who wrote those letters. Billy took the return boat to Juneau and Frances caught her train, clutching a last-minute cablegram from her husband promising that he would return from his Cuban mission to meet her in New York and escort her back to the "real honeymoon world" of Havana.

The Mystery
of the *Maine*

The Journalism That Acts

THERE WAS a Baby Huey quality about William Randolph Hearst. Like the oversize infant of comic book fame, he was quite capable of wreaking havoc in the spirit of innocent playfulness. Thirty-two years old when he moved to New York in the fall of 1895, Hearst was still very much under the influence of his mother, who controlled the bulk of the family fortune. His physical appearance suggested an overgrown boy, a child-giant who had never come to terms with his body. Six foot two and solidly built, he walked with a slight stoop, as if embarrassed to be taking up so much space. His otherwise strong-featured face was marred by closely set, pale gray eyes, suggesting an underdeveloped personality lurking inside, and his voice, startlingly high and thin, was described by *San Francisco Examiner* columnist Ambrose Bierce as "the fragrance of violets made audible."[1]

Society hostesses were baffled by him. As a bachelor and heir to one of America's great fortunes, Hearst was besieged by invitations during his first few months in New York. But he had no small talk, did not much care for dancing, riding, or drinking, and sat through dinner parties looking as if he were silently praying for the moment when he could politely say his good-byes and disappear. Before long, the society ladies had written him off as hopeless, and by the autumn of 1896 he had begun appearing at Sherry's and Bustonoby's in the company of two teenage sisters, Millicent and Anita Willson, who were appearing as featured dancers in the Broadway hit, *The Girl from Paris*.

Hearst's preference for dating *à trois* raised eyebrows around town, particularly after January 1897, when California Congressman Grove Johnson denounced Hearst in the House as a "debauchee" unfit for decent society, "erotic in his tastes, erratic in his dissipations."[2] Gossip about Hearst's private life would continue to circulate as long as he lived. However, there were a number of innocent reasons he may have preferred to date both sisters together. For one thing, Millicent Willson, the sister he was more interested in, was only sixteen. For another, Hearst could not afford to offend his mother by marrying a showgirl, and escorting both sisters at once no doubt made it less likely that he would be trapped into proposing. Also, the girls could always talk to each other, relieving him of the burden of entertaining a date half his age. Perhaps most important, Hearst simply lacked a sense of proportion.

His curse, as well as his blessing, was that he was the son of a lucky man. His father, George Hearst, was a self-taught mining engineer who parlayed a $450 claim into ownership of substantial mining interests in the Comstock Lode. In 1872, George Hearst and his two partners purchased the Ontario, a Utah silver mine that ultimately outproduced their Comstock Lode properties. A few years after that they put up seventy thousand dollars for a claim that became the Homestake mine, the richest gold strike in history. And again, in 1882, the partners spent thirty thousand dollars for a Montana mine known as the Anaconda.

When little Willie Hearst asked for ice cream money, his father would reach into his pocket and hand over whatever he happened to have on him at the moment, on one occasion, a twenty-dollar bill. When he wanted a pet dog, he was given a Newfoundland. And when he was ten, his mother, a former teacher and patron of the arts, decided that he needed a change of scene and took him off on a tour of Europe for a year and a half.

At Harvard, Hearst became business manager of the *Lampoon*, putting the magazine in the black for the first time in its history. He also had a penchant for practical jokes. Midway through the second semester of his junior year, he sent each of his instructors a personally engraved chamber pot, a prank for which he was promptly expelled. Far from being angry, George Hearst was delighted that his son's formal education had come to an end. He offered to make him manager of the Homestake mine ... or, if Willie preferred, of a little ranch of about forty-five thousand acres called San Simeon that he had recently purchased up near San Luis Obispo ... or of his million-acre ranch in the Mexican state of Chihuahua. Hearst considered the possibilities and rejected them all. The Homestake, he wrote his father, was "a wonderful mine"—perhaps the understatement of all time—and his father was "very kind" to offer it. "But I'd rather have the *Examiner*," he concluded.[3]

The *San Francisco Examiner* had been acquired by George Hearst in 1881, largely because he thought that ownership of a newspaper would help him in his efforts to get elected to the Senate. Will Hearst transformed it within a few years from a chronic money-loser with a circulation of about twenty-three thousand into one of the liveliest papers in the country. Although he was often accused of lifting all his ideas from Pulitzer—and then vulgarizing them—Hearst was a talented newspaperman with enlightened prolabor views and flair for putting together a paper that was lively without being shrill or ugly.

What made Hearst a lesser man than Pulitzer was not a lack of brains or even of ideals but his short attention span. Intellectually lazy, he rarely bothered to grapple with the details of any job. And almost as soon as the New York *Journal* was successfully launched he began to lose interest in the day-to-day grind of newspaper work, spending more and more of his time on projects that allowed him to indulge his fancy for role-playing.

In the summer of 1897, for example, Hearst was busy playing detective. He had set up a special "murder squad" and teams of *Journal* reporters visited the morgue every day looking for mysteries to solve. The squad's first big story came in late June, when reporter George Arnold visited the morgue to have a look at a headless, armless torso that had been found floating in the East River near 176th Street, wrapped in oilcloth printed in a distinctive cabbage rose design. By an amazing coincidence, Arnold recognized the torso as that of his masseur, or rubber, as he was called in those days, William Guldensuppe. *Journal* employees scoured the dry goods stores until they located a clerk who recalled selling the oilcloth in question to a Mrs. Augusta Nack. At this point, Hearst paid off the tenants who lived opposite Mrs. Nack's house and set up his own office in their parlor, so unnerving the suspect that she tried to flee, whereupon *Journal* staffers rushed out into the street and detained her until she could be taken into custody by the police.[4]

No sooner had the Nack murder case been solved, than Hearst became caught up in an even more dramatic scheme. Now he planned to rescue a political prisoner from a Havana jail. The prisoner was a seventeen-year-old girl from a prominent Creole family, Evangelina Cosio y Cisneros—invariably called "Miss Cisneros" in the American press, not out of ignorance but in order to emphasize her relationship to her great uncle, the first president of the provisional republican government. The timing of the *Journal*'s bold campaign, after six months without a major Cuban story, was no accident. Spain's conservative prime minister, Cánovas, had been assassinated in August by an Italian anarchist. The war hawk party in Madrid was on its way out, and there was little chance that Weyler would choose this politically delicate moment to threaten another American newspaperman with death.

The Cisneros case is invariably cited as an example of the cynicism and warmongering hysteria of the yellow press, but it began with the purest of motives. Early in 1897, the old Cuba hand George Eugene Bryson, now working for the *Journal*, discovered that the convent-educated teenager was being held prisoner in the Casa de Recojidas, a women's prison notorious as a dumping ground for prostitutes, murderers, and psychotics. Visiting Recojidas, Bryson and another *Journal* writer, the Englishman George Clarke Musgrave, found it to be a snake pit, the courtyard filled with howling, keening madwomen, many of them parading around in the nude and routinely taken advantage of by the prison guards. Genuinely shocked, Bryson asked Consul General Fitzhugh Lee to look into the situation.

On investigation, Lee discovered that despite the appalling conditions in the prison, Cisneros had been given a private room segregated from the other prisoners and was in no immediate danger. Moreover, there was some dispute about the nature of the charges against her. Before she was sent to Recojidas, Cisneros had been keeping house for her father, a prominent separatist who was under house arrest at the Spanish prison colony on the Isle of Pines. According to her friends, Cisneros's only crime was resisting the advances of Colonel Berriz, commander of the island, who had been pressuring her for sexual favors in return for better treatment for her father. The Spanish, however, told another story. Cisneros and her sweetheart, one of the numerous Betancourt clan, had been plotting an escape from the island, and Cisneros had lured Berriz to her room where he was overpowered and taken hostage. Soldiers passing in the street heard the commotion, and in the ensuing fracas several bystanders had been killed.

Bryson was probably the only American reporter in Havana who believed unreservedly in Cisneros's innocence. A well-meaning, slightly befuddled gentleman of the old school, he simply could not imagine that a well-brought-up girl, a mere child in his estimation, could have been part of such a plot. Furthermore, he had heard one of the Recojidas jailers make some off-color remarks about Cisneros, and he was convinced she was in danger of being assaulted if she remained locked up much longer.

Lee took up the case with General Weyler, who confessed that he was in a bind. A harsh sentence would turn the girl into a heroine of the revolution; on the other hand, if he released her, Junta propagandists would undoubtedly claim this as proof of her innocence. Weyler suggested that if the American press, for once, would refrain from making the case into a cause célèbre, a solution could be worked out, perhaps involving exile to Spain, where Cisneros could live with relatives and attend school.

Although by this time every American journalist in Havana was aware of Cisneros's incarceration, and most had visited her in jail, the press corps agreed to maintain their silence. Months passed, and Weyler did not keep his part of the bargain. By June of 1897, Bryson was becoming distraught, and he wrote to Scovel, then in Madrid, pleading, "Can't you do something to secure the pardon of the little girl in the Recojidas?"[5]

Scovel was called home before he could do anything to help, and by late July, Bryson and Musgrave, now co-bureau chief in Havana, had decided to take matters into their own hands. Bryson found a military judge who offered to order the señorita's release in exchange for a bribe of two thousand dollars, but while Bryson was trying to raise the money he was expelled from Cuba in connection with an unrelated story. Musgrave was afraid that the bribe offer would become known, precipitating the very threat he and Bryson had been trying to avoid, Cisneros's transfer to a Spanish prison camp off the coast of Africa. So he began to think in terms of organizing a jailbreak. He was now visiting the Recojidas every day, and the guards were so used to his presence that he thought he would be able to divert their attention by sending them out to buy cigars. Once they were gone, he planned to overpower the jailer and flee with Cisneros to the nearby house of a Cuban agent, who had arranged for her to be smuggled out of Havana by an engineer on the Matanzas railroad.

Cisneros, who was not the pale and passive child that Bryson imagined her to be, was all for the plan, but Musgrave could not quite work up his nerve. In a panic, he decided that the time had come to go public.

As soon as he learned of Cisneros's plight, Hearst was galvanized. The pages of the *Journal* were filled with calls for the release of the "Cuban Joan of Arc," who was also, somewhat prematurely, being called the "Cuban girl martyr." Mass meetings were organized in cooperation with women's clubs across the United States, and James Creelman was assigned to organize a petition drive. With his usual thoroughness, Creelman enlisted two hundred *Journal* stringers who collected ten thousand signatures within five days, bolstered by letters of appeal from President McKinley's mother, Mrs. Ulysses S. Grant, Mrs. William Tecumseh Sherman, Frances Hodgson Burnett, and Julia Ward Howe. But Creelman's coup was the recruitment of Mrs. Jefferson Davis, a cousin of Mrs. Pulitzer and the recipient over the years of financial help from the Pulitzer family.

In September, Fitzhugh Lee visited New York and gave an

interview to the *Commercial Advertiser* denouncing the *Journal*'s campaign as "tommyrot." The *World* obtained a statement from Weyler disavowing any plan to deport Cisneros to an African penal colony; it then observed that if the captain-general changed his mind the *Journal* would have only itself to blame. Even staffers at the *Journal* viewed the campaign as a cynical stunt, except for Hearst himself, who was caught up in the spirit of the thing. "I was in the office during the progress of this comedy and in daily contact with Hearst," wrote editorial page chief Willis Abbot. "He took the whole affair with utmost seriousness . . . and he brooked no indifference on the part of his employees, most of whom in his absence cursed the whole thing for a false bit of cheap sensationalism. But Hearst felt himself in the role of Sir Galahad rescuing a helpless maiden."[6]

The *Journal* had committed its honor, such as it was, to winning the freedom of Cisneros, and when Weyler ignored a plea from the pope himself, Hearst decided to revive the plan to break the girl out of prison. His choice to organize the escape was Karl Decker, a blond six-foot-plus square-jawed Virginian, the son of a Confederate colonel. Decker was thirty-three, a bit too old for such pranks, he thought, but the *Journal*'s managing editor Sam Chamberlain promised him that Hearst would reward his efforts with "ample appreciation."

Decker enlisted two accomplices, American businessman William McDonald and Junta agent Carlos Carbonell, who was also a naturalized American citizen. Carbonell rented a house on Calle O'Farrill, directly across from Cisneros's prison cell. On the night chosen for the rescue he and Decker suspended a twelve-foot-long plank between the roof of the house and the cell window. Perched thirty-five feet about the street, the burly Decker hacked away at the bars of the jail window until they weakened enough for him to bend them with a heavy stillson wrench. Cisneros squeezed through the opening and inched her way along the precariously balanced plank to safety. Three days later she was smuggled aboard the passenger steamer *Seneca*, disguised in men's clothes and smoking an enormous Havana cigar.

As insiders at the *Journal* later revealed, the jailbreak was somewhat less risky than it seemed. The warden and guards had all been bribed, and the elaborate plan was carried out chiefly to provide the prison personnel with a plausible alibi. Nevertheless, Cisneros arrived in New York to a tumultuous welcome, organized and paid for by the _Journal._ After a brief stop at the Waldorf, where she changed into a white gown provided by the _Journal,_ she was whisked off to a banquet in her honor at Delmonico's, hosted by mayoral candidate Chauncey Depew. Her escort for the evening was, of course, Karl Decker, her Yankee "d'Artagnan." Hearst, when he finally came face-to-face with the object of his chivalric gesture, was so overcome by shyness that he mumbled a few inaudible words of welcome, then fled in his French motorcar.

The _Journal_ now announced that Cisneros's fondest desire was to become an American citizen. "Please fix it for me to become a citizen," she was quoted as pleading. "Fix it quickly for me, tonight even. I do so want to march and sing, 'I am an American.' "[7] By special dispensation, she was allowed to take out her first naturalization papers on October 16, 1897, less than twenty-four hours after she first set foot on American soil. The next day, she was feted at a sold-out rally in Madison Square Garden, after which she departed on a national speaking tour.

Cisneros's sponsors faced the usual problems encountered by those who present radical activists to a middle-class audience. She was an authentic revolutionary heroine, but the effort to entrap Colonel Berriz was not the sort of thing one would describe to a women's club audience. Therefore it was necessary to present the teenage Judith as a passive victim, the fragile flower of Cuban womanhood rescued from rapacious Spanish jailers by a virile white knight of the American press. Though avoiding the facts of the case, the _Journal_ managed to fill some 375 columns of newsprint with trivia. Readers were entertained with the breathtaking saga of her "First Elevator Ride" and of a shopping trip to purchase a "superb trousseau" at Hearst's expense. They were informed of her favorite color (black), her childhood desire to become a nun, and her ambition to become an English teacher. Assured by Tomás Estrada Palma that the fuss was all for the good of the cause, Cisneros behaved like a good trooper, although she persisted in thinking that her name was Señorita Evangelina Cosio, not Evangeline Cisneros.

"Doubtless she knew she was being exploited," Charles Michelson wrote. Still, he was appalled by the callous way the *Journal* fawned over the teenager, only to drop her cold as soon as her speaking tour was ended. Her moment in the spotlight past, the girl found refuge in the Virginia homes of the Fitzhugh Lees and other sympathetic Americans, including Mrs. John W. Foster, widow of the former secretary of state. Against all odds, her story did end happily. In May 1898, she was married to Carlos Carbonell. After the war, during which Carbonell served as a captain in the U.S. Army, he and his bride settled in Havana, where he practiced dentistry for many years.[8]

This was a suitably upbeat last act to what Willis Abbot called the "magnificent farce" of the "Cuban Girl Martyr." Karl Decker, however, fared less well. The reward he had been promised never materialized. On the contrary, when Decker submitted his expense account, including claims for the bribe money he had paid the Recojidas guards, the *Journal* refused to reimburse him. Perhaps no one dared submit the account to Hearst, who was seemingly unaware that the escape was not the heroic adventure that had been reported. Thirty years later, Decker was still writing letters to the Hearst corporation, reminding them of the debt.

If there was anything sillier than the *Journal*'s self-adulatory coverage of the Cisneros escapade it was the reaction of Hearst's critics. Some conservative editorial writers seriously suggested that the United States ought to make amends for the incident by returning Cisneros to Havana, the last thing Spain wanted, one can be sure. In retrospect, George Eugene Bryson was probably correct in thinking that Weyler never intended to honor his gentleman's agreement with Consul-General Lee to release Cisneros, if only because he could not do so without incurring the wrath of his hawkish supporters in Spain. Advisable or not, the escape was organized by private citizens, and under existing treaties the United States had no obligation to extradite a political prisoner to Spain.

Hearst's boasts to the contrary, the escape did not bring the United States one day closer to war with Spain. But it was a shameful early example of the manufactured celebrity. Nothing about Cisneros was quite as advertised, from her own name on down, and the campaign helped to sell the American public on a false image of Cuba—a pale-skinned, upper-class virgin waiting breathlessly for a broad-shouldered American to rescue her and make her his.

While the Cisneros campaign was gathering steam, Joseph Pulitzer had become worried enough over the competition from the *Journal* to authorize assistant business manager Don Seitz to begin secret negotiations aimed at a price-fixing agreement. In the parlance of the *World* cable code, GENUINE and GERANIUM were talking about going to JAIL together.

Considering that Pulitzer was a vocal champion of antitrust legislation, this was a somewhat surprising move. However, the powers at the Dome (anticipating subsequent court decisions on the subject) had convinced themselves that antitrust principles did not apply to the newspaper business. A memorandum prepared by Seitz pointed out that the purpose of an agreement would not be "to kill off the next anaconda that may uncoil in the town," but to raise the price of the daily *World* to two cents so that "it can operate on its own lines of public service, pure politics and commonsense."[9]

Even if Hearst could not be persuaded to agree that both papers should sell for two cents, Seitz estimated that even a limited agreement—covering only advertising rates, payments for returns from news dealers, the limiting of bill posting and handbill distribution, and a few other items—could save the *World* $224,000 a year, and the *Journal* somewhat more. This was a considerable sum in 1897 dollars, but the editors at the Dome were so irrational on the subject of Hearst—and so determined to get revenge on Carvalho, who had defected to the *Journal* earlier in the year—that there was little chance of them actually securing an agreement. To begin with, Seitz proposed an offer to buy out and fold SENIOR GERANIUM (the morning *Journal*), which was "obviously unprofitable and destined to remain so." The *Journal* would then become an afternoon and Sunday paper. He had no illusion that such a proposal would be seriously entertained, Seitz wrote Pulitzer, but he intended to make it anyway "for the pleasure of seeing LOS [Carvalho] faint away."[10]

Ironically, the "nervous invalid" Joseph Pulitzer was at times more reasonable than his supposedly hardheaded employees, who were committed to crushing GUSH (Hearst) if it took the Boss's last dollar to do it.

Writing to editorial page chief William Merrill later that year, Pulitzer lectured, "I have known you to talk with the utmost contempt, or at least as much contempt as your benevolent nature will allow, about the very best things in GERANIUM [the *Journal*]." But it was imperative to dispel "the idea that GERANIUM owes its position simply to money, or as ANFRACTO [business manager John Norris] puts it very foolishly—that it is simply matching dollars. This is utterly false and the first thing to eradicate. Money of course is an extraordinarily important factor, but GERANIUM has brains and genius beyond any question, not only brains for news and features but genius for the self-advertising acts which have no parallel."

Pulitzer complained that ANFRACTO and other anti-Hearst executives were guilty of "self-complacency," but in the case of DART (Assistant news editor E. O. Chamberlin), refusal to face reality approached "semi lunacy": "He does not recognize GERANIUM at all —never did—says they are not in the field. This is not new.... I have talked to him 40 times over this and he actually denied the very figures."

The Boss implored William Merrill to appoint himself a "doctor of lunacy" and spend "an hour or two" acting as an amateur therapist every day until he had "cured DART." [11]

As late as August 1897, Artie Brisbane remained loyal to the *World* dogma that Hearst was an "unknown upstart" and anyone who went to work for him was committing "journalistic suicide." When his chief assistant, Charles Edward Russell, announced one day that he had decided to take the plunge, Brisbane invited him to his country house in Hempstead for the weekend and kept him up all night trying to persuade him not to go.

"Both of us are young," he warned Russell, "We've gone far, but we can't afford to spoil our future."

Brisbane's most fervent argument, Russell later recalled, was grounded in the science of phrenology. "Why just look at the difference in the heads of Pulitzer and Hearst," he urged. "Jo Pulitzer has a head as long as a horse. Compare that with Hearst's. Then you'll realize how obvious it is that Pulitzer will lick Hearst in short order." [12]

Russell was not convinced, and Brisbane, by early August, had begun to doubt his own reasoning. In return for his saving the Sunday edition, he had hoped that the Boss would allow him to write a signed column for the editorial pages. Pulitzer, however, subscribed to the old-fashioned view that all editorial opinions represent the voice of the owner, regardless of who actually wrote the words. "These newspapers belong to me," he cabled Brisbane, "and so long as I live, no one will express an independent editorial opinion in my newspapers."[13] This rejection, combined with the increasingly byzantine office politics at the Dome, was behind Brisbane's defection, but it was his admiration for Creelman's handling of the Cisneros case that provided the spark.

Within days of the first *Journal* stories on Cisneros, Brisbane sent a note to Hearst at his hotel. He had turned down several offers from the *Journal* in the past, but now he had a proposal. Hearst was preparing to close down the evening edition of the *Journal,* which was foundering with a circulation of about forty thousand. Brisbane offered to take over the edition for a salary of eight thousand dollars a year—about two-thirds of what he was getting from Pulitzer—on the condition that his contract include substantial bonuses. Hearst agreed, suggesting an escalator clause that would raise Brisbane's salary a thousand dollars for every ten thousand the evening *Journal* gained in circulation.

"The Spanish-American War was coming on and we went in for the war," Brisbane recalled many years later. "We gained four hundred thousand circulation in eight weeks."[14]

Champagne and Ice Cream

THE NATURE of the mission that brought Harry Scovel back to Havana in October of 1897 was so secret that Brad Merrill forbade him to reveal it even to his wife. Exactly what the *World* was up to will never be known, but apparently there was a plot to steal the *Journal*'s thunder by getting Evangelina Cisneros out of prison before Karl Decker did. However, the scheme went awry almost immediately. Someone, never identified, recognized Scovel on the street and tipped off the authorities. That same night, Decker, who had been in Havana for a month trying to work up his nerve to go through with the jailbreak, made his assault on Recojidas.

Scovel, meanwhile, was arrested, arraigned, and officially expelled from Cuba in record time: Within six hours of his coming ashore he was on his way back to the docks. The officer who escorted him made a show of rough treatment as he shoved his prisoner up the gangplank of the *Seneca*. "You are officially deported," he announced. Then, lowering his voice to a stage whisper, he added, "But you might as well turn around and come right back. Weyler is done for."[1]

The official was right: Weyler's recall was announced the next day. Harry remained in New York just long enough to meet the train that was bringing Frances back from Seattle before returning to Havana. The Liberal Party had come to power in Madrid, and Weyler's replacement, Captain-General Ramón Blanco y Erenas, was under orders to launch Cuba on the path to home rule and restore friendly relations with the American press. One of his first acts in office was a negotiated compromise with the *World*. Harry agreed to appear before a judge and was sentenced to six years in jail and a fine of six hundred dollars, then immediately paroled and issued accreditation papers permitting him to work as a correspondent. By mid-November, Frances had joined him in his suite at the Hotel Inglaterra.

The Cuba that Harry introduced his wife to that November bore little resemblance to the shadow world of jungle camps and secret agents he had known on previous assignments. As Frances put it, suddenly all was "champagne and ice cream." There were weekend sailing parties with the American expatriate crowd that frequented the Havana Yacht Club and official receptions at the governor's palace. The general responsible for organizing the dragnet that captured Harry the previous February actually paid a courtesy call to express his regrets, and when the Scovels traveled outside the city they found that, in Fran's words, the Spanish officers they met were "almost crazy and did everything they could for us."[2]

Even so, Frances did not find Havana quite the "honeymoon world" she had been promised. During her first week in Cuba, she and Harry made a tour of Havana Province in the company of Harry Brown, who had been on the island since early October working on a special *World* series on the plight of the *reconcentrados*. In a letter to the St. Louis *Post-Dispatch*, Frances wrote of the horrible scenes she had witnessed: "In some places, these poor people would get on a train, their feet swollen and sore and their bodies nothing but skeletons.... They cried around the café so that one cannot eat a mouthful of food and [the waiters] shut the doors and windows so that we could eat in comfort.... In one town before ten o'clock in the day Mr. Scovel had seen twenty-three dead people, and in [Havana] a woman was dying right on the street, another dying under the portico of the palace."[3]

Brown estimated that thirty thousand people, mostly women and children, had died from starvation during the several weeks he had been in the country, and he had taken hundreds of photographs of children in the last stages of malnutrition, with toothpicklike limbs barely able to support their grotesquely puffed-up bellies. The *World* had one of its staff artists translate these photographs into illustrations, and even though the details were toned down the pictures made a tremendous impact. The public in the 1890s was not accustomed to such realism, and the *World* received hundreds of letters of protest. Pulitzer apologized to his readers in an editorial, but justified the decision to publish the illustrations, observing that the issue containing Brown's article had been passed around the table at a meeting of the president's cabinet on November 10.

Several weeks later, Scovel was making small talk with Blanco at a party at the governor's palace, when he mentioned that it was a dream of his to introduce his bride to his dear and respected friend, Máximo Gómez. According to Frances, the captain-general was so flabbergasted by "the idea of a woman going out there" that he gave permission for the journey.

The story that Harry took Frances to see Gómez on their "honeymoon trip" would become one of the legends of the era of the yellow kid press. Of course, it went without saying that the journey was more than a social call. The Associated Press reported that Secretary of State John Sherman, acting on orders from President McKinley, had asked Scovel to sound out Gómez once again on the possibility of the Cuban separatists accepting a U.S.-guaranteed settlement, based on home rule. Taking note of this story, the *World* denied that Scovel was carrying any official letters from McKinley but did not bother to refute the rest of the AP's information.

Blanco, meanwhile, had granted the Scovels permission to undertake a compassionate errand on behalf of the widow of the late Charles E. Crosby, a representative of the Chicago *Record* killed in action the previous March 9. Crosby's personal effects, including $350 in gold, were in the possession of Gómez, who had promised to turn them over to an authorized representative of the

United States government, and since Scovel had no official government connection, he cajoled Blanco into allowing Rafael Madrigal to join the expedition.

The four-day journey into the Sierra de Escambray mountains was fraught with danger. Although the travelers displayed a 10" x 24" American flag, the largest they could find, there was a very real risk that they and their Cuban guides would be fired on by a Spanish patrol. In addition, Rafael Madrigal weighed over three hundred pounds and was suffering from a heart condition that made any exertion dangerous. Nevertheless, Scovel's account of the journey in the *World* was filled with lyrical descriptions of the joys of riding across prairies lush with guinea grass and of camping at night under the stars. *World* readers, who had still not been informed that Scovel was traveling with his wife of six months, must have wondered how to account for his romantic mood.

On the second day of the journey, the group reached the camp of a brigadier general in the insurgent army where they staged an impromptu ceremony. "I was allowed to carry the little American flag," Frances wrote proudly, "and salute the single star banner, the first time it has ever been done."[4] A day later, at Gómez's headquarters on a large stock farm near Arroyo Arenas, the ceremony was repeated, but this time, while two Cuban buglers played a somewhat garbled version of the "Star-Spangled Banner," it was Madrigal who "dipped the flag," a gesture that implied official recognition of the rebels.

Even so, the mission was not a success. The Liberal cabinet in Madrid had recently announced that it planned to grant Cuba autonomy as of January 1, 1898, and Scovel had been asked by the State Department to urge the insurgents to participate in the new government. But Gómez, who had seemed amenable to this idea a year earlier, now wanted no part of home rule. Spain was bankrupt, and the rebels were convinced that it could not keep an army in Cuba much longer. "In a few weeks," Gómez predicted, "Spain will either evacuate Cuba or fight the United States." He added, "I think that the United States will only want Cuba commercially. Frankly, if Cuba were annexed tomorrow, I don't think there is an American statesman that would know what to do with her."[5]

On their return journey, the Scovels and Madrigal paused to celebrate Christmas day by sharing a meal with their guides, who managed somehow to procure a small pig. The next morning, as they were packing their saddlebags after breakfast, a rebel officer rode into their camp to warn them of a rumor that the train they were planning to take back to Havana might be bombed. Hastily changing their plans, the party headed for Tunas, where they caught a commercial steamer bound for the capital. The ship was "an old tub," awash in odors so "marvelous," wrote Fran, that she and Harry abandoned their cabin to sleep on deck. By the time the Scovels reached Havana on December 27, the AP was reporting that Scovel was dead, hanged by order of Gómez who was outraged that he had come to demand the surrender of the insurgents.

The rumors of Scovel's death, greatly exaggerated as usual, were a symptom of the hysteria that had erupted in Havana as the deadline for the Liberal Party's autonomy plan approached. Home rule had long been the solution to the Cuban problem favored by moderates on both sides. But as Gómez had pointed out, there were very few moderates left on the island. The Cuban separatists had vowed never to cooperate with autonomy, and the Loyalists in the cities, seeing that Spain no longer had the will to fight the insurgents, were beginning to look to the United States to save them from the rebels.

In a cable to the State Department, Fitzhugh Lee reported a recent conversation with "a rabid violent ... colonel of volunteers. He said he 'tried to be a Reformist at first' and then he told the Palace people he 'would try and be an Autonomist.'

"What next?" asked Lee.

"Yankee," replied the colonel.[6]

Complicating the situation, German warships were active in the Caribbean. In Haiti the German minister, Count von Schwerin, had suddenly become solicitous of the rights of one Emile Luders, a Port-au-Prince resident who was, through his German father, a subject of the Reich. Luders had been jailed a few months earlier after a melee at the livery stable he operated, and Count von Schwerin had demanded Luders's immediate release and repatriation. The Haitians complied, but now von Schwerin had come up with some additional demands. He wanted the judge who convicted Luders removed from the bench, a twenty-thousand dollar settlement, a formal apology, a twenty-one-gun salute in honor of two German naval training ships that just happened to have arrived in the harbor and, the final humiliation, the Haitian flag that flew over the Palais National was to be struck and a white flag flown in its place.

It did not take a great deal of imagination to interpret the symbolism behind these demands. The Haitian government appealed to Washington to lend its "moral influence" in the form of a warship capable of intimidating the Germans, but on December 6, before the United States cruiser *Marblehead* could reach Port-au-Prince, the Haitians were forced to capitulate. Determined not to be caught unprepared a second time, Assistant Secretary of the Navy Theodore Roosevelt ordered the North Atlantic Squadron to begin maneuvers in the Gulf of Mexico.

Coincidentally, the United States and Spain had been discussing an exchange of battleships to symbolize the resumption of normal, or at least relatively normal, relations between the United States and the Spanish liberal government. The Spanish battleship *Vizcaya* would visit several East Coast ports, and the USS *Maine*, a second-class battleship, would be dispatched to Havana.

Everyone agreed that the presence of an American warship in Havana harbor would be a powerful symbol. But of what? Fitzhugh Lee had been arguing vigorously for an American naval visit for the past six months on the grounds that an American presence was desirable to protect the lives and property of U.S. citizens in the event of civil disturbances. But in the United States, noninterventionists like Carl Schurz wondered in print if the real purpose was not to provoke the Loyalists into calling for a U.S. protectorate.

Havana was rife with plots, both pro- and anti-American. At one point that winter, dynamite was discovered in the Casa Nueva, the office building that housed both the offices of the *Journal* and the American Consulate. Shortly before Christmas the police attempted to question George Clarke Musgrave, who was temporarily in charge of the *Journal*'s Havana operation, about his alleged connection to an attempt to bomb the Consulate. Musgrave responded with a story calling the charges nonsense and saying that the real target of the bombing attempt had been the *Journal* offices. The British press, meanwhile, was reporting that Hearst was at last planning to mount a filibuster expedition, to be commanded by Karl Decker. The *Journal* issued an official denial on December 4, stating, "It is scarcely necessary to say that the *Journal* has no belligerent intentions toward Cuba."[7]

On the morning of January 12, to no one's great surprise, the resentments against the Blanco government erupted into violence. Rioters surged through the streets shouting, "Down with Blanco!" and "Long Live Weyler!" The *Journal* reported that the disturbances were directed against American citizens, but other American papers contradicted this account, noting that the actual targets were the offices of Havana's four proautonomy newspapers. Scovel's story in the *World* bitterly condemned "sensationalist" coverage and suggested that the demonstrations were being secretly stage-managed by a cabal of pro-Weyler officers.

On the theory that the arrival of an American ship would only provide another pretext for demonstrations, Fitzhugh Lee asked that the *Maine*'s visit be temporarily postponed. The battleship was to remain in Key West until and unless its captain, Charles D. Sigsbee, received a message from Lee containing the code phrase "two dollars."

Despite this precaution, Lee did not expect any more serious trouble in Havana until late February, when elections were scheduled to be held under the new constitution. Scovel agreed. In fact, he was so confident that the troubles had died down that he was planning to take his long-deferred vacation. In contrast to the *Journal,* which now had seven full- or part-time correspondents in Havana, and the *Herald* and *Sun,* which each had four, the *World* had only Scovel, who still managed to get more scoops than all the other papers combined. He wanted to hire an assistant, however, and had decided that taking a leave to visit New York was the only way to force Brad Merrill to send another reporter to Cuba.

But the day before he and Frances planned to sail, Harry came down with chills and a high fever, a recurrence of the malaria he had contracted crossing the Majana swamp. He insisted that she go on to New York alone, promising to join her as soon as possible.

A few days later, on Saturday, January 22, he was well enough to send the *World* a story praising Fitzhugh Lee for his restraint in refusing to summon the *Maine* on the day of the riots. By keeping his head, said Scovel, Lee had probably averted war between Spain and the United States.

That same evening, "homesick" for Frances he wrote her:

> My Darling—I am just on the point of deciding to cable Merrill that things are sure to be quiet here until the elections (a month ahead) and ask for permission to come home for a vacation.
>
> However I have one scheme to put through first i.e. get a war ship down here. All the Doctors and American citizens want it and I am getting up a big petition to McKinley. By getting Blanco to say he would like a U.S. man of war to come (so as to show there is no anti-American feeling here (?)) [*sic*] I hope to work both sides for a good end. For a ship will be needed next time.[8]

Two days later, Consul-General Lee received a visit from John R. Caldwell, the chief Havana correspondent of the New York *Herald.* Caldwell showed Lee a cablegram he had just received from his editors in New York: "Send report Cuban cane crop. Want for main section." All the newspapers used codes to foil the Spanish censors, and Caldwell told Lee that according to the *Herald* codebook, this message meant that the *Maine* was on its way to Havana.

"Nonsense," snorted Lee. "The government would never send a navy vessel here unless I requested it, which I haven't done."[9]

But within hours, Lee had confirmation from Washington that the battleship was on its way.

To this day, no one knows exactly what inspired President McKinley's decision to order the *Maine* to Cuba. G. J. A. O'Toole, who attempted to reconstruct the events leading up to McKinley's action in *The Spanish War,* suggests that the triggering event was a report from William F. Powell, the American minister in Port-au-Prince, noting the presence of four German warships in Haitian waters. This suggestion makes sense, although it does not entirely explain the State Department's failure to consult with Lee beforehand, as it had promised to do.[10]

When he learned of the battleship's imminent arrival, Lee

protested to Washington that the timing of the *Maine*'s visit could not be worse. Blanco had recently left on a two-week tour of the island and the aides he had left in charge, some of whom were suspected of being members of the ultra-Loyalist faction, could not be trusted to keep their heads in the event of the unexpected arrival of an American battleship.

John Caldwell began to wonder whether he might have inadvertently caused the president's decision through a garbled coded message he had sent to the *Herald* area manager in Key West. As Caldwell confided to the AP's Walter Scott Meriwether, the *Herald*'s Key West office manager, Fred Burgin, had smuggled him a revolver through secret channels but had neglected to send any ammunition. Realizing that a request for bullets could never get by the censors, Caldwell had cabled: "Camera received, but no plates." It happened that nearly all of the codes used by correspondents in Havana involved requests for money or equipment, and the *Herald* office boy who received Caldwell's message in Burgin's absence leafed through his codebook and, through some mix-up, deciphered it as a warning that the American Consulate was under attack. This false report was forwarded to Washington where Harry Brown, who had recently left the *World* to become chief of the *Herald*'s Washington bureau, duly informed the Department of the Navy.

For years afterward, Havana insiders would be convinced that Caldwell's cable message was the "real" reason the *Maine* was dispatched when it was. There is no direct evidence that this cable or Scovel's lobbying had anything to do with the president's decision. (A curious facet of Scovel's "scheme," however, is that Blanco was out of town, as everyone knew; how he planned to get the captain-general to request a warship when he was not even in Havana is mysterious.)

For whatever reasons, the *Maine* was on its way, and at midday on January 25th, it appeared outside the entrance to Havana harbor. Three hundred and nineteen feet long, with large smokestacks amidships and tall masts fore and aft, its hull painted white as was traditional for U.S. Navy vessels in peacetime, the *Maine* was an impressive sight, easily dominating the other vessels in the harbor, and an excited crowd gathered on the quays to watch the battleship's arrival. The ship had been dispatched so hastily that it did not even have the required documents certifying that its crew was free of yellow fever, but Fitzhugh Lee hurried to the governor's palace, cajoling the bureaucrats in charge into accepting the battleship's presence as a fait accompli.

The anti-American demonstrations Lee had feared failed to materialize. A week later the city was still calm, so quiet, in fact, that Don José Canalejas, an editor of the Madrid *El Heraldo* who had been in Havana on a fact-finding trip, decided to cut short his visit and return to Spain. Canalejas's private secretary was busy packing his boss's papers when a Cuban acquaintance, Gustavo Escoto, dropped by and offered to help. Unbeknownst to the secretary, Escoto was actually an agent of the Junta. When Escoto spotted a compromising letter from Enrique Dupuy de Lôme, the Spanish minister to Washington, among Canalejas's correspondence, he quickly pocketed it, taking the next boat to New York, and then turning the document over to Horatio Rubens.

The letter was a political bombshell. Among other injudicious comments, Dupuy de Lôme implied that Blanco's autonomy plan was a sham—exactly what the Cubans had been saying all along —and he insultingly referred to President McKinley as "weak and catering to the rabble, and besides, a low politician."[11]

As a reward to the *Journal* for its efforts on behalf of Evangelina Cisneros, Tomás Estrada Palma personally delivered the first facsimile of the letter to Sam Chamberlain. The *Journal* gleefully launched a "de Lôme go home" campaign, pillorying the Spaniard while at the same time assuring that his libelous views on McKinley received the widest possible circulation. Dupuy de Lôme had no choice but to resign, an event celebrated by the *Journal* with a Homer Davenport cartoon showing the Spanish minister being booted out of the country by Uncle Sam. "The flag of Cuba Libre ought to float over Morro Castle in a week," the caption predicted.

On February 11, 1898, the same day Dupuy de Lôme left Washington, the *Journal*'s 138-foot yacht *Buccaneer*, successor to the *Vamoose*, was boarded by harbor police as it attempted to dock in Havana. The police were looking for Karl Decker, who was rumored to be on board, but found instead another *Journal* correspondent, Julian Hawthorne, the author of such best-selling novels as *Bressant* and *Idolatry* (and son of the less commercially successful novelist, Nathaniel). Even though Decker was not on board, the *Buccaneer* was found to be fitted with several small artillery pieces and was seized. The *Journal* expressed outrage, and an article on the incident in the morning editions of February 12 ran under a headline that announced the declaration of THE SPANISH-*JOURNAL* WAR. But the paper seemed almost as angry with Captain Sigsbee of the *Maine* as with the Spanish harbor police, complaining that the seizure of the *Buccaneer* "right under the guns of the *Maine* was regarded as almost incredible." [12]

The *Maine* Is Still Your Ship

I N HAVANA, February 15 was the second day of Carnival, and not even the troubles of the past month could keep the population from enjoying its last fling before the beginning of Lent. By nine-forty in the evening the streets around the Parque Central were filled with promenaders decked out in finery and masks, and from the fashionable cafés to the lowliest side-street cantinas, the city throbbed with revelry.

The music and laughter drifted out into the harbor where no doubt they provoked some bitter reflections among the crew of the *Maine* who had already retired to their quarters for the night. In order to avoid any pretext for trouble, the enlisted men had been denied shore leave in Havana. Cooped up on board with few duties and little recreation, they had spent the past three weeks gazing longingly at the bustling palm-lined streets of a port well known for its wide-open night life—legal gambling, smooth rum, and tempestuous women. They had endured the boredom in the belief that by Mardi Gras, February 17, they would be in New

Orleans, only to discover, a few days before, that the *Maine*'s departure had been postponed. Consul-General Lee had warned the Navy Department that it would be a mistake to withdraw the ship before arrangements were made for another vessel to take its place. Instead, the *Maine* had been resupplied by the torpedo boat *Cushing*, which promptly returned to Key West, leaving the 354 officers and men on board the battleship feeling more isolated than ever.

It was a still, moonless night and banks of high clouds blotted out all but the brightest constellations. Lieutenant John Hood, the chief watch officer, was sitting on the port side of the deck, his feet up on the rail, contemplating the lights of Havana. Suddenly, he "felt more than heard" a tremendous explosion, which seemed to be coming from underwater, near the forward section of the starboard deck. "I instantly turned my head," Hood recalled, and "there was a second explosion. I saw the whole starboard side of the deck and everything above it as far as the aft end of the superstructure spring up into the air with all kinds of objects in it —a regular crater-like performance with flames and everything else coming up."[1]

In the brightly lit café of the Inglaterra overlooking the park, Harry and Frances Scovel were having dinner with George Rea when they noticed that their crystal wine glasses had begun to vibrate. Seconds later, they felt the shock wave of a powerful explosion. Windowpanes shattered, causing patrons to dive under the tables and strollers in the plaza to run for cover. The sky over the harbor lit up with a brilliant white flash, followed by a barrage of smaller explosions.

After making sure that Frances was all right, Scovel and Rea sprinted toward the harbor, pushing their way through the panicky crowds. Scovel had recently rented an office in the customs house, so the two of them had no trouble getting past the guard post there. As they ran out onto the wharves, they saw the black silhouette of the *Maine*, illuminated by a fire burning amidships. The foremast and smokestacks had toppled, the superstructure had settled on its side, and the entire bow section had been reduced to a jumble of twisted steel. Six-pound shells from the ship's magazines were still going off in bursts, exploding over the heads of sailors from the Ward Line steamer *City of Washington* and the Spanish cruiser *Alfonso XII,* who were circling the wreck in lifeboats, looking for survivors.

Colonel José Paglieri, chief of the Havana police force, had commandeered a rowboat and was about to shove away from the dock. Paglieri had arrested Scovel on more than one occasion, but he maintained a good-humored tolerance of American journalists and he motioned for him and Rea to jump aboard. Rowed by two very nervous oarsmen, the boat approached what was left of the *Maine.* "The superstructure alone loomed up, partly colored by the red glare of flames glancing upon the black water," Scovel wrote of the scene.[2] Someone on the wharf turned on a search-light, and as the beam raked the water around their boat, the men saw that they were surrounded by dismembered bodies.

"Great God! They are all gone!" Rea heard Scovel gasp. "This is the work of a torpedo, and marks the beginning of the end."[3]

Captain Sigsbee had reluctantly agreed to be ferried to the *City of Washington* where several dozen wounded were being cared for on deck. Recognizing Rea, he scrawled a message in pencil and asked him to see that it got on the cable to Washington as soon as possible: "Tell admiral *Maine* blown up and destroyed. Send lighthouse tenders. Many killed and wounded. Don't send war vessels if others available."[4]

Rea and Scovel borrowed Paglieri's boat and headed back to the cable office, which was jammed with American newsmen waiting for the clerk to be rounded up at his home. Rea waved the official message from Sigsbee and the crowd parted, sending him and Scovel to the head of the line. Despite a good deal of pushing and shoving, no one was worrying much about who put his story on the wire first since the Spanish censors were notorious for not honoring filing times.

At this moment, however, Scovel demonstrated the cunning that made him such a successful correspondent. Several weeks earlier, he had obtained from a Cuban sympathizer in the censor's office a blank cable form prestamped with the censor's seal of approval. He had been carrying the blank form in his pocket ever since, waiting for just such an emergency.

In New York, Ernest Chamberlin was on night duty in the city room at the Dome when news of the disaster came over the wires. The first report on the cable was a hundred-word bulletin by F. J.

Hilgert of the Associated Press. Scovel's story, the first report by a journalist who had actually been at the scene of the disaster, came through minutes later, in time for the five A.M. edition. It read in full:

> The United States battleship *Maine* was blown up in Havana harbor shortly before 10 o'clock this evening.
> Many of those on the *Maine* were killed and many more injured.
> The injured do not know what caused the explosion.
> There is some doubt as to whether the explosion took place ON the *Maine*.
> The battleship was practically destroyed, but little of her being left above the water.[5]

Except for Sigsbee's cable, which was relayed to Navy Secretary John Long shortly before one A.M., Hilgert's and Scovel's dispatches were the only ones to get through from Cuba that night, and Chamberlin, who wrongly assumed that the cable had been worded partly for the eyes of censors, saw innuendos that were not intended. The headline he wrote for the front-page story stressed: "... It Is Not Known Whether Explosion Occurred On or UNDER the *Maine*." The emphasis left no doubt as to where the *World* thought the explosion had originated.

Arthur Brisbane, an early riser, first learned of the disaster at four-thirty the next morning, when he left his room at his downtown club and, as was his custom, picked up an early edition of the *World* on his way to the office. Hearst had already been informed of the news by phone and had ordered the morning *Journal* to devote its entire front page to the story, but the task of coming up with the first in-depth coverage on the disaster would fall to Brisbane. As he cheerfully admitted in later years, the evening *Journal*'s staff at this point consisted of only two reporters, one of whom was assigned to stand outside the Dome and snatch up new editions of the *World* as they came on the street. For news from Havana, Brisbane would have to rely on the morning *Journal* team, headed at the moment by George Eugene Bryson, no one's idea of a competent investigator.

Brisbane's first act that morning was to cable Scovel renewing the *Journal*'s offer of a job. Since he realized there was virtually no chance that Scovel would desert the *World* in the middle of a breaking story of this importance, Brisbane added a personal plea, asking him to find some man who could send the evening *Journal* "all the news." Minutes later, he sat down and wrote his editorial for the early afternoon edition: "Until further facts are known, we are bound to accept the accident theory." These were the last measured words the *Journal* would ever print on the subject of the USS *Maine*.

The "accident theory" Brisbane referred to was familiar to any reasonably well-informed reader. The navy's new coal-powered warships, particularly first-generation models like the *Maine*, whose keel had been laid in 1888, were designed in such a way that coal bunkers were located near the ship's magazines. Heat generated by spontaneous-combustion fires in the bunkers could all too easily spread to the magazines, creating the potential for the ship to blow itself up. There had been at least a dozen reported incidents on American ships in the previous year, and during one fire, on board the cruiser *Cincinnati*, sparks actually ignited wooden ammunition crates before the blaze was brought under control.

Analysts in the navy's Bureau of Ordnance assumed from the first that a bunker fire was the most reasonable explanation of the *Maine*'s destruction. Two days after the tragedy, Philip R. Alger, the navy's leading expert on explosives, told the Washington Evening *Star* that "no torpedo such as is known to modern warfare, can of itself cause an explosion as powerful as that which destroyed the *Maine*. We know of no instances where the explosion of a torpedo or mine under a ship's bottom has exploded the magazine within."[6]

Alger's explanation was quickly taken up by opponents of the McKinley administration's military spending. Speaker of the House Thomas Reed saw a clear moral to the disaster: Battleships were inherently dangerous; therefore, the United States ought to stop building them. Assistant Secretary of the Navy Roosevelt, infuriated by Alger's public comments, accused him of taking the "Spanish side." Roosevelt had already concluded that the sinking of the *Maine* was "an act of dirty treachery" on the part of the Spanish, but a letter to the chief of the Bureau of Ordnance, Rear

Admiral Charles O'Neil, ten days after the disaster indicates that he knew the merits of Alger's argument but was determined to downplay them. "All the best men in the Department agree that, whether probable or not, it certainly is possible that the ship was blown up by a mine," he wrote. And he added, suggestively, that perhaps the exact cause of the explosion would never be determined.[7]

Similarly, American correspondents in Havana were well aware of the merits of the "accident theory." But they also knew that the city was teeming with Loyalist conspiracies, and the Loyalists had everything to gain from provoking a conflict between Spain and the United States. If Spain won, so much the better, and if the United States were the victor, the Loyalists would still prefer an American protectorate to the rule of the insurgents. To think that there was no connection between the hostility of the ultra-Loyalists and the loss of the *Maine* was almost too much to ask.

When the correspondents explained their suspicions to navy officers on the scene, they were assured that a technical investigation of the wreckage would produce some answers in short order. As Scovel explained in a story written on the day after the tragedy:

> The cause of the blowing up of the ship will not be known until divers go down and examine the wreck. If their investigation shows that the indentation in the hull is inward, the conclusion that the magazine was exploded by a bomb or torpedo placed beneath the vessel is inevitable.
>
> If the indentation is outward, it will be indicated that the first explosion was in the magazine. This will be determined within twenty-four hours.[8]

This was one of the more inaccurate predictions of all times. The cause of the *Maine* disaster would not be definitively set forth in twenty-four hours or twenty-four years; and even today there remain many unanswered questions about the sequence of events leading up to the most humiliating incident in the history of the U.S. Navy. It simply was not possible to determine the cause of an explosion from looking at the debris to see whether the force of the explosion was from the outside-in or the inside-out, and this amateurish misconception would wreak havoc with the navy's fact-finding efforts.

Unrealistic expectations of getting quick answers only compounded the frustration that Americans in Havana felt about the navy's response to the accident. On the morning of February 16, even while some portions of the wreck were still smoldering, the Havana harbor police established a cordon around what was left of the ship. A few hours later, a team of Spanish navy divers arrived and began exploring the harbor bottom in the vicinity. The divers were collecting evidence for Captain-General Blanco's official investigation, but they had not been authorized to remove the bodies of the victims, many of which were still trapped in the wreckage.

By late afternoon a colony of vultures had come to roost among the twisted steel plating of the *Maine*'s hull. Spectators on the docks watched in horror as the birds lazily swooped down from their perches to pick at the flesh of corpses pinned near the surface of the water.

On the second morning, more bodies, many of them hideously charred and bloated, began surfacing and were washed up against the seawall by the incoming tide.

The lighthouse tender *Fern*, whose senior officer Lieutenant Commander William S. Cowles was Teddy Roosevelt's brother-in-law, had arrived from Key West the previous afternoon. But the *Fern* did not have a team of divers on board. And because the rest of the North Atlantic Squadron was still on maneuvers in the region of the Dry Tortugas, additional help was not expected until the next day. In any case, when sailors from the *Fern* tried to approach the wreck they were turned back by the harbor police.

Since the keel of the battleship was resting on the harbor floor, Captain-General Blanco was pushing for a joint U.S.-Spanish investigation, with the bulk of the recovery work on the scene to be done by Spanish personnel. Fitzhugh Lee knew that the chances of Washington accepting such an arrangement were slight, but so far he had received no firm instructions. In the interim, Lee urged Captain Sigsbee to assert his control over the wreck.

But Captain Sigsbee was in a daze. He had been given a cabin aboard the passenger liner *City of Washington*, and he sat on deck hour after hour, gazing across the water at what remained of his ship. The explosion had torn open the superstructure, opening it up like a peeled banana. On one section of the wreckage that had formerly been a ceiling, he could make out two human forms outlined against the white paint—"mere dust," he noted in his journal.

Sigsbee, an unfailingly courteous man who in happier times had displayed flashes of an almost elfin sense of humor, was an object of sympathy to the press corps who defended him in print while recognizing privately that he was completely out of his depth. They and the rest of the American community in Havana had less patience with the sluggish response of the Navy Department. Uninjured survivors of the disaster, including officers who had been on shore leave at the time, had been evacuated to Key West on the Plant Line steamer *Olivette*, but the navy had sent no hospital ship or nurses, and no vessel to transport the bodies of the deceased.

The more severely injured sailors, some with third-degree burns, were spread among several Havana hospitals, where there were no English-speaking nurses to comfort them or take down messages to their families. In the absence of any official assistance, Frances Scovel and some of the other American wives volunteered to act as nurses and interpreters.

One task that could not be delayed was that of burying the bodies that had been pulled from the harbor after they washed up against the seawall. Nineteen corpses were lined up in the customs house, and on the morning of February 17, Captain Sigsbee accepted an offer from Blanco to inter the dead sailors in a military cemetery. The funeral was carried out that afternoon with full honors. Blanco himself, accompanied by the bishop of Havana, walked in the procession, following the nineteen hearses as they made their way from the governor's palace to the cemetery in the suburb of Colón. Father Chidwick, the Catholic chaplain of the *Maine*, conducted the service and Captain Sigsbee read from an Episcopal prayer book. Washington seemed unaware that there were no Protestant clergymen in Havana, and the failure of the navy to send a Protestant chaplain to officiate at the service or minister to the injured was another sore point with the American community.

By now all three major New York papers, the *Journal*, the *Herald*, and the *World*, had hired teams of divers. But all of them were prohibited by the harbor police from approaching the wreck. So, too, were the navy divers who finally arrived on the morning of February 18. On learning that the navy had been turned away, Sigsbee made up his mind to visit the remains of his ship, but he, too, was refused permission to pass through the cordon. The harbormaster suggested that Sigsbee apply to Captain-General Blanco for a pass, exactly what Fitzhugh Lee did not want, since to make such a request would imply that a captain of the United States Navy needed permission to visit his own vessel.

That afternoon, Lee and Sigsbee went to the governor's palace to lodge a protest. Blanco continued to insist that the wreck was his jurisdiction, since the hull was resting on the bottom of the harbor. Sigsbee and Lee argued with equal fervor that the *Maine* was still an American ship. Maritime law on this point was complicated but, as Lee anticipated, Blanco did not want war and was in no position to dictate conditions. By the end of the meeting, it had been agreed that each nation would conduct its own inquiry and the harbor police would no longer interfere with the U.S. Navy's efforts. Late that afternoon, an American ensign rowed out to the wreck and raised the Stars and Stripes.

Aside from their concern for the recovery of the dead, the American correspondents were frantic over the thought that the Spanish navy divers had been working unhindered for three days, with more than enough opportunity to remove telltale evidence of a mine. American correspondents had been hanging around the docks, keeping as close a watch as they could and, ironically, the one tidbit of interest they did pick up concerned a discovery that even the Spanish took to be evidence of a mine.

As George Eugene Bryson reported in a story smuggled out to Key West by the purser on the *Olivette*, the divers had found a hole eight inches in diameter, "the flanges of the wound bent inward," in the vicinity of the forward compartment of the berth deck. The excitable Bryson concluded that the mystery of the *Maine* was now solved. "The *Maine* was destroyed by a torpedo," he wrote, using the word, as was common at that time, to refer to any submarine explosive device. "The whole city knows it and is waiting almost with baited breath for what must follow."[9]

The *Journal*, hungry for a scoop, pounced on Bryson's conclusion. Brisbane, who twenty-four hours earlier had favored the accident theory, ran Bryson's story under the headline WAR! SURE! And beneath this: MAINE DESTROYED BY SPANISH . . . THIS PROVED ABSOLUTELY BY DISCOVERY OF THE TORPEDO HOLE!

Did Brisbane believe this? Probably not, since his opinion of Bryson remained as low as ever and he continued to send flattering messages to Scovel to woo him over to the *Journal*. In the meantime, Bryson's "proof" of Spanish complicity became the basis for the most hysterical newspaper campaign in America's history. The evening *Journal* took the lead, exceeding even the morning *Journal* in screaming for war. Brisbane disguised the lack of substance in Bryson's reports by printing his stories double spaced, under headlines so large that the composing room no longer had any brass type large enough to print them and staff artists had to be called on to draw the letters.

Despite tremendous pressure from their editors, most American correspondents were doing their best to stay calm and avoid a rush to judgment. Captain Sigsbee had asked the divers hired by the various newspapers to go to work with the navy team that was to begin recovering bodies on February 19, so at least the members of the press corps could report to their home offices that they were doing *something* to assist the navy's efforts. But that morning at ten A.M., when Scovel showed up at the docks with the divers, he discovered that Blanco had extracted a promise from Sigsbee that no representatives of the American press would be allowed to take part in the operation.

Frustrated by Sigsbee's tendency to say yes to the last person who managed to get his ear, Scovel fired off a testy note: "the *Maine* is still *your* ship." In another letter the next day he reminded the captain that the *World*'s divers "are the same men the Merritt Wrecking Co. used to raise the Ward Line steamer *Seneca*, and dive naked except for helmet, air pump [and hose]."[10]

Walter Scott Meriwether, now of the *Herald*, was equally annoyed that Sigsbee had lacked the courage to tell him outright about his promise to Blanco, instead muttering something evasive about "complications" that had arisen. And the *Journal*, as usual stressing the most lurid aspect of the situation, complained that the Spanish, by slowing down the progress of the rescue effort, were "protecting these foul birds," the vultures who were dining on the flesh of the American dead.

By February 20, more than a hundred bodies had been hauled from the water; many too decomposed to be identified. In the meantime, a second team of navy divers, arrived from Key West on the *Olivette* the previous afternoon, had begun searching the wreckage for clues to the nature of the explosion. Officers from the *Fern* were inspecting the wreckage that remained above the waterline, among them Ensign Wilfred Van Nest Powelson, a trained naval architect who had been asked to make detailed drawings of the damage for the use of navy investigators.

Scovel, deciding that the moment had come to test the harbormaster's ban on journalists, borrowed a dinghy, and after paying a call on the Spanish cruiser *Alfonso XII* that was docked nearby to announce his intentions to the captain, he began rowing himself toward the wreck. About three hundred feet away he was stopped by a Spanish patrol boat. "I intend to exercise my right as an American citizen to get as close to a piece of American soil as desired," Scovel informed the officer on board.[11] Whether or not such a right actually existed, the officer declined to contest the point, and Scovel was allowed to cross the cordon and approach to within five yards of the hull.

Scovel's gesture of defiance was applauded by the navy officers working around the wreck, who were still irate over the harbor police's treatment of Sigsbee. A day or so later, the "newspaper divers" were officially hired by the navy as contract employees of the Merritt Wrecking Company to perform salvage work, and Ensign Powelson promptly asked the *World* correspondent to serve as interpreter. Although the navy's investigation was supposedly confidential, as the result of his cooperation with Powelson, Scovel was able to report, accurately as it turned out, the consensus of "naval experts" on the scene that "nothing could have destroyed the *Maine* so peculiarly but a submerged mine of large size."[12]

* * *

On the home front, war hysteria was on the rise. The Spanish battleship *Vizcaya* had arrived in New York on February 18 to carry out its planned reciprocal visit, and the *Journal* celebrated the event by introducing its readers to a new card game, "The Game of War With Spain," the object of which was to sink the *Vizcaya*. The *World,* though more restrained than the *Journal* in its daily news coverage, published a Sunday feature solemnly reminding New Yorkers that the *Vizcaya,* while moored off the Battery, was capable of lobbing shells as far away as the Harlem River and the "suburbs of Brooklyn." A map was provided so that readers could determine whether or not they were within range of the Spanish guns.

In Havana, the Spanish investigation, conducted under the authority of Admiral Manterola, was fast moving toward the conclusion that the explosion was the result of an on-board accident. It was generally accepted in Washington that only a similar finding by the U.S. Navy's Court of Inquiry could avert war. Unfortunately, it was difficult to see how the navy court could exonerate the Spanish without reaching the conclusion that its own personnel or procedures were at fault. To admit that it had lost a battleship through negligence in the course of the most sensitive mission the navy had been assigned in decades would be humiliating to say the least.

After dithering for days about the composition of the court, Secretary of the Navy Long decreed that the panel would begin its deliberations on Monday, February 21, meeting in Havana harbor on board the U.S. lighthouse tender *Mangrove.* In addition to the judge advocate, who was a former executive officer of the *Maine,* the court would consist of three experienced officers: Captain French Ensor Chadwick, an expert in naval intelligence as well as a former chief of the Bureau of Equipment; Lieutenant Commander William Potter, a graduate engineer; and Captain William T. Sampson, who was chosen directly by Secretary Long in place of one of Admiral Sicard's original nominees. Sampson was a former Bureau of Ordnance chief but, significantly, not connected with the current bureau staff, which was stubbornly adhering to the accident theory.

All three officers were honest men, but as everyone seemed

to overlook at the time, their investigation was conducted under a flawed mandate. The court was not asked to determine what had happened to the _Maine,_ only to decide the narrower question of whether the ship had been lost through negligence on the part of its officers or crew. It approached its task less in the spirit of a fact-finding panel than as a judicial body, determined to regard the personnel of the _Maine_ as innocent until proven otherwise.

The first witness to appear before the court on Monday morning was Captain Sigsbee. To put it mildly, he was not an impressive witness. There were questions he could not answer and numerous details he could not "personally recall." The most telling comment on Sigsbee's performance is that made by another navy man, Admiral Hyman Rickover, who reexamined the Court of Inquiry transcripts in connection with his 1976 study of the _Maine_ disaster. "From [Sigsbee's] testimony," observed Rickover, "emerges a portrait of an individual who was unfamiliar with his ship.... Whatever the reasons, he appears to have been isolated from the day-to-day routine."[13]

Though vague about so much, Sigsbee volunteered the information that on the day before the explosion he had been in the port-wing passage adjacent to coal bunker 16 and made an informal test for excessive heat by resting his hand on the quarter-inch steel plating. This testimony created a dilemma for the court. It could no longer declare the disaster to be the result of a coal-fire accident without implying that Captain Sigsbee had perjured himself.

In the meantime, the court's efforts to decide whether the damage was consistent with an internal or external explosion was not going well. Damage to the forward section of the _Maine_ was so extensive that the navy divers, hampered by poor visibility, were having trouble getting their bearings underwater, much less making any close observations. The divers had no training in damage assessment and little knowledge of ship construction so that it was difficult for them to interpret what they saw.

The task of making sense of the divers' reports fell to Ensign Powelson, and on Saturday, at the end of the divers' first week of work, he finally had something interesting to report. A portion of the _Maine_'s keel about fifty-nine feet from the bow had been thrust upward into an inverted V shape.

Wilfred Van Nest Powelson was a young man whose energy and knowledgeability had made him influential beyond his rank. He had studied naval architecture in Glasgow before entering Annapolis, and when the _Maine_ was commissioned in 1895, he had taken a special interest in the new battleship's design on the hunch that he might someday be assigned to serve on it. As his superiors soon realized, Powelson was more familiar than many of the ship's own officers with the details of the _Maine_'s construction. Powelson was not an expert in damage assessment or ordnance, and in his testimony he correctly avoided expressing any opinions as to the cause of the damage. But when pressed by Captain Sampson for an opinion, he volunteered the obvious conclusion: "I think that the explosion occurred on the port side somewhere about frame 18 . . . and that this was under the ship." [14]

Despite a supposedly impenetrable veil of secrecy, correspondents in Havana knew about the discovery of the imploded bottom plating and the recovery of unexploded six-inch shells as well as intact copper ammunition cases from the ten-inch magazines—all interpreted by the divers as an indication that the source of the explosion was outside the _Maine_'s hull. As A. Maurice Low of the London _Chronicle_ wrote to Secretary of the Navy Long, even the most skeptical members of the press corps were coming around to the belief that the _Maine_ had been destroyed by a mine.

Besides what they were able to glean from sources close to the official investigation, the press could not help but be influenced by rumors and gossip. Basically, the rumors divided into two scenarios: Either the _Maine_ had been blown up by a fixed mine, planted at buoy four months earlier and detonated by remote control, or else the destruction of the ship was the work of a crude floating mine, constructed and planted at the last minute by ultra-Loyalist conspirators.

Captain Sigsbee was by now utterly convinced that buoy four, reportedly the "least used buoy in the harbor," where the _Maine_ was docked had been mined long in advance. In apparent support of this hypothesis, a former crew member of the _City of Washington_ had written Scovel claiming to have witnessed French and Spanish divers laying mines in the harbor the previous summer. There was nothing inherently implausible about this—many nations did take the precaution of planting their harbors with mines. But it was strange that such activity would not have been known to the American Consulate, which was receiving reliable information from Cuban spies in the governor's palace, including one who worked in the office of the Spanish censor.

Possibly for that very reason, Fitzhugh Lee favored the crude mine theory. Holding forth every midday at his reserved table at the Inglaterra café, Lee speculated that a device as crude as a barrel stuffed with guncotton might have done the job.

This hypothesis was bolstered by an anonymous letter to Lee shortly after the explosion, outlining a conspiracy allegedly instigated by "some merchants in Murallo Street" who had offered six thousand dollars to an experienced diver improbably nicknamed Pepe Taco (later, somewhat more plausibly identified as Pepe Barquín). This diver, according to the letter writer, had hired two accomplices, men "with the worst antecedents as harbor thieves," to help him plant a mine in the vicinity of the *Maine.*

"But they did not come out of the adventure well," the letter continued, "having been attacked as they were retiring." The alleged attackers were dissident Spanish officers who approved of the plot's aims but were determined to see that the saboteurs would not go free to tell the tale. Pepe Taco, or rather Barquín, had escaped and was in hiding, in fear of his life. The second accomplice, wounded in the attack, was being held in detention where "he is being given morphine constantly to see if he will die or give evidence." [15]

The letter was studded with suggestive details, and if it was a hoax it was a very clever one. Lee took it seriously enough to ask Henry Drain, a member of his staff, to appear before the navy court on February 26 and read the letter into evidence. Drain told the navy panel that the letter, signed "An Admirer," had been passed on to the Consulate by a source he considered completely reliable, an American citizen named Charles Carbonell. This of course was Carlos Carbonell, the Junta agent who had assisted in arranging the escape of Evangelina Cosio y Cisneros.

"How do you suppose he knows so much about this?" the judge advocate asked.

Drain wasn't sure. He explained that since Consul-General Lee lacked a budget for secret service work, he had attempted to

conduct his own investigation of the letter's claims and had succeeded in discovering only that Pepe Barquín had since died.
Unvetted and unsupported by evidence, the letter was included
in the official investigation transcript.

At the end of its first week of hearings, the court temporarily
adjourned to Key West to take statements from the survivors
there, and by March 17, after hearing just eighteen days of testimony, it was ready to begin composing its final report. Four days
later, its work was done. The court's brief report concluded that
the *Maine* had been destroyed by a submarine mine, but it offered
no explanations, technical or circumstantial, of how this might
have been accomplished. Moreover, the court conceded that it
had been "unable to obtain evidence fixing the responsibility...
upon any person or persons." [16]

The court's findings sufficed to bring U.S.-Spanish relations
to the breaking point, and in the long run they raised more questions than they resolved. Ironically, through an interesting process
of evolution, American writers unfamiliar with Cuban politics have
tended to pin the blame for the *Maine* disaster not on disaffected
Loyalists who, as everyone at the time knew, had both motive and
opportunity, but on the Separatists. Even the Pulitzer Prize–winning biographer W. A. Swanberg got it wrong, speculating that "it
was most reasonable to suspect those who stood the most to gain
from the crime—the Cuban rebels." [17]

Another vein of speculation, seldom argued in print but believed by many in both Cuba and the United States, is that William
Randolph Hearst was somehow the instigator of a plot to blow up
the *Maine*. Like most persistent conspiracy theories, this one is
bolstered by a kind of loopy plausibility. After all, it was on February 12, just three days before the disaster, that the *Journal*
declared its private war on Spain in response to the seizure of the
Buccaneer, in the process expressing considerable resentment
against the *Maine* for not interfering to defend the rights of a U.S.
flag vessel. Then, too, there were the prevalent rumors that the
Journal was responsible for the abortive bombing of the Casa
Nueva.

Another reason for the persistence of belief in a Hearst connection is that over the years some *Journal* correspondents
seemed to take a perverse pleasure in encouraging it. This was

especially true of James Creelman: "The time has not yet come when all the machinery employed by the American press on behalf of Cuba can be laid bare to the American public. Great fortunes were spent in the effort to arouse the country to a realization of the real situation. Things which cannot be referred to even now were attempted."[18]

Another *Journal* veteran, Willis Abbot, provides a sample of the sort of leading anecdotes Creelman was given to circulating among acquaintances. As Abbot tells it, back when Creelman was still with the *Herald*, he had been friendly with Paul Boynton, an amateur diving enthusiast and the owner of a seafood bistro known as The Ship, located in Manhattan's West Thirties. Creelman recalled that he was having dinner at The Ship one evening when there happened to be a British man-of-war in New York Harbor, whose presence offended Boynton's Irish sensibilities. Boynton began boasting about how easy it would be for a trained diver to get near enough to attach a mine to the ship's hull. Creelman bet it couldn't be done, and the argument ended with Boynton promising to settle the question that very night.

Using a weighted keg to represent a mine, the two men borrowed a boat and rowed as close as they dared to the mooring of the British ship. Boynton then entered the water and began towing the keg toward the hull. He was within a hundred yards of his destination when a spotlight raked the water and an excited sentry sounded an alarm. Both he and Creelman ended up being interrogated by the British navy, which failed to see any humor in the situation.

According to Abbot, Creelman insisted that he told this story only to illustrate his conviction that it would have been *impossible* for conspirators to plant a mine in the vicinity of the *Maine* without being detected. But as Creelman no doubt realized, the story was more likely to be interpreted as a hint that Creelman knew a lot more about mine-laying and sabotage then he cared to admit.[19]

Similarly, George Clarke Musgrave, who had been accused by the Spanish authorities of having something to do with the attempted dynamitings in the Casa Nueva, hinted that Karl Decker had been in Cuba shortly before the explosion organizing a *Journal* invasion of the French prison camp on Devil's Island in

French Guiana, the object of which was to liberate Captain Drey-fus.[20] While no evidence confirming this has ever been found, the Dreyfus case was indeed very close to the heart of the French-educated Arthur Brisbane, who had written a series of evening *Journal* editorials on the case, strongly suggesting that Americans ought to take matters into their own hands.

When the *Maine* exploded, the fun rather went out of such hijinks. Assuming that there was some truth to the persistent rumors that the *Buccaneer* was carrying dynamite in Caribbean waters, and probably they were true, some nervous *Journal* staffers may even have wondered whether the explosives had fallen into the wrong hands and been used to kill American sailors. At any rate, as long as the official explanation for the tragedy was a mine of unknown origins, it would have been impolitic in the extreme to admit publicly any *Journal* involvement in munitions smuggling.

The best argument against the existence of any Hearst connection is that it is impossible to imagine that other correspondents in Havana would not have heard of it. Contrary to the image of fierce competition fostered by their papers' home offices, American journalists in Havana, along with consular officials, interpreters, Junta agents, and certain prominent Cuban-Americans, formed a close-knit community. The man who worked for the *Journal* today might find himself tomorrow on the staff of the *Herald*, the *Sun*, or the *Chicago Tribune*. Indeed, a few correspondents were surreptitiously writing for more than one paper at a time. Under the circumstances, journalists treated the race for scoops as a sporting proposition governed by gentlemen's rules. It is inconceivable that rumors of *Journal* involvement in such a plot would not have reached the ears of representatives of other papers, and equally inconceivable that they would have kept quiet about them.

Moreover, as numerous technical experts then and since have pointed out, blowing up a battleship with a single mine is no easy task. The harbor bottom at buoy four was only fourteen feet beneath the *Maine*'s keel; a fixed mine would have had to have had a very large charge, one hundred pounds of dynamite or more, to explode the ship's magazines, and even then it would have to be virtually resting on the harbor floor in order to produce the upward-thrusting of the keel observed by investigators. The possibility that a homemade mine could have caused such extensive damage was even more remote. On the other hand, the inverted V shape of the wreckage has since been shown to be consistent with damage from an internal-combustion fire.

Considering the various conspiracy theories that have sprung up regarding the loss of the *Maine,* it is ironic that little attention has been paid to a far more plausible possibility, that Theodore Roosevelt was responsible for masterminding a cover-up. Roosevelt had many admirable qualities, but a dispassionate concern for truth was not among them. He considered war with Spain not only inevitable, but desirable, and he dreaded a Court of Inquiry verdict that might have jeopardized the navy's commitment to building more coal-fired ships. Admiral Rickover mentions that some members of the family of ordnance expert Philip Alger were convinced that Alger had prepared a confidential report on the *Maine* tragedy, a report suppressed on Roosevelt's orders. Whether or not such a report ever existed, it was hardly accidental that no representative of the bureau was appointed to serve on the Court of Inquiry and none was called to testify. The narrow wording of the court's mandate, the exclusion from the court and from testimony of representatives of the Bureau of Ordnance, the pressure for a hasty decision, and even the prominent role played by the lighthouse tender *Fern* and its junior officer Powelson—all these suggest a managed verdict.

No doubt the true opinion of the court's members is reflected in their subsequent actions. Captain Sampson, when he became admiral of North Atlantic Squadron during the war with Spain, made sure that Sigsbee was relegated to the command of the *St. Paul,* a civilian liner converted for use as a scout ship. Nor, surely, was it a coincidence that another court member, Captain Chadwick, ordered extra bulkheads installed between the coal bunkers and the magazines of his own ship, the *New York,* a change incorporated in all navy ships commissioned after 1899.[21]

While the Havana press corps was blinded by its admiration for the new navy, the press back in the States did raise questions about the hasty conclusion of the court. On March 25, for example, the Brooklyn *Eagle* published a story, attributed to its Washington correspondent, noting that a certain Brooklynite, "a prominent figure here and at home who has served the city faithfully and well," was extremely dissatisfied with the navy panel's conclusions and had telephoned the president's private secretary, J. Addison Porter, to lodge a protest.

According to the _Eagle_, the unnamed Brooklynite was distressed that the report failed to mention a bunker fire that had occurred aboard the _Maine_ in August 1897, on an evening when he happened to be dining on board the ship as a guest of Captain Sigsbee. That party was interrupted by the watch officer, who entered the captain's quarters and whispered an urgent message to the executive officer and then to Sigsbee himelf. Immediately, one of them exclaimed, "My God!" and they both rushed out of the room. Minutes later, Sigsbee returned and apologetically told the guests that they would have to be sent ashore because there was a fire burning in one of the coal bunkers. The source particularly remembered Sigsbee saying, as he ushered his guests toward the gangway, "Gentlemen, you have had a narrow escape tonight."[22]

Of course, an anecdote told by an anonymous source hardly counts as evidence, but the story demonstrates that the _Eagle_ was well aware of the kind of questions the navy had failed to pursue. But the protest of the Brooklyn politician was not mentioned again in the pages of the _Eagle_. America was drifting closer to war with Spain, and further criticism of the navy during an hour of national crisis would have seemed disloyal.

War Fever

WHILE the Naval Court of Inquiry was still conducting hearings aboard the *Mangrove,* Havana had already begun to prepare for war. The long-silent guns of the harbor batteries were being readied for action and the army had scheduled its first gunnery practice in years. Anti-American feeling was running high. Correspondents were automatically suspected of being Yankee spies, and *Harper's Weekly* photographer J. C. Hemment narrowly escaped being shot at when he was spotted aiming his camera in the direction of Morro Castle, Havana's most prominent landmark.

In some cases, the suspicion was justified. One day Harry Scovel and Ensign Powelson left the city before dawn to hide in a secluded spot in the hills where they were able to peer down at the Santa Clara battery and watch the Spanish gunners firing their cannon at targets being trolled about two miles offshore. The proportion of hits, Scovel noted, "was not very satisfactory," and he and Powelson were especially encouraged to see that the Span-

ish gunners seemed to be having serious problems with the formidable Krupp guns, whose shells invariably dropped harmlessly
into the water about fifty yards short of their target. Once they
had written up their observations, Powelson and Scovel weren't
sure what to do with them. Captain Sampson was the senior American officer in Havana, but he had given orders that neither members of the press nor witnesses called by the court were to
attempt to speak with him. They were still debating when Powelson received a summons to reappear before the court to clear up
certain questions about the navy divers' findings. Powelson gave
his testimony and then, after he had been officially dismissed, he
approached the table where members of the court were sitting,
placed his report in front of Sampson, and left the room without
saying a word.

Scovel had expanded the *World*'s staff by hiring two additional correspondents, Henry M. Carey and, much to the surprise
of knowledgeable observers in Havana, George Rea. Rea's charge
that Scovel had been duped by the insurgents, published the previous fall in *Facts and Fakes About Cuba*, had received good
coverage in Cuba's Loyalist press and it was widely assumed that
the two men were enemies. In fact, they had never let their differences of opinion interfere with their friendship, and in any case
the wheel of politics had taken one of its dizzying turns, bringing
the proinsurgent Scovel and the ultraconservative Rea into essential agreement. Both favored limited intevention in Cuba but opposed annexation—Scovel and the *World* on the grounds that
U.S. foreign policy should encourage self-determination throughout Latin America, and Rea because he saw no need for the United
States to take on responsibility for Cuba's myriad social and economic problems when there were easier ways for American sugar
interests and other investors to obtain all the concessions they
needed. At any rate, Scovel was already looking ahead to the
possibility of using the *World*'s news gathering activities as a
cover for a military spy ring, an adventure Rea would not have
missed for anything.

Soon after he was hired, Rea departed for Puerto Rico. Ostensibly he was to do a series of articles for the *World*, but according
to a biographical entry some years later in *Who's Who*, the purpose was to gather information that might be useful to the U.S.

government. Rea filed one dispatch from San Juan, then dropped out of sight until April 12, when the *World* received what it aptly described as an "eloquent" cable announcing his safe arrival in St. Thomas and summarizing his experience in twenty-four words: "Arrived Puertorico hot impossible cable truth since your fortification message police surveillance eluded vigilance midnight bicycle coach horse schooner smuggler's boat here hope satisfactory."[1] Interpreting this message for the benefit of its readers, the *World* explained that it was a cable from the Dome to Rea in San Juan, asking for a description of military fortifications, which had blown his cover, forcing Rea to escape to St. Thomas.

In addition to collecting military intelligence, the hyperactive Scovel was arranging not just the *World*'s coverage of the developing crisis but the *Journal*'s as well. On behalf of Artie Brisbane he negotiated a *Journal* contract for the New York *Sun* correspondent Honoré Lainé, a great favorite of Frances Scovel, who referred to him as "that dear, mournful man."

Dignified and gracious, with impeccable manners, Lainé was a magnet for bad luck. Early in the rebellion, after his plantation was burned by the insurgents, he had been held hostage in the wreckage of his home for eight days. Hired by the *World*, he had been captured by the Spanish and given up for dead. In actuality, Lainé had spent thirteen months being shuttled from one provincial jail to another, and by the time he was released in the spring of 1897, he had become bitterly anti-Spanish and pro-republican. Fleeing to the United States, he had settled in Philadelphia, where he became a publicist for the Junta and dabbled in various unsuccessful business deals, hoping to recoup his lost fortune.

Lainé had been a Spanish prisoner far longer than Scovel and had suffered more than almost anyone, but although he had written several articles about his experiences and was working on a book, no American publisher was interested. Scovel could do nothing to help on that score, but in a cable to Brisbane he explained that Lainé, while continuing to write for the *Sun*, would be willing to send stories to the *Journal* as well.

Since Lainé also happened to be a Junta agent involved in smuggling correspondence from Havana to the United States, this was a good bargain for the *Journal*. Within a matter of days Lainé forwarded to Brisbane a letter allegedly written by General Weyler to a friend in Havana, Don Francisco de Santis Guzmán, hinting that Havana harbor had been secretly mined and predicting darkly that some dramatic event was forthcoming that would restore him to power.

Lainé was identified as the source of the letter almost immediately. He was arrested on March 4, but this time the *Journal* and the U.S. Consulate obtained his release and a week later he was in Washington, testifying before the Senate Foreign Relations Committee. Although the Guzmán letter was widely denounced as a fraud, it was taken seriously by congressmen eager for some context that would justify the conclusions of the naval court's finding.

Dizzy with success, the *Journal* escalated its rhetoric, impugning the motives of anyone whose hispanophobia failed to measure up to the paper's own high standards. When Mark Hanna dared to suggest that war might yet be averted, the paper accused him of considering the murder of American sailors and the starvation of innocent children "of less importance than the fall of two points in a price of stock."[2]

The *Journal* was raising a fund for a memorial to the *Maine* dead, and Hearst had dispatched his latest yacht, the *Anita*, to Cuban waters, carrying a delegation of U.S. congressmen on a fact-finding junket. Among the passengers was Mrs. John W. Thurston, wife of a Nebraska senator, whose regular letters to the *Journal* included heartrending descriptions of starvation among the *reconcentrados:* "Oh! Mothers of the Northland... think of the black despair that fills each Cuban mother's heart as she felt her life-blood ebb away, and knew that she had left her little ones to perish from the pain of starvation...," etc.[3] But it was Mrs. Thurston's heart that gave way first. She collapsed and died from a coronary while the *Anita* was moored in Matanzas harbor, and the *Journal* announced that she was yet another victim of Weyler's cruelty, killed by the strain of witnessing his horrible handiwork.

Although the *World* never came close to matching the *Journal*, either in typographical shrillness or editorial expressions of jingoist sentiment, the mood of hysteria had infected the Dome. Ironically, in November 1897, Hearst had actually offered to join the *World* in a price-fixing agreement, with both papers raising their newsstand price to two cents, but Pulitzer had rejected the offer in the mistaken belief that the *Journal* was on the point of bankruptcy. Now the time for compromise had passed and the *World* was in the impossible position of trying to outshout the *Journal* without quite matching its rival's jingoistic excesses.

For Ernest Chamberlin, who had not responded to William Merrill's attempts at amateur therapy, the strain was too much. One day in mid-March, after working nearly round-the-clock, Chamberlin burst out of his office shouting, "War is declared! War is declared!" Pandemonium erupted. Then someone thought to check the AP wire and learned that the declaration of war existed only in Chamberlin's troubled mind. Led out of the office by two colleagues who suggested that he take a few days of bed rest at home, Chamberlin never did return to work. By the end of the summer he was dead.

Some years later, Arthur Brisbane would defend the techniques he employed during this period, replying to a *Collier's* interviewer who asked him to define yellow journalism by saying: "Whatever is new, especially if it succeeds, disturbs old fashioned people, above all, if it compels them to pay their employees more, from top to bottom. That's what yellow journalism does when it's successful."[4]

Cynical as he was, Brisbane had a point. The anti-intervention press during this period seemed less interested in putting forth its own views of the crisis than in attacking the "yellow" competition. The mandarin critic E. L. Godkin, self-appointed voice of the public interest, thundered, "Every one who knows anything about 'yellow journals' knows that everything they do and say is intended to promote sales. No one—absolutely no one—supposes a yellow journal cares five cents about the Cubans, the *Maine* victims, or anyone else."[5]

Godkin's claim to moral superiority was undercut by the fact that he had never seen the devastation of Cuba as anything worth getting excited about, and he was simply wrong in saying that the personnel behind the yellow journals didn't care about the Cubans or the *Maine* victims and in implying that Hearst and Pulitzer were foisting war on a reluctant public. The *World*, during an informal survey of American women in ten cities across the country, discovered—to its amazement—that nine out of ten favored war with Spain. Congress had passed a mobilization act on March 9, without even waiting for the results of the naval court's investigation. Volunteers were thronging army recruitment stations. Even the Brooklyn *Eagle* got caught up in the excitement, announcing that it had hired teams of operators who were standing by to call every telephone subscriber in Brooklyn and on Long Island—all seventy-five hundred of them—the moment war was officially declared. The *Wall Street Journal* ruefully admitted that "the street" had become the last bastion of antiwar sentiment, the kiss of death in any public policy debate.

In Madrid, the American minister Stewart Woodford had informed the Spanish foreign minister that the United States would settle for nothing less than "an immediate honorable peace" in Cuba. The Sagasta government was ready to negotiate a cease-fire—"They know Cuba is lost," Woodford cabled Assistant Secretary of State William R. Day on March 29[6]—but it was not quite ready to declare its unilateral withdrawal, and the Cuban Junta, despite "intense pressure" from the McKinley administration, refused to accept anything less.

The view of the Junta—a view held by Cubans to this day—was that the United States had been playing a double game all along. For three years the United States had remained neutral, all the while crying crocodile tears about the poor, suffering Cubans, only to step in and rob them of their independence at the very moment when it was finally within their grasp. There was a degree of truth to this accusation. Although the situation had become intolerable, the prospect of Spain's withdrawal, leading to continued domestic turmoil and, for all anyone knew, the opportunity for Germany to meddle in Cuba's politics as it had in Haiti's, was equally appalling. Democracy for Cuba had never been, per se, a goal of U.S. policy; stability in the Caribbean was.

For once, "large policy" conservatives, who wanted to pick up the pieces of the crumbling Spanish empire, and Congressional liberals, concerned about the suffering of the *reconcentrados*, were in agreement. Had it not been for the *Maine* disaster, or rather the navy's interpretation of it, the United States would no doubt have continued to muddle through. But the explosion in

Havana harbor had plunged the nation into a psychological crisis
that could be resolved only by definitive action.

On April 9, Easter Saturday, McKinley ordered the last remaining Americans—mostly journalists and consular officials—to
leave Havana for Key West. The following Monday morning, the
president's war message was delivered to the capitol.

When the report was read to a joint session of Congress it
was found to be unexpectedly mild in tone, and like most concili-
atory documents, it contained something to offend everyone. Although the logic of the president's message made war inevitable,
McKinley stopped short of actually requesting a declaration of
hostilities. Congressmen who knew they were going to end up
voting for war in any case, were angered because McKinley, by
citing Spain's willingness to accept an armistice, had failed to give
them a justification that they could take home to their constitu-
ents. Pro-intervention congressmen, meanwhile, were furious that
the report did not call for recognition of the Republic of Cuba.

The report was a perfect example of the sort of fence-strad-
dling that had caused Speaker of the House Thomas Reed to say
of the president that he "had all the backbone of a chocolate
eclair." But though his actions gave the appearance of weakness,
McKinley had actually managed the situation rather neatly: The
pro-Cuban faction was stuck with voting into existence a war
whose strategy would be determined by Roosevelt and the "large
policy" Republicans. If everything turned out well, McKinley could
take the credit; if not, he could always blame both the Democrats
and Roosevelt Republicans for dragging him kicking into a conflict
he had never wanted.

Longtime Cuba supporters like Congressman Hugh A. Dins-
more of Arkansas were not about to give up on the recognition
issue without a fight. He pleaded: "We talk about liberty. Then let
us give the Cubans liberty. We talk about freedom. Let us give
them the right to establish a government which they think will be
a free government, and which does not reserve to us, the Government of the United States, the right to say, after it is established,
'Ah this is not a "stable government." ' "[7]

Nevertheless, on April 19, after a week of acrimonious debate,
the House and Senate finally passed a joint war resolution, quali-

fied only by the Teller Resolution, by which the United States disavowed any intention of exercising sovereignty over Cuba once the island had been successfully pacified.

In Madrid, at ten thirty-five A.M. on April 21, Ambassador Woodford was asked by the Spanish foreign minister to surrender his passport.

That same day, in New York, the stock market fell one percent, a drop considered dramatic enough to rate a front-page headline in the Brooklyn *Eagle*.

At the Key West Naval Station, Admiral Sicard, the aging commander of the North Atlantic Squadron, had been informed by Secretary Long that the navy would accept his resignation on the grounds of "poor health." His replacement was William Sampson, a mere captain who, cynics charged, was being rewarded for steering the Court of Inquiry to the "right" conclusion, one that exonerated the service. The bluejackets were already hard at work painting the navy warships a dull black, the traditional wartime color, and Sampson's first order was to start all over again, repainting the hulls lead gray, a shade more difficult to detect at a distance, especially at twilight. The order was controversial among old-timers, who considered the use of camouflage colors undignified and even unsporting, but it won wholehearted approval of the younger officers, who recognized the change as a symbol that a new era in the navy's history had begun.

In spite of the optimism of the men and younger officers, there was a serious question of whether the navy was prepared to fight a major war. As French Ensor Chadwick, captain of the *New York* and the author of a definitive military history of the war, later observed, the United States in 1898 was "not even a second rate naval power."[8] The army was even less prepared. Limited by law to twenty-five thousand men, it had not seen action against a foreign power since the Mexican-American War a half-century earlier.

By contrast, the press was the essence of readiness. Correspondents had begun arriving in Key West as early as the second week of May and representatives of the major papers and news syndicates had been actively lining up transportation and selling berths to journalists whose papers were too small to have their own boats. The *Journal* already had two yachts, the *Buccaneer* and the *Anita*, although only the latter was in Key West at the moment, and would eventually have eight boats in the war zone. The *Herald* had chartered the *Sommers N. Smith*, a handsome steam yacht that Richard Harding Davis pronounced "as big as [Commodore] Benedict's."[9] The *World*, typically, refused to hire a yacht, but Henry Carey had managed to line up two tugboats, the *Triton* and the *Confidence* (later replaced by the *Three Friends*), whose crews were experienced filibusters.

Frances Scovel, who arrived from Havana in late March, found the Key West Hotel already so crowded that correspondents were paying five dollars a night for the privilege of sleeping on cots in the hallway. Daytime temperatures in town were hovering around 100 degrees, and the influx of visitors had brought about a water shortage, so that street vendors were getting up to fifty cents a gallon for fresh water, and those who could afford it were using Apollinaris mineral water for everything from mixing drinks to brushing their teeth. There was nothing to read and less to do; magazines and papers arriving at the local newsstand were snapped up within minutes. The food served in the hotel dining room was meager and poorly prepared.

But no one was complaining. The air was electric with excitement. "The correspondents," wrote Frances, "were kicking up their heels," eager for the war to begin.[10]

On Secret Service

****

At Havana's Gate

AS CAPTAIN (soon to be Rear Admiral) Sampson awaited orders to establish a blockade of Havana, he was faced with the problems of conducting a modern naval operation with communications and intelligence systems that were antiquated at best. He had no charts of the Cuban coastline, only the vaguest information about shore fortifications and troop deployments, and no means of contacting the insurgents, even though the American plan of action called for resupplying the Cubans in exchange for their cooperation.

In 1898, the only civilian agency involved with espionage and intelligence gathering was the Secret Service, a branch of the Treasury Department, whose chief responsibility in peacetime had been tracking counterfeiters. McKinley's first military appropriations bill had included an allocation of five thousand dollars for the service, later augmented by fifty thousand dollars, a sum considered "sufficient to maintain the force for several months."[1] By early April, agency chief John Wilkie and his tiny staff were busily processing unsolicited applications for the position of secret agent, at a maximum salary of four dollars per diem plus an additional three dollars in expense money. "Many of the writers confessed to an absolute ignorance of detective work," wrote Wilkie, "and apparently overlooked the fact that we were dealing with a foe whose language was not our own.... Among the hundreds and hundreds of letters, there were many whose authors were even at sea as to the general qualifications necessary for the work. One man advanced the statement that he had been married four times—possibly to emphasize the fact that his courage was beyond question. Another pointed out that, being the fortunate possessor of 'Spanish whiskers,' he could work among the enemy with absolute safety."

Even after the staffing was completed the Secret Service was still, in Wilkie's words, "smaller than the local staff of a large metropolitan newspaper."[2] Throughout the war it would devote most of its resources to breaking a spy ring operating out of the Windsor Hotel in Montreal under the direction of the former Spanish minister to the United States, Luis Polo de Bernabé.

On the military side, the job of collecting information about Spanish ship movements had devolved on the Office of Naval Intelligence (ONI). Founded in 1882, the ONI had never done fieldwork; it merely collected statistics on the status of the world's navies. After the loss of the *Maine*, however, two enthusiastic young ensigns, William S. Sims in Paris and John C. Colwell in London, began recruiting agents in Spain, the Canary Islands, and Port Said. Most of these agents were foreign nationals who were paid one thousand to two thousand dollars a month for their information. They apparently earned their salaries—one was reported "disappeared" in Spain, another "wounded" at Cádiz.

In the meantime, no one was concentrating on intelligence gathering in Cuba. Captains Sampson and Chadwick had been impressed by the unsolicited report compiled by Ensign Powelson and Scovel, and on April 15 when the officers of the North Atlantic Squadron came ashore to attend a party in their honor sponsored by the Key West press corps, they made it a point to meet Scovel and ask him whether he knew any American who might be willing to risk infiltrating Havana.

Scovel knew just the man. He was Charles Thrall, a Yale graduate who had been living in Cuba since 1891, where he was manager of the American-owned Havana Electric Company. Before evacuating to Florida, Thrall had spent several weeks loitering in the vicinity of the Havana forts, bribing suspicious sentries with cigarettes in order to get close enough to have a look at the gun emplacements. He believed he had discovered a weakness in the harbor defenses: The fixed guns in the batteries on the western side of the harbor entrance all pointed north. By staying close in to shore, ships approaching from the west might well be able to sneak inside the guns' range and bombard the forts with impunity.

Sampson listened eagerly to Thrall's information, which confirmed his own hunch that a naval assault on Havana from the west would throw the city into a panic and bring a quick end to the war with minimal loss of life on either side. Unfortunately, Thrall was unable to answer many of Sampson's technical questions, but he readily agreed to try to reenter Havana to take another look at the forts.

Thrall was confident of his ability to slip in and out of Havana undetected, unrealistically so, considering that as a prosperous American bachelor who made no secret of his ardent *independentista* sympathies, he was well known in the capital. And even if Thrall were not actually recognized, there was the language problem to contend with. Francis Nichols, who had recently joined the *World* staff in Key West, praised Thrall for being so fluent in Spanish that "he knows he speaks it with a foreign accent." Small comfort, one would think, for a man whose life might depend on being able to pass as a native.

Thrall reentered Havana as a stowaway on the bark *Matanzas*, one of the last cargo ships to land in Cuba before the U.S. blockade went into effect. He had memorized his instructions, but for unknown reasons it became necessary within a matter of hours for the navy to change its plans for the mission, and Scovel was asked to find a second volunteer to carry new instructions to Thrall. This time, Scovel came aboard the admiral's flagship with George Francisco Hyatt, the nineteen-year-old son of the American-born mayor of Guanabacoa.

Unlike Thrall, Hyatt was a nervous spy, and Scovel, who knew the boy's father, was soon suffering pangs of conscience for having recruited him. Hyatt had studied German in school, and to provide him with a cover story in case he was captured, Scovel fabricated a press credential identifying him as one George Heilberg, supposedly a German correspondent on assignment for the *World.* Further, to minimize the risk of Hyatt being picked up by a military patrol, Scovel was determined to put him ashore as close to the center of Havana as possible. The site he chose was just five hundred yards east of Morro Light, directly under the batteries of the old fortress. Unfortunately, there were submerged reefs in the vicinity and the beach consisted of a coral shelf, jagged and unwelcoming. When the *Triton* had come as near to the shore as the skipper dared, Hyatt, Scovel, and four navy seamen who had volunteered for the mission jumped into the tug's longboat and began pulling for shore. Scovel described the scene some years later in a letter to Captain Chadwick:

> The surf was running fairly high, and young Hyatt was deathly seasick. About 50 yards from the beach . . . the iron boat began to pound the bottom between the rollers. It seemed absolutely impossible for the courier to reach the shore. Mate Benjamin, a man from Bath, Me., jumped overboard with young Hyatt in his arms, and, on being thrown against the coral ledge by the first big breaker, he threw Hyatt clear upon the ledge, with force enough to roll him back several feet inland out of reach of the surf—where he lay stunned and unconscious for several hours.[3]

When Hyatt regained consciousness it was shortly before dawn and he saw a circle of curious faces examining him by the light of a fisherman's lantern. By an amazing coincidence one member of the group that had found him was a former *reconcentrado* who had been saved from starvation by Hyatt's father. He recognized the son of his benefactor and talked the others into sneaking Hyatt past the Morro Castle sentries, hidden in the bottom of their boat under a pile of nets.

The *Triton,* meanwhile, had left the vicinity immediately since its presence in the area would draw attention to Hyatt as he lay helpless on the coral shelf. As the tug steamed back toward Key West, all hands were speechless with dismay over the failure of their mission. Assuming that Hyatt had been taken prisoner,

Scovel decided to provide him with a cover story. The next day, April 19, the *World* prominently featured a long account under Scovel's byline describing how the plucky "*World* scout," George Heilberg, had been deposited on the beach, directly under the sweeping searchlight of Morro Castle. The narrative of course omitted any mention of the presence of navy personnel on the *Triton* and included a stirring description of the correspondent swimming ashore through the breakers.

The tale of Heilberg's landing in Cuba captured the imagination of a news-hungry public. However, thoughtful readers wondered how the paper could be so irresponsible as to send a reporter into the enemy's capital and then reveal his presence there while his fate was still in doubt. The *World*'s chief rivals, those with press contingents in Key West, knew the truth, but editors of smaller papers were sharply critical of Pulitzer for taking unnecessary risks with the lives of his staff, a charge that rankled all the more because Pulitzer could not defend himself without compromising the secrecy of the mission.

On the same day that the account of "Heilberg's" disappearance came out, *McClure's Magazine* photographer Jimmy Hare was strolling the docks in Key West when he encountered Scovel. A forty-two-year-old Englishman, barely five foot two, Jimmy was the son of George Hare, the designer of a line of costly hand-crafted cameras. At a time when the typical photojournalist used a bulky 8 x 10 view camera and required an assistant to help carry his gear, Hare was working with one of his father's portable models, so compact that it could be concealed under his coat. He had been in Havana photographing the wreck of the *Maine* when he first met Scovel, himself an inept though enthusiastic photographer, and during the trip back to Florida the two of them had spent a good part of the voyage swapping stories. It was Hare's ambition to photograph Gómez, and he readily agreed to Scovel's suggestion that he join the *Triton*'s next voyage. The plan was for the tug to make its way eastward toward the vicinity of Gómez's camp in Santa Clara Province, with Hare taking reconnaissance photographs while Scovel and Nichols took soundings for a nautical chart.

Before heading south, the *Triton* paid a call on the flagship

New York and Hare realized for the first time that the voyage would include a stop at Mosquito Inlet west of Havana to pick up Hyatt and Thrall.

Night had fallen by the time the *Triton* reached the appointed meeting place. The sea was calm and the stars brilliant overhead, and the *Triton*'s skipper had no trouble locating the landmarks leading to the spot where Hyatt and Thrall were supposed to be waiting. The *Triton* reduced its engine speed by two-thirds and began nosing in toward shore. Sure of his position now, Scovel ordered the skipper to cut the engines so that the tug could drift toward the beach.

Unfortunately, they had just missed Thrall and Hyatt. The two men had been scared off the beach minutes earlier by the approach of a Spanish patrol. By the time they emerged from their hiding place in the bush, Scovel, who did not dare linger in the area for fear of attracting the attention of Spanish gunboats patrolling in the vicinity, had already decided to patrol the coast between the inlet and Havana on the chance that the two men had gotten off to a late start and were waiting some ways down the beach.

The tug was showing no lights, and in the darkness its engines sounded fearfully loud. "Suddenly," wrote Scovel later, "right on our port bow, the shore shot up distinct and clear and right upon us." The captain attempted a sharp turn to starboard, but before the slow-moving tug could react, it came to a lurching halt, its bow snagged on a submerged reef.[4]

In a frantic effort to lighten the boat, all hands began tossing overboard the bags of coal that were piled on deck. Little Jimmy Hare, struggling to hoist the two-hundred-pound sacks, watched the others tossing them around "like footballs" and began to wonder whether he really belonged on this expedition.

After all the coal that could be spared had been dumped, everyone began shifting what was left to the stern, in the hope of raising the bow enough to lift it off the bottom. This too failed, and the captain next tried dropping the half-ton anchor from the ship's rowboat, a precarious operation, and using a hawser rigged between the anchor and the capstan to pull the tug off the reef. The futile maneuver took up most of the night. At last, shortly after three A.M., the tide turned and it became obvious that the rising waters would eventually refloat the boat. The only question was whether this would happen before a Spanish patrol boat arrived on the scene. It was already growing light, and the efforts of the *Triton*'s crew had attracted the attention of early-morning strollers on the beach.

Scovel decided that the crew's chances of escaping a Spanish firing squad would be better if they were not caught in the company of the notorious *World* correspondent. He boarded the boat's dinghy and prepared to head down the coast on his own. There was also the matter of Hare's incriminating photography equipment. "Toss that thing over," he shouted, pointing to Hare's camera. Hare indignantly refused. Not even a Spanish gunboat could induce him to destroy his camera, so he jumped into the dinghy with Scovel.

The two of them had rowed only a short way when a swelling wave lifted the *Triton* off the reef and the crew waved them back. The tug had survived a close call, but it was now so low on fuel that the skipper was unwilling to risk another foray close in shore.

Later that day, Nichols and Hare were about to take the longboat and row to the beach when Scovel offhandedly mentioned that the distance was about twenty miles. Quite suddenly, it occurred to Nichols that the ideal guide for their mission had been left back in Key West, and he suggested returning there to pick up Gómez's bodyguard, Captain W. D. Smith. "Why, we're greenhorns," he reminded Hare, who was all too amenable to abandoning the plan. "That fellow knows Cuba as we know Broadway!"[5]

Scovel, who considered twenty miles a reasonable distance for two men to row, was none too pleased, but the *Triton* returned to Key West. At six o'clock that evening, April 21, the long-awaited word arrived from Washington that the war had officially begun. Captain Sampson was immediately promoted to rear admiral and ordered to mobilize the fleet for a blockade of the north coast of Cuba between Bahia Honda and Cárdenas.

More unexpectedly, Scovel and Nichols found a disagreeable surprise awaiting them at the Key West Hotel: Ralph D. Paine had just arrived on the steamer from Tampa carrying a telegram from Don Seitz giving him permission to travel aboard the *World*'s dispatch boats. Paine was aware of Scovel and Nichols's secret work for Sampson and wanted desperately to be included. He had asked his editor to negotiate a deal with the *World* whereby he would be permitted on the *Triton* in exchange for a fee plus syndication rights to his articles.

All the newspapers with their own boats were making similar arrangements to help defray their expenses, much to the disgust of their staff managers in Key West who saw no reason why they and their correspondents should have to serve as tour guides for the competition. Seitz either didn't know about the *Triton*'s secret work for Admiral Sampson or didn't see why it should make any difference. However, Brad Merrill, who for some reason did not like Paine any more than Scovel did, wanted him nowhere near the Thrall-Hyatt story and he sent a curt telegram instructing Scovel to "sidetrack" the new arrival.

Ditching Paine was not going to be easy, but Scovel had an inspired solution. On the morning of the 22nd when Paine showed up ready to board the *Triton,* Scovel told him that he had made other plans. "You are not to go aboard the *World*'s dispatch boat with me," he said. "I have made different arrangements. You will sail on Admiral Sampson's flagship *New York,* and you had better hustle yourself aboard."[6]

The admiral's flagship was supposedly a choice assignment, but for the ambitious, active Ralph Paine it was torture. Sampson clearly had no recollection of discussing Paine's assignment with Scovel, so Paine was in the embarrassing position of having come aboard the admiral's ship without permission, about the worst gaffe it was possible to commit. What's more, shortly after he settled in, Richard Harding Davis arrived with a letter of introduction from Assistant Secretary of the Navy Roosevelt and began holding court in the officer's dining room, driving Paine, *McClure's* Stephen Bonsal, and the AP's Chappie Goode to share the inferior food of the enlisted men's mess.

Scovel showed up frequently to confer with Sampson and Chadwick and to interrogate prisoners from captured ships—the absence of a single interpreter or Spanish-speaking officer on the admiral's staff was another of the Navy Department's oversights —but on April 26, when the *New York* took part in the shelling of Matanzas, the navy's first combat engagement since the Civil War, the *World*'s dispatch boat was nowhere in sight. Paine watched in frustration as the celebrated RHD completed his description of the shelling, wrapped his copy in a waterproof oilskin packet, and tossed it onto the deck of the *Herald*'s boat, the *Sommers N. Smith.*

Recalling the occasion more than two decades later, Paine complained that "destiny had properly scuppered him" at the moment of the greatest opportunity of his life. But according to Frances Scovel, Paine knew very well that Scovel had deliberately kept him away from the spy ring's activities. "Paine never forgave Harry," she recalled.[7] In his memoir, *Roads of Adventure,* Paine got his revenge. Among other inaccuracies, Paine complained that Scovel's unexplained "errands" for the admiral caused him to neglect his duties to the *World.* This was disingenuous. Not only was the Thrall-Hyatt expedition successful from the intelligence standpoint, it was the basis for a series of front-page exclusives, the only major scoops by any reporter since the beginning of the war. So far at least, Scovel was successful in juggling his two roles, spymaster and correspondent.

While Ralph Paine cooled his heels on board the *New York,* Charles Thrall and George Hyatt had been located. On April 22, the *Triton* was waiting at the last of the previously agreed on meeting places, a deserted stretch of beach near Hyatt's hometown of Guanabacoa, when the missing spies appeared out of the bush, accompanied by a detachment of insurgents. Hyatt was content to be rescued, but Thrall, when he learned that war had been declared, insisted on returning to Havana to gauge the mood of the city. He and Scovel set up another series of rendezvous points, as before agreeing on three different locations where they would attempt to meet on successive nights.

Paradoxically, now that war was declared, the *Triton*'s nighttime forays into enemy waters had become somewhat less risky. Admiral Sampson had assigned the *Triton* an armed escort, the torpedo boat *Porter,* commanded by Lieutenant John C. Frémont, Jr., son of the late explorer and first U.S. senator from California. But in spite of the *Porter*'s assistance, the next several attempts to make contact with Thrall did not go well. Thrall would arrive on the beach in time to see the *Porter*'s signal lanterns winking in the distance and the silhouette of the *Triton* itself as it made regular passes closer to the shore, but because of unusually cloudy weather the signal fires he lit on the beach could not be seen by either boat. Scovel and the four navy crewmen who had volunteered for the undercover mission actually took a dinghy ashore and searched the beach, but they failed to find Thrall. In the meantime, the Signal Corps telegraph operator in Key West had learned from the army's Cuban spy in the Havana cable office that Thrall had been recognized on the streets of Havana. Chased by the police, the American had managed to disappear into a crowd of shoppers. Captain-General Blanco had offered a two-thousand-dollar reward for his arrest and the police were diligently searching the homes of Havana's foreign residents.

Since Thrall had kept the faked press credential originally given to George Hyatt, the *World* now ran another cover story, "revealing" that the mysterious correspondent "Heilberg" was still active in Havana. The story described the secret meeting on the beach near Guanabacoa in exciting detail, though again certain facts were deliberately garbled to mislead the Spanish. Most confusingly, Thrall, who had previously been identified by the alias "Holmes," was now called "Heilberg," and Hyatt, consequently, was called "Holmes."

In spite of this elaborate attempt at obfuscation, it seemed likely that Thrall had been shot by a patrol while trying to make his way back to the city. Writing from on board the *Porter* on April 27, Scovel noted grimly that the "*World*'s daring Havana correspondent" was still missing and believed dead.

Because of the search for Charles Thrall, a week went by before Scovel and Nichols were able to organize another party of journalists to visit Gómez. During that time, however, the trip had taken on a sense of urgency. A war conference at the White House had discussed a plan for General William Rufus Shafter to land a major expedition at Tunas on Cuba's southern coast. The expeditionaries would deliver arms to Gómez, who in turn would lead his followers in a cross-country push toward Havana. The Junta, meanwhile, overcoming its disappointment over the failure of McKinley to extend recognition to the Cuban republic, had signed an agreement placing the Liberation Army under the command of the U.S. invasion forces.

Astonishingly, no one had bothered to inform Gómez that he was supposed to be taking orders from the Americans. In hindsight, the obvious reason was that the McKinley administration feared that Gómez, once face-to-face with an official representative of the U.S. government, might demand something in return for his cooperation. The possibility that deliberately insulting the leader of the insurgency by ignoring his existence might do more to sour U.S.-Cuban relations in the long run does not appear to have been considered. However, this point was not lost on the Spanish military governor, Blanco, who sent an open letter to Gómez, calling on him to make common cause with Spain in repelling "the foreign enemy." Blanco suggested that whatever their differences, the Cubans and the Spanish still shared a common cultural heritage. Moreover, if the rebels now sided with Spain, the mother country would show its gratitude by granting independence. After the war, he wrote, "Spain as a loving mother, will open her arms to a new daughter of the Nations of the New World which speaks her language."[8]

Rejecting this offer, Gómez wrote: "We are fighting for an American principle, the principle of Bolívar and Washington. You say that we belong to the same race and invite me to fight against a foreign invader, but you are again mistaken because there are no differences of blood or of race. I believe in only one race: humanity."[9]

During the week after the American blockade was established, two emissaries of the army's Bureau of Military Information did arrive in the Caribbean, but neither of them was carrying an official message from President McKinley to the insurgent commanders. As one of the pair, Lieutenant Andrew Rowan, put it, their mission was simply "to bring the military data up to date." Traveling disguised as a "British sportsman," though this was hardly the moment for sports fishing in Cuban waters, Rowan sailed from Jamaica on April 23, heading for southeastern Cuba where he hoped to meet Calixto García, the insurgent general in command in eastern Cuba. Rowan's partner, Lieutenant Henry Whitney, was in Key West, preparing to leave for Gómez's stronghold in Santa Clara Province. But for reasons as mysterious now as they were to Admiral Sampson at the time, Whitney's orders from Washington were delayed and he kept postponing his departure.

Admiral Sampson, who was expecting the Spanish fleet to arrive in Cuban waters any day, had no patience with the army's dilatory tactics, and on the morning of April 28, just hours after Charles Thrall had been given up for lost, the admiral hosted a briefing in his quarters on the *New York* for the party of journalists who had volunteered to establish communications with Gómez. In addition to Francis Nichols and Jimmy Hare, the group included George Lynch of the London *Chronicle* and H. J. Whigham, a celebrated Scottish amateur golfer who was covering the war for the *Chicago Tribune*. Like Jimmy Hare, Whigham and Lynch were British subjects, which might offer them some protection against a charge of espionage if they fell into Spanish hands. Scovel would not be joining the group because he was determined not to abandon the search for Thrall until he had definite news one way or the other, so Major W. D. Smith was recruited after all to guide the newspapermen into the interior. Sampson and Captain Chadwick had ordered the *Triton* outfitted with a navy howitzer for the voyage, and before the members of the "Gómez Commission" departed, the admiral solemnly shook their hands and presented each of them with a brace of pistols.

"You'll need these when you start going through the jungle," he remarked, a prediction Jimmy Hare fervently hoped would turn out to be mistaken.[10]

Late in the afternoon, the *Triton* steamed eastward to the vicinity of Punta de Caguanes, twenty miles beyond Caibarién. This stretch of coast was protected by a maze of barrier islands and submerged reefs. The tug's Cuban pilot, a native of Havana, was doing his best to thread the maze but the crew was terrified of a repetition of the *Triton*'s last misadventure.

Major Smith, who impressed H. J. Whigham as quite thrillingly "piratical," saved the situation by hailing a passing fishing boat and forcefully haranguing the crew into taking his party ashore. Unfortunately, except for Nichols, the newspapermen expected Gómez to welcome the news that the United States had joined the war against Spain, and when he did not, they were disheartened. Jimmy Hare was doubly disappointed, first by Gómez, who was in no mood to sit for a photograph, and second by the food in camp, which consisted solely of boiled *jutia*, "the possum of Cuba."

The ultraconservative Whigham, who had earlier described the Junta organizers of Tampa as "amusing children," pronounced Gómez "a man of remarkable width of vision considering his narrow field of action." But, he added, Gómez "had the face to tell us that he did not want a single American soldier landed on the island. With the fleet keeping up the blockade he was quite prepared to finish the war, provided he were given the proper supplies and a little artillery." Further, he quoted Gómez as predicting that after the Spanish surrendered:

> The [cease-fire] request would be granted, because the Americans were so humane—this he said with an air of contempt for so foolish a quality—and that was exactly what the Cubans did not want. They desired an eye for an eye and a tooth for a tooth. Theirs was not a civilized war—these were his very words—but a war of extermination, and no Cuban would be satisfied until every Spaniard was killed or driven from the island.[11]

If Gómez actually said this, and in the heart of anger he may well have, he had certainly done his part to justify the diplomatic cold shoulder he was getting from Washington.

It was only three days since the Gómez Commission had left the battleship *New York*, but the U.S. strategy for the war was quickly turning in the direction of a major land invasion. At a second planning session in the White House, McKinley and his advisers had adopted a new strategy: Shafter's expedition via Cape Tunas to supply the rebels was to be undertaken as soon as possible, followed by an immediate American invasion, to begin with the landing of fifty thousand troops on the beaches near Mariel.

In a front-page article published in the *World* on April 30, Scovel denounced the planned land invasion as "criminal," on the grounds that American draftees would end up suffering the same fate as their Spanish counterparts, getting bogged down in an unwinnable war in a hostile tropical climate. Although he had his doubts about the ability of the insurgents to form a stable government, he reasoned that they were the only force with a mandate to govern the country. As for Gómez, Scovel had argued all along that the insurgent commander's more rabid statements were not the true measure of the man. The general was seventy-two years old and ailing, and he wanted desperately to be known as the father of Cuban independence.

"Ask [Gómez] what he wants, and let him have it," the *World* advised. Unfortunately, the paper published this advice under a banner headline that promised, "Gómez Will HAMMER AT HAVANA'S GATES," a phrase that evoked the very fears of a bloodbath that the article was meant to allay.

Which was the "real' Gómez? Scovel had seen both sides and he was convinced that the old man, exhausted from too many years of campaigning, would accept a U.S. role in a transitional government, provided he was assured that America intended to allow the Cubans the right to self-determination. Unless peace came soon, Gómez's dream of going down in history as the George Washington of Cuba would never be fulfilled.

By April 30, with Lieutenant Whitney still awaiting his orders from Washington, Sampson decided on his own authority to open direct communications by sending the Cuban general a personal letter:

> Sir,
>
> I have the honor to inform you of the presence of the Squadron under my command off the coast of Cuba. Desiring information for my government, I would be very much pleased to have you inform me as to your ideas concerning cooperation, and your needs as to arms, munitions and supplies in general.
>
> The bearer, Mr. Sylvester Scovel, is empowered to treat with you in my name.[12]

Scovel was dispatched aboard the speedy torpedo boat *Porter* to deliver the letter and bring the members of the Gómez Commission back to the blockade line. As the *Porter* prepared to shove off, Sampson bid an emotional, if laconic, farewell to Scovel, saying, "You be sure and take good care of that boat." Seppings

Wright, a British journalist, happened to be standing nearby, and he was so carried away by the intensity of the moment that he impulsively leaped onto the *Porter*'s deck as it was pulling away from flagship, begging to be allowed to go along for the ride.

Off Caibarién, the *Porter* was forced to cut its engines to maneuver through the shallows. The torpedo boat had a draft of seven feet four inches, the deepest sounding the mate could make was eight feet, and there was a Spanish garrison not half a mile away. Scovel, warning that the *Porter* was bound to be spotted poking its way through the channel, persuaded Lieutenant Frémont to put him and Wright ashore at a sugar plantation some miles from Punta de Caguanes. From there, they would hike to the rendezvous with Major Smith's party. Frémont would return to pick them all up in a week, by which time Scovel would have had time to deliver Sampson's letter to Gómez and rejoin the group.

Almost as soon as the *Porter* was out of sight, Scovel and Wright realized they had miscalculated. The promontory on which they had chosen to land was separated from the mainland by a marsh several miles wide. They had no choice but to ford the swamp, wading their way through three-foot-deep muck and foul-smelling stagnant water. Every step required an effort of will. When they finally reached the mainland, Major Smith's group was in the vicinity, but so were five heavily armed Spanish gunboats, lying in wait to ambush the *Porter* on its return.

Scovel was determined to find some way to get himself and his companions back to the fleet in time to prevent the torpedo boat from sailing into a trap. This left no time for him to make the round-trip to Gómez's camp. Fortunately, Frederick Somerford, a *Herald* correspondent who had been with Gómez for several months, had come down to the coast with Major Smith's party. Somerford, wrote Scovel, "had been reduced by starvation to great attenuation and was most anxious to get back in communication with his paper and to participate in the newspaper side of the war."[13] Nevertheless, he volunteered to return to Barrancones with the admiral's letter while Scovel tried to figure out an escape route.

A few hours after Somerford's departure, two Cuban fishing

boats appeared in the channel and tied up at an anchorage several hundred yards from the spot where the Americans were camped. "We're going to take those boats," Smith announced. This was piracy indeed, but by now this seemed a minor detail. Five members of the Cuban escort that had brought them down from Barrancones were still in camp, and Smith stationed them and the correspondents at strategic locations in the bush. On his signal they came charging out, shooting their pistols in the air and yelling whatever battle cries came to mind, invoking the honor of Uncle Sam, Her Majesty, and the highland clans. Seventeen fishermen were captured and were no doubt startled to learn that they were being taken prisoner in the name of the New York *World* and *Chicago Tribune.*

As the correspondents prepared to shove off in the largest and fastest of the boats, Fred Somerford appeared on the beach waving his arms and signaling to be picked up. He had run into Gómez, who was moving his headquarters nearer the coast, and had brought back one of Gómez's aides, who was carrying a reply to Admiral Sampson and a letter of greeting to McKinley. Somerford and the aide somehow got on board and they all stripped to their trousers, hoping to pass for a crew of fishermen as the sloop sailed past Caibarién under the nose of the Spanish gunboats.

After a dangerous three-day journey, hopscotching down the coast to avoid Spanish ships, the correspondents reached Key West, just hours before the torpedo boat *Ericsson,* a substitute for the *Porter,* departed for Punta de Caguanes.

Hare, Nichols, and the others had been gone just eleven days, but when they returned to Key West they might as well have been stepping out of a time warp.

On May 1, the U.S. Navy's Asiatic Fleet under the command of Commodore George Dewey had defeated the Spanish at Manila Bay. The Hong Kong–Manila cable was cut shortly after the battle, and for six days no news reached the western hemisphere apart from an inconclusive bulletin from Madrid that mentioned "heavy losses" but did not say who had won. The nation waited, suspense mounting, and on the morning of May 7, the New York *Journal* reported "Great Nervousness Is Felt In Washington Because Nothing Is Heard From Dewey." But a few hours earlier, the first boatload of American correspondents had reached Hong Kong, and as so often happened, it was a *World* man, Edwin Harden, who stole a beat on the competition by filing his dispatch on the battle at the "urgent" rate of $9.90 a word. His copy went out on the cable even before Dewey's official report to Washington, and the *World*'s early edition on the same morning the Gómez Commission returned trumpeted the news: OLD GLORY WAVES OVER MANILA! Later that day, the *Journal* followed with a lengthy narrative account of the battle, written by Charles Michelson, who had improvised the entire story from a six-hundred-word dispatch put on the wire by a correspondent for the Chicago *Record.*

Dewey's triumph inspired delirium. Dozens of popular songs were written to celebrate the victory—forcing hard-pressed lyricists to rhyme "Dewey" with "truly" and "Hooray!"—and inspiring Rudyard Kipling to write his famous poem, "The White Man's Burden," which Theodore Roosevelt called "mediocre poetry but uncommonly good sense."[14]

> Take up the White Man's burden—,
>   Send forth the best ye breed—
> Go, bind your sons to exile
>   To serve your captives' need;
> To wait in heavy harness
>   On fluttered folk and wild—
> Your new-caught, sullen peoples
>   Half-devil and half-child.

The victory in Manila changed overnight the psychology of the war. Roosevelt's "large policy" had proved rewarding beyond anyone's wildest dreams—except, possibly, his. Roosevelt celebrated by announcing that very day that he was resigning his post with the Department of the Navy to accept a commission with the First Volunteer Cavalry, the regiment of cowboys, Indian fighters, and Ivy League sportsmen being organized by Colonel Leonard Wood in San Antonio, Texas.

* * *

The Gómez commissioners had missed other major developments as well. Admiral Sampson had taken a flotilla of ships off the blockade line and sailed east toward the Windward Passage, hoping to find the Spanish fleet of Admiral Pascual Cervera, which was reliably reported to have left the Cape Verde Islands on April 30.

Major Smith was surprised to read, in the same edition of the *World* that proclaimed Dewey's victory, a report of his own death, based on a rumor that he had been arrested as a spy in Havana. When he dropped in at the Eagle Tavern to celebrate his safe return he found another "dead man," Charles Thrall, seated at a rear table.

Thrall was not an articulate individual, but a *World* correspondent, probably Alex Kenealy with some help from Stephen Crane, was able to extract enough information to piece together the ghostwritten account of his activities that appeared in the *World* on May 8 as, "The Thrilling Adventures of A World Scout in Cuba." Thrall had studied the fortifications and the disposition of ships in Havana harbor, learning, for example, that the armored cruiser *Alfonso XII* was disabled. He had bicycled and hiked twenty-nine miles down the coast on at least six occasions in vain attempts to attract the attention of his contacts on the *Porter*. Finally, he was found by chance when an American patrol boat noticed him signaling on the beach. Thrall volunteered to return to Cuba just seven hours later to supervise the first landing of supplies for the insurgents on the beach west of Havana. There he assisted two Cuban scouts in carrying cases of live ammunition while under fire from a detachment of Cuban cavalry.

Captain French Ensor Chadwick later called the *World-Tribune*'s commission to Gómez "a bold and gallant adventure upon the part of all concerned, a marked instance of the spirit of the newspaper correspondent, who has so generally shown himself ready to dare with the best." [15]

As for Charles Thrall, he had never been a correspondent and his only motive in infiltrating Havana had been to serve his country. But he could not have succeeded without the help of Scovel and Nichols and Joseph Pulitzer's generous loan of the *Triton* to the government.

Ironically, the *World*'s contributions to the war effort won the paper no gratitude in Washington. The policy of cooperation with the insurgents had been adopted mainly for political and diplomatic purposes, and in fact the last thing the McKinley administration wanted was for Gómez to succeed in wresting control of Havana.

It Has to Be Written Later . . .

THE AMBIENCE on board the battleship *New York*, where the band played the "Star Song" from *Die Meistersinger* during the evening promenade hour, had struck Dick Davis as exquisitely fin de siècle. But the Tampa Bay Hotel, officers' headquarters for the army mobilization, reminded him of nothing so much as a Civil War reunion. Aging officers who had not seen action since they fought on opposite sides of the War Between the States had installed themselves in the row of white wicker rocking chairs on the main veranda, puffing their cigars, sipping port, and fairly bursting the seams of their dress uniforms, their decades-old reminiscences of courage and carnage forming a gruff counterpoint to the waltz tunes played by the regimental band in the adjacent pavilion. The general staff was divided between Union Army veterans such as William Rufus Shafter, who would be in command of the army of invasion, and O. O. Howard and such former Confederate stalwarts as Fitzhugh Lee, recently recommissioned as a major general, and "Fightin' Joe" Wheeler, whose cavalry had once harried General Sherman's troops on their march to Atlanta, now a thin, stoop-shouldered sixty-two-year-old, who wore a linen duster over his uniform even in the hundred-degree-plus heat. McKinley had appointed the grizzled veterans in the hope that their leadership would symbolize the healing of the wounds of the Civil War.

Choosing field commanders for one war in order to memorialize the last was a rather whimsical strategy, but then never had war been plotted in more fanciful surroundings. The Tampa Bay Hotel was a magnificent Spanish-Moorish-Victorian structure, five stories tall, its red brick facade encircled by broad verandas and topped by thirteen silver minarets said to symbolize the months of the Moslem calendar. Peacocks wandered among the fragrant oleanders on the lawn. Mediocre but genuine Renaissance bronzes peeked from behind the potted palms and rubber plants in the lobby. The five-hundred-room hotel had its own golf course, formal gardens, and a casino, known as the Oriental Annex, complete with a dance hall and a swimming pool. It even boasted outdoor electric lights strung on the veranda and around the casino, a novelty that made it possible for guests to extend after-dinner strolls and, an unheard-of indulgence, enjoy midnight swims in the pool. As one correspondent quipped, the place reminded you of a Turkish harem without women.

The hotel was the pride and joy of Henry Bradley Plant, owner of the Plant Line steamers that traveled regularly to Key West and Cuba and the railroad magnate responsible for bringing the first rail line to Tampa in 1884. At the time, Tampa had been an obscure military outpost whose wooden plank streets were often piled with drifting sand. With remarkable prescience, Plant concluded that what the town needed was an amusement park. He developed one called Picnic Island, which was followed shortly by a dockside hotel, the Tampa Bay Inn, where guests were encouraged to fish from their bedroom windows. In the meantime, besides an influx of adventurous tourists, the railroad brought an influx of Cuban emigrants, among them V. Martínez Ybor, who opened the first cigar factory and founded the Cuban neighborhood known as Ybor City. By 1890 Tampa was a boomtown. The streets were paved and lighted by electric streetlamps, double-deck streetcars carried commuters downtown, and Plant had persuaded the city to construct the Lafayette Street Bridge, providing access to a undeveloped tract west of the river where he was building his dream hotel, constructed for the ages around a super-structure reinforced with steel cables and railroad ties and deco-rated by Mrs. Plant, who spent more than a million dollars on a whirlwind European buying tour.

When the hotel opened in 1891, the consensus was that Henry Plant had been too long in the Florida sun, a judgment reinforced by his statement that the hotel would be worth every penny he'd spent even if it never made a profit. Now, at seventy-nine, Plant was on hand with his wife at his side to welcome the officers of the Fifth Army and savor his moment of vindication. "Plant's Folly" was rapidly filling its five hundred rooms.

By mid-May there were 129 credentialed correspondents. Among them were at least two women—Anna Northend Benjamin of *Leslie's* magazine and a Canadian free-lance reporter, Kathleen Blake Watkins. In the face of considerable hostility, particularly from Arthur Brisbane who turned down several dozen women eager to represent the *Journal* at the front, both Benjamin and Watkins were determined and highly professional. "I know what you think," Benjamin told British correspondent Charles Hands when he questioned her seriousness. "You think it ridiculous my being here, you are laughing at me wanting to go, that's the worst of being a woman. But just let me tell you, I'm going through to Cuba and not all the old generals in the world are going to stop me."[1]

And despite the army's efforts to scuttle her mission, Benja-min did manage to get to Cuba before the fighting was over. Left behind when the army sailed from Tampa, she went to Key West and bribed the skipper of a collier to take her to the war zone. Subsequently, Benjamin moved on to the Pacific where she cov-ered the Philippine insurrection, reported from China and Japan, and then returned to Europe via the Trans-Siberian Railroad. She became a popular author and lecturer but died of cancer at the age of twenty-seven.

Kathleen Watkins also eventually earned her male colleagues' grudging respect as "one of the boys." Indeed, while many of the boys spent their afternoons drinking iced tea on the hotel veranda, Watkins tirelessly patrolled the campgrounds on Picnic Island, striking up conversations with the enlisted men and culling human interest stories. When an eight-foot-long alligator burrowing in the sand to find water surfaced inside a private's tent in the middle of the night, Watkins was the first to hear of it. At dinnertime she reappeared "looking cool as a watermelon," and worked the lobby until she knew everyone worth knowing. By the end of her first evening at the hotel, a British colleague noted with some chagrin, "she was introducing *us* to generals and colonels."[2]

After his brief stint on the admiral's flagship, Davis had arrived in Tampa on May 3 in high spirits. He was covering the war for the *Herald, Scribner's,* and the London *Times* as well as for a book of his own, and had written to his family, predicting with the lightest touch of self-satire, "I expect to get rich off this war." His first act in Tampa was to buy a Kentucky filly, which he renamed Gaiety Girl, and he was already entertaining fantasies that "when this cruel war is over" Gaiety Girl would be famous as the horse who "carried the news of the fall of Havana to Matanzas, fifty miles under fire."[3]

Several days later, Davis's good spirits were crushed: He received notification that President McKinley wanted to commission him as a captain in the U.S. Army. Meant as an honor, the offer threw Davis into a tailspin of self-doubt. The problem was not that he was a coward, as many of his colleagues supposed, but that he found any major life decision paralyzing. Every irrevocable choice was a frightening reminder that he had only one life to live, one chance to be RHD. Quite irrationally, Davis fretted that if he chose the army he would be assigned to staff duty, counting canteens and soda crackers at Fort Chickamauga or keeping the books in Gretna Green. More to the point, no doubt, he feared he was too old (at thirty-four), too spoiled by his life of "excitement and freedom," and too cynical overall "to make the sacrifices other men can make." And what if, after all, the war went on for a year or more? "It would bore me to death."

In an agony of indecision, he shut himself up in Fred Remington's hotel room with Remington and Colonel Arthur Lee, the British military attaché, and rehearsed the pros and cons of the offer for two hours, until a bleary-eyed Colonel Lee drafted a telegram of rejection. Davis signed, but no sooner was the tele-

gram sent off to the president than he began to reproach himself
for taking Lee's bad advice and missing "the chance of a lifetime."

"It's a question of character entirely," he reflected, "and I
don't feel I've played the part at all. It's all very well to say you are
doing more by writing, but are you?"[4]

Davis's funk deepened when he learned that his byline would
be sharing the *Herald*'s front page with that of a writer he detested, the arrogant and infuriating Poultney Bigelow. The son of
diplomat John Bigelow, Poultney had been reared in Berlin where
he and Kaiser Wilhelm II were boyhood playmates, re-enacting
the adventures of Uncas and Leatherstocking out of the pages of
James Fenimore Cooper as they took turns stalking each other
through the marbled halls of the Neues Palais with a bow and
arrow set that Mrs. Bigelow had brought her son as a souvenir
from a visit to Niagara Falls. Despite a subsequent falling out with
the kaiser, Bigelow remained an admirer of Bismarckian Prussia,
a society untouched by pacifism, feminism, and socialism—or any
of the "modern fads that make us weak"—and where no Jew
could hold "high office of any kind." He had no use for blacks
either, and once wrote that the abolitionists had cynically cooked
up sob stories about the sufferings of the slaves in order to provide a rationale for a war that would establish New England's
commercial domination over the South. He did, however, have a
good word for the Catholic religion: "As God made 85 per cent. of
His creatures morons or mental defectives, He necessarily provided religions adapted to their capacities; and papacy persists
because it is a product of human infirmity."[5]

Another of Bigelow's particular dislikes was Teddy Roosevelt,
who had been a fellow student at Columbia Law School. Bigelow
once described Roosevelt as "an excellent specimen of the genus
Americanus egotisticus." Some years, later, and more insightfully,
he recognized Roosevelt as "the first American President that has
from the very threshold of his political career cultivated Press
notices as an important element in the achievement of power. He
made himself the hero of a dramatic episode such as Richard
Wagner would create for a Nibelungen Siegfried."[6]

"Big" Bigelow arrived in the hotel dining hall on his first
evening at Tampa to find RHD—*the* War Correspondent *par
excellence*"—presiding at the head of a table of journalists and

wearing a row of medals on his jacket. Davis was not at all pleased to see his *Herald* colleague. "He knew that I knew the Roosevelts by inheritance," Bigelow speculated, "and perhaps suspected a rival in the Rough Rider entourage."

During a lull in the conversation, Davis abruptly announced, "It seems to me Bigelow that we are too crowded here. Don't you think we had better scatter?"

"Dickey," Bigelow retorted, "you are quite right.... Suppose you begin the scattering."[7]

Later Bigelow happened to run into Captain H. J. Dorst and learned that an army expedition to supply the insurgents with arms was sailing from Port Tampa that very night. Except for the *Leyden* mission, which had been supervised by Charles Thrall, this would be the first officially sponsored filibuster. Bigelow wanted to be part of the expedition in the worst way. Dorst had already promised Davis that he would have an exclusive on the mission, but Bigelow confronted his rival in the lobby of the hotel and somehow bluffed him into giving up the berth. No doubt the reason was that the Rough Riders were due to arrive any day, and Davis wanted to make sure that he, not Bigelow, would be covering their activities for the *Herald.*

A few hours later, Bigelow arrived at the docks carrying his portable typewriting machine in a sailor's bag slung over one shoulder. The *Gussie* turned out to be a forty-year-old side-wheel double-deck riverboat painted a bright red with green shutters and trim. Her cargo hold and staterooms were loaded with an estimated five million dollars' worth of arms and ammunition, her mirror-lined saloon was transformed into an officer's quarters, and the two companies of infantrymen assigned to provide armed cover for the landing were packed shoulder to shoulder along the upper and lower promenade decks. A few bales of hay piled on the upper deck completed the *Gussie*'s transformation into a ship of war.

Bigelow had been promised that he and the *Harper's Weekly* illustrator Rufus Zogbaum would be the only representatives of the press to cover the *Gussie*'s voyage, but the naturally garrulous Captain Dorst was no match for the persistent Kathleen Watkins, who managed to wheedle the entire story out of him. Realizing that she would never be permitted to go along on the expedition herself, Watkins had passed the tip on, and by sailing time the roster of newsmen included Stenie Bonsal, Ralph Paine, C. E. Akers of the London *Times,* and James F. J. Archibald of the San Francisco *Post.*

The "secret" expedition had become the talk of Tampa. A crowd was gathered on the dock to witness the *Gussie*'s midnight departure, and the mission was announced the next morning in newspapers across the country. A typical story, featured on the front page of the Atlanta *Constitution,* carried the headline "Cuban Invasion Begins Today."

Bigelow had known Captain Dorst for years and described him as "a man who knew not fear, and was famous more for his reckless daring than military science."[8] The army's decision to place him in charge of supplying the Cubans, and to assign him no better ship than the *Gussie* for the purpose, was an indication of its priorities. The mission seemed designed if not for actual failure, at least for ignominy, and the press, taking the cue, treated the voyage as an occasion for snide humor. Stenie Bonsal led the chorus, complaining that the *Gussie* looked more fit for a Sunday school outing than a landing on a hostile coast and suggesting that the newsmen petition the army for a name that was not quite so "suggestive of a seminary for young ladies."[9]

The *Gussie*'s departure for Key West was set for midnight on May 9, but for unexplained reasons was postponed until noon the next day. Then, the expedition faced another delay. The navy had agreed to provide an escort for the voyage into Cuban waters, but as the result of a garbled wigwag message, orders meant for the revenue cutter *Manning* were missent to the lighthouse tender *Mangrove.*

While waiting for the mix-up to be straightened out, Captain Dorst sought out Harry Scovel, who had befriended him during the Greco-Turkish War. He found him aboard the *Triton* with Charles Thrall and a *World* illustrator, Hayden Jones. Thrall had volunteered to attempt another landing in Cuba, accompanied by Jones, and the two of them were busy with barbers' shears, trying to change each other's appearance in the hope that they would be able to pass as British merchant seamen stranded in Cuba by the blockade. When he heard from Dorst that the *Gussie* was already a day behind schedule, Thrall offered to act as a courier. He would land first from the *Triton,* find the Cuban detachment that was supposed to pick up the *Gussie*'s cargo, explain the delay, and make sure they were prepared to remove the munitions from the beach as quickly as possible.

Scovel was doubtful. It was most unlikely that the Cubans would remain in the vicinity of the staging area during daylight hours, and if they had taken the risk, they would probably have been spotted by Spanish sentries. There was a good possibility that the *Gussie* would be sailing into an ambush. But Dorst refused to scuttle the mission, and at ten P.M. the *Triton* gave the *Gussie* a tow out of Key West harbor.

A few miles out to sea they parted company, and the *Triton* steamed directly to Baracoa, arriving just before daybreak. Thrall and Jones were put ashore, where they learned that exactly what Scovel feared had taken place. The Cubans had waited so long for the *Gussie* to show up that a Spanish patrol had caught up with them. There had been a skirmish, and the Cubans had scattered and were hiding out in the bush.

The *Gussie,* meanwhile, could not keep up with its naval escort, the *Manning.* A squall blew up, and the two ships were separated. According to Ralph Paine, Captain Dorst seemed never to have heard of blackouts. The skipper, who a few weeks earlier had been taking excursion parties up the Mississippi, was quaking with fear. The *Gussie* "blazed grandly with lights from every port-hole, like a hotel afloat," making an inviting target for the ships on the American blockade line that had not been informed of the *Gussie*'s identity. The side-wheeler was fired on by seven different American vessels in the space of about four hours, making for a very "entertaining night," Paine wrote.

Scovel, after dropping Thrall and Jones on the beach, had taken the *Triton* back out to sea and was waiting near Baracoa, as planned, for the *Gussie*'s arrival. Shortly after sunup, much to his surprise, he saw the side-wheel steamer running close in to shore, still lit up like a party boat and proceeding decorously at a speed of barely six knots in the direction of Cabañas, where the harbor fort was garrisoned with at least two thousand Spanish soldiers.[10]

For reasons that mystified everyone, and much against the advice of his Cuban scouts, Dorst had decided to attempt a landing on Arbolitas Point, just west of the entrance to Cabañas harbor. The first landing boats snagged on a hidden sandbar two hundred yards from shore, and while the crew struggled to pull the boat free, a mounted patrol appeared on the beach and began shooting at them. Ralph Paine, who was attempting to save one of the horses, was nearly trampled, and James Archibald was shot in the arm, the first land casualty of the war.

Rufus Zogbaum, sketching the action from the deck of the *Gussie*, turned the tumultuous scene into a highly admired illustration entitled "Landing Through the Surf Under Fire from the Shore." But Paine later wrote that while accurate in substance, the drawing failed to convey the emotional turmoil he had felt at the time. "Art has its limitations."

Scovel had spent the night searching unsuccessfully for Thrall and Jones. Convinced that his friends had been captured, and blaming Dorst's recklessness for their loss, he returned in disgust to Key West. Even now, however, Dorst refused to take the advice of his scouts, insisting on making yet another try in the vicinity of Matanzas. After failing to find any insurgents who could accept delivery of its cargo, the paddle wheeler tooled around in the bay for most of the day taking reconnaissance photographs.

Topping off the feckless journey, when the correspondents returned to Tampa they learned that Dorst had been promoted in his absence to the rank of lieutenant colonel.

Poultney Bigelow had completed his account of what he called the "Battle of Cabañas" while the *Gussie* was still at sea, and as soon as he reached Port Tampa he handed it to a Pullman porter of a train bound for New York, thus bypassing military censorship. In an unbylined account in the *Herald*, he summed up the voyage: "That the failure was unattended by any loss of life on our part seems more due to good luck than to good judgment. When the war is over some comic opera librettists can find inspiration in the adventures of the *Gussie*, whose movements from the time she left Key West until she returned were as frivolous and flighty as her name." [11] Stephen Bonsal and Ralph Paine were hardly less critical. In a piece carried by the *World*, Paine wrote: "I have been pretty well around the island in the filibustering industry, but I never saw a worse place chosen for a landing party than the harbor entrance to the village of Cabañas." [12]

Although a number of correspondents also criticized the press for breaching security by publicizing the mission ahead of time, the Spanish hardly needed to read about the *Gussie*'s mission in the newspaper. Her parade down the coast had been self-advertisement enough. Nevertheless, Lieutenant John D. Miley, who as General Shafter's aide-de-camp was responsible for coordinating the *Gussie* expedition, blamed its failure on the U.S. Navy and the press, not necessarily in that order.

The immediate consequence of the *Gussie* fiasco was the tightening of censorship. In New York, Lieutenant Colonel Joseph Maxwell, the Signal Corps officer in charge of monitoring commercial cable traffic, was replaced by Lieutenant Colonel George O. Squier. Previously, only obvious cipher messages and explicit information about current military operations had been forbidden, but Squier was obviously under orders to take a hard line with the press. "The whole system of censorship had taken on a scope wider than ever known before," charged the *World.*[13] Among the scores of messages that Squier refused to allow was one from the *World* to William Shaw Bowen in St. Thomas, which read in full: "Cervera's fleet reported in Puerto Rico. Try ascertain truth." Editors and publishers complained that the new system made even routine communications with field correspondents impossible, but some congressmen thought the army had not gone far enough. On May 18, the House debated a bill that would have made it a crime, punishable by ten years in prison and a twenty-five-thousand-dollar fine, to transmit any information about the strength of military fortifications in the United States, including pictures of guns. The bill was returned to committee after Representative Richard P. Bland of Missouri pointed out that the bill was so vaguely worded that it would prevent even Congress from receiving such information.

In Tampa, the new censorship regulations were enforced by Lieutenant Miley. When the steamer *Florida* departed on May 21, carrying four-hundred Cuban volunteers from Tampa as well as a shipment of arms, Miley made sure that only one correspondent, Clyde Hunt of *Harper's Weekly,* was allowed to go along. Further, he threatened that the first correspondent to get out of line would be denied credentials to accompany the army to Cuba.

Miley's threat had a chilling effect on the correspondents in Tampa. The exception was the outspoken Poultney Bigelow.

The multiprejudiced Poultney had a brother, Captain John Bigelow, who was, of all things, a white officer in an all-black unit, the famous Tenth Cavalry "buffalo soldiers," who before the war had been stationed at forts Custer and Assiniboine in Montana. John Bigelow was a staunch admirer of the fighting ability of the black soldier and outraged on their behalf at the treatment they were receiving at their training camp near Lakeland, Florida. Local shopkeepers refused to serve black soldiers and an officer of New York's socialite-led National Guard unit, the "Gallant Seventy-first," had actually lodged a complaint that having black troops in the same campground was "humiliating" to his men.

Despite his differences with his brother on certrain subjects, Poultney was a champion of the career officer. He had moved out of his room at the Tampa Bay to bivouac with the troops on Picnic Island, and on March 28, he followed up his account of the "Battle of Cabañas" with an exposé of conditions in the camps where troops bound for a campaign in the tropics were being issued winter weight uniforms, shoes that dissolved the first time they got wet, hats that were too large, rifles without ammunition or vice versa, and finally, greasy tinned pork that laid low whole regiments with diarrhea.

Bigelow went on to question the wisdom of staging the embarkation from a city serviced by only a single narrow-gauge rail connection. Boxcars loaded with munitions and commissary supplies were backed up as far as South Carolina, and there was no end to the confusion in sight. Bigelow suggested that the selection of Tampa had more to do with Henry Plant's political influence than the suitability of the site, and he attacked the doling out of commissions to the volunteers, another blatant form of political patronage. According to Bigelow, he had actually met one newly commissioned major who did not realize that his rank was superior to a captain's.

"Nobody dares complain for fear of appearing unpatriotic," Bigelow wrote of the mess in Tampa. "Still it will do no harm to hear a little of the truth."[14]

Bigelow's facts were indisputably correct, but he was guilty of telling the truth at the wrong time and being the wrong individual to tell it. Lieutenant Miley retaliated by revoking Bigelow's press credentials and Richard Harding Davis attacked him in a June 6 article in the *Herald*, calling his charges "untrue... un-American... and calculated to give courage to the enemy."

But as Davis admitted in a letter to his brother Charles, his scorn for Bigelow was mixed with envy. He had been tempted to write a similar article himself. The "readiness of the volunteers to be sacrificed" was a "pathetic spectacle." But an exposé now would serve no purpose and would undermine morale at home. "It has to be written later," he rationalized. "... If I started to tell the truth at all, it would do no good, and it would open up a hell of an outcry from all the families of the boys who volunteered." [15]

Another victim of the new censorship regulations was Harry Scovel, who in a bizarre twist of events was accused of stowing away on the navy's armed tug *Uncas*. The "Uncas affair," much publicized at the time, was frequently cited by critics of the yellow press as an example of the irresponsible behavior of correspondents in the war zone. The facts of the case, never before published, tell a different story.

When Scovel returned to Key West after the *Gussie* expedition, he learned that Captain Dorst's incautious leadership had indeed led to the capture of the advance scouts Charles Thrall and Hayden Jones. Fortunately, Thrall had become so haggard looking that he was not recognized by the same spy who had spotted him in Havana a few weeks earlier. Both he and Jones were being held in Morro Castle, and the chief Spanish censor in Cuba, Ramón Méndez, who happened to be a rebel sympathizer and a friend of Scovel's in spite of his high position in the colonial government, was doing his best to look out for prisoners' interests.

To its credit, the Department of the Navy moved quickly to authorize a prisoner exchange: Two of the Spanish naval officers who were being held as prisoners of war in Fort Thomas, Georgia, were to be offered in return for the New York *World* "correspondents." The *Uncas*, commanded by a Lieutenant Brainard, was to be sent to Havana the next day, May 14, to negotiate the details of the exchange. Commodore Watson, who had been left in charge of the spy ring activities by Admiral Sampson, suggested that

Scovel follow in the *Triton*, remaining within call of Havana in case he was needed.

To keep the *Uncas*'s destination secret from the rest of the press corps, Watson had specified that the *Triton* was to sail from Key West separately under cover of darkness and rendezvous with the navy tug at sea. But at six o'clock on the evening before he was to depart, Scovel was suddenly informed by Lieutenant McKinstry, the master of the port, that the *Triton*'s permit to enter and leave the harbor during the curfew hours of eight P.M. to four A.M. had been rescinded. There was no particular reason for the curfew except that McKinstry's superior, Commodore Remey, commander of the Key West Naval Station, happened to be feuding with Commodore Watson over the traffic problems caused by the newspaper boats. Nevertheless, McKinstry refused Scovel's request for an exemption and by the time the *Triton*'s firemen could be rounded up from the local bars where they were celebrating the end of the *Gussie* fiasco, it was after eight P.M.

At this point, Lieutenant Brainard sent Scovel an invitation to come to Havana on the *Uncas*. E. F. Knight, a British journalist who had credentials from the Spanish government, had already received official permission to travel on the navy tug, and Brainard obviously thought that as long as he had one journalist on board, a second would do no harm.

Brainard's negotiations in Havana went well, and when the *Uncas* returned to Key West, Scovel jumped from the deck and sprinted for the cable office to file his story while correspondents from the other papers gathered around Brainard, who, much to their annoyance, refused to answer their questions.

Someone, it is not known who, rushed off to file a complaint with Commodore Remey, and when Scovel emerged from the telegraph office an hour or so later Remey was waiting to confront him.

"Were you aboard the *Uncas*?" Remey demanded.

"I was."

Remey, hopping mad, replied that he was personally going to see to it that Lieutenant Brainard was stripped of his command.

Visions of Jonesey, whose promising career had been ruined as a result of their boyhood bargain back at the Michigan Military

Academy, must have flashed through Scovel's mind. "Lt. Brainard wasn't at fault," he told Remey quickly. "I thought they might need an interpreter, so I stowed away and he couldn't very well throw me overboard."[16]

To further protect Brainard, Scovel had E. F. Knight send a telegram to the Navy Department backing up the stowaway story.

Lieutenant Brainard's career had been saved, but on May 18, Secretary of the Navy Long issued an order *permanently* barring Scovel from all naval vessels and naval installations. In addition, the secretary forbade all naval personnel to have "any conversation whatever on the subjects in any way pertaining to the navy with representatives of the press."[17] This sweeping order was intended as a reproof to Admiral Sampson, whose reliance on the press was disapproved of by Long. But Long clearly had no concept of Sampson's problems. The navy had entered the modern age in every area except communications. Electronic ship-to-ship communications did not exist, and navy planners had grossly underestimated the need for auxiliary vessels for carrying messages, communicating with on-shore telegraph offices, and performing intelligence functions. Although the *Triton*'s role as a spy vessel had been unique, all the newspaper boats had been co-opted to one degree or another to do errands for the navy, and still Secretary Long insisted on viewing them as nuisances.

As for Scovel, overnight he became a hero to the press corps. No one had ever accused the *World*'s star correspondent of being self-effacing and his ability to garner more exclusives than the rest of the correspondents combined was the cause of no little jealousy. Even so, he was generally liked, and the feeling in Key West was that Lieutenant Brainard, in allowing Scovel to take the blame for what was after all his decision, had violated the gentleman's code.

Scovel had the means to clear himself if he really wanted to. A meticulous collector of documents, he had saved notes written to him by Brainard and McKinstry as well as a photograph of himself and Knight posing on deck of the *Uncas* in navy caps.[18] Nevertheless, he had made up his mind to protect Brainard. While the *World* protested vigorously that Long's action was a violation of the "freedom of newspaper correspondents" (meaning, one presumes, freedom of the press), Scovel was quoted in a front-

page story as saying that he knew he had violated a navy regula-
tion and was prepared to "take my medicine uncomplainingly."[19]

In the end, Sampson decided simply to ignore Long's orders.
He was the admiral, after all, and no civilian, not even the secretary of the navy, was going to tell him who was allowed on *his*
ships. At the admiral's insistence, Scovel continued to visit the
New York and to use the navy vessel, the armed tug *Tecumseh*,
to make secret landings on the Cuban coast for the purpose of
gathering intelligence from the insurgents.

Scovel was understandably nervous about his situation. For a
time he insisted on having written authorization from Sampson or
Captain F. E. Chadwick for each of his missions, but in the rush of
events over the next few weeks, this precaution was sometimes
forgotten. The Navy Department made no attempt to enforce
Long's exclusion order, and everyone in the war zone from Admiral Sampson on down assumed it had become a dead letter.

****

The Minstrel Boy
to the War Has Gone

The minstrel boy to the war has gone,
In the ranks of death you'll find him.
His father's sword he had girded on,
And his wild harp slung behind him.

—Private Dryden,
"the most useful crazy man in the United States Army,"
Stephen Crane's "The Sergeant's Private Madhouse"

MUCH TO HIS DISGUST, Admiral Sampson had been ordered not to risk his fleet by attempting to capture Havana but to maintain the blockade until Admiral Cervera's fleet chose to make an appearance in the Caribbean. Calm descended on the blockade line, but there was no calm in the newspaper offices in New York. The war was *the* story of the moment—all other news and features had been suspended for the duration—and editors were desperate for copy. As Stephen Crane later wrote: "We were fought by our managing editors tooth and nail...and we were urged...to remember that the American people were a collection of super-nervous idiots who would immediately have convulsions if we did not throw them some news—any news."[1] Eager to appease their bosses, the correspondents resorted to puffery. As Crane put it, news that arrived in Key West as a mouse was invariably cabled north as an elephant.

Stephen Crane had been recruited personally by Joseph Pulitzer who offered him three thousand dollars to come from England to cover the war for the *World*. On reaching New York, Crane first attempted to enlist in the army but was unable to pass the physical. Only then did he check in at the Dome, which sent him on to Key West along with former drama critic Alex Kenealy and Adolph Koelble, at one time a reporter for the *World*'s German-language edition.

Harry Scovel learned of Crane's imminent arrival in a letter from Cora.

Dear Harry,

Stephen is coming on the ship that carries this letter to America, as correspondent in the U.S.-Spain row. I suppose you will see him as doubtless Key West will be the headquarters for the newspaper men. We have thought it best for me to remain in England. I am writing to ask you and your good wife—if she be in the same town, to look after him a little. He is rather seedy and I am anxious about him for he does not care to look out for himself. Adoni goes with him but you know what the Greek servant is. And if he should be ill I beg you to wire me.[2]

When Crane arrived he immediately gravitated to the roulette room of the Eagle Tavern, where he became the center of an admiring circle of newspapermen. One who was not impressed, however, was Frances Scovel. She had been hearing Stephen Crane stories since the early days of her courtship, but Crane in person was a disappointment. He was, she decided, a "quicksilver" personality, a "queer little man with much ego, some vanity, and an inferiority complex."[3]

Her husband's attitude toward Crane, she later recalled, was, " 'That's my little brother, isn't he smart?' . . . I don't think they had a moral between them, but they did have ethics, and traditions of honesty and bravery."[4]

But Frances was infuriated that none of the correspondents, Harry included, seemed to grasp that Stephen was a sick man. Having been a volunteer nurse, she recognized the peculiar glassy color of the whites of his eyes as a sign of TB, and she was convinced that the "out of this world" manner that the men mistook for a low-grade buzz of intoxication was a symptom of his illness.

At his wife's urging, Scovel did try to protect Crane by assigning him to replace Ralph Paine on board the *New York*, but this arrangement ended when the secretary of the navy ordered all correspondents except the AP's Chappie Goode off the flagship. At this point, Crane joined the *World*'s number-two dispatch boat, the *Three Friends*.

As a result of an agreement with the *Herald*, which gave Scovel and Kenealy access to that paper's yacht, the *Sommers N. Smith*, the passengers on the *Three Friends* included *Herald* reporters Harry Brown and Ernest McCready as well as Ralph Paine. Crane was intrigued by the coincidence that he, Brown, McCready, and Paine were all ministers' sons. There the four of them were, apostates from the faith of their fathers, tooling around warship-infested waters in an unarmed tugboat, an activity, Crane thought, that would have been better reserved for men who believed in God's power to protect them from harm. They wore their pajamas day in and day out, and with nothing much to write about, they passed the time drinking warm beer and making up obscene lyrics to half-remembered sea chanteys.

On May 1, Admiral Sampson detached a flotilla from the blockade line and began sailing east toward the Windward Passage and Puerto Rico in the hope of finding the Spanish fleet. Despite an attempt to keep the plan a secret, the press learned of the admiral's intentions and all the dispatch boats came racing out of Key West to catch up with the flagship. But the flotilla's progress was painfully slow, mostly due to mechanical troubles with the unwieldy monitors *Amphitre* and *Terror,* and one by one the press boats gave up and deserted the convoy. Four days out of Havana, some crewmen from the converted yacht *Hornet* visited several of the boats and began regaling the bored newspapermen with the story of their recent run-in with a Spanish gunboat in Matanzas Bay. The *Hornet*'s misadventure was scarcely newsworthy, but with nothing better to do the crew chiefs of the *Three Friends* and the AP boat *Dauntless* decided to order a quick trip back to Key West to file copy on the incident. A race developed, continuing even after the cabin of the *Three Friends* was set on fire by sparks from its red-hot funnel. The tug's fire hose was steam driven and skipper Montcalm Broward, caught up in the spirit of the race, strictly forbade the passengers to waste steam in attempting to douse the flames. The *Three Friends* arrived in Key West blazing merrily away but in time for Ernest McCready to leap onto the dock and race the fastest of the AP reporters to the door of the cable office. McCready won, but repairs to the tug took several days, causing the *World-Herald* team to miss the American shelling of San Juan.

The *Journal*'s boat *Anita*, meanwhile, had also separated from the flagship, heading to Cap-Haïtien, Haiti, to take on coal. Before it had gone very far the *Anita* was hailed by the battleship *Indiana* and asked to take on a passenger, Lieutenant Henry Whitney, the Bureau of Military Intelligence officer who had been trying to get to Gómez's camp since the beginning of the war. According to *Leslie's* correspondent Edwin Emerson, Jr., who was a passenger on the *Anita*, Whitney had been on board for some hours when a chance remark of his brought out that he wanted to go to Cape Mayti (Cape Maisí) on the eastern tip of Cuba, not Cape Hayti (Cap-Haïtien). The confusion seems incredible—Cape Mayti, being in Spanish hands, was not a logical destination for a dispatch boat—but the story is typical of the hapless misadventures that marked Whitney's "mission to Gómez."

Edwin Emerson's father and namesake was the author of such popular boys' adventures as *Dingle the Outlaw, or the Secret Slayer* and *Dusky Darrell, Trooper, or the Green Ranger of Yellowstone*. Of the various American reporters who became involved to one degree or another with intelligence work for the navy, Emerson's case was unique. A strange, sardonic man, he had a grudge against the *Journal*, which he believed had overcharged him for passage on the paper's dispatch boats. In fact, the only person in Key West for whom he had a good word was "Sylvester Scovel's pretty wife," with whom he danced at the press corps party at the Key West Hotel on April 15. He had no journalistic experience—at the time the war began he was the secretary of the School of Education at Columbia University—but Teddy Roosevelt, a friend of the family, had personally signed his press credential. Reading between the lines of Emerson's cryptic autobiography, *Pepys' Ghost*, one infers that he was a spy first and a correspondent second rather than the other way around.

According to Emerson, he and Whitney first tried to get to Santiago, Cuba, on a banana boat. When they failed, they changed their plans—on whose authority Emerson never said—and headed for Puerto Rico to make contact with the insurgents there. With the help of the British consul in the Virgin Islands, Whitney reached Ponce disguised as a stoker on the British vessel *Adenrose*. Emerson, who was born in Dresden, entered San Juan with forged papers identifying him as a German reporter named Emile Ennersohn. Crossing the island by foot and on horseback, Emerson was arrested in Caguas but escaped by bribing his guard and stealing a horse from a livery stable across the town square from the jail. After a wild ride, he reached the insurgents, who helped him to escape to St. Thomas hidden among a cargo of sugarcane.

Emerson's exploit was one of the better-publicized spying missions of all time. His plan was announced in the St. Thomas papers at the time of his departure for Puerto Rico, and he later described the journey extensively in a series in *Leslie's*, in *Century* magazine, and in his autobiography. "Happily," Emerson wrote, "there need be no conflict between my duty to my country and the steadfast loyalty by which war correspondents are spurred to do their utmost duty."[5] Nevertheless, his accounts read like a travelogue and none discloses the nature of his contacts with the insurgents.

Another spy active in Puerto Rico was George Rea. After his first escape from the island in April, he attempted to return as a passenger on the French flag vessel *Rodrigues*, bound from St. Thomas to Jamaica. The Spanish authorities learned of his plans, and only the presence of a French naval vessel in San Juan Harbor saved him from being taken off the *Rodrigues* and, most likely, shot. Despite being unable to go ashore, Rea managed to take photos of the harbor fortifications through his porthole window and compile a report that was used by Sampson to direct the naval bombardment of San Juan on May 15.

However, Sampson's flotilla failed to find Cervera's fleet, and another eighteen days would pass before the Spanish warships were located. Finding the enemy had always been one of the challenges of naval warfare, but in the age of telegraphy the delay seemed agonizingly long. The New York *Herald* with its worldwide network of stringers actually outperformed U.S. government intelligence in tracking Cervera's fleet. A *Herald* reporter in the Cape Verde Islands followed the Spanish ships for twelve hours in a chartered boat when they departed from St. Vincent on April 29, and another *Herald* stringer in Martinique was the first to report its arrival in the western hemisphere. Shortly thereafter, the U.S. War Office had confirmation from its agent in the Havana cable office that Cervera's ships were refueling at Santiago de Cuba.

Even so, the War Office was not sure its Havana spy was credible. Commodore Winfield Scott Schley's Flying Squadron, which had been held at Norfolk in case the Spanish should decide to attack the American coastal cities, was dispatched to patrol the southern coast of Cuba in search of Cervera. Schley was possessed by the fixed idea that the enemy was inside Cienfuegos harbor, and despite indications to the contrary from Key West, the stubborn, befuddled old commodore set up a cordon around the harbor entrance and sat tight.

Harry Scovel, who had faith in the power of systematic observation, reasoned that a sure way to locate the Spanish would be to circle the island in a fast boat. As usual, the *World* was remiss about forwarding expenses so he spent several thousand dollars of his own money to fuel and provision the *Sommers N. Smith* for a joint *World-Herald* expedition.

During a week when the Caribbean was swept by torrential storms and fifty-mile-an-hour winds, the yacht, which Richard Harding Davis had compared favorably with Commodore Benedict's, succeeded in circumnavigating Cuba in seven days, covering a distance of 1,586 miles. On several occasions it was mistaken for a Spanish vessel and fired on by U.S. ships. On one occasion the USS *Dolphin* fired a warning from a distance of three miles. The cannonball passed between the masts of the moving yacht, clearing the deck at an elevation of fifteen feet.

After all this, the expedition failed. The *Smith* was accosted off Santiago by the scout ship *St. Paul.* After assuring the correspondents that Cervera was not at Santiago, the *St. Paul*'s captain, who was none other than Charles Sigsbee, strongly advised them to get out of the area. Assuming that Sigsbee must know what he was talking about, Scovel, Hare Whigham, and the rest of the expedition returned to Key West on the morning of June 1. As they tied up, a newsboy appeared on the dock hawking a morning paper with the headline, SPANISH FLEET BOTTLED UP AT SANTIAGO!

After a series of blunders so egregious that Schley would later be investigated by a navy court of inquiry, the commodore at last reached Santiago where, as both the AP and the *Herald* had been reporting for days, he found Cervera's fleet in the harbor. Sampson hurried south with his flotilla, and on the way he and a young ensign, Richmond Hobson, planned the war's first "thrilling exploit," as the memoirists called it. Assisted by seven volunteers, Hobson transformed the disabled collier *Merrimac* into a floating bomb by festooning the hull with ten watertight cans, each loaded with seventy-eight pounds of dynamite. In the predawn hours, the volunteer crew glided the craft into the channel at the mouth of Santiago harbor where Hobson detonated the dynamite. This was considered a suicide mission by everyone except Hobson, who brought along a small catamaran in which all hands made their escape. Taken prisoner by the Spanish, the bluejackets were grinning from ear to ear, amazed to be alive.

Practically speaking, Hobson's plan was a failure since he was not able to block the entrance to the harbor. Nevertheless, the young engineering graduate was the first genuine hero of the war, and the newspaper boats rushed to file their stories. Most headed southward to the cable office in Port Antonio, Jamaica, but Montcalm Broward of the *Three Friends* decided to make for Le Môle St. Nicholas, Haiti. The presence of warships in the Caribbean had unsettled Haiti's precarious political equilibrium, and the correspondents arrived in Le Môle St. Nicholas just as the army was in the last stages of putting down a coup attempt. The governor's palace was cordoned off, the cable office was closed, and the local merchants were unwilling to load coal on an American ship. Fortunately, when the governor's bemedaled, gold-epauletted chief of staff made his appearance, Stephen Crane got him talking and discovered that the official had formerly been a butler for a family in New Rochelle, New York. Suddenly, Crane and the butler were the best of friends, and the visit ended with the correspondents throwing a party on the beach for the entire provincial army, with rum at forty cents per gallon dispensed via a hose.

Crane hadn't bathed in weeks and his breath was described by Ernest McCready as "circumambient." Yet, to the amazement of his companions, he was the center of attention everywhere he went. Laughing children followed him, the chief of staff thought him a capital fellow, and during the party he was continually approached by attractive young women, disappearing with several of them for long stretches of time. In all the excitement, he never got around to writing anything about Hobson, but this did not bother Crane, who complained that anyhow he could not see the point of so many competing writers scrambling to cable home news stories that were essentially the same.

Back in New York, the navy spy Edwin Emerson arrived by ship from St. Thomas on June 8. Ragged, sunburned, and alarmingly "bushy" looking, Emerson had not a penny in his pockets and had to hike up Broadway from the docks to the Union Square office of *Leslie's* publisher, Frank Arkell. There he learned that Arkell's firm had gone into receivership that very day. *Leslie's* would survive under new ownership, but no one in the office had the authority to issue Emerson his back pay.

This experience only confirmed Emerson's sour impression of journalism as a profession. A week later, however, he enjoyed a moment of revenge. Called to Washington to brief Secretary of War Alger and General Miles on his mission to Puerto Rico, Emerson found himself sharing a couch in the secretary's waiting room with none other than William Randolph Hearst. At the beginning of the war, Emerson had paid three hundred dollars to Arthur Brisbane on the understanding that he would be allowed to sail on the *Journal's* fine 130-foot yacht, *Buccaneer.* Days later, Hearst donated the *Buccaneer* to the war effort, and Emerson was stuck on the much inferior *Anita.* Now it developed that despite the gift of the *Buccaneer,* Hearst had been left cooling his heels in every waiting room in Washington. At a time when it seemed that every postmaster's second cousin was being offered a commission—and John Jacob Astor, who also donated a yacht, had been made a lieutenant colonel—Hearst was told that he would have to await the decision of the "review board" that was supposedly debating the merits of his request.

The humiliating treatment of Hearst had nothing at all to do with the administration's disapproval of the yellow press. He was being punished for having supported William Jennings Bryan and for all those wicked political cartoons lampooning McKinley and Mark Hanna. Amazingly, considering the shrill, often bullying tone of his newspapers, Hearst in person was a self-effacing man, one who had all he could do to talk face-to-face to the powerful, much less take advantage of his own wealth and position to obtain favors.

Hearst's navy commission did not come through until after the war was over. In the meantime, he was pursuing his own schemes to further the war effort. One of his bright ideas was for James Creelman, who was in London when the war broke out, to purchase "some big English steamer" and sink it in the Suez Canal, thereby preventing the Spanish from sending Admiral Camara's fleet to the Philippines to fight Dewey. Despite some qualms that the plan might draw Britain into the war on Spain's side, Creelman set about looking for a suitable ship. Hearst's idea, he later wrote, was "a piece of heartfelt, practical patriotism combined with a Napoleonic stroke of advertising."[6] Moreover, if it resulted in saving Dewey's fleet from destruction, few would quibble about the legalities.

Spain ultimately decided not to send Camara to the Pacific after all, and Creelman sailed for the United States to join Hearst in another adventure. Realizing at last that he was not going to be made an officer, Hearst had decided to go to the front as a reporter. He was to travel in yet another chartered steamer, the *Sylvia*, a luxury edition of a dispatch boat fitted out with fresh fruit, ice, medical supplies and, according to one passenger, "enough chemicals to start a photographic laboratory."[7] A few cynics noted that Hearst, who was suspected of having political ambitions, had an obvious motive for having lots of photographs taken of himself touring the war zone, but on the whole, public reaction to the junket was favorable.

Aside from promoting Hearst's image as a patriot and giving him a chance to play war correspondent, the *Sylvia* venture did have a serious purpose. In addition to Hearst's friend and secretary George Pancoast, a camera buff, and photographer J. C. Hemment, the yacht's passengers included two Biograph cameramen who planned to make a moving picture record of the war. Unfortunately, the film they took of the action has been lost.

* * *

While Hearst was preoccupied with getting into the war, Arthur Brisbane, his star in the ascendent at the *Journal,* was pumping up the evening edition's circulation to dizzying heights. He had become infatuated with the fudge box, a pressroom innovation that made it possible to insert new material without recomposing an entire page. With the benefit of fudging, the evening *Journal,* increasingly the dominant voice of the paper, was able to issue as many as forty-three editions in a single day, the first hitting the streets as early as eight A.M. Obviously, there could never be enough genuine war news to justify so many extras, so the desperate editors resorted to outright fabrications. The embarkation of the troops from Tampa was announced on a half-dozen occasions. Other favorite "scoops" were the fall of San Juan, Puerto Rico, and the destruction of Santiago's defenses—each reported several times.

One might think that the public would resent being hoaxed and stop buying the paper. Much to Brisbane's surprise and delight, this never happened. At the height of the frenzy the evening *Journal* sold 1,868,000 copies in a single day, and it could have sold more, Brisbane boasted, if only the printers had not run out of paper. Since the daily *Journal* was still selling for a penny, no one was making money from this madness but Brisbane, whose bonus clause had pushed his salary for the year up to the $140,000 range.

Over at the Dome, the editors of the *World* had fallen into the trap of trying to match the *Journal* edition for edition. The *World* had missed its chance to negotiate an end to the price war the previous autumn. Now even a unilateral truce had become unthinkable because the paper's old two-cent rival, the *Herald,* was thriving, making the most of its network of Caribbean stringers and the services of such big-name correspondents as Dick Davis and Poultney Bigelow.

Pulitzer was so distraught over the *World*'s financial troubles that he canceled his usual summer stay in Bar Harbor and took a house in Amagansett. So in addition to coping with the crisis at the office, editors and business executives from the Dome were kept busy shuttling out to Long Island. The rented house, owned by the W. A. Miles family, commanded a breathtaking view of the sea, but visitors found the atmosphere inside grim. The Pulitzers were still mourning their daughter Lucille, who had died in December 1897 after being stricken with typhoid just two weeks after her coming-out party.

Adding to the gloom, the elderly Mrs. Jefferson Davis and her daughter Varina were also visiting. Joseph and Kate Pulitzer had at one time taken a warm interest in Varina, supporting her secret engagement to a Yankee and generally doing their best to rescue her from her unsought role as the "Daughter of the Confederacy." But Varina had given in to the advice of friends and broken the engagement. Now in her early thirties, she was a sad, spinsterish woman who seemed to become more ethereal by the day. During the course of the summer she became bedridden, and on September 18, she died.

No matter how bad his personal and business problems, such things seldom had the power to plunge Pulitzer to the depths of depression. Only a political defeat could do that, and before the war was fairly begun he had already come to regard it as a major disaster. Pulitzer had supported the war against Spain under the impression that it would be fought for a just cause, the liberation of Cuba. Now the refusal of the United States to make an alliance with Gómez and the absence of any serious effort to send relief to hungry civilians anywhere on the island convinced him that he had been betrayed.

In early June, the *World* was still hopefully reporting as imminent the invasion of Havana by an army of forty thousand men commanded by Fitzhugh Lee. On the editorial page, however, the paper denounced the "famine blockade of Havana" and hinted that something sinister was going on in Washington: "Why rob ourselves of the fruits of victory [by] refusing to take Havana? Why descend from the sublime of Hobson's heroism to the ridiculousness of corpse-stabbing?"

Accompanying the editorial, the paper published a "calendar," which read in part:

MAY—
19—Nothing done.
20—Nothing done.

21—Nothing done.
22—Nothing done.
23—Nothing done.
24—Nothing done.
25—Seventy thousand more volunteers called out. Nothing
    done.
26—Nothing done.
27—Nothing done.
28—Nothing done.
29—Nothing done.
30—Nothing done.
31—Schley released from "orders from Washington," shuts Cer-
    vera in Santiago Harbor.[8]

The implication was that Schley's seeming incompetence was part of a deliberate conspiracy to prolong the war until the United States had time to occupy the Philippines and Puerto Rico. Although the *World* was going too far in suggesting that Schley was malingering, it was true that the McKinley administration was in no hurry to end the war before San Juan and Manila had been secured. Saying this outright, however, was considered shocking —even the *Journal* restrained its criticisms of the administration while American troops were actually in the field—and both Pulitzer's Republican opponents in Washington and the pro-Bryanite *Journal* wasted no opportunity to attack the *World* as unpatriotic, even treasonous.

The *World*'s counterattacks against the *Journal* were equally nasty. When American troops in Tampa took possession of Hearst's donated yacht, the *Buccaneer,* the *World* published an item entitled ZEAL BY THEFT IN NEWS-GETTING THWARTED AT TAMPA, charging that the yacht had been seized because, "It is said that correspondents on that vessel are suspected of having obtained government plans and documents and intended to sail for some port where they could send the matter by wire."[9] Hearst responded to this canard by filing a half-million-dollar libel suit against the *World.*

If there was one thing that the editors of the *World* and the *Journal* agreed on during this period it was that field correspondents were, at best, a necessary evil. Both Artie Brisbane and the

World's Don Seitz, in magazine articles written after the war, would complain bitterly of the high costs of gathering news in wartime. In one widely quoted piece in *McClure's Magazine,* Brisbane estimated that salaries, cable fees, the rental of press boats, and coal bills cost the *Journal* a minimum of three thousand dollars a day. Of course, Brisbane did not mention that his own salary was about three thousand dollars a week, and in any event, the cost of news gathering did not begin to account for why the *Journal* had lost eight million dollars in its first three years of operation.

A few literary stars like Stephen Crane and Richard Harding Davis still enjoyed the luxury of writing long, descriptive essays that were forwarded north by mail, but most of their colleagues knew that their jobs might depend on getting their stories on the cable five minutes before the competition did. Under the circumstances, it is hardly surprising that correspondents sometimes promoted rumors to the status of fact.

The *World* staff, which never numbered more than six correspondents at any one time—in contrast to the *Journal,* which had two dozen correspondents and twelve boats—was under especially heavy pressure. Unable to compete with the sheer volume of copy wired north by *Journal* men, crew chief Francis Nichols settled in at the Titchfield Hotel in Port Antonio, Jamaica, where he devoted himself to the time-honored journalistic art of rewriting the competition's stories. Artie Brisbane himself was no slouch at cribbing—he later boasted that when he took over the evening *Journal* he had only two correspondents, one of whom was assigned to stand outside the Dome and snatch up copies of each new edition of the *World* and race them back to the *Journal*'s offices. Nevertheless, he pretended to be morally outraged by Nichols's actions.

Resorting to a ruse he had learned from Pulitzer, who had used it to embarrass a rival paper during his early days in St. Louis, Brisbane planted a story in the *Journal* about the death of a certain Austrian artillery officer, Colonel Reflipe W. Thenuz, who had been killed at Aguadores, near Santiago, where he was serving with the Spanish army under Colonel Ordonez (odor-nose). Sure enough, a few days later the *World* duly reported the tragic demise of Thenuz, whereupon the *Journal* came forward with the announcement that Reflipe W. Thenuz was an anagram, more or less, for "We pilfer the news." Sarcastically, the *Journal* announced plans for a "Thenuz Memorial" and began soliciting artists' designs for an appropriate monument. For days it printed letters, a few possibly even authentic, denouncing Pulitzer and his employees as plagiarists.

The Thenuz hoax is arguably the best-known practical joke in the annals of journalism, but there is a twist to the story that previous published accounts fail to mention. Mysteriously, the "news" of Thenuz's death appeared at the end of a long story about Haiti that carried the byline of Ralph Paine. In punishment, Paine was banished from the *World*'s dispatch boats for the rest of the campaign and his replacement on the *Three Friends* was ...Francis Nichols. Considering that Brad Merrill and Scovel had been trying to get rid of Ralph Paine since the day Seitz signed him up, one can't help but think that this turn of affairs was no accident.

Despite such finagling, the correspondents in the field were doing their best under difficult circumstances, trying to satisfy the hysterical demands of their home offices while serving Admiral Sampson virtually as a naval auxiliary. In addition to the intelligence-gathering work done by the *World* staff, most of the newspaper teams were kept busy ferrying messages between ships and to nearby cable offices for transmission to Washington. For these services they received no appreciation; the Department of the Navy could not acknowledge the contribution of the press without implicitly admitting its own failure to provide proper support services for its modernized fleet. In the meantime the shrill rhetoric and constant trading of wild charges indulged in by their editors devalued their work, providing ammunition for those who considered the presence of correspondents in the theater of war undignified and unnecessary. The image of the correspondents fostered by critics such as E. L. Godkin and perpetuated in many subsequent books was that they were irresponsible scalawags who cared nothing about the welfare of the troops and would not hesitate to violate censorship in pursuit of a good story.

This could not have been more unfair. If anything, the correspondents erred on the side of unquestioning devotion to the "new Navy," which in their eyes could do no wrong. So far, only a few of the most senior correspondents had given much thought to the possible conflicts between truth-telling and patriotic boosterism. But with the landing on the Cuban coast only days away, that situation was about to change dramatically.

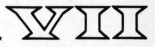

The Conquest
of Santiago

Guantánamo

But to get at the real thing! It seems impossible!
—Vernall, the correspondent
in Stephen Crane's "The Sergeant's Private Madhouse"

ONE YEAR and eight months after he signed up with Irving Bacheller to become a correspondent in Cuba, Stephen Crane finally found his war. On June 7, 1898, an advance party of 150 marines accomplished the first landing of American troops on Cuban soil at Guantánamo, forty miles west of Santiago. The landing was made late in the day, and the marines' commander, Colonel Huntington, had chosen a site on high ground on the eastern arm of the bay. When the *Three Friends* arrived close on to nightfall, Crane was struck by the contrast between the steel blue of the water and the ominous glow of the palm trees, their fronds turned into giant "crimson feathers" by the reflected glow of the soldiers' campfires. Down at the shoreline, a few parties of marines were still unloading their three-inch fieldpieces. As they worked, they sang "There'll be a hot time in the old town tonight," the popular song that had become the unofficial anthem of the campaign.

In addition to the *Three Friends*, the *Anita*, the *Sommers*

303

N. Smith, and the *Sun's* boat *Kanapaha* were on the scene. But oddly, considering how eager all the newsmen had been to see some action, only a handful of reporters stayed with the marines when the boats returned to Haiti and Jamaica to file their stories. Among this small group was H. J. Whigham, who remarked to the others that Huntington's choice of a campsite on an exposed hillside surrounded by higher peaks seemed to offer a perfect opportunity for enemy snipers.

Whigham's fears proved correct. About three thousand Spanish irregulars were in the vicinity. The next afternoon at about three o'clock, the shooting started. Many of the marines were bathing in the bay and had no chance to grab their clothes or shoes as they sprinted up the hill to their posts. Colonel Huntington ordered some of them to charge the spot in the jungle where the firing seemed to be coming from. "This was no fun for naked men," observed the *Journal* correspondent on the scene, but the enemy had vanished.

The sniper fire continued off and on all evening until shortly before midnight when the *guerrilleros* opened fire in earnest. When the action started, Crane was on his way to see army surgeon John Blair Gibbs, who had noticed that Crane was not well and had begun treating him with quinine. Gibbs was thirty-nine years old, a well-known yachtsman, and a socially prominent citizen of New Brunswick, New Jersey. His father, a major in the cavalry, had perished with Custer at Little Big Horn, and when war was declared he became the first physician to volunteer for duty.

Gibbs was standing just inside his tent door talking to Thomas Steep, a correspondent from *Leslie's.* "Well, I don't want to die in the place . . ." Before he could finish his sentence, he was shot through the head.

Gibbs fell forward and someone scurried from cover and pulled him into the same trench Crane had just dived into. For the rest of the night the men in the trench lay in total darkness, about seven feet apart, Crane and several marines listening helplessly while Gibbs gasped in his death throes. "He took a long time to die," wrote Crane. "He was long past groaning. There was only the bitter strife for air. . . . I held my own breath in the common unconscious aspiration to help. I thought this man would never die. I wanted him to die.

"I was," he wrote, "a child who, in a fit of ignorance, had jumped into a vat of war."[1]

On June 10, another five hundred marines arrived on the USS *Panther,* joining the advance party and a detachment of insurgents sent by Gómez to assist in the landing. The Spanish were not heard from until the next night, Saturday, when they once again surrounded the camp. This time the enemy was so close that its front lines were within revolver range of the marines' tents. When night fell Crane found himself near a position where four marine signalmen were sending wigwag messages to the *Marblehead* and the *Dolphin,* which had trained their guns on the *guerrilleros'* positions in the hills. The signalmen used two lanterns, one set up on a cracker box and the other moved by hand to create various signal patterns. Naturally, the lanterns made ideal targets, and Crane found himself mesmerized by the businesslike way the marines went about sending their messages, apparently oblivious to the danger of their situation. "I could lie near and watch the face of the signalman, illumed as it was by the yellow shine of lantern light, and the absence of excitement, fright, or any emotion at all upon his countenance was something to astonish all theories out of one's mind."[2]

In all his writing about the war, Crane unsparingly described his own fears, even admitting that he stayed awake at night hoping he would be struck with some serious illness to spare him from getting close to the shooting. But these private terrors were not at all apparent to those around him. Captain George Elliott was so impressed by Crane's cool behavior under fire that when he was ordered to take two companies of men inland to destroy the irregulars' water supply, he asked him to come along. During the fighting, Crane acted as a runner, carrying messages between the company commanders. Captain Elliott later submitted a letter to the secretary of the navy officially commending Crane for his contribution to the fight, and another officer, Major Charles McCawley, wrote to him in 1899, saying, "I, in company with all my brother officers, have always looked back with pleasure and pride upon your service with us in Cuba, for you were the only outsider who saw it all, and we regard you as an honorary member of the Corps."[3]

Out of Crane's days at Guantánamo came one of his best sketches, "The Red Badge of Courage Was His Wig-Wag Flag," published in the *World* on July 1, 1898. The paper should have been satisfied, but it was not. Crane did not finish his sketch until June 22, and in the meantime, when Paine, McCready, and Harry Brown returned from Haiti, they found it frustratingly difficult to elicit from Crane a concise account of what had gone on while they were away. Crane came on board the boat looking incredibly haggard, his mind already full of images for his "wig-wag" sketch, while McCready desperately tried to get him to dictate the facts of the sniper attack and Dr. Gibbs's death.

"It was a ridiculous scene," Paine recalled later. "McCready, the conscientious reporter, waiting with pencil and paper—Crane, the artist, deliberating over this phrase and that, finicky about a word, insisting upon frequent changes and erasures, and growing more and more suspicious. Finally he exclaimed: 'Read it aloud, Mac, as far as it goes. I believe you are murdering my stuff.'

" 'I dropped a few adjectives here and there, Steve,' McCready retorted. 'This has to be *news*, sent at cable rates. You can save your flub-dub and send it to New York by mail.' "[4]

After Guantánamo, Crane reported, "I fell into the hands of one of my closest friends."[5]

This of course was Scovel, who had shown up at Guantánamo with Alexander Kenealy in the *Triton*. He was going on a scouting mission for Admiral Sampson in the hills above Santiago and he offered Crane a chance to come along.

Sampson was eager to know the exact position of Cervera's ships in the harbor, and either to verify or disprove a rumor that the Spanish battleship *Vizcaya* had slipped out past the blockade during the night. Lieutenant Victor Blue had gone ashore a few days earlier but had been unable to get closer than three and a half miles to the harbor. Scovel thought he could do better, and, said Crane, "he mercilessly outlined a scheme for landing to the west of Santiago and getting through the Spanish lines."[6]

On the morning of June 17, Scovel, Crane, and Kenealy reached Playa Juan Gonzalez, thirteen miles west of Santiago.

Scovel and Kenealy planted a *World* banner on the beach, establishing what the *World* grandly proclaimed as its "first permanent headquarters on Cuban soil." They also raised the single-star banner of the Cuban republic. The U.S. government may not have recognized the existence of the Cuban government, but the New York *World* had, no doubt much to the annoyance of the McKinley administration.

While Kenealy returned to Jamaica, Scovel and Crane made the trip up Mount St. Augustín, two days of hard climbing. Scovel had brought two Jamaican polo ponies with him and they made the first part of the journey on horseback, marveling at the boundless energy of their ragged Cuban guides who informed them that they had eaten nothing but mangoes for three weeks, yet still scrambled up and down the steep trails "like rats." The scenery was so lush that even Scovel, who seldom wasted words on mere description, could not resist extolling the pristine air, the clear mountain streams, and the dazzling profusion of tropical flowers. In camp, Crane and Scovel lay awake in their hammocks long into the night, smoking and listening to the Cuban music (some "afric wail," Crane called it) and contemplating the stars, which seemed as "big as coconuts."[7]

Their sense of having entered a different world, remote from war and politics, was jolted when Scovel got into a conversation with one of the camp sentries, a tall, muscular black man who was patiently removing a day's accumulation of thorns from the thickly calloused soles of his feet. "Where are your shoes?" Scovel asked in Spanish. "I lose dem in de woods," the sentry replied in English accented with the unmistakable echoes of the Bowery. To Crane's delight, the Cuban explained that his name was Joe Riley and he had lived for a time on Mulberry Street.[8]

The next morning the correspondents left their ponies in camp and covered another six miles on foot, sneaking past a line of Spanish pickets, until they were able to descend the side of the mountain to a good vantage point overlooking the harbor. And "there upon the bosom of the green-fringed harbor," Scovel wrote, "lay Cervera's once-dreaded fleet."[9]

One of the Cuban guides had been carrying a mysterious parcel wrapped in a dirty towel and tied up with vines. Carefully unwrapping it, he produced a telescope and handed it to Scovel, who climbed a tree and began sketching a map of the ships' locations while Riley and the others fanned out to stand guard.

Crane lay down in the grass to rest. He had been feeling weak all day. Now he realized that his legs had turned to "dough." His spine burned like "a red hot wire." In agony, he forced himself to remain ambulatory as far as the camp where they had left their ponies.

Ironically, he and Scovel had been discussing how healthy the mountain air was, and how Mount St. Augustín might make a good spot for a TB sanitarium after the war. Of course, it is quite possible that whatever fever Crane had was contracted only days earlier; nevertheless, it is curious that Crane and Scovel, who got sick later, would eventually die of similar complaints, with symptoms that may well have been complications of a tropical disease.

In the short run, Crane was feeling much better by the time Kenealy returned with the dispatch boat to take them to Port Antonio, and he kept quiet about his illness for fear that the Jamaican authorities might be motivated to quarantine the *World*'s boats.

Scovel, meanwhile, was jubilant. On the way down the mountains, the Cuban guides had shown him a promontory from which one could see both the coast and an observation point that looked down into the harbor. Scovel speculated that a team of wigwags could be established to relay messages to a ship offshore in order to direct a naval bombardment of Cervera's ships inside Santiago harbor. The Spanish fleet, he suggested, could be "annihilated" where it lay by "plunging fire over the coast bluffs."[10]

A Great Historical Expedition

O N JUNE 19, while Crane and Scovel were still reconnoitering on Mount St. Augustín, the Fifth Army arrived from Tampa, a great armada consisting of 48 ships, including 32 transports carrying 16,072 enlisted men, 815 officers, 89 correspondents, 2,295 horses and mules, 10 million pounds of rations, 4 light artillery batteries and various fieldpieces including Gatling guns and howitzers. Theodore Roosevelt had called the fleet a "great historical expedition.... If we are allowed to succeed (for we shall certainly succeed if we are allowed) we have scored the first great triumph in what will be a world movement." [1] No one, however, had called it a great military expedition.

The shortcomings of the Fifth Army were epitomized by its commanding general, sixty-three-year-old William Rufus Shafter. A Medal of Honor winner who had risen through the ranks after enlisting as a private, the gruff, plainspoken Shafter had been a colorful and certainly very visible officer. Weighing in at something over 330 pounds, he was well known for his parade appearances on a seventeen-hands-tall bay stallion that was said to be the largest horse in the army. Shafter was a lifelong cavalryman, presiding over an army whose most combat-ready units, for example, the Ninth and Tenth Regiment Buffalo Soldiers, were also cavalry. But because of space limitations, these units' mounts had been left behind in Tampa—along with those of the celebrated volunteer cavalry regiment, the Rough Riders, who would be fighting on foot. As for Shafter, even his loyal and very protective aide, Lieutenant John Miley, would later acknowledge that the veteran of so many rough-and-ready cavalry charges had no concept of the logistics of a major amphibious landing. The general, wrote Miley, "was extremely anxious to push on to Santiago with the utmost haste, and at first did not realize it would take a week to completely disembark the command and supplies."[2]

Lieutenant Miley already blamed the press for its criticisms of the handling of the *Gussie* expedition, and no doubt anticipating that this landing would be less than a textbook operation, he had made sure that the order for disembarkation listed the correspondents last. The newspapermen had been on board the transports for eight days, most of them sharing the troop's diet of "embalmed" beef and canned tomatoes, and now they were to be stuck on the transports, far from the shore, without so much as a briefing.

To Miley's dismay, however, he had no control over the press boats. At nine-forty on the morning of June 22, when the headquarters ship raised the blue peter to call for the preliminary shelling of the beach, the press boats were already bobbing just offshore. As soon as it became apparent that the Spanish defenders had fled during the night and the shelling had stopped, the boats lowered their dinghys and the correspondents of the AP, the *World*, the *Journal*, the *Herald*, and the *Sun* all swarmed ashore, taking up positions on the beach.

Presently, General Demetrio Castillo of the Cuban army appeared on the ridge behind the hamlet, accompanied by a mounted escort. Castillo's party was displaying a large Cuban flag, which the advance party of American scouts mistook for the Spanish colors. The Americans opened fire and got off about twenty shots before the yelling, gesticulating correspondents managed to get the message across to the scouts that they were firing on their allies.

In the meantime, the first of the boats from the transports were approaching the beach. Daiquirí, the site chosen for the landing on the advice of the Cubans, was a hamlet some sixteen miles east of Santiago that had formerly been the seaward end of a rail spur operated by the American-owned Spanish American Mining Company. The facilities on shore consisted of two piers. The first, an iron structure used for on-loading iron ore, was too high to be of any practical use. The second, a modest wooden dock, had been set on fire and vandalized the previous night by Spanish soldiers. The extent of the damage was not apparent to the Americans approaching in the first boat and as their craft rose on the crest of the swelling wave, the troops, weighed down by their bedrolls, rations, and one hundred rounds each of ammunition, leaped ashore as best they could. Some were lucky enough to land on solid planking; others went crashing through the gaps, suffering gashed legs and twisted knees and ankles before they had even set foot on Cuban soil.

The first of these mishaps may have been unavoidable. But as the day wore on, and wave after wave of boats discharged their passengers at the pier, the scene was repeated scores of times, to the horror of the watching correspondents. The *Journal*'s Edward Marshall, who had managed to hitch a ride ashore from one of the transports on the press boat *Anita*, complained that "although there were thousands of feet of loose boards piled on shore, our men were in too great a hurry to nail them to the bare timbers."[3]

As the afternoon wore on and the tide began to ebb, it was no longer possible even to jump to the pier. Soldiers flung themselves at the timbers and pulled themselves up onto the top of the pier as best they could. Two cavalrymen from the Tenth Regiment fell back into the water and were drowned. Luckily, most of the injuries were relatively minor, though to the soldiers who were about to begin a march through the jungle during the rainy season with open wounds on their shins and swollen knees, their injuries probably seemed serious enough.

For reasons no one understood, the army engineers, who

might have supervised on-the-spot repairs, had been dispatched down the coast to build pontoon bridges for the Cuban army, even though more urgent Cuban demands, such as for emergency food relief, had been denied. Worse yet, Shafter had failed to take into account that the transports were chartered boats with civilian captains and crews who could not be relied on to follow military discipline. In no hurry to have the honor of being first to approach the beach, many of the captains had taken their ships as far as five miles out to sea, where they remained until rounded up by navy torpedo boats. As a result, the troops were hitting the beach in no particular order, and some crucial cargo, including all the army's field ambulances, was never unloaded at all.

Moreover, once the units did reach the beach there was no one to tell them where to assemble and pitch camp. As Captain John Bigelow recalled, the sense that no one was in control was already having an affect on morale.

> I was looking at this time for a general order congratulating the troops on the success of the expedition thus far, commending them for their behavior on the transports, giving them some information about the enemy, and perhaps a hint of the plan of operation, and appealing to their pride and ambition to answer the extraordinary demands to be made upon them. As many of the officers had never been in the presence of their commanding General, I thought there would be a review, or that the General would take occasion to ride with his staff along the front of the troops drawn up in line, so that he could see them, and they him. But there was no inspiring or congratulatory order; and I, for one, never saw General Shafter during the campaign.[4]

Amazingly, despite the lack of direction, the landing was an overall success. Thanks to the good sense of the junior officers and men, and the absence of any resistance from the enemy, six thousand troops made it ashore by nightfall, with only two fatalities. What's more, by the following morning two regiments of the Second Division Infantry had already occupied Siboney, eight miles to the east, and some of the remaining transports were able to begin sending their men ashore there.

As for the press, Lieutenant Miley's fears proved groundless. Richard Harding Davis had kicked up so much fuss over the restrictions on the correspondents that Miley had finally given permission for him and an elite group including Stephen Bonsal and Fred Remington to be ferried ashore. Far from allowing his resentment to color his view of the day's events, Davis compared the operation to a regatta and the scene on the beach to "Coney Island on a hot Sunday."[5] Other newsmen followed suit, judging that this was not the moment for naysaying. Edward Marshall, for example, saved his criticisms for later and joined several of the Rough Riders in their project of scaling a thousand-foot peak in the hills behind Daiquirí to raise the Stars and Stripes over a deserted Spanish blockhouse, an escapade featured in many of the press accounts filed that day.

Among the few attempts at serious analysis, as opposed to cheerleading, was Scovel's bylined account that mentioned the accidental firing on the Cubans and warned that the approach to Santiago might be hampered by the lack of mule batteries and "bushwhacking teams." Nevertheless, he described the landing as "miraculously easy" and reported that the Cubans were "extremely happy despite the loss of a man's arm."[6]

While exercising a degree of self-censorship in writing about the failings of the commanding officer, the press had little trouble finding good stories. The best, of course, was the saga of the Rough Riders, the volunteer cavalry unit composed of wild West cowboys and Ivy League athletes. The enterprising Edward Marshall had attached himself to the Rough Riders during the race up the mountain to the Spanish blockhouse, and he was camped with the regiment the next night at Siboney when it received orders from General Joseph Wheeler. Cuban army units reported that they had chased the Spanish to a position about four miles west of Siboney. The Rough Riders, along with the regular army's First and Tenth Cavalries (all on foot since there had been room on the transports for only the officers' horses), were to push westward and knock out the Spanish gun emplacements to clear the way for a general advance. When the order to move came at 5:40 A.M., Marshall was part of the select group of correspondents invited to join the march, along with Kennett Harris of the Chicago *Record*, John Dunning of the AP and, inevitably, Richard Harding Davis.

Stephen Crane and Francis Nichols had spent the night at

the *World* tent in Playa del Este, where navy engineers had just managed to repair a severed cable, restoring telegraph communications with the United States. They arrived in Siboney just in time to see the regular army units heading down the main road while the last of the Rough Riders disappeared up a secondary trail that climbed the bluff behind the camp. While Nichols joined the regular cavalry, Crane hurried to catch up with "Teddy's Terrors," as he called them.

Despite his differences with Roosevelt over the Dora Clark affair, Crane greatly admired him for leaving a safe post in the Department of the Navy to come to the front. Nevertheless, he was terrified by the contrast between the professionalism of the marines he had marched with on their search-and-destroy mission at Guantánamo and the boisterous volunteers who were ambling along as if on their way to a picnic—"babbling joyously, arguing, recounting, laughing; making more noise than a train going through a tunnel."[7]

From time to time, when the clamor died down, one could hear the tremulous cooing of the wood dove deep in the forest. Crane recognized the species: This was no bird, but the "Spanish guerrilla wood-dove," whose call he had heard at Guantánamo. "Incidentally, I mentioned the cooing of the doves to some of the men, but they said decisively that the Spaniards did not use this signal. I don't know how they knew."[8]

Up ahead, the leaders of the march had stopped to rest in a glade. Dick Davis, who had been in eastern Cuba before, was delivering an impromptu lecture on the local flora and fauna to the regimental commander, Colonel Leonard Wood. Edward Marshall was sitting with Roosevelt, who was telling a funny story about meeting William Randolph Hearst at a luncheon at the Astor House in New York. As he talked, Roosevelt was idly examining some strands of the barbed-wire fence that ran between the trail and the grassy field on the left. The shiny ends of the cut wire caught his attention, and he held them up a few inches from his nose, peering at them intently through his thick glasses. "My God," he said, interrupting his own anecdote, "these wires have been cut today."[9]

About ten minutes later, Colonel Wood returned from a conference with his point man, Captain Allyn Capron, Jr., and quietly began deploying troops on either side of the trail. Before the men had moved out very far, the Spanish opened fire. For the next hour, the Spanish raked the Rough Riders' position while the Americans blindly stumbled forward through the thick brush, trying to locate the enemy position.

When the shooting was over, eight Rough Riders and eight regulars from General Samuel Young's column on the main road had been killed. Among the former were Captain Capron, a well-known amateur boxer and one of the most popular soldiers in the regiment, and Ham Fish, a grandson and namesake of Ulysses Grant's secretary of state and a former captain of the Columbia University rowing team.

Also among the casualties was Edward Marshall, who had suddenly found himself sprawled on the ground, unable to move his legs. He had heard no shot and he had felt no pain. He did not even feel surprised. He just lay there in shock, "perfectly satisfied and entirely comfortable in the long grass."[10]

Some time later, still lying where he had fallen, Marshall was examined by the regimental surgeon who suggested that if he had any messages he wanted sent home, "you better write 'em. Be quick." He was calmly dictating his third letter when the significance of the doctor's advice suddenly dawned on him.

By the time Stephen Crane reached the clearing where the shooting had taken place, someone yelled out to him, "There's a correspondent up there all shot to hell." Crane knew Marshall well. Before the publication of *The Red Badge of Courage*, when he was a starving free-lancer, Marshall had been with the *New York Post*, and one of the first editors to give him steady work.

"You'll be all right old boy," he told his friend. "What can I do for you?"

"Well, you might file my dispatches," Marshall replied. "I don't mean file them ahead of your own, old man—but just file 'em if you find it handy."

At that moment Crane was sure that Marshall was dying. "No man could be so sublime in detail concerning the trade of journalism and not die," he later quipped.[11]

Although there was still shooting going on, Crane turned back immediately, covering the five miles to the cable office at top speed to put Marshall's story on the wire to New York. As soon as the story was on its way, Crane rounded up Acton Davies of the *Sun* and Walter Howard and George Coffin of the *Journal* to take a stretcher back into the jungle and fetch their colleague. Several hours later, euphoric from shock, Marshall was carried aboard the hospital ship *Olivette* booming out the chorus of "On the Banks of the Wabash Far Away." Army surgeons reported that the bullet he had taken was too near his spine to be removed and predicted that he would never walk again.

Scovel thought Crane's transmission of Marshall's copy "a grand gesture." The Dome might have been more appreciative if Crane had bothered to write a story himself. The seven-sentence report he did file neglected to give the number of dead, their names, or to mention that units of the regular army had been involved in the fighting.

Ironically, it was the one accurate statement in Crane's dispatch that embroiled the *World* in a controversy. Crane called the action an ambush and "a gallant blunder." This was consistent with other early accounts, including that of Dick Davis, who used the word *ambush* in his story for the *Herald*. The consensus of these reports was that the Rough Riders had moved too fast, ignoring the advice of their scouts and allowing themselves to get out ahead of the regulars. Overeagerness was not the worst fault one could charge to amateur officers leading their first combat patrol. Nevertheless, Colonel Wood and Roosevelt were indignant over the implication that they might have been even partially responsible for the deaths of Fish, Capron, and the others.

Within twenty-four hours a revisionist version of the skirmish, by now being called Las Guásimas, had come to the fore. Wood and Roosevelt put all the blame on the Cuban scouts. According to a story by Stephen Bonsal in *McClure's*, the Cubans had misled the Rough Riders into thinking that the Spanish gun emplacement was half a mile farther down the road than it actually was.

Dick Davis, in a letter to his brother, acknowledged that the Cubans *had* given a warning. But, he wrote, "I thought it was a false alarm and none of us believed that there were any Spaniards this side of Santiago."[12] Davis, however, had been in the advance of the charge at Guásimas and had been commended for heroism in helping to locate the source of the enemy fire. Sensitive to the suggestion that he had impugned the judgment of Wood and Roosevelt, he devoted a subsequent dispatch to *Scribner's* to a rather tortuous explanation of the "vast difference between blundering into an ambuscade and setting out with full knowledge that you will find the enemy in ambush."[13]

Since the Cubans had been active in the area for years and had skirmished with the Spanish along the same road not forty-eight hours earlier, the charge that they had misled the Americans about the Spanish position was a serious one, implying either deliberate treachery or extreme dereliction of duty. Coming on the third day of the U.S. Army's presence on Cuban soil, the accusation dealt the coup de grace to the rapidly deteriorating relationship between the U.S. troops and the Cubans.

Despite all that had been written about starving Cuba, many of the better-educated Americans, officers and correspondents alike, had been more influenced by romantic tales of the Evangelina Cisneros variety. Landing at Daiquirí, they had expected to be welcomed as liberators by grateful dark-eyed señoritas and cheering crowds of "sturdy patriots" from the republican army.

Outlook magazine correspondent George F. Kennan, a Cuban sympathizer, wrote: "The Cubans disappointed me, I suppose, because I had pictured them to myself as a better dressed and better disciplined body of men, and had not made allowance enough for the hardships and privations of an insurgent's life." American soldiers were less tactful, describing the Cubans as "half-breed mongrels," "villains," and "mango-bellied degenerates." Wrote one American lieutenant: "The valiant Cuban! He strikes you first by his color. It ranges from chocolate yellow through all the shades to deepest black with kinky hair. The next thing you notice is the furtive look of the thief.... Next you notice that he is dirty.... He is infested with things that crawl and creep, often visibly, over his half-naked body."[14]

But not all of the bad feeling could be blamed on the prejudices of the Americans. General García had been greatly offended to learn that Shafter planned to use his men primarily as porters, hostlers, and trench diggers. "My men are soldiers, not laborers," García complained, and he made no effort to get his officers to enforce the arrangement. To the Yankees, not one in a hundred of whom had any notion that their intervention in the war had not been wanted to begin with, this attitude was infuriating. "The very

first time you suggest anything like manual labor," wrote one officer, " ...[the Cuban's] manly chest swells with pride and he ex-
claims in accents of wounded dignity, 'Yo soy soldado.'"
Americans complained bitterly that while they dug trenches in
the sweltering hundred-degree heat, Cuban units sat by gorging
themselves on the rations that had been distributed by the American commissary.[15]

And indeed, García's army had more than its share of hang-
ers-on—petty thieves, scroungers, and just plain desperate, hungry men who would steal anything in sight in their effort to
provide for hungrier families hiding out in the bush. Stephen
Crane could scarcely recognize the surly, unmotivated Cuban soldiers he met on this campaign as belonging to the same army as
the disciplined and courageous "stealthy woodsmen" he had seen
in action at Guantánamo. He correctly predicted that the situation
would have tragic implications for Cuba's future. "If [the Cuban
soldier] stupidly, drowsily remains out of these fights, what weight
is his voice to have later in the final adjustments? The officers and
men of the army, if their feeling remains the same, will not be
happy to see him have any at all."

Crane's prescription was simple and to the point: "The situation needs a Gómez."[16] But of course, Gómez's reputation as a
martinet was part of the reason the Americans wanted no part of
him. When it came to living up to the Americans' idealized image
of the patriot-soldier, the Cubans were between a rock and a hard
place.

However justified many of the complaints against the Cubans
might be, the charge that Castillo's scouts had led the Rough
Riders into danger at Las Guásimas went too far. On the evening
of the skirmish, George Bronson Rea, the last man to be preju-
diced in favor of the insurgents, interviewed the Cubans who had
been accused of dereliction of duty. He reported in the *World*
their complaint that Colonel Wood, in his hurry to keep ahead of
General Young's regulars, had refused to heed their advice. As a
result, there was no opportunity to execute a maneuver the Cubans had had in mind, which would have resulted in trapping the
Spanish position between the two American columns. Considering
that Rea's reputation had been built on his scathing assessment

of the Cubans, it was a bizarre twist that he now became the only American correspondent of any standing to raise his voice in their defense.

William Randolph Hearst, meanwhile, had decided to solve the mystery of General Shafter's absence from his own campaign. A few hours after the shooting ended at Las Guásimas, the *Journal* yacht *Sylvia* located the *Seguranca* several miles off Siboney. A rope ladder was lowered from the headquarters ship, and Hearst, six foot two and notoriously uncoordinated, scrambled awkwardly up onto the deck, followed by James Creelman, Jack Follansbee, photographer John Hemment, and two assistants, who were struggling to keep from being pulled backward into the sea by the bulky camera equipment strapped to their backs.

Shafter's well-known contempt for the press did not apply to Hearst, with whom he had a friendly relationship going back to the days when Shafter, then a colonel, had been stationed at Fort Ord. The *San Francisco Examiner* had given Shafter rafts of free publicity and he was returning the favor now by granting Hearst an exclusive interview.

Stripped down to his flannel shirt and trousers, Shafter greeted the *Journal* contingent in what had formerly been the main salon of the converted passenger liner. It soon became evident to his visitors, however, that Shafter would have little to say that was printable. A courier had just come on board with a report on the casualties at Las Guásimas and the general, as John Hemment noted, "was in a mood not truthfully to be described as pleasant." [17]

Despite his size, the sixty-three-year-old Shafter had been reasonably fit until he was stricken with an attack of gout during the journey from Tampa. After that, however, the campaign had quickly degenerated into an agonizing ordeal. On June 20, the day after the fleet's arrival, Shafter had gone ashore to confer with Admiral Sampson and the Cuban regional commander Calixto García at his headquarters high in the cliffs above Aserredero beach. He had been humiliated to discover that the Cuban camp could be reached only by climbing a steep switchback trail, an impossible task with his gouty leg. There were no horses available, and after a long delay the Cubans had finally produced a white mule—small but *"con mucho corazón,"* they assured him—that had managed to haul Shafter up the trail.

No doubt it was Shafter's desire to avoid a similar embarrassing display of his disability that had prompted him to remain on board the *Seguranca.* After thirty-eight years in the service he was not about to miss his chance to make history, as he surely would have been urged to do if his condition became known to General Miles in Washington.

The *Journal* contingent was shocked by Shafter's physical condition, his moodiness, and his apparent determination to run the campaign without setting foot on Cuban soil. "It occurred to me," Hemment wrote, "that as our forces were on shore, this ship was not the proper place for the general of the Fifth Army Corps." Nevertheless, Hearst personally wrote up an account of the visit to the *Seguranca,* praising the commanding general as a "bold, lion-headed hero . . . a sort of human fortress." This was followed a few days later by a profile in the *World,* based on interviews with veterans of Shafter's old First Infantry command, which described the General "jumping about lively as a cricket . . . [the sort of officer] who always has his coat off when anything is doing."[18]

Later the press would have many unkind things to say about Shafter, seeing his bloated, misshapen body as a metaphor for the campaign as a whole. But for the moment, he was being gently treated by correspondents who felt that to mention his singular remoteness from the action would be unpatriotic and bad for morale.

★★

The Chute of Death

ARMY OFFICERS and the press weren't alone in wondering what was going on with General Shafter. Admiral Sampson had met with the general just once, at the Cuban headquarters on June 20. Most of that conference had been concerned with plans for the landing. The strategy for the remainder of the campaign had been discussed only briefly, just long enough to create a misunderstanding. Sampson was under the impression that the army's objective would be to capture the forts guarding the entrance to Santiago harbor. Shafter, on the other hand, would always maintain that he had never voiced any such idea. He was planning a blunt, all-out assault on the city from the landward side.

Regardless of who was right—and there were arguments for both strategies—Shafter was certainly responsible for the breakdown in communications between the services. At their meeting, the general and his aide had made it clear that the army had primary responsibility for the campaign and that when Sampson's help was needed, Shafter would contact him.

By June 28, six days after the landing, Sampson had still heard nothing. Since an assault on the harbor forts would necessarily have to be supported by a naval bombardment, Sampson was mystified by the army's failure to provide him with up-to-date maps of the coastal fortifications. Etiquette prohibited sending a senior navy officer ashore without an invitation, so Sampson asked Scovel to lead a reconnaissance party consistiing of a navy topographic artist and two Cuban scouts.

Scovel took the precaution of paying a call on the *Seguranca* where Shafter signed a letter giving him permission to go ashore. In Siboney, however, his party ran into Lieutenant Miley, who was in camp making arrangements for Shafter to disembark from his headquarters ship for the first time. The task of preparing the way for the ailing general was not an easy one. Among other arrangements, Miley had ordered the construction of a platform that the general would use to mount his horse. The lieutenant was not in a good mood, and when he spotted Scovel, whom he associated with the *Gussie* fiasco, he blew up. Scovel explained their mission and produced his written orders, but Miley waved them away, insisting he had no business on the island.

The navy man, an ensign, took exception to being ordered around by an army lieutenant and a tremendous quarrel ensued, with Scovel in the middle. When it was over, and the navy party retreated to the *Triton*, they still had no inkling of Shafter's intentions.

The absence of good maps was also high on the mental list of the campaign's shortcomings that Dick Davis was quietly compiling. His horse had finally been unloaded from the transports on June 27, and despite an excruciating attack of sciatica, he and General Adna Chaffee had ridden together to the conical hill known as El Pozo about seven miles out of Siboney where American and Cuban pickets had established the invaders' forward lines. Just beyond El Pozo the Sevilla Road divided, the right fork snaking up into the foothills of the Sierra Maestra to the village of El Caney, while the left, the main route to Santiago, led down into the valley of the Aguadores River, where it disappeared from view, hidden by the impenetrable canopy of jungle vegetation.

Beyond, on the far side of the valley, rose the San Juan heights, the key to a land approach to Santiago. At first glance, Davis was impressed by the peaceful appearance of the red and blue farmhouses that clung to the side of San Juan Hill. Even the small Spanish blockhouse visible on the heights resembled "a Chinese pagoda," more quaint than threatening. But as he and Chaffee studied the scene through their field glasses, its aspect changed. Lines of men streamed out of the blockhouse and began digging trenches, opening up long yellow scars along the side of the heights. Davis could see well enough to count the straw sombreros of the workmen bobbing up and down as they wielded their spades.

General Chaffee pulled out a trail map and began puzzling over some markings that apparently showed that the road to Santiago divided again some distance into the jungle. "Of course the enemy knows where those two trails leave the woods," Chaffee complained. "They have their guns trained on the openings. If our men leave the cover and reach the plain from those trails alone they will be piled up so high that they will block the road."[1]

Davis complained that the existing maps of the area were so inaccurate that "they rank(ed) with America's best efforts in fiction."[2] But despite many volunteers, Miley showed no interest in mounting scouting expeditions.

On the afternoon of June 29, Shafter finally managed to reach El Pozo, and after a brief look at the Spanish fortifications across the valley he ordered the attack for the next day. A Spanish relief column rumored to consist of eight thousand men (actually it was only about half as large) was on its way from Manzanillo, and it was vital to capture the San Juan heights before the enemy could reinforce itself.

The following morning, after a second visit to El Pozo, Shafter summoned his generals and brigade commanders to a conference at headquarters where he laid out his plan for an assault to begin the next morning at dawn. "There was no strategy at all," he later wrote, "and no attempt at turning their flanks. It was simply going straight for them."[3]

At dawn on July 1, a division of infantry—about 5,400 men supported by a light artillery battery commanded by Allyn Capron, Sr., father of one of the Rough Riders killed at Las Guásimas—

was to knock off El Caney, the Spanish blockhouse that commanded the alternate route to Santiago through the mountains. In the meantime, a second light battery commanded by Captain George Grimes would begin shelling the San Juan heights from El Pozo while the rest of the infantry and the dismounted cavalry marched across the valley and took up its battle positions. By that time, El Caney should have fallen, and Lawton's soldiers would be free to join the main attack force.

In addition, a third force would conduct a diversionary feint in order to prevent the Spanish from withdrawing their troops from the harbor forts and sending them to defend the San Juan heights. The Thirty-third Michigan Volunteers had been one of the last units to land and was still back at Siboney, assigned to guard the camp. When morning came, the Thirty-third was to march down the coast road until challenged and pin down the Spanish defenders for as long as possible. A detachment of officers had been summoned ashore from the flagship *New York,* and Shafter handed them a note addressed to the admiral, asking him to bombard the Aguadores ravine in support of the Michigan regiment's advance. For the first time, wrote AP correspondent Goode, "it began to dawn upon the navy that Shafter was not feinting inland, but was going to try to capture the city."[4]

Finally, the generals gathered in Shafter's tent took care of a few personnel changes. Two generals, Wheeler and Young, had come down with fevers, probably malarial, and so junior officers were promoted to take their places. Young's brigade was given over to Colonel Leonard Wood who received a field commission as brigadier general, a decision that left Teddy Roosevelt in charge of the Rough Riders.

It was past noon when Shafter's strategy session came to a close and the general officers withdrew to their tents to draw up the regimental orders. By the time couriers delivered their messages to the units, it was already three o'clock. The confusion as twelve thousand enlisted men hastily struck camp and then jostled for a position on the narrow, muddy road was indescribable. It took some units more than eight hours to cover the three miles to their assigned forward positions.

Dick Davis, riding near the front of the march with the officers of the Rough Riders, was mesmerized by the Signal Corps' reconnaissance balloon that was hovering directly above the vanguard of the moving men at an altitude of one thousand feet. The balloon, which was equipped with a telephone system, was tethered to earth by a cable fed by a huge wooden reel carried on the flatbed of a wagon. The balloon was the pride and joy of Lieutenant Colonel Maxwell, and apparently he and Lieutenant Colonel Derby, another of Shafter's aides, were determined that whatever reconnaissance was needed could be done by them from the air.

The balloon was still aloft at sunset, and some of the units were still backed up along the trail at ten o'clock that night. When the order finally came to fall out, the men simply dropped down in the first clearing they found and fell asleep, without bothering to have dinner.

The Rough Riders managed to get as far as El Pozo hill, where Davis stayed awake until after midnight working on a dispatch for the *Herald*. Through the mist that had settled over the valley he could see the glow of the streetlights of Santiago. "Above us," he recalled later, "the tropical moon hung white and clear in the dark purple sky, pierced with millions of white stars."[5]

Before he saw that moon again, one out of six of the men who were sleeping on the hillside around him would be either killed or seriously wounded.

The next morning at dawn, four teams of sweating, straining horses began dragging artillery pieces up the hill to the spot where Captain Grimes had decided to establish his battery. Burr McIntosh, a photographer for *Leslie's*, set up his tripod about fifty feet away from Grimes's position, and when the firing began he calmly set about trying to capture the shapely white plume of smoke that was emitted from the barrels of the cannons. Engrossed in his work, he took no notice of answering volleys from the Spanish batteries on the heights, which killed several Cubans and sent the Rough Riders sprinting for cover.

Led by General Kent's First Infantry Division, the troops were pouring down the Sevilla Road. At the bottom of the hill, they emerged from the jungle onto the valley floor, blinking and momentarily disoriented by the bright sunlight, and found themselves standing on the bank of the Aguadores River, a sluggish stream about ten yards wide. In some spots the river was only inches deep, but because of the press of the traffic behind them many of the soldiers fanned out from the fords to wade through waist-high water. On the far bank was a thin border of trees and a stretch of tall swamp grass where they could take cover, but again, the pressure of moving men behind them made it impossible to hold their positions. Inevitably, they were pushed out onto the sunlit plain, where they crouched in the grass in full view of the Spanish trenches. The infantry was deployed to the left where they faced San Juan Hill, directly across the valley. The dismounted cavalry units ranged to the right, where there was intermediate hill between them and the heights proper. Later, the Americans would call this Kettle Hill, a reference to the gigantic iron kettles once used for boiling down sugarcane that lay overturned on the summit.

Once the first units had taken cover in the grass, no one quite knew what to do. The officers' only order was to "await further orders." Behind them, other units were continually emerging from the forest, pushing them forward. The sun was high overhead, the heat stifling. Spanish sharpshooters hidden in the trees began firing, and the Americans, many of whom had no experience with smokeless powder, were frustrated by their inability to pick out the snipers' positions.

Up at the command post on El Pozo, General Edward John McClernand was watching in frustration. The ailing General Shafter was attempting to direct the fight from his tent three miles to the rear, but the field telephones were not working, making it necessary to wait while Lieutenant Miley carried messages back and forth.

One possible maneuver to speed things up, obvious to every trained officer, would have been to send an infantry battalion or two around to the left flank. The army maps showed no trails through the jungle on that side, but Lieutenant Colonel Derby, who was aloft in the observation balloon with Lieutenant Colonel Maxwell of the Signal Corps, thought he spotted a path and ordered the balloon moved down the road closer to the river.

Richard Harding Davis watched in horror from the command post as the wagon carrying the balloon's cables and field telephone connection began to make its lumbering way down the trail. Overhead, the balloon bobbed and turned on its tether. "The observation balloon came up the trail on its go-cart and succeeded in blocking the trail for an hour. The place for a balloon is, properly, two miles in the rear.... This one was raised by a Col. Derby, a protégé of Shafter, immediately over the line of our men, about a hundred feet above the tree tops. It disclosed and established our exact position to the enemy."[6]

At length, the balloon drifted directly over the spot where troops were fording the river. Stephen Crane, who was with Davis at the observation post on the hill, was fascinated by the sight of the varnished silk bubble—"huge, fat, yellow, quivering"—at once grand and terribly vulnerable as it hung in the shimmering midmorning heat, a perfect target for the Spanish riflemen across the valley.

Almost simultaneously, the same thought occurred to General Wood, who was waiting on the slope of the hill with the Rough Riders. Before he had the chance to spread the alarm, a Spanish shell plummeted into a small blockhouse nearby killing several Cuban volunteers who had taken shelter there. Shrapnel flew everywhere, and Colonel Roosevelt noticed, almost in passing, that one piece had hit his hand, raising a welt "the size of a hazelnut." Everyone scrambled over the crest to take refuge on the far side of the hill.

Minutes later, the Spanish began to fire on the troops who were backed up along the trail, waiting for the men in front of them to ford the river, opening a corridor of devastation several hundred yards long. In a matter of seconds, four hundred soldiers were killed or severely wounded. Miraculously—or perhaps perversely, from the point of view of the soldiers down below getting shot at—Derby and Maxwell in the balloon were unscathed. They continued to stand upright in the basket, waiting patiently for the punctured balloon to descend as bullets whizzed all around them.

Lieutenant Derby, meanwhile, had spotted a trail forking off to the left. As soon as General Kent got the word, he hurried to and ordered the New York Seventy-first National Guard to shunt off onto the subsidiary trail. No sooner had the first company of guardsmen started down the narrow path than an artillery shell burst through the jungle canopy, killing twelve men. In the confusion that followed some of the officers ran away, and General Kent ordered the regiment to fall out to the sides of the trail while the regulars pushed on through. Lieutenant William Rockwell, describing the incident later in the company history, recalled a curious sense of indifference. "I remember falling asleep and dozing for some time in that storm of fire. . . . It is a sort of fatalism. A feeling of such utter helplessness against the display of mighty powers that no one place seems safer than another."[7]

At the command post on the hill, the correspondents could hear heavy firing from the direction of El Caney. The blockhouse, which had been expected to surrender within an hour, was still holding out. One P.M. came and went, and McClernand was still waiting for word from Shafter. Wrote Dick Davis: "Our troops could not retreat, as the trail for two miles behind them was wedged with men. They could not remain where they were, for they were being shot to pieces. . . . A series of military blunders had brought seven thousand American soldiers into a chute of death from which there was no escape except by taking the enemy who held it by the throat and driving him out and beating him down."[8]

At last, Lieutenant Miley, who had been shuttling back and forth, appeared and gave the long-awaited order to proceed with the attack. The job of carrying the order to the men fanned out in the grass beyond the ford was delegated to the fearless, if easily flustered, Lieutenant Colonel Dorst. One of the first units Dorst reached was the Rough Riders. He barked out the command that the volunteers were to "support the advance of the regulars."

Roosevelt had been sitting in the hot sun for what seemed an eternity, watching some of his best men get picked off by snipers. Dorst's words set his adrenaline pumping. He jumped into the saddle and began urging his men forward. Soon he had reached the rear platoons of the Ninth Cavalry buffalo soldiers. Having as yet received no orders, they were patiently staked out in the grass, holding their position in the face of the enemy fire. One can only imagine their astonishment when Colonel Roosevelt came galloping up, the polka-dot bandanna on his hat flying out behind him, and ordered them in his peculiar high-pitched braying voice to "Charge or let my men through!"

The men of the Ninth stayed where they were as the Rough Riders came hurtling past them—amateur soldiers, many of them middle-aged men used to riding horseback but not at all accustomed to covering so much distance on foot, running bolt upright, clutching their rifles tightly to their chests, their eyes all but popping out from the exertion and the heat, yet in their irrational excitement grinning madly. Seeing that the advance had already started, some of the troopers got up and followed Roosevelt; others waited until they saw their captains give the signal, then scurried to catch up.

Up on El Pozo someone shouted, "By God! There go our boys up the hill!"

Stephen Crane felt "a thrill of patriotic insanity.... Yes, yes they were going up the hill, up the hill. It was the best moment of anyone's life." [9]

Dick Davis, standing nearby, saw the charge through an older man's eyes: "It seemed as if someone had made an awful and terrible mistake. You felt that someone had blundered and that these few men were blindly following out some madman's mad order. It was not heroic then, it was merely pathetic. The pity of it, the folly of such a sacrifice was what held you." [10]

This was the famous charge up San Juan Hill that would propel Roosevelt into the presidency. Whatever doubts the more experienced reporters on the scene may have had, the news that the colorful politician and outdoorsman had been the first up the hill was a ready-made lead. Later, a host of illustrators, essayists, and editorial writers would supply some of the heroic elements missing from the actual scene—the gleaming bayonets, upraised sabers and, in some cases, horses, since the public found it difficult to imagine that the Rough Riders, in their moment of glory, were not actually riding.

Roosevelt had no admirers among the regular army men, however. He had exceeded his orders by pushing on ahead of the regular cavalry units, a sin he compounded later that afternoon when he accosted two black troopers of the Tenth Cavalry who had been sent to the rear for entrenching tools and loudly accused them of cowardice. Some regular army officers also suggested that the Rough Riders, in their haste and excitement, had actually been firing on their own side.

After the war, Poultney Bigelow, whose brother John sustained three gunshot wounds in the charge up the hill, virtually made a career out of denouncing "our cowboy Napoleon." But

Bigelow's efforts to expose the "myth of San Juan Hill," which was glorified by Frederic Remington and other illustrators, was doomed to defeat. It was ironic that Roosevelt, who had made his early reputation on the issues of civil service and police reform, had no empathy for professionals and no respect for process, but the fact was, this was exactly why the public loved him. He was the archetypal inspired amateur, the living embodiment of the can-do spirit. And the lesson of San Juan Hill seemed to be that the can-do spirit was enough to see America through a crisis, a particularly dangerous lesson for a nation that was making its debut as a major world power.

The fight to secure San Juan heights dragged on into the afternoon, and the correspondents who had been watching from El Pozo decided to strike out down the hill to see the rest of the action at closer range. Dick Davis wandered off with *Herald* artist Floyd Campbell while Stephen Crane, Henry Whigham, Jimmy Hare, and Burr McIntosh hurried down the trail to the ford of the river, the spot the soldiers were already calling "Bloody Bend." There they found Harry Scovel jotting down a brief account of the battle while George Larsen, his servant, stood nearby holding the reins of his horse, prepared to race back to Siboney with the first news of the successful assault.

Scovel's report to the *World* was euphoric. "The Americans have carried all before them," he wrote, and the fall of Santiago was only "a matter of hours" away. Nevertheless, Crane and the others found him in a grim mood. He had been at "Bloody Bend" when the weather balloon drew the fire of the Spanish. The carnage had been horrific—witnesses noted that, coming down the trail, one of the first sights one saw was a severed penis lying in the dirt—and Scovel was furious because it had all been unnecessary, another blunder by one of Shafter's arrogant staff officers.

Scovel was also obsessed with the fate of the Seventy-first Volunteers. By some mysterious process, word of the Seventy-first's panic had already spread through the ranks, and members of the regiment were being subjected to taunts, and sometimes outright threats of violence, from men belonging to other units. He had been close enough to the confusion at the fork in the trails to be convinced that the entire incident was the fault of a few inept officers. The subject was not one that belonged in his first dispatch on the battle—even to bring it up would be to blow the incident out of proportion—but something would have to be written later on in defense of the regiment's reputation.

Despite Scovel's warnings about sniper fire, McIntosh, Hare, and Crane ventured out onto the plain on their way to the heights. McIntosh was coming down with fever, and the postbattle scenes had a surreal aspect. He saw a man who had been shot through the jaw; another, through the knee. Then, making his way back to El Pozo, he ran into General Shafter, who had left his sickbed to have a look at the battlefield.

Hearing firing in the distance, Shafter turned his horse and asked what the noise was. The Spaniards, McIntosh told him.

A little farther on, McIntosh came to a clearing in the jungle where he found a sometime rival, *Journal* photographer J. C. Hemment, in a sunny clearing sitting down to a picnic lunch supplied from the pantry of the *Sylvia*. Hemment had a complete spread, including linen napkins, real china, a servant was standing by with an umbrella to shield him from the sun, and he was decorously eating a chicken sandwich.

After McIntosh turned back, Crane and Jimmy Hare had separated from Whigham and pushed on to the top of the San Juan ridge where, wrote Crane, "the two lines of battle were royally whacking away at each other."[11] Dick Davis was interviewing some of the Rough Riders and General Leonard Wood. Hare began taking photographs and Crane wandered away from the group to a spot on the crest where he could gaze directly down onto the city. Crane was wearing an ankle-length India rubber mackintosh and smoking a pipe, and Davis could not help noticing that he had chosen an especially exposed spot, exactly the sort of promontory that a wigwag might have used for signaling.

Wood shouted for Crane to lie down. "You're drawing fire on these men."

Crane seemed not to hear.

"What's the idea, Steve," shouted Hare. "Did you get a wire from Pulitzer this morning reading, 'Why don't *you* get wounded so we can get some notices, too'?"

Crane still didn't move, and Davis called out, "You're not impressing anyone by doing that, Crane."[12]

But of course Crane was making a very big impression on Dick Davis. Everything that Crane did was grist for the gossip mills, and after the war some would speculate that he had a death wish and had deliberately tried to get himself killed in Cuba. In fact, Crane's bravado was far from unique. It was still popularly believed that gentlemen did not take cover. A number of officers, including Rough Rider Bucky O'Neill, the cowboy mayor of Scottsdale, Arizona, had died that day because they disdained to shield themselves from enemy bullets. Davis subscribed to this view. He was too sensible to push the principle to its logical extreme, but in an earlier dispatch he had insisted, mistakenly, that the late Ham Fish had died because he refused to duck in the face of enemy bullets. Struck with admiration for Crane's bravado, Davis forgot his objections to his unconventional morals and manners.

Over at El Caney, meanwhile, the fight for the little blockhouse, which had now become irrelevant in military terms, was still going on. The battle was in its tenth hour, and of 520 Spanish defenders only 82 were still alive. Yet the survivors refused to surrender.

James Creelman and Hearst were part of the *Journal* contingent that had decided to cover El Caney in the mistaken belief that the fighting would be over in plenty of time for them to go on to El Pozo. Two years earlier, when he found himself staring down at the decaying bodies of murdered peasants in Campo Florida, Creelman had vowed that someday he would personally take up arms to end Spanish rule in Cuba. Like many correspondents of the day, Creelman carried a sidearm, and all afternoon long he had been begging General Chaffee for permission to join the charge on the fort. When the time finally came, Chaffee motioned to Creelman to go along.

The scene inside the blockhouse was horrible—dead and dying men lying in their own blood, the few soldiers left alive so stunned that it was difficult to tell if they knew what was going on. Creelman began looking around for the Spanish flag, which the Americans had been staring at in frustration all day long. "I wanted it for the *Journal.* The *Journal* had provoked the war, and it was only fair that the *Journal* should have the first flag captured in the greatest land battle of the war." [13] Spotting the flag lying in the grass behind the blockhouse, still attached to a length of shattered flagpole, he impulsively picked it up and waved it tauntingly in the direction of El Caney, where a few dozen Spanish soldiers were still entrenched, then threw it to some soldiers, who began passing it from hand to hand "cheering like madmen." The Spaniards in the village, who had all but ceased firing now that the blockhouse was in enemy hands, responded with a tremendous volley.

A bullet struck Creelman, passing through his left arm and lodging in his back. He was carried down the hill to where the rest of the American wounded were lying, and someone came and threw the captured Spanish flag over him. As he lay there, waiting for a surgeon, he slipped into a state of shock. There was "a strange yellow glare on everything. Voices of thunder...blurred figures...a horse twenty feet high....Little fiery blobs kept dropping down from somewhere and the world was whirling upside down." Then someone was asking him about copy. "Copy! copy! an hour to spare before the paper goes to press!"

Creelman opened his eyes and saw his boss kneeling beside him, wearing a panama hat with a bright ribbon tied around it. Hearst was clutching a notebook, "his face radiant with enthusiasm."

"I'm sorry you're hurt," said Hearst. "But wasn't it a splendid fight? We beat every paper in the world."[14]

Creelman spent the night in the field hospital in Sevilla, meditating on the fact that the greatest story of his life had been written by his boss, who generously praised Creelman's role in the fight but nonetheless took the byline for himself.

At El Pozo, a group of the more prominent correspondents were invited by Scovel to share a box of food that George Larsen had brought from Siboney. The food was canned "fat hog meat" and coffee, but surprisingly, after all they had been through, everyone had a good appetite. Besides Crane, Davis, Whigham, Hare, McIntosh, and *Journal* contributor George Clarke Musgrave, the group included George Rea, who had spent much of the day with the Cuban forces on the road beyond El Caney, and Francis Nichols, who had followed the Ninth and Tenth regiments up San Juan Hill. As the correspondents exchanged stories, the photographer, McIntosh, found himself regretting that it was impossible to take down a word-for-word record of the conversation. They had seen so much that day, and their perspectives were so different, that their talk would have made a book in itself.

By now some of the optimism of the early afternoon had worn off. American troops were spread out thinly along the length of the ridge, vulnerable to an attack from Santiago, especially if the Spanish decided to dismount guns from Cervera's ships and move them into position to fire on the heights. The more experienced regular army officers were so uneasy about the new position that when General Wheeler toured the trenches just before nightfall, a number of officers had appealed to him to have Shafter order a pullback.

By nine o'clock everyone was exhausted. Stephen Crane settled down on a pile of saddles and Scovel simply went to sleep on the bare ground. McIntosh and Davis had wandered down the side of the hill to the Rough Riders' camp where they found an empty tent and made themselves at home. The next morning, they learned that the tent had belonged to Bucky O'Neill, the popular cowboy captain who had been killed by a Spanish sharpshooter just before the charge.

Davis had taken the previous night's conversation to heart, and after touring the rifle pits the next morning with General Wheeler, he compared the infantry's chances of taking Santiago to "open[ing] a safe with a pocket pistol." He concluded that the time had come to dispense with morale building and tell the truth to the folks at home. In a dispatch to the *Herald* datelined that evening from "the trenches of San Juan," he summed up the campaign so far as "prepared in ignorance and conducted in a series of blunders." He warned: "Another such victory as that of July 1 and our troops must retreat.... This may sound hysterical, yet it is written with the most serious and earnest intentions.... This is written with the sole purpose that the entire press of the country will force instant action at Washington to relieve the strained situation." [15]

To Davis's dismay and shock, the *Herald* withheld the dispatch, judging it too inflammatory to print. For RHD, this was unprecedented.

VIII

Regulars Get No Glory

Scovel Arrested

WITH THE DISCOVERY that Cervera's fleet was at Santiago, the newspapers had shifted their field headquarters from Key West to Port Antonio, Jamaica. Frances Scovel and Mrs. Harry Brown, the only two correspondents' wives still at the Key West Hotel, were determined to see their husbands as often as possible, and Mrs. Brown managed to charter a boat, the schooner *Kate,* formerly Key West pilot boat #6, to take them south. By the time the *Kate* sailed it had acquired a full complement of passengers: Jimmy Hare; the *World*'s Adolph Koelble; the Russian military attaché, Prince Levin; the Swedish attaché, Captain Anderson; John Randolph Coolidge, a young American who had been turned down for enlistment and was determined to take his case directly to General Shafter; and finally, a teenage "newsboy" (probably an orderly for one of the correspondents) who, recalled Frances Scovel, regaled his fellow passengers with the tale of how he had climbed Mount Pelee and stared down into the mouth of the volcano.

The *Kate*'s nervous skipper steered a course that took the schooner in such a wide arc around Cuba that the journey, provisioned for four days, lasted twice that long. And Jimmy Hare, still not recovered from the hunger he had suffered on the expedition to Gómez's camp, groused that the ladies seemed to regard the hardships of the voyage as "glamorous."

Frances Scovel, at least, was certainly in high spirits. She had solved what she considered the number one obstacle to a woman's freedom to travel, the "under linens" problem. The typical petticoat of the day contained between four and five yards of material and women normally wore four of them at a time. After her trip into the interior to meet Gómez, Frances had commissioned her Havana seamstress to run up a set of petticoats in extralight cambric, and now, with her denim skirt, Eton jacket, and something she called her "sat-upon Knox sailor top," she felt ready to face any adventure.

The *Kate*'s skipper wandered into the Bahama Channel, then fell asleep at the wheel, beaching his vessel on a sandbar. Luckily, the schooner did not encounter any Spanish gunboats, but it was fired on by the USS *Dolphin*, whose sailors made up for the error by gathering on deck to give three cheers for the correspondents' wives. Each day's single meal consisted of a carefully rationed portion of "cold salt horse" and a cup of tea. Nevertheless, wrote Frances, "At night when the sails were filled, and she was heeling over a little and the stars hanging down like diamonds on strings out of a blue beyond, the *Kate* was beautiful."[1]

Harry Brown had reserved a suite of rooms for the women at the Titchfield, Port Antonio's best hotel, and Frances, who did not share her husband's enthusiasm for Cuba, found Jamaica the tropical paradise of her dreams. All was well until the day after the battle of San Juan heights when the *Three Friends* returned to Jamaica and Harry Scovel was not on board. Convinced that her husband would not have remained in Cuba unless something were seriously wrong, Frances insisted on making the return trip to Siboney. "As there was only one cabin with four bunks," she wrote, "and four tired men to occupy them, I would not take it. They gave me a mattress, which was put under a lifeboat and I slept on deck."[2]

On Sunday morning, the Fourth of July, the newspaper boat

was approaching Cuban waters when it was hailed by a navy yacht.

"Hullo! Hear the news?" a bluejacket shouted over the megaphone.

"No, what is it?"

"The Spanish fleet came out this morning."

"Of course it did," said one of the correspondents sarcastically.

"Honest."

"Yes I know. Well, where are they now?"

"Sunk."[3]

The news seemed incredible, but it was true. At nine thirty-five A.M., the Spanish flagship *Infanta María Teresa* had come steaming out of the harbor, followed at ten-minute intervals by the battleships *Vizcaya, Cristobal Colón,* and *Almirante Oquendo* and the destroyers *Plutón* and *Furor.* Surveying the scene from the deck of the *Brooklyn,* Associated Press correspondent George Graham felt that he had been propelled backward in time to the days of the Spanish Armada. Unlike the U.S. Navy, the Spanish warships were painted in the traditional battle colors, their hulls a glossy black and their figureheads and insignia shining with freshly applied gilding. Sallying forth from the harbor, they looked as if they were ready for a regatta, their immense silk battle pennants flying, brightly colored awnings unfurled over the decks, their crews standing at attention on the yardarms.

One by one, Cervera's ships turned westward in a futile attempt to escape from the blockade, only to be chased down and run aground by the Americans. Only one American sailor lost his life in the one-sided fight, but 323 Spanish sailors perished, and the toll would have been much higher if the captains of the American ships had not realized early on that victory was inevitable and begun to concentrate on rescuing survivors. "Don't cheer boys, those poor devils are dying," was the day's most memorable order, issued by Captain J. W. Phillips of the battleship *Texas.*[4]

Like so many really stupid things done in wartime, the suicide of the Spanish fleet was motivated by the desire to avoid a loss of face. Captain-General Blanco had sent orders to Cervera and General Arsenio Linares, the ranking army officer at Santiago, that no matter what happened, they must avoid the humiliation of having the fleet scuttled inside the harbor. Four centuries of Spanish naval power must not be allowed to end with a whimper. "If we should lose the squadron without fighting," Blanco had cabled Linares, "the moral effect would be terrible, both in Spain and abroad." Admiral Cervera protested that he would never consent, "for I should consider myself responsible to God and history for lives sacrificed on the altar of vanity, and not in the true defense of country." When Blanco refused to change his orders, Cervera gave in but ordered the maneuver to take place in broad daylight, a bad time for an escape at sea but a good one for picking up survivors in the water.[5]

Although no one said so for publication, the Americans generally agreed that Cervera had saved the day for the United States. Had General Linares been allowed to dismount the ships' big guns and use them to shell the San Juan heights, a move he favored, the city might have been able to hold out indefinitely. This was certainly the view of Shafter, who had cabled the War Department on Saturday morning that he was considering pulling back his troops from the territory they had captured the previous day.

It was typical of the war that after the sea battle the Americans expressed respect, even a measure of affection, for their inept enemy, while bitterly quarreling among themselves and with their Cuban allies. After being ignored by Shafter for nearly two weeks, Admiral Sampson had finally been called ashore for a parley with him that morning. The flagship *New York* had been steaming toward Siboney when the Spanish fleet came out of the harbor, causing Sampson to miss the only major naval engagement of his command. Commodore Schley, meanwhile, left temporarily in charge, had ordered his ship, the *Brooklyn*, to execute a sharp turn to starboard, nearly colliding with the battleship *Texas*, an unorthodox maneuver that many observers interpreted as an attempt to run away.

Another controversial incident, meanwhile, had occurred on the beach at Aserredero, where the *Vizcaya* ran aground after being fired on by the battleship *Iowa*. According to the *Iowa*'s captain, Robley Evans, scores of Spanish sailors were swimming to shore when a dozen or so insurgents came down to the water's edge with their rifles and began picking them off like ducks in a shooting gallery. Robley's account is supported by a number of normally reliable witnesses, including W. A. M. Goode, who witnessed the scene from the deck of the *New York*. Cuban sources then and now adamantly deny that such a thing ever happened, pointing out with some justice that the incident was never mentioned by Admiral Cervera, who later thanked both the Americans and the Cubans for their conduct toward his shipwrecked sailors. Interestingly, it was William Randolph Hearst, the strident champion of the Cubans, who took the lead in publicizing charges that the insurgents were slaughtering Spanish prisoners. The day after the sea battle, the *Sylvia* was inspecting the sunken hulls of Cervera's fleet when someone pointed out a group of Spanish sailors encamped on the beach. Hearst had a crew member row him ashore and, with J. C. Hemment recording the moment for posterity, he leaped out of the boat, waded ashore, and informed the twenty-nine Spaniards that he was taking them prisoner in the name of the U.S. government. It being the Fourth of July, Hearst ordered the Spaniards to give three cheers for George Washington before they were delivered to officers on the U.S. scout ship *St. Louis*.

Although the presence of twenty-nine sailors on the beach a full day after their ship went down suggests that there was no wholesale slaughter of the stranded Spaniards, Hearst wrote in his bylined story that the sailors "seemed to dread the Cubans far more than the Americans." He amplified this comment by mentioning that forty prisoners taken at El Caney and turned over to the insurgents by U.S. troops had been beheaded.

Hearst reported this action with apparent approval, even a degree of relish, prompting indignant editorials in both the *World* and the *Herald*, and leading to an official U.S. inquiry. In the meantime, *Journal* correspondent Honoré Lainé pointed out to his boss that the story had been mangled in the translation. There were four, not forty prisoners. Moreover, they had been *guerrilleros*, native-born Cubans who fought out of uniform and were thus considered turncoats by the Liberation Army. Far from expressing embarrassment over the error, the *Journal* charged that both Pulitzer and James Gordon Bennett were guilty of treason— "traitors in instinct [and] traitors in deed"[6]—for failing to show sufficient enthusiasm for the war. This would remain the paper's position as long as Hearst was in the war zone, where he would inevitably be personally associated with any critical commentary.

The *Three Friends* had taken time for only a quick tour of the wrecked Spanish ships before going on to Siboney. When it arrived, a courier rowed out in a dinghy with a message from Scovel: Don't land. Three soldiers of the Michigan National Guard had just been diagnosed as having yellow fever, and if the *Three Friends'* crew came ashore there was a good chance that they would not be allowed to dock at Port Antonio when they returned to Jamaica.

The tug prepared to return immediately to Jamaica. But when Harry did not even appear on the beach to wave good-bye, Fran Scovel began to suspect that something was seriously wrong. She persuaded one of the tug's firemen to row her within a few yards of the beach, and from there she scrambled ashore through the surf.

She found her husband in a dirt-floor hut on the outskirts of the camp, too weak to leave his hammock. Along with Burr Mc-Intosh and George Larsen, Scovel was apparently suffering from a particularly virulent strain of malaria, not the more serious yellow fever, but the strain was bad enough to cause an abrupt reversal of the army's policy on female nurses in camp. Just a week earlier, on June 26, when a contingent of trained nurses under the direction of Clara Barton, the formidable seventy-six-year-old founder of the American Red Cross, had landed at Siboney, they had received a chilly welcome from the army's head surgeon, the aptly named Dr. Winter, who informed them that their assistance was "not desired." Refusing to be discouraged, Barton had promptly offered her services to General Castillo, and the entire Red Cross contingent, which included a male surgeon, went to work at the Cuban field hospital. By July 4, with battle casualties still being brought in from the front lines and new fever cases showing up at the hospital almost hourly, the camp commander made no objection to Frances Scovel's decision to remain in Siboney to nurse members of the press corps, a service for which, incidentally, she received neither pay nor any official word of thanks from the

World. As for Miss Barton, she was summoned to the First Division field hospital, where a regimental band was called out to play at an official welcoming ceremony.

Francis Nichols, the only member of the *World* staff who had managed to remain reasonably healthy, covered the welcoming ceremony for the *World*, and the occasion prompted him to unleash by far the harshest criticism of the army that had appeared in the paper so far. Seventeen wounded men had died the previous night, Nichols wrote. Medicines of all descriptions were in short supply, and quinine tablets were so scarce that they were being sold on the black market for several dollars apiece. Worse yet, scores of wounded were still waiting in aid stations at the front for transportation back to Siboney. "Why ambulances that should have been at the front are now in the holds of transports, why there is no field hospital within two miles of the front, are questions that men have asked as they died out in the cactus under the blazing sun—died because there was no one to care for their wounds," Nichols wrote. "Someone has blundered and blundered badly."[7]

There was another army field hospital at El Caney and Nichols asked Stephen Crane to ride out to see what the situation was there. Crane found the village packed with hungry refugees who had fled Santiago and the army hospital set up in the church of San Luis El Caney, a historic landmark where Cortés was said to have prayed before departing on his conquest of Mexico. The church, which had been used as a fort by the Spanish earlier in the campaign, was now presided over by a veteran army surgeon, Dr. Bangs, who was in the habit of popping his glass eye out of its socket and cleaning it on his pants leg. The wounded, many of them Spanish prisoners of war, were lined up in the chancel under a statue of Our Lady of Sorrows waiting for their chance to be operated on. When their turn came they lay down on the altar, where Dr. Bangs, surrounded by assistants wearing oversize white aprons, wielded his scalpel with lightning speed in a grotesque parody of a black mass.

From El Caney, Crane went to the front where he met up with Dick Davis. A week of living in the trenches with the Rough Riders had brought out the better side of Davis's nature, transforming him from a self-absorbed fussbudget into a good sport. The rainy season had now begun in earnest and the troops devoted most of their energy to staying dry, a serious concern given the prevailing belief that malaria and yellow fever were caused by "vapors" rising from the pits. "It was not at all an unusual experience," Davis later wrote, "to sleep through the greater part of the night with the head lifted just clear of the water and the shoulders and one-half of the body down in it."[8] Nevertheless, nothing disturbed Davis's serenity more than the news that some soldiers' wives back home were holding canned bacon and hardtack luncheons to show their loyalty to their husbands at the front. What the women didn't understand, Davis wrote his family, was that the "sauce of appetite" made almost anything palatable in the trenches. The ladies' sacrifice was touching, but unnecessary.

On July 6, the sun came out in time for General Shafter's first appearance on the heights, and Davis and Crane were on hand to watch him preside over an exchange of prisoners, which included, on the American side, Lieutenant Richmond Hobson and the crew of the *Merrimac*. Tall, bearded, and strikingly pale in contrast to the sunburned troops in the rifle pits, Hobson received a spontaneous tribute as entire battalions stood at attention and doffed their hats as he passed by. Crane had never liked Hobson, believing him to be a glory hound—perhaps accurately, since Hobson's father soon received a postmastership and Hobson himself was later elected to Congress—and he was disgusted to see that Hobson acknowledged the salute with deep bows, playing to the crowd like an actor or a politician and reducing a solemn moment to "rubbish."

On the ride back to Siboney, Davis began lecturing Crane. The public needed ceremonies; it needed heroes, too. It was wrong to blame Hobson for playing the part fate had dealt him. Crane wasn't paying much attention. The dizziness and backache that had tortured him during his trip to the mountains with Scovel had suddenly returned, and he was trying to stave off the pain by taking regular nips from a flask of brandy. Soon the flask was nearly empty and Crane was sliding out of the saddle.

George Rea and Scovel came along, the latter himself out of his hammock for the first time in a week, and they managed to carry Crane to a grassy spot where he could rest. After spending the night at Shafter's headquarters in Sevilla, they reached Siboney the next evening after the cable office had closed for the night and Nichols had taken the *Three Friends* back to Jamaica. Crane, still semidelirious, found Davis hard at work as usual, writing up the story of Hobson's tumultuous welcome, and he began teasing him about his competitiveness. Since he couldn't file his own story, he announced, he was going to see to it that Davis couldn't write either. Davis recalled that Crane "did everything he could to break me up, but I worked on. Finally, he began to tell a story of the Greek war. Now, there was no one would ever tell a story like Stephen Crane, and time after time I would find myself stopping to listen to the narrative."[9]

At the *World*'s camp that night, Crane's talking jag continued. He was full of resolutions: From now on he was going to be more productive, he promised Scovel and Rea... he would get his stories done... he would even get them done on time... he would learn to acquire that "tranquility in occupation" displayed by the wigwags, and he now saw, by Davis, the consummate professional, who had managed to finish his article despite Crane's best efforts to distract him. After listening to him rave on for most of the night, Rea and Scovel forcibly hauled Crane off to the military hospital, where a doctor diagnosed yellow fever.

Even while he was lying in the hospital, Crane's mind was racing. He heard two men on stretchers near him matter-of-factly discussing the death of an anonymous private, and he became enraged thinking of all the fuss over Hobson and all public breast-beating over the death of the socialite soldier Ham Fish while no one was paying the slightest attention to the sacrifice of the "unknowns." Propping himself up on his cot, he called for some paper and a pencil and began scribbling the article that became "The Regulars Get No Glory."

The public wants to learn of the gallantry of Reginald Marmaduke Maurice Montmorenci Sturtevant, and for goodness sake how the poor old chappy endures that dreadful hard-tack and bacon. Whereas the name of the regular soldier is probably Michael Nolan and his life-sized portrait was not in the papers in celebration of his enlistment. . . . It will probably take us three more months to learn that the society reporter, invaluable as he may be in times of peace, has no function during the blood and smoke of battle.[10]

The next morning George Rea put Crane aboard the transport *City of Washington,* which was bound for the military hospital at Old Point Comfort, Virginia. The army doctor on board was so terrified of yellow fever that he refused to let anyone come near Crane, even to give him food.[11] Even so, Crane was lucky. Most of the civilian captains of the ships chartered to transport the wounded were refusing to carry yellow fever victims at all. Those who did get on board, malaria sufferers and battlefield casualties, found conditions scandalously bad.

Fran Scovel, who came down with malaria the day after Crane's relapse, left Siboney on July 14 aboard the *Seneca,* one of the worst of the "horror ships." The captain was drunk, the crew surly and intimidating, the drinking water suspiciously murky. There were more passengers than bunks, and one ailing correspondent, William Paley, who had come to Cuba to take movies for Vitascope, lay on deck for three days without even a blanket over him at night.

Before sailing, there was a tremendous argument on deck when several reporters came up the gangway carrying Burr McIntosh, who had been diagnosed, probably erroneously, as suffering from yellow fever. Despite their pleas, followed up by a near brawl, the captain refused to sail until McIntosh was taken off the ship. Ironically, McIntosh eventually recovered, while A. W. Lyman of the Associated Press, one of the friends who tried to help him, died of yellow fever a few days after the *Seneca* reached New York.

Frances Scovel herself had to pay a ten-dollar bribe to an army corpsman just to get a few quinine pills. When she arrived in New York after a miserable six-day voyage and checked into the Waldorf-Astoria, she was careful not to let the hotel staff know that she had come from Cuba, for fear that they would refuse to take her in.

General Shafter, meanwhile, was negotiating with the Spanish for the surrender—or, as the Spanish insisted on calling it, the "capitulation"—of Santiago, under the supervision of senior army general Nelson Miles, who had recently arrived from Washington. The arrangements, which were to be ratified on the morning of July 17, reflected the administration's view of the correct distribution of the credit.

The Cuban Army of Liberation, which had been fighting under the impression that it was a U.S. ally, and despite its crucial role in delaying the arrival of the Spanish reinforcements under Coloniel Escario, was not to be permitted to enter the city for the surrender ceremonies.

Members of the press were also to be excluded. Not only were reporters not welcome at the ceremony, Shafter told one of them, but they would "god-damned never" be allowed in as long as he had anything to say about it.

More surprisingly, the U.S. Navy was also snubbed. Admiral Sampson had to officially request the text of the articles of capitulation, and the copy he received was prominently and pointedly marked "for your information."

Then, on the morning of the ceremony, after he had already offended everyone concerned, Shafter changed his mind and sent out invitations. By the time Admiral Sampson and Captain Chadwick received theirs it was too late for them to reach Santiago in time for the ceremony.

The Cuban general, Calixto García, another last-minute invitee, decided to swallow his pride and attend. Accompanied by an honor guard, he was on his way into the city when he encountered an army roadblock. A private wearing the khaki uniform of the First Volunteer Cavalry, the Rough Riders, stepped forward, drew a derringer from his belt, pointed it at García, and informed him that he would have to turn back. One of García's companions, probably Honoré Lainé, argued with the soldier in French, the only language they had in common, but the private reiterated that he was under orders not to let any Cuban soldiers enter Santiago.

Curiously enough, the private was none other than Teddy Roosevelt's protégé, Edwin Emerson, Jr. He had returned to Cuba on July 10 and was sworn in as a trooper in the Rough Riders by Roosevelt. His supervision of the roadblock detail that morning was his first and only active duty as a member of the U.S. Army.

In his postwar memoir, *Pepys' Ghost*, Emerson insisted that his presence was coincidental and that he had not recognized General García. García, however, did not believe his exclusion from the city was an accident. Convinced that he had been deliberately humiliated, he returned to his headquarters and dictated a letter to Gómez resigning his command. Informally, he urged his officers not to lay down their arms but to continue the struggle by taking on the "army of the intervention." [12]

Another last-minute decision on Shafter's part was to grant passes to a few carefully selected journalists. George Clarke Musgrave, the English correspondent who had been in Cuba since 1897, was one of the "favored few," as he put it, but he decided to boycott the ceremony rather than cooperate with a system he considered unfair. "The reason for this suppression of one of the great chapters in American history seemed inexplicable," he wrote. Instead, Musgrave chose to spend the day on the San Juan heights, touring the impromptu celebrations staged by the various regiments. He found the cheers of the Cubans—*"Viva los americanos"*—especially poignant. One Cuban officer told him, "By the exclusion of our leaders and flag from today's ceremony we feel as the patriots under Washington would have felt had the allied armies captured New York, and the French prohibited the entry of the Americans and their flag." [13]

Musgrave's gesture proved hollow. More than a hundred of the officially "excluded" correspondents ignored the Shafter's edict and followed the American troops into the city. The press had learned that Shafter was as capricious about enforcing his own orders as he was in issuing them, and just as they suspected, no one made the slightest effort to stop them from following the parade to the governor's palace.

Except for Louis Seibold, who had recently come down from New York to take over the duties of the ailing Francis Nichols and Alex Kenealy, the *World* contingent at the ceremonies was a weary group. Scovel and Adolph Koelble were planning to leave for Puerto Rico as soon as the flag-raising formalities ended in order to cover the activities of the U.S. invasion force that was to be personally directed by General Miles. George Rea was also packed to leave Cuba that afternoon, headed for the Philippines where the shaky alliance between the U.S. Army and nationalist insurgents was already disintegrating. All of them were exhausted, and most had suffered dramatic weight losses from dysentery and other ailments. Scovel was in the worst shape; he was down to 130 pounds, about 50 pounds less than he had weighed at the start of the campaign four months earlier. Still badly dehydrated, he couldn't keep food down and had slept only four hours during the last two days. Nevertheless, after seeing his wife aboard the *Seneca*, he rode out to Aserredero to interview General García and say good-bye to a number of Cuban acquaintances. The visit to García was troubling. He found the general distraught over the news that the United States did not plan to allow the insurgents in the peace settlement, an especially worrisome situation in view of the fact that García had attempted suicide in his despair over the Cuban defeat during the Ten Years War.

The parade into Santiago was a disorganized affair, with the conquering troops zigzagging their way through a maze of barbed-wire and sandbag barriers erected during the siege. The troops broke ranks going through the barriers and then never quite re-grouped. As one correspondent wrote, they ambled rather than marched down the cobblestone streets to the governor's palace. There, however, Shafter's staff had taken some care to arrange a dignified ritual worthy of the occasion. After a luncheon in the palace, senior officers of both armies came out together to the courtyard where an honor guard of General McKibbin's Ninth Regiment stood at attention. At the moment the Stars and Stripes was hoisted over the palace, the honor guard would present arms while the regimental band played the opening notes of "Hail, Columbia."

Captain McKittrick, who happened to be Shafter's son-in-law, was to have the honor of actually hoisting the colors, assisted by Lieutenant Wheeler, the son of General Joseph Wheeler, and Shafter's aide, Lieutenant Miley. Scovel, who was determined to have a good view of every detail of the ceremony, was standing so near the palace that he gave Lieutenant Miley a boost up onto the roof. He then went around to the side of the building, about thirty feet away from the flagstaff, and shinnied up a tree. Notebook in hand, he pulled himself up so that his head and shoulders were above the roofline but still out of sight of the officers in the square in front of the building.

Lieutenant Wheeler noticed Scovel, bowed in his direction, and smiled.

"Who is that man?" asked McKittrick.

Scovel spoke up, giving his name, and Miley glowered, recognizing him for the first time. "Get down from there!" he ordered.

Scovel scrambled back into the tree and began to climb down, but not quickly enough to suit Miley. "There's a man here on the roof, and he won't get down!" he shouted.

"Then throw him down," Shafter yelled back.

Scovel, however, was already down.

The flag went up, the band played, and Shafter's senior officers took turns offering him their formal congratulations. Scovel, meanwhile, had rejoined Rea, Seibold, and Koelble. Shafter, a few feet away, paid no particular attention. No one seemed to know what to do next, so the *Sun* correspondent De Armas suggested that the troops be allowed to cheer the flag. "Good idea," muttered a few of the reporters, and Shafter signaled McKittrick to give the order.

But McKittrick, the proud son-in-law, either misunderstood or decided on his own that the moment had come for the commander to enjoy some recognition. "Three cheers for General Shafter!" he announced.

The men cheered, but faintly. A number of soldiers smirked and elbowed one another. Shafter looked none too happy.

The *World* contingent was ready to leave, but Scovel felt that it would not be right to go without apologizing to Shafter. Unaware of the general's mood, Scovel approached and began to explain that he had been the man on the roof and that he had not meant to cause any trouble.

"You son of a bitch," Shafter interrupted. "You and all your tribe are goddamned nuisances."

This, Scovel would realize in retrospect, would have been a good moment to remain silent and "put his feelings in his pocket." Instead, he protested, "You shouldn't use such language to me, sir."

Shafter turned suddenly toward him and swung. Shafter later described the movement as "a flamboyant gesture of dismissal." Witnesses described it as a punch. At any rate, the blow hit Scovel full in the face, knocked off his hat, and sent him staggering backward.

Caught completely off guard, Scovel impulsively swung back. Then, anticlimactically, he heard himself saying, "You!! A Major General of the United States Army! You ought to be ashamed of yourself!"

Scovel knew immediately that he had gone too far. Shafter went berserk, screaming in his peculiar tinny, high-pitched voice, "Let no one see that man. Let no one speak to him."

"The next thing I knew," Scovel later told Louis Seibold, "about 281 marines were all over me. For the first time since I came to Cuba, I was really scared."[14]

Lord Tholepin
Conquers Puerto Rico

STEPHEN CRANE spent the sea voyage back to the States lying on the deck of the troop transport *City of Washington,* shunned by everyone including the ship's doctor, dreaming tortured dreams of ice cream sodas—cool, delicious, and unobtainable. To everyone's surprise, he was still alive when the ship docked in Virginia. Along with several hundred wounded soldiers, he was transferred to Fort Monroe, where an army doctor brusquely informed him that he did not have yellow fever after all.

Crane was recuperating at a civilian hotel nearby when on July 16 the *World* published a brief dispatch summarizing the results of its Cuban staff's inquiry into the actions of New York's Seventy-first Volunteers during the battle of San Juan. The article quoted members of General Kent's staff as charging that only one officer from the Seventy-first had remained with his troops throughout the advance. The headline of the front-page story sarcastically summed up the performance of the others: "Investigation Shows That the Men were Ready to Fight, but the Officers, Perhaps, Were More Modest."

As might be expected, the charge of dereliction of duty created an uproar. The intent of the article was clearly to *defend* the much maligned enlisted men, albeit at the expense of their officers. But within hours, the *Journal*, willfully misinterpreting the story, accused the *World* of printing "slurs on the bravery of the boys of the 71st."

Crane returned to New York a few days later, by which time the controversy had been exacerbated by the news of Scovel's arrest in Santiago. On his way to talk to Brad Merrill, he dropped into the business office to file a voucher for twenty-four dollars, the cost of a new suit of clothes to replace the sweat-stained rags he had worn on the hospital ship.

"Don't you think you have had enough of Mr. Pulitzer's money without earning it?" business manager John Norris asked gruffly.

Muttering something on the order of "if that's the way you feel about it," Crane turned on his heel and walked out.

Minutes later, Norris poked his head into the office of his assistant, Don Seitz, and crowed, "I've just kissed your little friend Stephen Crane goodbye."

Years later, explaining Norris's reasons for goading Crane into quitting, Seitz wrote that while in Cuba Crane "sent only one dispatch of any merit and that, accusing the Seventy-first regiment of cowardice at Santiago, imperilled the paper."[1] As Crane's admirers never tire of pointing out, this is inaccurate. Crane in fact had sent the *World* over two dozen stories, including several long essays that are still in print today, almost a century later.

Nevertheless, it is true that Crane was a failure when it came to reporting hard news. His sketches, whatever literary value they may retain, did not reach New York until weeks after the incidents they describe, and even then they offended many readers. The public at home, the wives, parents, and sweethearts of the men at the front, did not care to read realistic descriptions of what it was like to be shot at.

Crane's biographers have also argued that he could not possibly have written the story about the disgrace of the Gallant Seventy-first, since the dispatch was not sent from Jamaica until after he was shipped home. But the unsigned story represented the research and views of the entire *World* staff, and chances are it was completed long before Crane left Cuba. The story was filed on July 13, because Spain had begun armistice negotiations and the first wounded veterans of the Seventy-first were about to reach the States aboard the *City of Washington*. Crane probably did not personally write the dispatch, but he was partly responsible for its contents, and since Scovel already had problems enough, he may well have taken the blame.

Fired by the *World*, Crane walked across the street and signed a contract with the *Journal*, which had no compunctions about hiring one of those responsible for the story it was publicly denouncing as a "slur" on the honor of New York's gallant National Guard.

By the end of July, Crane was in Pensacola, Florida, where he joined a team of reporters led by Charlie Michelson covering General Miles's invasion of Puerto Rico. Michelson was shocked by Crane's appearance, his concave chest, his wasted muscles, his "legs like pipestems ... one of the most unprepossessing figures that ever served as a nucleus for apocryphal romances ... the very antithesis of the conquering male."

Nevertheless, Crane was eager to see action, so eager that when the commander of the USS *Prairie* suggested that the *Journal* tug make a sortie near the mouth of San Juan harbor in the hopes of luring a Spanish destroyer into coming out to give chase, Crane managed to goad the skipper into going along with the idea. "You don't think I'm going to let this damned frayed tholepin think he's got more guts than me?" the captain groused to Michelson. Crane had been telling his fellow reporters about Brede Place, the manor house in Sussex that Cora had just rented from her friends the Moreton Frewens. As a result, his colleagues joshingly nicknamed him Lord Tholepin of Mango Chutney, a nickname that stuck with him throughout the campaign.[2]

Aside from a few exciting moments baiting Spanish warships on the blockade line, the conquest of Puerto Rico produced little high drama. The Puerto Ricans, whatever their private feelings about U.S. intentions, were so happy to be rid of Spanish rule— and so eager to avoid pointless bloodshed—that they welcomed U.S. troops as liberators. According to Richard Harding Davis, the city of Ponce surrendered four times in a single day, including once to three officers who had wandered into the city by mistake. "Indeed," he wrote, "for anyone in uniform it was most unsafe to enter the town at any time, unless he came prepared to accept its unconditional surrender."[3]

In fact, Davis and Crane were drinking together at an inn in Ponce on the first night of the American occupation when Crane happened to remark that capturing a Puerto Rican town was so easy even a mere newspaperman could do it. Davis, intrigued, pulled out a map and pointed to a likely candidate for conquest, the town of Juana Diaz, halfway between Ponce and Coama. The two of them agreed to get up at sunrise the next morning in order to have plenty of time to conquer Juana Diaz before the advancing U.S. Army arrived to steal the moment of glory.

The next morning, however, Davis slept in, and Charlie Michelson, aghast at Crane's lack of competitive spirit, refused to allow him to haul his colleague out of bed. If the *Herald* correspondent couldn't get out of bed in time to cover a story, that was his problem.

So, wrote Davis, "while I slumbered, Crane crept forward between our advance posts, and fell upon the doomed garrison." Appearing in the town square dressed in a military looking khaki suit with leggings, Crane was met by the mayor, who ceremoniously presented the "conqueror" with the keys to the town jail. According to Davis, Crane then lined up the male population of the town and randomly divided them into "good fellows" and "suspects." The good fellows were invited to take part in a victory celebration. The suspects were ordered confined to their homes. Wrote Davis: "From the barred windows they looked out with envy on the feast of brotherly love that overflowed from the plaza into the by streets, and lashed itself into a friendly carnival of rejoicing. It was a long night, and it will be long remembered in Juana Diaz."[4]

This, at least, was Davis's version. But since the prank sounds arrogant and meanspirited, and Crane was extremely popular with the local populations wherever he went, perhaps Davis got the story wrong.

After Puerto Rico, Crane went on to Havana. Although a half-dozen other correspondents, including Ralph Paine, were interned on ships in Havana harbor, forbidden to enter the city, Crane arrived via the Bahamas disguised as a British tobacco merchant and had no trouble getting past customs. Crane found the population of the city in an uproar over an announcement by the Spanish government that when the official transfer of power took place in a few weeks, the bones of Christopher Columbus would be removed from their place of honor in the cathedral and repatriated to Madrid. No matter that the bones in question were not authentic—the real ones were reposing in Santo Domingo; for the Loyalists of Havana, who had stood by the mother country through decades of incompetent leadership and broken promises, this was the final betrayal. On September 3, a Havana newspaper printed up copies of the U.S. Constitution and began hawking them through the streets. The mood of the city, Crane wrote, was summed up by the proverb one heard everywhere: "Better a lion's tail than a rat's head."

A week later, Crane abruptly disappeared from his hotel and the Jacksonville *Times-Union* printed a story noting ominously that "the police had been shadowing him for several days before he disappeared." Cora had not heard from him since August 16, when he cabled her announcing his safe departure from Puerto Rico. When a friend forwarded a copy of the *Times-Union* story, she was frantic. Immediately, she began firing off appeals to anyone who might be able to help: Secretary of War Alger, the American ambassador to Britain, the British consul in Havana, Harry Scovel, William Randolph Hearst, Stephen's New York agent Paul R. Reynolds, James Creelman.

Cora's appeals put Reynolds and Creelman on the spot. Both of them knew very well that Stephen was in no danger. In fact, his dispatches were still appearing regularly in the pages of the morning *Journal.* If Crane had not been seen recently in Havana, it was only becuse he had moved into the boardinghouse run by Mary Horan, the Irish-American widow who had hidden Scovel and later Charles Thrall when they were being sought by the Spanish authorities.

But while Crane was in no physical danger, there was definitely something very strange going on. Although he was receiving a good salary from the *Journal* and had sent nothing to Cora for months, Crane was bombarding Reynolds with desperate appeals for cash. "I have got to have at least fifteen hundred dollars this month, the sooner the better," went one such appeal. "For Christ's sake get me some money quick here by cable," went another.[5]

Crane's mysterious behavior may never be explained. He had been playing high stakes poker while he was in Puerto Rico with Charlie Michelson, so perhaps he needed money to pay off gambling debts. Or perhaps he was being blackmailed. It was during this period that Crane talked of writing a long novel about the experiences of a boy prostitute—he planned to call it *Flowers of Asphalt*—and given his record of blundering into trouble while engaging in "research," he may well have become the victim of an extortionist. Almost a year went by before Frances Scovel had occasion to return to Havana. When she did, she found her and Harry's friends still buzzing with disapproval over Crane's scandalous behavior. She never did find out exactly what had happened because no one would discuss the details in front of her, or at least so she claimed.

Whatever the problem, it was finally solved in mid-November when Crane's British publisher forwarded him an advance of fifty pounds, and Stephen took the next steamer for New York. For several weeks, he and Cora carried on a "duel at long range, with ink." Cora had recently taken in the orphaned children of their good friend Harold Frederic and was deeply in debt. Naturally, she was hurt that she had been forced to inquire of the British consul in Havana to learn that he was still alive. When Stephen informed her that he had decided to return to live with her at Brede Place after all, she wasn't even sure she wanted him back. In the end, however, she relented, and was waiting for him on the pier when his ship docked at Gravesend. "There is no spirit of Evil," she wrote in her diary. "We are betrayed by our own passions and the chief of these passions is love. It is the nemesis that stalks the world."[6]

An Engineer by Training, a Newspaperman by Accident

FOR SCOVEL, the night of July 17 was like old times. Once again he was in jail in Cuba, the prisoner of a frustrated general who did not quite know what to do with him. Following the flag-raising ceremony, Shafter had at first vowed to have the *World* correspondent shot by a military firing squad. There would later be some debate in the press over whether he would have had the right to do this, but overnight his aides had convinced him that the wiser course would be to drop the charges. When morning came, Scovel's guard, Lieutenant Charles Dudley Rose, was ordered to fetch him from the "moss grown calabozo" where he was being held and deliver him to Siboney in an army tug, where he was put aboard the next transport to New York.

And this was very nearly the end of it. Nearly one hundred correspondents had witnessed the quarrel between Shafter and Scovel, yet not one word about it appeared in press accounts of the ceremony. Those on the scene unanimously felt that the incident reflected badly on Shafter, and the consensus was that to insert a description of the incident into a story that was rightfully a celebration of America's moment of triumph would be unpatriotic and in poor taste. It happened, however, that *Herald* correspondent Thomas F. Millard, who had not been present, heard about the fight the next day from Shafter and McKittrick. Both officers claimed that Scovel had struck the first and only blow, landing a roundhouse punch to the general's jaw. Guessing correctly that the disgrace of the *World*'s star "special" would be of interest to his editors, Millard wrote up an account that put Scovel's behavior in the worst possible light. The story broke before Scovel landed in New York, and when he reported to the Dome he was informed that he was out of a job.

Quite possibly the Shafter brouhaha was only an excuse. Arthur Brisbane had warned Scovel as early as the summer of 1897 that as soon as Cuba was no longer news he would become a casualty of the intraoffice wars at the Dome. The Seitz faction at the paper was always looking for ways to get rid of Brad Merrill's high-salaried favorites, and they had already managed to dump Stephen Crane. By any standards, however, Scovel had managed to give his enemies the perfect pretext.

But if the *World* hoped to protect itself from the controversy by firing Scovel, the tactic failed. Anti-interventionist papers across the country picked up the *Herald* account, using it as an occasion for editorials denouncing the excesses of yellow journalism. "One of the most obnoxious features of the war in Cuba from the first has been a fellow named Sylvester Scovel," editorialized the San Francisco *Call*, which went on to complain that before the United States entered the war Scovel had specialized in inventing news of the insurgents from the safety of Key West, one charge of which he was certainly not guilty.

From his room at the Waldorf-Astoria, where he and Frances were both still recovering from malaria, Harry watched the gathering storm, first with a certain bemusement, then with alarm. The *World* had made him into a "personality," and now it refused either to defend him or give him space to defend himself. Furthermore, aside from the harm that was being done to his reputation, the paper owed him four thousand dollars in expenses, which Don Seitz now claimed he had never authorized.

On the recommendation of Horatio Rubens, Scovel consulted Bourke Cockran, a former U.S. congressman and prominent attorney well known for his support of the Irish Republican cause. Harry wrote Frances, who had recently returned to St. Louis to visit her parents, saying that Cockran was urging him to sue Pulitzer for breach of contract. But, he confessed, "I know I never will." In spite of everything, he still revered "the chief."

While Scovel tried to decide what to do, his colleagues were already beginning to come to his defense. George Rea had sailed for the Philippines immediately after the truce, but when he belatedly learned that Scovel had been fired he wrote a letter of protest to Pulitzer. More important, Rea still had influence at the *Herald,* and that paper, perhaps partly out of fear of a libel suit, came forward with a partial retraction. Quoting Rea's account of the fight, the *Herald* now admitted that Shafter had swung first, after calling the *World* correspondent a "——— nuisance," "you ———," and a "———, ———, ———."

Richard Harding Davis was so incensed over Shafter's public temper tantrum that he spent the boat trip to Puerto Rico writing a dispatch that lambasted the general as a self-promoting incompetent and a "coward" who used his rank to bully those who could not defend themselves.

> It does not matter what was Mr. Scovel's offense—that he had presumed to tell the truth about this gross Falstaff in his paper was probably the real offense, but whatever it might have been Gen. Shafter knew when he struck Mr. Scovel that he had 16,000 men behind him to protect him, and that if Scovel struck him in return he did so at the risk of being legally shot. And yet knowing this, this officer and gentleman struck the civilian in the face. And Scovel, knowing that he might be shot, struck him back.[1]

This was too much for the *Herald.* For the first time in Davis's career, one of his dispatches was rejected in its entirety.

But public opinion was beginning to turn against the army. Few could be as philosophical as Ralph Paine, who observed that "a democracy is always unready for war."[2] By September of 1898 the same newspapers that had formerly gloried in the war were publishing exposés of the horrible condition of the returning troops at Montauk Point and Chickamauga and loudly accusing Secretary Alger of murder. The odd thing about this outcry was that the United States had won a great victory, even if largely by dint of luck, and American casualties were comparatively few. Even counting fatalities due to the various tropical diseases, only 5,462 American soldiers had lost their lives in 1898, and the percentage of deaths due to disease was actually less than during the opening months of the Civil War. To a great extent, these belated exposés represented a sublimated debate over other issues. Conservatives like Dick Davis regretted that they had not spoken out earlier in favor of a strong standing army. Former Liberty League members like Samuel Gompers and Andrew Carnegie and Jane Addams, who were transferring their allegiance to the Anti-Imperialist League, regretted supporting the war in the first place. Pulitzer, though never as enchanted with Emilio Aguinaldo and the Philippine insurgents as he had been with Gómez and the Cubans, opposed the annexation of the Philippines and placed himself firmly in the anti-imperialist camp.

Within two weeks of firing Scovel, Pulitzer was already beginning to wonder whether he had made a mistake. He asked Rea, Louis Seibold, and Adolph Koelble, all of whom had been present at the surrender ceremony, to submit written statements about the events of that day, "as if under oath and for his private information." When all three backed Scovel, he was invited to publish a letter to the editor giving his side of the story. Striking a placatory note, Scovel admitted that he had acted "thoughtlessly and without premeditation," adding, "I had not signed the Articles of War, having never applied for a military license. Nevertheless, I was under military control and should have borne the blow." However, he insisted that he was "not alone in the wrong. . . . Had I really done the things ascribed to me I should and certainly would have been shot."[3]

Scovel's letter was syndicated by the *World* and turned the tide in his favor. Scores of pro-Scovel editorials appeared across the country. Even E. L. Godkin of *The Nation* called for Scovel's reinstatement. Although a month earlier Godkin had been of the opinion that Scovel deserved to be shot, he now professed to be mystified at Pulitzer's lack of loyalty to his employee: "It will puzzle most thoughtful men to justify the New York *World* in its act of repudiation and rebuke."[4]

The Washington *Chronicle* was even more outspoken: "Is the *World* a cowardly parvenu? The moment it was informed [of Scovel's arrest] it should have turned its batteries on upon Shafter and portrayed him as he is—a pudgy, featherbrained, irritable old granny; a bully and a blackguard. It would have been the natural, manly thing, if Scovel had *shot him down instantly* when Shafter struck Scovel in the face."[5]

After seeing the favorable response to Scovel's letter, Pulitzer offered him the assignment he had wanted so badly a year earlier, chief European correspondent, permanently stationed in London. To Pulitzer's dismay, Scovel turned down the job. He had often said that he was "an engineer by profession and a journalist by accident" and the events of the last few months had convinced him that he had no stomach for the office politics necessary to stay on top in the newspaper game. He shared the prevailing opinion that "Cuba was a place where a lot of money was waiting to be made" and he had decided to settle down in Havana and go into business.[6]

Unfortunately, he had a problem. At the moment, the island was under U.S. military rule, and as a result of the Shafter and *Uncas* incidents, he was now officially banned from *both* navy and army installations. On the advice of Bourke Cockran, Scovel spent the month of October at the home of his in-laws in St. Louis, compiling a dossier to support a personal appeal to President McKinley. Fortunately, he had kept the evidence explaining the truth about the *Uncas* affair as well as supporting letters from Admiral Sampson and E. F. Knight. Fourteen additional witnesses provided accounts of the events of July 17, including Acton Davies of the *Sun,* Malcolm McDowell of the Chicago *Record* and Thomas F. Millard of the *Herald.* Millard acknowledged that he had heard Shafter admit to striking Scovel, adding that he was dropping his threat of a court martial because if he persisted "the incident might create an awful stink and there was no telling where it would end."[7]

Interestingly, Scovel never suggested publicly that his problems with Secretary Long and Shafter had anything to do with his proinsurgent views. Speaking to the University of Michigan Alumni Association in December 1898, Scovel attributed all his difficulties during the war to his personal feud with Lieutenant John Miley and, more generally, to his bad luck in getting caught up in the rivalry between Admiral Sampson and General Shafter and between pro- and anti-Sampson factions within the navy. Bourke Cockran obviously thought otherwise because the synopsis that was submitted along with Scovel's appeal stressed the political credentials of those who had contributed affidavits: George Rea was described as "perhaps the most conservative correspondent in the country"; H. J. Whigham was "a most conservative Scotchman"; Bryan Leighton "an English officer and a baronet," and so on. Help from another conservative source came on December 1, when Dick Davis's long-suppressed dispatch attacking Shafter was finally published in the Washington *Times* and became the talk of the capital. On December 15, Scovel received word that the navy and army's orders against him were being officially rescinded.[8]

By New Year's Day, 1899, Scovel was back in Havana, and he wrote the front-page story for the *World* describing the formal transfer of power as the Spanish colors were lowered for the last time and the American colors were raised in their place by a U.S. honor guard. Over the next several months, he continued to send the *World* long accounts of the travails of U.S.-occupied Havana. "There are more swindlers in Havana than in Skagway," he wrote in a story datelined January 7. One such con artist was a man named Hammond, who claimed to have been appointed "Bishop of Havana" by the U.S.-based denomination, the Christian Church in America, and was assiduously soliciting funds for church relief efforts. Through his father, who was active in interdenominational affairs, Scovel was able to establish within hours that Hammond had no connection with the Christian Church and had run similar scams in the States.

The *World*, among other papers, was printing stories that suggested that America's new possessions offered opportunities for the unemployed. JUST OUT OF WORK? the headline of one feature story asked. "THEN FORWARD MARCH!! And Join the Industrial Army for Cuba, the Philippines, Porto Rico, Hawaii." The article went on to estimate that there were jobs waiting in the new possessions for 200 carpenters, 400 plumbers, 100 barbers, 500 stevedores, 1,500 clerks, 10,000 laborers, and so on. Scovel did his best to rebut such nonsense. Laborers in Cuba worked for far less than any American workman would accept, and there were dozens of overeducated applicants vying for every clerical post. Nor, he added, was there any truth to the suggestion that there was a shortage of barbers in Havana.

The major story of the winter was Gómez's decision to disband the insurgent army, following negotiations with Robert B. Porter, the first official emissary of the McKinley administration ever dispatched to confer with the insurgent chief. Although he was denounced by Separatist leaders, Gómez's acceptance of the pact made him a national hero. His journey to Havana to sign the final papers was a triumphal march. In February, the Havana paper *Diaria de la Marina*, formerly ultra-Loyalist and then proannexationist, had come out in favor of Cuba Libre. Scovel reported this "startling political change" in a cable dispatch to the *World*, arguing that there could be no further justification for continuing the U.S. occupation: "With ultra-Spaniards and Cubans united in sentiment [there is] absolutely no further use United States [in] Havana or Cuba.... Fact that Cubans have been able to preserve order and not wreak revenge is ample proof that present combination [of] all nationalities in Cuba permanently successful.... This means Cuban independence now, or bad faith United States. When Spanish businessmen and property owners willing to trust to Cuba Libre, the annexation jig's up."[9]

Joseph Pulitzer sympathized with these sentiments. Like Scovel, he had no use for annexation. But Cuba's troubles under U.S. rule was not a subject that sold newspapers. The *World* felt it could not afford a full-time correspondent in Havana. Brad Merrill offered Scovel a choice: Accept reassignment or resign. He chose to resign.

Harry remained in Havana, where Frances eventually joined him in June. He had received an appointment as a consulting engineer to the U.S. occupation government, and he and George Rea, who was once again employed by the O. B. Stillman consortium, worked together on the construction of public elementary schools in Santiago. Scovel also founded his own firm, Scovel Maquinaria, which imported American plumbing systems and, later, a wide range of American-made goods, from steam boilers and arc lamps to bronze statuary. In 1901, Scovel wrote his father-in-law that he was hoping to begin selling hardware distribution franchises to Cuban nationals. And in 1902, he became Havana's first automobile distributor. The slogan for this venture was "A Ride With Sylvester Scovel," a phrase that evoked memories of his days as a daring horseman and hero of the rebellion.

The Scovels continued to socialize with their friends from the Havana Yacht Club and with American navy personnel. Among the yacht club's guests was Captain Charles Sigsbee who, his reputation restored, had been given command of the battleship *Texas*. On one of the *Texas*'s visits to Havana, Sigsbee invited the Scovels and other members of the Havana press corps on a cruise down the coast and Scovel found himself sharing the men's cabin with Edward Marshall. Refusing to accept doctors' predictions that he would be paralyzed for the rest of his life, Marshall had found a New York surgeon who was willing to risk attempting to remove the bullet lodged near his spinal cord. The operation was a success. Marshall still walked with a cane, but he had been able to return to journalism and a career as an editor, correspondent, and adapter, specializing in novelizations of successful stage plays.

The Scovels also saw a good deal of "Papa Gómez," as Harry called him. As irascible as ever, Gómez had few close friends but, Harry confided in a letter to Frances, the "Old Man" was secretly supporting dozens of impoverished Cubans, among them Dona Trina, the widow of Rafael Madrigal, who died of a heart attack shortly after the war.

On his frequent business trips to New York, Scovel was amazed to discover that the newspapers were still rehashing the case of Shafter versus Scovel. As the press began to regret some of the nastier things they had said about Shafter after the war, the pendulum began to swing back in the general's favor, and in the fall of 1899 the *Herald* ran a story accusing Scovel of risking American lives during the *Gussie* expedition. In a letter to his father-in-law, Scovel wrote that he was planning to sue the *Herald* for libel, an action that he hoped would publicly establish once and for all that he had been acting on orders of Admiral Sampson throughout the war. However, he had as little enthusiasm for lawsuits as ever, and against Bourke Cockran's advice he let the matter drop.

The following March, while Harry was again in New York on business, Frances gave birth to a son. Writing to Captain French Ensor Chadwick a few days after his return to Havana, Scovel reported "the youngster is just now beginning to do well. Mrs. Scovel wishes to be remembered to you, and says that she is going to make Sylvester III an officer in the U.S. Navy, and that she only hopes that he will be as good a man as her good friends therein." [10]

Three months later, the Scovels learned of the death of Stephen Crane at the age of twenty-eight. The cause of death was not tuberculosis, but the continuing effects of what Cora called "the Cuban fever," complicated by an abscess of the bowels. Rutherford Corbin, assistant secretary of the U.S. Commission in the Philippines, and a press colleague of Crane's during the war, wrote Scovel on the day the news reached Manila: "I feel like the devil about Crane. It seems many kinds of a sorry trick of fate that he should die in this way after accomplishing so much and having risked so much to accomplish it. He was a dear old boy and I shall not ever forget his and your many kindnesses to me that month on the hillside at Siboney." [11]

The Scovels had little time to mourn their friend. Harry, too, had suffered a relapse of the fever, and no sooner was he feeling better than the baby developed a series of troubling illnesses. Sometime during the winter of 1901–02 the child died, and Frances, grieving and exhausted, returned to St. Louis for an extended visit.

The American occupation, meanwhile, was drawing to a close. On May 20, 1902, the Republic was officially proclaimed and Tomás Estrada Palma took office as Cuba's first elected president. Havana, once the stronghold of anti-independence sentiment on the island, celebrated the event in an outpouring of joy and pride. Máximo Gómez, tears streaming from his eyes, took the place of honor at the ceremony and raised the single-star banner over Morro Castle. [12]

The euphoria was short-lived. Writing to Frances later that summer, Harry struck a pessimistic note. The Cuban economy had never rebounded after the war as expected, and businessmen, both American and Cuban, who relied on selling manufactured goods to the Cuban market were going through rough times. Cuba's continued poverty could hardly be blamed on the United States: Four centuries of colonialism and slavery, followed by an economically devastating war, were not easily overcome. But the island's prospects for development were complicated by reciprocal trade agreements with the United States, the effect of which was to perpetuate the deadening influence of the sugar economy. Harry complained bitterly of the malign influence of the annexationists who were interested in nothing except "the pocketbooks of 'naturalized' sugar estate owners." Their strategy for promoting union with the States, he wrote, seemed to be to place Cuba and the Cubans in the worst light possible, in the hopes that their American friends would rescue them from their countrymen.

"Palma is getting used to being President—to being abused, and goes right on showing just the qualities you've heard me quote Rubens as saying Palma had—'Honest as can be and stubborn as a mule.' " Palma had recently asked the United States to withdraw its army artillery units from the island, Scovel added. "I suppose there will be a big howl over this in our mis-informed U.S.A. But it is no more than right. They are not needed...and their uniforms on the streets certainly do not tend to make the Cubans 'we have freed' feel any 'free-er.' "

In the middle of this tirade, Scovel came out with a surprising admission: "God knows, I want annexation as much as anyone, but I believe there are better, surer and more honest ways of securing it."

This was indeed a "startling political change." No American writer on Cuban affairs had been more consistently opposed to annexation than Scovel. However, he explained, he had come to believe that annexation—"but only as a state," he emphasized— would at least give the Cuban people some voice in U.S. policies that were shaping their nation's future. The Cubans might see the advantages of this course, he went on, if only the annexation option were presented in terms that did not insult their pride and their love for their homeland. Perhaps the time was ripe for a new annexationist party, but one whose voice would be "moderate, always moderate."

Although he admitted that the chances of a proannexation party succeeding were remote, Harry mused half-seriously that he might be in a unique position to lead such a movement. He suggested that when Fran returned to Havana, as she was planning to do soon, he might consider devoting more time to politics and less to the automobile business: "How would you enjoy Washington as the wife of the senator from Cuba?"[13]

Advisable or not, this scheme came to nothing. For the next year and a half, Scovel was preoccupied trying to save his failing automobile business, and in the fall of 1904, when he was thirty-five, he was bedridden with yet another bout of malaria. The doctors diagnosed an abscess of the liver and on February 1, 1905, they operated to remove it. Eleven days later the wound had become badly infected and the doctors tried surgery again. This time Scovel did not survive the operation. He was buried in Wooster, Ohio, on February 20, in a service organized by members of the First Cleveland Troop, since renamed McKinley's Own. The tombstone the Reverend and Mrs. Scovel had ordered was inscribed with the name Sylvester Henry Scovel. Frances was dismayed when she saw it. It did not seem possible that Harry could ever rest easily under a stone that identified him as Henry. But there was no point now telling his parents how much he hated that name.

Postscript:
Still Filibustering
and Revoluting

ON AUGUST 20, 1898, the *World* welcomed the victorious ships of the North Atlantic Squadron to New York harbor by sponsoring a day-long "Naval Pageant" highlighted by a parade of warships up the Hudson River. In honor of the occasion, Joseph Pulitzer had wooden arches draped with red, white, and blue bunting erected on Park Row. Also, according to the *World*, "a Cuban flag or two gave historical significance to the color scheme."

The wording was telling. The formal peace accord had not even been signed, but to the American public the idea of Cuban annexation was already a historical footnote. And so it would remain, despite Scovel's fantasy as late as 1902 of becoming the first senator from Cuba. The reason was not that a majority of Cubans opposed annexation, although by that time they certainly did oppose it. Nor was it the Teller Resolution, which could have been circumvented if the will to do so had been strong enough. The problem was simply that a consensus in favor of annexation did not exist in the United States. The Philippines, regarded as the magic "key to China," were far enough away to be seen through a haze of romantic illusions about helping out "little brown brothers." Cuba, by contrast, was too close, its problems too well known and, not incidentally, its population too predominantly black. Moreover, through trade agreements, the United States already had the best of the bargain; as New York Congressman John De Witt Warner observed as early as 1896, America had the milk of the coconut. So why bother with the shell?

The immediate consequence of the war on the domestic scene was the spectacular rise of the man Joseph Pulitzer called GLUTINOUS. Teddy Roosevelt was elected governor of New York State in 1899 then stood for vice president and succeeded to the presidency on the death of McKinley. Roosevelt's view of America's place in world affairs was the antithesis of Pulitzer's. But for all that, he was a worthy opponent, and the *World* was never so exciting as during the years when Pulitzer and Roosevelt locked horns over the issues of the Panama Canal and trust-busting.

For Hearst, a few weeks reporting from Cuba had satisfied his craving for adventure. He was on to bigger things, dreaming of the White House.

According to a September 1904 article in *The Journalist*, it was Arthur Brisbane who encouraged Hearst to believe he had a chance of becoming president. In the postwar years, Hearst went through a period of loneliness. George Pancoast married and Jack Follansbee, another bachelor friend, was dispatched to Mexico to take over the running of the Babicora, the Hearst family's million-acre ranch in the state of Chihuahua. Brisbane became Hearst's closest confidant, even moving into "the shanty," Hearst's huge half-empty house on Lexington Avenue. Although he was ambitious to enter politics, Hearst loathed public speaking and had no talent for glad-handing. Brisbane, the eternal optimist, managed to convince his boss and mentor that these deficiencies didn't matter.

Ironically, it was one of Brisbane's celebrated sharp-tongued editorials in the evening *Journal* that did the most to ruin Hearst's chances for political success. In a moment of rhetorical excess, a comment on the McKinley campaign included the line, "If bad men and bad institutions can be gotten rid of only by killing, then killing must be done." Although Hearst ordered the presses stopped when he learned of the contents of the editorial, he was too late to prevent it from appearing in early editions of the afternoon paper. Five months later, McKinley was killed by a mentally unbalanced anarchist and even though the assassin claimed he had been inspired by a speech by Emma Goldman, not the Hearst press, the *Journal* was widely boycotted and Hearst received so many threats that he took to carrying a gun. Thanks to a last-minute deal with Tammany, he still managed to win election to Congress in 1903, but his campaign for the Democratic presidential nomination a year later fizzled when even Bryan, for whom he had done so much, failed to support him.

Brisbane, meanwhile, had become the highest salaried journalist in America. When his contract with Hearst was renegotiated after the war, he was awarded a $50,000 salary. By 1906, he was making $100,000, and by 1936, $260,000. In addition, he had made a fortune as an investor in midtown Manhattan real estate, and he was quite possibly the most widely read writer in the world. His column "Today," which ran on the front page of the Hearst newspapers, dispensed self-help nostrums and pseudohomespun comments on current events and earned him the nickname "the Shopgirl's Addison." Nevertheless, Brisbane never got over the notion that he was staying with Hearst only until he could accumulate a nest egg that would buy him the freedom to write as his conscience dictated.

According to his Genesee Valley friend David Gray, "In the Nineties, Brisbane used to plan his life like this: He would live to be a hundred. Biologically the normal life of man ought to be that and his father had taught him the secret. It was good soup, plenty of salad, good red wine, not smoking, and wearing Jaeger flannels. He would experiment with life for fifty years, then he would marry and give twenty years to educating his children. After seventy he would begin his mature work."[1]

Brisbane carried out the first two phases of this plan, but not the third. Although, according to Gray, Brisbane received many tempting offers over the years, including one that would have given him editorial control of *McClure's Magazine,* he never felt secure enough to launch himself on an independent career. Perhaps the ultimate comment on his character was made by Thomas

Edison, who wrote in a 1925 letter to him, "There are very few men whose forethought is so long that it sags in the middle.... But you must have an awful sag."[2]

In 1928, when Brisbane was sixty-four, Hearst wrote him complaining, "You give me the blues by continually referring to wasted opportunities and stating what you might have done but have not." Eight years later, Brisbane was still churning out his "Today" columns, even while vacationing with Hearst in Italy and despite the boss's gentle hints that Brisbane's minilectures on getting rich through thrift were outdated. During the course of that Italian sojourn, both Brisbane and Hearst were afflicted with dysentery. Hearst recovered in short order, but Brisbane did not. Returning home to his upper Fifth Avenue apartment, he suffered several heart attacks before dying in his sleep on Christmas Day.

Richard Harding Davis came out of the war determined to make major changes in this life. After finishing the book he had contracted to write for Scribner's, he went off to London to recuperate from the sciatica that had been bothering him ever since the Santiago campaign. While there, he made up his mind that the time had come for him to marry. Typically, the proposal was announced to newspaper readers on two continents days before the bride-to-be heard of it. Davis bet his English friends that his fourteen-year-old servant, Will Jaggers, could deliver the letter of proposal to the lucky young lady in Chicago faster than the mails could. Jaggers departed, someone called the *Daily Mail* to inform them of the bet, and soon the boy's transoceanic dash was being featured on all the front pages. By the time Jaggers returned to London he was so famous that he was awarded a gold medal by the duchess of Rutland and the queen herself had asked to meet him.

As for the bride, no one had ever heard of her. Neither a celebrated ingenue nor one of the glittering social lionesses who had been linked with Davis in the past, Cecil Clark was the daughter of friends of Davis's parents. In some respects, the match seemed promising. Like RHD, Cecil was meticulously, even compulsively neat. Here was one woman who would never be caught with a smudge on her gloves.

She was also a lesbian. Her interests were painting, breeding show dogs, and her servant, a woman named Hubert. She made it quite clear before the proposal that she was interested only in what was called in those days a spiritual marriage. Unfortunately, Davis, used to being pursued, took these statements as evidence of maidenly modesty, another challenge for RHD to meet and overcome.

When his wife did not change her mind, Davis, to his credit, continued to admire her character and enjoy her companionship. But his later years were not happy ones. His attempts to produce more serious literary work were willfully, almost cruelly misunderstood by the critics. Then, in 1908, he met and fell in love with Bessie McCoy, a Broadway comedienne known as "the Yama Yama Girl," after a novelty song she sang in the musical review, *The Three Twins*. Bessie's comedic charms included what one critic described as "a quaint sort of haw-hawy voice."[3] It took Davis four agonizing years to arrange an amicable divorce from Cecil Clark and convince Bessie, a Catholic, to marry him.

In January of 1915, Bessie Davis gave birth to a nine-and-a-half-pound girl, who was named Hope after the tomboyish heroine of *Soldiers of Fortune*. Four months later the *Lusitania* was sunk and Richard, who the previous year had toured the battlefields in France and the Balkans for his book, *With the Allies*, decided to promote the cause of military preparedness by doing an article for *Collier's* on a paramilitary camp in Plattsburg, New York, that promised to give tired businessmen a month of rigorous drill. Now fifty-one, he made it a point of pride to go through all the routines himself. By the end of a month of forced marches carrying a forty-pound pack and vigorous calisthenics under the midday sun, he was suffering chest pains. Nevertheless, he made a second tour of the French front that autumn. By the time he returned home, he was bothered almost daily by attacks that he diagnosed as "acute indigestion," which he treated by drinking warm champagne. He spent the last day of his life, April 11, 1916, reading page proofs, interviewing nursemaids for his baby daughter, and answering letters. He was on the phone talking business with a colleague when he suffered his final attack.

Of the other members of the yellow kid generation, few remained active as correspondents. As George Rea later observed, "after Harry punched Shafter at Santiago, the bottom fell out of the war correspondent business."[4]

Charles Michelson defected to Pulitzer after the war and ran the *World*'s Washington bureau for some years before resigning to become publicity director for the Democratic Party and a speechwriter for Franklin Roosevelt. Thomas Alvord, who had once jokingly signed his letters to Scovel "That God of a Man," dropped out of the newspaper business to become a successful advertising executive. Alex Kenealy returned to his native England, where he founded the *Daily Mirror*, the first English illustrated halfpenny daily. George Eugene Bryson engaged in business in Havana, where he also owned and managed a small independent news bureau.

Francis Nichols, one of the few to continue as a correspondent, went to China as a representative of the *Christian Herald* and wrote a book about his travels in remote areas of Shensi Province, where he died in 1904 at the age of thirty-six.

Ralph Paine also remained active, covering the Boxer Rebellion in China and sailing with the Allied Naval forces in 1917–18. For the most part, however, he lived quietly in New Hampshire where he devoted himself to writing fiction and nonfiction on seafaring subjects.

James Creelman, another defector to Pulitzer, wrote editorials for the *World* until 1906, then served briefly as the president of the New York Municipal Civil Service Commission. Ever a Hearst admirer, he then returned to the *Journal* and was on his way to cover World War I for the paper when he died suddenly in 1915.

Poultney Bigelow, his anti-Semitic and antiblack views unmellowed by age, remained abroad, living in Switzerland until his death in 1954 at the age of ninety-eight. Bigelow had few friends; indeed, he and his wife were convinced that they were constantly being victimized by thieving servants, professional rivals, even entire social classes. Their constantly refreshed indignation seemed to keep them young.

Oddly enough, however, Bigelow and his wife did befriend Cora Taylor, at a time when she had few allies either in Europe or at home. After Stephen Crane's death, social acquaintances who had been willing to overlook the fact that she and Stephen were not legally married for the sake of befriending a genius, wanted nothing to do with her. Worse yet, Stephen's will treated her shabbily and despite the Bigelows' help, her efforts to earn a living as a free-lance writer and, later, by acting as the British representative of the Curtis Brown literary agency, were a failure. In April 1901, she returned to the United States, where she soon drifted back to Jacksonville and opened another "nightclub." In 1905, Cora, thirty-nine, married twenty-five-year-old Hammond McNeil, the alcoholic son of a socially prominent family. Abusive and wildly jealous, Hammond became convinced that Cora was having an affair with a nineteen-year-old boy. Surprising them on the beach, he got off four shots, missing Cora but killing the boy. Cora fled to England to avoid testifying in the case, and Hammond was found not guilty by reason of self-defense. Before Cora could return, Hammond repaid her misguided loyalty by divorcing her and marrying another woman—who shot and killed him five years later in a quarrel over a gun. Cora, too, died young, succumbing to a stroke at the age of forty-five.

In 1934, George Rea learned the whereabouts of Frances Scovel, whom he had not seen since he left Cuba in 1903, and he wrote to bring her up to date on his life since they had last met. After resigning from his job with O. B. Stillman, he had settled in the Philippines, where he held minor posts with the U.S. occupation government and, in 1904, founded the *Far Eastern Review*. During World War I, he served as a military attaché in Spain where, he wrote, he "fought the war in Madrid with frequent excursions to Andalucia ostensibly and officially to ferret out German submarine bases." He found no German spies, but he did meet a twenty-one-year-old beauty, Francesca Ruiz-Morón. His first wife having died some years earlier, he "finally got revenge" on the Spanish for wounding him twice during the time he was with Maceo by marrying "the sweetest girl I could find and taking her away with me."

In 1918, Rea and his bride settled in Peking, where he served as an adviser to the Chinese government, returning to the States periodically to lecture against what he called "the uplift element," the missionaries and YMCA organizers whose criticisms of American and European trading practices in China he denounced as "emotional hysteria." Rea opposed renegotiating the treaties that granted special privileges to various foreign nations, on the grounds that anything that discouraged the flow of capital into China, on whatever terms, would hinder its economic development. Frustrated that the Chinese did not see fit to take his advice, he eventually left to accept the post of counsellor to the Japanese puppet state of Manchukuo. The wheel of political fortune having come full circle, Rea was also sending occasional dispatches to the Hearst press, and during his visits to the United States had been Hearst's guest at the 110-room Santa Monica beachfront "cottage" he had built for his lover, Marion Davies.

Rea confessed that his new post in Manchukuo was "the kind of job I have always wanted. The whole world is 'agin me.' " And he added, "I am still filibustering and revoluting, the same 'wild Irishman,' always looking for a fight and not particular whose fight it is, as long as it is a good one.... If I lose, there will probably be another war. I am willing to lose out and go under, if I can stop it."[5]

Rea's letter reached the former Frances Scovel at her home in Long Beach, California. She was glad to hear from an old friend even though she did not find his logic persuasive. ("Poor man," she later commented, "he was completely taken in by the Japanese."[6]) Frances herself had returned to St. Louis after Harry's death to care for her ailing father, and in 1909 she became the society columnist for the St. Louis *Post-Dispatch*. Several years later one of her columns happened to come to the attention of Captain William F. Saportas. Billy Saportas had given up prospecting to join the army in 1898. He became a career officer, serving at various posts in the Far East, but he had never forgotten the "pretty little Frances." The two of them corresponded off and on for years and in 1917, when Saportas returned to the States where he was stationed at Governor's Island in New York harbor, they were married.

The Saportases lived happily in New York and California until Billy's death in 1947, after which Frances returned to St. Louis to be closer to the family of her nephew, former Marine Corps correspondent Ted Link. At the age of "seventy eight minus three months," a self-described "old war horse," she wrote to John Berryman, reminiscing about the old days in Cuba. Looking back, she mentioned only one regret: "I have always admired Cora, and I would like to have known her. I don't care whether she was married to Stephen or not.... She gave so much more than many wives I have known."

As for herself, "I feel fresh—I mean fresh. It is such a lovely day with the leaves popping out on the trees, a cardinal whistling way up in one of them, and I can almost hear the Pipes of Pan, and I would like to go out and swing from limb to limb."[7]

She lived until 1959, the last survivor of the yellow kid generation.

Notes

In the notes the following abbreviations are used:

AB   Brisbane Papers. George Arents Research Library, Syracuse University, New York.

CC   Crane Collection. Rare Book and Manuscript Library, Columbia University, New York.

JB   John Berryman Papers, Manuscripts Division, University of Minnesota, St. Paul.

JP   Pulitzer Papers, Columbia University, New York.

NYW   New York *World* Collection, Columbia University, New York.

SS   Sylvester Scovel Papers. Missouri Historical Society, St. Louis.

Introduction

1. Creelman, *On the Great Highway*, pp. 177–78.
2. Davis, *Novels and Stories ("The Exiles")*, pp. 251–53.
3. Paine, *Roads of Adventure*, pp. 255–56.
4. Ibid., p. 250.
5. Mason, *Remember the Maine*, p. 263–64.
6. Frances Saportas to John Berryman, n.d., JB.
7. Ibid.

Chapter 1 The Go-Ahead Spirit

1. Blanchet and Dard, *Statue of Liberty*, p. 98.
2. Ibid., p. 94.
3. Martí, "Dedication of the Statue of Liberty," *Inside the Monster*, pp. 133–57.
4. *New York Times*, Oct. 29, 1886.
5. Seitz, *Joseph Pulitzer*, p. 52
6. O'Brien, *The Story of the Sun*, p. 246
7. Juergens, *Joseph Pulitzer and the New York World*, p. 12.

Chapter 2 Tall Enough to Spit on the *Sun*

1. Cockerill, "Some Phases of Contemporary Journalism," *Cosmopolitan*, Oct. 1892.
2. Emery, *The Press and America*, p. 415.
3. New York *Sun*, Aug. 24, 1871.
4. Barrett, *Joseph Pulitzer and His World*, p. 124.
5. Sacks, *The Man Who Mistook His Wife for a Hat*, p. 97.
6. Dr. Hermann Pagenstecher to Kate Pulitzer, 1904, JP.

Chapter 3 A Climax to Recent Victories

1. Pulitzer to W. H. Merrill, n.d. but probably 1897, JP.
2. Seitz, *Joseph Pulitzer*, p. 194.
3. Roosevelt to Henry Cabot Lodge, Dec. 20, 1895, Morison, *Letters*, vol. 1, Letter #602, p. 500.
4. Seitz, *Joseph Pulitzer*, p. 204.
5. Morison, *Letters*, p. 504.
6. Barrett, *Joseph Pulitzer and His World*, p. 172.

Chapter 4 A Young Man Who Can Scan Every Ode of Horace

1. Unpublished autobiographical memo, AB.
2. Ibid.
3. Ibid.
4. Carlson, *Brisbane*, pp. 92–93.
5. Gray, David, "The Early Arthur Brisbane," AB. This twenty-six-page typescript, apparently never published, was submitted to Brisbane at a time when Gray was hoping to write Brisbane's biography.
6. Albert Brisbane to Arthur, Mar. 3, 1889, AB.

7. Crowther, Samuel, "A Talk with Arthur Brisbane," AB. Quoted material is from the unedited typescript of the article, which eventually appeared in *Collier's*, Dec. 5, 1925.
8. New York *World*, May 1, 1898.
9. Ibid., Feb. 23, 1896.
10. Carlson, *Brisbane*, p. 97.

Chapter 5   The Peanut Club

1. Quoted in True. For Martí's life and organizational work with the Cuban Revolutionary Party, see Mañach. For a selection of his prose writings, see *Our America*.
2. Rubens, *Liberty*, p. 30.
3. Ibid., pp. 205–6.
4. New York *Herald*, Dec. 16, 1897. Quoted in Pérez, *Cuba Between Empires*, p. 98.
5. Foner, *Spanish-Cuban-American War*, vol. 1, p. 171.

Chapter 6   With the Insurgents

1. Autobiographical memo to Joseph Pulitzer, undated but written in April 1897, SS.
2. Brown, *The Correspondents' War*, p. 21.
3. Rubens, *Liberty*, p. 202.
4. Frances Saportas to John Berryman, n.d. but spring or summer 1949, JB.
5. Autobiographical memo, SS.
6. Saportas to Berryman, JB.
7. Autobiographical memo, SS.
8. The New York *World*, Feb. 7, 1897.
9. *The Wooster Quarterly*, Apr. 1905, p. 207.
10. Autobiographical memo, SS. Additional quoted matter, pages 63–66, is from the same source unless otherwise cited.
11. Undated clipping, Scovel scrapbook, SS.
12. Foner, *The Spanish-Cuban-American War*, vol. 1, p. 21. Foner translates this phrase: "the chains of Cuba have been forged by her own richness."
13. The New York *World*, Dec. 1895.
14. Atkins, *Sixty Years in Cuba*, p. 214.
15. Quoted matter on pp. 72–76 is from Rea, *Facts and Fakes About Cuba*, pp. 236 ff.
16. Ibid., p. xvi.

Chapter 7   Cuba's Bloodless Battles

1. All quotations are from Halstead, *Story of Cuba*, pp. 200–13.
2. Quesada to the editor of the *New York Post*, March 11, 1896. *Publicaciones del Archivo Nacional de Cuba. Correspondencia Diplomática*, p. 46.
3. Guiteras, *Free Cuba*, p. 526.
4. Michelson, *The Ghost Talks*, p. 85.

Chapter 8   James Creelman's Midnight Journey

1. Rea, *Facts and Fakes About Cuba*, pp. 162–65.
2. Ibid., p. 211.
3. New York *World*, April 5, 1896.
4. New York *Journal*, June 5, 1896.
5. Creelman, *On the Great Highway*, p. 146.
6. Swanberg, *Citizen Hearst*, pp. 174–75.
7. Creelman, *On the Great Highway*, pp. 161–62.
8. Ibid., p. 163.
9. Quoted in Merrill's memo to Scovel, March 9, 1896, SS.
10. Ibid.
11. *Partido Revolucionario Cubano*, vol. 4, p. 78. Author's translation.
12. Creelman, *On the Great Highway*, p. 167.
13. Ibid., p. 168.
14. New York *World*, June 10, 1896; see also Scovel's article of May 27.
15. Affidavits collected by Sylvester Scovel, SS. In some instances the original affidavits are accompanied by English translations, apparently the work of Scovel's interpreter Juan Betancourt.
16. New York *World*, July 19, 1896.
17. Undated clipping, Scovel scrapbook, SS.
18. New York *World*, Nov. 9, 1896; see also major articles of Nov. 13, 18, and 21.

Chapter 9   Shrapnel, Chivalry, and Sauce Mousseline

1. The New York *Journal*, Nov. 3, 1896.
2. The New York *World*, Nov. 8, 1896.
3. Older, *William Randolph Hearst*, p. 166. Although Older's work contains many historical inaccuracies, the author had access to the private papers of Phoebe Hearst, and her family anecdotes were drawn from this reliable source.
4. Crane, *Active Service*, p. 50.

5. Downey, *Richard Harding Davis: His Day*, p. 2. Downey attributes this quotation to an unnamed "caustic critic."

6. Davis, *Novels and Stories*, vol. 4, introduction by Augustus Thomas, p. ix.

7. Langford, *The Richard Harding Davis Years*, p. 47.

8. The remark is found in *Gallegher*. See also *Novels and Stories*, p. viii.

9. Langford, *The Richard Harding Davis Years*, p. 108.

10. Ibid., p. 135.

11. Ibid., p. 157.

12. Ibid., p. 148–61.

13. Ibid., p. 105.

14. Ibid., p. 143.

15. Richard Harding Davis to Charles Belmont Davis, May 1896, *Adventures and Letters*, pp. 180–83.

16. Richard Harding Davis to Rebecca Harding Davis, Jan. 1, 1897, ibid., pp. 189–91.

17. Paine, *Roads of Adventure*, p. 60 ff.

Chapter 10 A Tale of the Tenderloin

1. Crane, "Adventures of a Novelist," in *Prose and Poetry*, pp. 865–70.

2. Stallman, *Stephen Crane*, p. 225.

3. Ibid., p. 15.

4. Ibid., p. 30.

5. Crane to Nellie Crouse, Jan. 26, 1896, in *Letters*, pp. 102–6.

6. Theodore Roosevelt to Crane, Aug. 18., 1896, CC.

7. Stallman, *Stephen Crane*, pp. 227–28.

Chapter 11 The Sins That March to Music

1. Gilkes, *Cora Crane*, pp. 25–27.

2. Ernest McCready to Benjamin J. R. Stolper, Jan. 22, 1934, CC.

3. All quotations of Cora Crane are from her notebooks, CC. Also quoted in Gilkes, passim.

4. Cable, *World* to Scovel, Dec. 2, 1896, SS. The story of the abortive voyage of the *Scooter* and Scovel's voyage to Cuba with Captain Morton unfolds in a series of cablegrams between Brad Merrill and Scovel, dated Dec. 3 through 20, as well as in several letters of instruction from Scovel to Morton. Stallman and Gilkes misidentify Morton as the bellboy or clerk at the St. James hotel.

5. Stallman, *Stephen Crane*, p. 4.

6. Ralph Paine's account in *Roads of Adventure* is disingenuous. He attributes a slightly cleaned-up version of this remark to Gómez, saying it was later "credibly reported" to him. The report can only have come from Scovel, whose name Paine assiduously avoids mentioning in connection with the events of the winter of 1896–97.

7. Paine wrote Scovel out of his version of the *Three Friends* escapade. However, the unbylined first-person account of the voyage published in the *World* (Dec. 25, 1896), in which the author refers to his earlier travels with the insurgents, is obviously by Scovel. Frances Saportas also places Scovel on the *Three Friends* in her correspondence with Berryman; however, she confuses the tug with the schooner *Martha,* on which Scovel had sailed in the spring of 1896.

8. The interviewer was Odell Hathaway of the Daytona *News-Journal.* Quoted in Stallman, *Stephen Crane,* pp. 252–53.

9. Ibid., p. 256.

10. Crane, *Letters,* p. 138.

Chapter 12　His Luck Had Run Out

1. Richard Harding Davis to Rebecca Harding Davis, January 15, 1897, in Davis, *Adventures and Letters,* p. 192.

2. Ibid., p. 193.

3. Ibid., January 16, 1897, pp. 194–95.

4. Ibid., p. 196.

5. New York *Journal,* Feb. 12, 1897.

6. See "By War Alone," Scovel's account of his mission to Gómez written in Madrid in June 1897, SS.

7. New York *World,* Jan. 19, 1897.

8. "Private letter from T. G. Alvord to the editor of the *World,*" Trinidad de Cuba, January 22, 1897, SS.

9. Alvord to the editor of the *World,* January 21, 1897.

10. "Private letter from Alvord to *World.*"

11. New York *World,* February 27, 1897.

12. R. Morton to "my dear Harry," February 15, 1897, SS.

13. New York *World,* Feb. 14, 1897.

14. "Letter from Calaboose #1," February 28, 1897, SS.

15. Ibid.

16. New York *World,* March 3, 1897.

17. Smith to Scovel, February 16, 1897, SS.

18. Rea to Scovel, February 16, 1897, SS.

19. Rea, *Facts and Fakes About Cuba,* p. xix.

Chapter 13   The Greco-Turkish War

1. Notebook, SS.
2. Rev. Sylvester Scovel, Sr., to Harry, Mar. 10, 1897; also, Harry Scovel to Merrill, Mar. 11, 1897, SS.
3. The holograph text of this wedding announcement, scrawled on the back of a business card, is found in Box 225, SS.
4. Pulitzer to Brad Merrill, Apr. 13, 1897.
5. Autobiographical memo to Joseph Pulitzer, Apr., 1897, SS.
6. Scovel scrapbook, SS. Cora's journal refers to an American correspondent, "SS," who accompanied her and Mrs. Ruedy on the journey from Munich to Constantinople, and who saved them from being turned back for lack of travel documents by flourishing his American passport. Stallman and Gilkes speculate that "SS" was Scovel; however, Scovel was still on the *New York* on April 28. Possibly the correspondent was Stanhope Sams of the New York *Times*.
7. Davis's unflattering comments about Cora Taylor were not included in *Adventures and Letters*. See Langford, *The Richard Harding Davis Years*, p. 186.
8. New York *Journal*, May 14, 1897; reprinted in Stallman and Hagemann, *The War Dispatches of Stephen Crane*, pp. 26–27. In a misguided effort to prove that Imogene Carter's dispatches were actually written by Crane, numerous scholars have pointed out similarities to his style. However, "Carter's" dispatches also echo Scovel. Her first, datelined April 29, begins with the phrase "I start today," a lead that had virtually become Scovel's trademark.
9. Harry Scovel to Frances, May 19, 1897, SS.
10. Richard Harding Davis to "Family," May 16, 1897. *Adventures and Letters*, p. 207.
11. New York *Journal*, May 11, 1897. See also Stallman, *Stephen Crane*, pp. 282–83.
12. Cable, Merrill to Scovel, May 17, 1897, SS.
13. Cable, Scovel to Merrill, May 19, 1897, SS. "I wonder how Mr. Pulitzer is satisfied..." is from Scovel to Frances, May 19, SS. Additional quoted matter pp. 163–64 is from this same twenty-page letter.
14. "The Man in the White Hat," Reprinted in Stallman and Hagemann, *The War Dispatches of Stephen Crane*, pp. 83–87.
15. Richard Harding Davis to "Family," Apr. 28, 1897, *Adventures and Letters*, p. 202.
16. Scovel to Frances, SS.
17. Scovel to Merrill, June 7, 1897, SS.

18. "By War Alone"; typescript, in English, of a letter prepared by Scovel for publication in the Madrid newspaper, *El Liberal*, SS.
19. Cable, Merrill to Scovel, June 8, 1897, SS.
20. Scovel to Pulitzer, June 11, 1897.

Chapter 14   Klondike Adventures

1. Chamberlin to Scovel, July 8, 1897, SS.
2. Typescript by Frances Scovel, text of an article written for the St. Louis *Post-Dispatch*, SS.
3. Ibid.
4. New York *World*, Aug. 27, 1897.
5. Scovel to Pulitzer, Oct. 2, 1897, SS.
6. Cable, Merrill to Scovel, Sept. 19, 1897.
7. Cable, Merrill to Scovel, Sept. 21, 1897.
8. Scovel to Frances, Sept. 21, 1897.
9. Scovel to Billy Saportas, n.d. but Sept. 21, 1897, SS.
10. Letters quoted on pages 180–82 are dated Sept. 21–29, 1897, SS.
11. "Skagway, Scovel, and the Inevitable Result," *Alaska Mining Record*, n.d., SS.
12. New York *Journal*, clipping, n.d., SS. For Miller's misadventures, see Berton, *The Klondike*.
13. Cora Crane to Scovel, Oct. 17, 1897, JB. A typed transcript, by Frances Scovel, is found in the John Berryman papers. The original of this letter has apparently been lost.
14. Bonsal, *The Real Condition of Cuba Today*, p. 107.
15. Typescript by Frances Scovel, SS.
16. Holograph note, dated by Frances Scovel, Sept. 30, 1897. SS.
17. Frances Scovel to Julia Cabanné, Sept. 26, 1897, SS.

Chapter 15   The Journalism That Acts

1. Swanberg, *Citizen Hearst*, p. 43.
2. Ibid., pp. 93–94.
3. For Hearst's family and early life, see Swanberg, *Citizen Hearst*. For his romance with Millicent Willson, later Mrs. Hearst, see Chaney and Cieply, *The Hearsts*.
4. For major stories on the Nack case, see New York *Journal*, June 28 and 30, July 1, 2, and 3, 1897, morning and evening editions. For Hearst's role in the case, see *Collier's*, September 20, 1906.
5. Bryson to Scovel, June 10, 1897, SS.
6. Abbot, *Watching the World Go By*, p. 216.

7. New York *Journal*, October 16, 1897.

8. Michelson, *The Ghost Talks*, pp. 88–89.

9. Undated memo, by internal evidence prepared between Carvalho's departure and the *Maine* disaster, NYW.

10. Joseph Pulitzer to "My Dear Old Man" (identified from context as William Merrill), December 26, 1897, NYW.

11. Carlson, *Brisbane*, p. 108.

12. Ibid., p. 101.

13. Crowther, "A Talk with Arthur Brisbane," AB.

Chapter 16   Champagne and Ice Cream

1. Harry Scovel to Frances, Oct. 10, 1897, SS.

2. Typescript by Frances Scovel, n.d., SS.

3. Frances Scovel to St. Louis *Post-Dispatch*, n.d., SS.

4. Ibid.

5. New York *World*, Jan. 2, 1898.

6. Perez, *Cuba Between Empires*, p. 161.

7. Brown, *Correspondents' War*, pp. 108–9. See also New York *Journal*, December 22, 1897.

8. Scovel to Frances Scovel, January 22, 1898, SS.

9. "Remembering the *Maine*," United States Naval Institute Proceedings, May 1948.

10. O'Toole, *The Spanish War*, pp. 115–16.

11. New York *Journal*, Feb. 9, 1898. See also the account in Rubens, and Swanberg's *Citizen Hearst*, pp. 134–37.

12. New York *Journal*, Feb. 11, 1898.

Chapter 17   The *Maine* is Still Your Ship

1. *Report of the Naval Court of Inquiry*, p. 119.

2. New York *World*, Feb. 17, 1898.

3. Rea, "The Night of the Explosion in Havana."

4. Ibid.

5. Rea sent the original of this message, in Sigsbee's handwriting, to the *Herald*, which published it in facsimile.

6. Rickover, *How the Battleship Maine Was Destroyed*, pp. 46–47.

7. "An act of dirty treachery...," Roosevelt to Henry Cabot Lodge, Morison, *Letters*, letter #927, pp. 774–75; for a discussion of the O'Neill letter and its timing, see Rickover, *How the Battleship Maine Was Destroyed*, p. 47.

8. New York *World*, Feb. 17, 1898.

9. New York *Journal*, Feb. 17, 1898.
10. Scovel to Sigsbee, Feb. 20, 1898.
11. New York *World*, Feb. 19, 1898.
12. Ibid.
13. Rickover, *How the Battleship Maine Was Destroyed*, p. 55.
14. *Report of the Naval Court of Inquiry*, p. 109.
15. Ibid., p. 291.
16. Ibid., p. 281.
17. Swanberg, *Citizen Hearst*, p. 137. By contrast, Cuban schoolchildren during the 1960s were taught that the U.S. Navy blew up its own ship, after sending nonwhite personnel into Havana on shore leave.
18. Creelman, *On the Great Highway*, p. 186.
19. Abbot, *Watching the World Go By*, p. 223.
20. Musgrave, *Under Three Flags in Cuba*, p. 96.
21. Rickover, *How the Battleship Maine Was Destroyed*, p. 125.
22. Brooklyn *Eagle*, Mar. 25, 1898.

Chapter 18   War Fever

1. New York *World*, April 11, 1898.
2. New York *Journal*, Feb. 24, 1898.
3. New York *Journal*, March 13, 1898.
4. Crowther, "A Talk With Arthur Brisbane," manuscript report of interview for *Collier's*, December 1925, AB.
5. *New York Post*, March 17, 1898.
6. Pérez, *Cuba Between Empires*, pp. 175–76.
7. Quoted in O'Toole, *The Spanish War*, p. 170.
8. Chadwick, *The Relations of the United States and Spain*, vol. 1, p. 28.
9. Richard Harding Davis to Rebecca Harding Davis, April 24, 1898, *Adventures and Letters*, p. 227.
10. Frances Scovel to John Berryman, n.d., JB.

Chapter 19   At Havana's Gate

1. Young, *Reminiscences and Thrilling Stories of the War*, p. 309.
2. Ibid., pp. 361–62.
3. Scovel to French Ensor Chadwick, Mar. 19, 1901, SS. Scovel addresses Chadwick as "Fredrick"; no doubt he was misled by Chadwick's nickname, which was Fred.
4. New York *World*, Apr. 21, 1898.
5. Carnes, *Jimmy Hare*, pp. 20–48.

6. Paine, *Roads of Adventure*, pp. 194–95.
7. Frances Saportas to John Berryman, n.d., JB.
8. Quoted in Foner, *The Spanish-Cuban-American War*, vol. 1, p. 277.
9. Ibid., pp. 277–78.
10. Carnes, *Jimmy Hare*, pp. 20–25.
11. Whigham, "Preliminary Incidents," *The Spanish-American War... By Eyewitnesses*, pp. 11–31.
12. Sampson to Máximo Gómez, April 30, 1898, SS.
13. New York *World*, April 30, 1898.
14. Roosevelt to Henry Cabot Lodge, Jan. 12, 1899, Morison, *Letters*, vol. 2, letter #1101, p. 909.
15. Chadwick, *The Relations of the United States and Spain*, vol. 1, p. 152.

Chapter 20   It Has to Be Written Later . . .

1. Quoted in Brown, *The Correspondents' War*, pp. 210–12.
2. Ibid.
3. Richard Harding Davis to Nora Davis, May 3, 1898, *Adventures and Letters*, p. 238–39.
4. Davis's second thoughts about rejecting the commission are from R. H. D. to Charles Belmont Davis, May 14, 1898, *Adventures and Letters*, p. 240–41.
5. Bigelow, *Seventy Summers*, vol. 1, p. 95.
6. Ibid., pp. 273, 280, 282.
7. Ibid., pp. 285–87.
8. Bigelow's judgment of Dorst in *Seventy Summers* was echoed by Ralph Paine, who complained that the impetuous cavalryman could not seem to accept the necessity of avoiding an all-out battle with Cuban troops on the beach: "It was all Dorst could do to restrain himself from telling the bugler to sound 'Boots and Saddles.'..."
9. Brown, *The Correspondents' War*, pp. 214–15.
10. Scovel to Chadwick, Mar. 19, 1898, SS.
11. Quoted in Brown, *The Correspondents' War*, p. 220.
12. Ibid., p. 216.
13. New York *World*, May 19, 1898.
14. *Harper's Weekly*, May 28, 1898.
15. R. H. D. to Charles, April 29, 1898. *Adventures and Letters*, pp. 241–44.
16. Affidavit of Sylvester Scovel, "Facts About the Uncas Affair," Oct. 1898, SS. Prepared for submission to the Secretary of the Navy, Scovel's affidavit is accompanied by supporting statements by Ad-

miral Sampson, Edward Hooker, Kenneth Bellairs of the Scripps-MacRae syndicate, Albert Hunt of the AP, and the Key West cable clerk, John Atkins.

17. New York *Tribune*, May 16, 1898.
18. Scovel's false confession to stowing away on the *Uncas* appeared in the *World*, May, 17, 1898. Brainard's note, Knight's statement, and other documents are attached to the Scovel affidavit, SS.
19. New York *World*, May 18, 1898.

Chapter 21   The Minstrel Boy to the War Has Gone

1. Crane, *Prose and Poetry*, p. 1134.
2. Cora Crane to Sylvester Scovel, March 28, 1898. JB.
3. Frances Saportas to John Berryman, n.d., JB. Saportas wrote four lengthy letters to Berryman, all undated; however, the correspondence began in April, 1949.
4. Ibid.
5. *Leslie's Illustrated Weekly*, June 23, 1898. See also the issues of June 23 and 30 and July 14.
6. Creelman, "The Real Mr. Hearst," *Pearson's Magazine*, Sept. 1906. A facsimile of Hearst's letter is found in *On the Great Highway*, p. 190.
7. For Hemment's account of the *Sylvia* expedition, see *Cannon and Camera*, pp. 66–76.
8. "Kind-Hearted War," New York *World*, June 7, 1898. See also editorial, same day.
9. New York *World*, June 7, 1898.

Chapter 22   Guantánamo

1. Crane, "War Memories." This account was not published until Dec. 1899, when it appeared in the *Anglo-Saxon Review*. Reprinted in Stallman and Hagemann, *The War Dispatches of Stephen Crane*, pp. 267–95.
2. Crane, "Marines Signalling Under Fire at Guantánamo," *McClure's Magazine*, February, 1899; reprinted in Stallman and Hagemann, *The War Dispatches of Stephen Crane*, pp. 148–54.
3. Stallman, *Stephen Crane*, p. 372.
4. Paine, *Roads of Adventure*, p. 246
5. Crane, "War Memories," Stallman and Hagemann, *The War Dispatches of Stephen Crane*, p. 274 ff.
6. Ibid.
7. "Hunger Has Made the Cubans Fatalists," New York *World*, July 12,

1898. Reprinted in Stallman and Hagemann, *The War Dispatches of Stephen Crane*, pp. 161–67.

8. Ibid., p. 165.
9. "Cervera's Squadron Discovered by *World:* Scovel's Story," New York *World*, June 19, 1898.
10. Ibid. Like many naval officers of the day, Scovel may have overestimated the potential of naval bombardment; however, the shelling of Cervera's fleet from the blockade line was also anticipated by Sampson.

Chapter 23 A Great Historical Expedition

1. Quoted in O'Toole, *The Spanish War*, p. 246. For complete text of this June 15, 1898, letter, see Morison, ed., *The Letters of Theodore Roosevelt*, pp. 843–44.
2. Miley, *In Cuba With Shafter*, p. 70.
3. Marshall, *The Story of the Rough Riders*, p. 65.
4. Bigelow, John. *Reminiscences of the Santiago Campaign*, pp. 82–83.
5. Davis, "The Landing of the Army," *Scribner's*, Aug. 1898.
6. "Our Men Must Fight All The Way To Santiago," New York *World*, June 24, 1898.
7. "Stephen Crane At The Front For The *World*," New York *World*, July 7, 1898. Reprinted in Stallman and Hagemann, *The War Dispatches of Stephen Crane*, pp. 154–60. This article carried a June 24 dateline; whether it was actually dispatched on this date is a matter of speculation.
8. Ibid.
9. Marshall, "A Wounded Correspondent's Recollections of Las Guásimas," *Scribner's*, Sept. 1898.
10. Ibid.
11. "Stephen Crane at the Front...," ibid.
12. Richard Harding Davis to Charles Davis, June 26, 1898, *Adventures and Letters*, pp. 247–52.
13. "The Rough Riders' Fight at Guásimas," *Scribner's*, Sept. 1898.
14. Pérez, *Cuba Between Empires*, pp. 199–200.
15. Ibid., p. 203.
16. "Stephen Crane's Vivid Story of the Battle of San Juan," New York *World*, July 14, 1898. Stallman and Hagemann, *The War Dispatches of Stephen Crane*, p. 182.
17. Hemment, *Cannon and Camera*, pp. 74–75.
18. New York *World*, July 4, 1898.

Chapter 24   The Chute of Death

1. Davis, *The Cuban and Porto Rican Campaigns*, p. 182.
2. Washington *Times*, December 1, 1898.
3. Shafter, "The Land Fight at Santiago," *The Great Republic*, vol. 4.
4. Goode, *With Sampson Through the War*, p. 187.
5. Davis, *The Cuban and Porto Rican Campaigns*, pp. 193–94.
6. Washington *Times*, ibid.
7. Elmdorf, *Memorial Souvenir*, p. 44.
8. Davis, "The Battle of San Juan," *Scribner's*, Oct. 1898.
9. Stallman and Hagemann, *The War Dispatches of Stephen Crane*, p. 176.
10. Davis, *The Cuban and Porto Rican Campaigns*, p. 218.
11. Crane, "War Memories," Stallman annd Hagemann, *The War Dispatches of Stephen Crane*, p. 284.
12. Stallman, *Stephen Crane*, p. 394. The anecdote was originally told by Davis in *Notes of a War Correspondent* (1911).
13. Davis, New York *Journal*, July 4, 1898.
14. Creelman, *On the Great Highway*, pp. 211–12.
15. Davis's article was eventually published on July 7, 1898, by which time the situation at Santiago had changed dramatically.

Chapter 25   Scovel Arrested

1. Frances Saportas to John Berryman, n.d., JB.
2. Ibid.
3. Stallman, *Stephen Crane*, p. 399. Stallman erroneously places Scovel on board the *Three Friends;* it was Mrs. Scovel who was present.
4. O'Toole, *The Spanish War*, p. 336.
5. Ibid., pp. 284–83.
6. "Treason," editorial in the New York *Journal*, July 11, 1898.
7. New York *World*, July 5, 1898. See also July 7 and 8.
8. Davis, *The Cuban and Porto Rican Campaigns*, p. 281.
9. Stallman, *Stephen Crane*, p. 403.
10. Stallman and Hagemann, *The War Dispatches of Stephen Crane*, pp. 187–90.
11. Crane, "War Memories," ibid., p. 292.
12. Pérez, *Cuba Between Empires*, pp. 209–10.
13. Musgrave, *Under Three Flags in Cuba*, pp. 347–56.
14. Scovel's account of this incident appeared in the New York *World*, Aug. 10, 1889. Supporting eyewitness accounts by Louis Seibold,

George Rea, Sir Bryan Leighton, and others were attached to Scovel's subsequent appeal to the Secretary of the Army. SS. Ralph Paine, who was not present, gives a very different version in *Roads of Adventure*.

Chapter 26   Lord Tholepin Conquers Puerto Rico

1. Seitz, *Joseph Pulitzer*, p. 241. See also Seitz, "Stephen Crane: War Correspondent."
2. Michelson, introduction to Crane, *Works*, vol. 12.
3. "The Puerto Rican Campaign," *Scribner's*, Nov. 1898. Davis blundered into the town of Coamo twenty minutes ahead of the army and found himself accepting the mayor's surrender.
4. "How Stephen Crane Took Juana Dias," Stallman and Hagemann, *The War Dispatches of Stephen Crane*, pp. 196–99.
5. Stephen Crane to Paul Revere Reynolds, October 20, 1898, *Letters*, p. 189.
6. Cora Crane, notebook, CC.

Chapter 27   An Engineer by Training, a Newspaperman by Accident

1. Washington *Times*, Dec. 1, 1898, SS.
2. Paine, *Roads of Adventure*, p. 263.
3. New York *World*, August 10, 1898.
4. Quoted in the Washington *Chronicle*, Aug. 13, 1898.
5. Ibid. Over 1,000 clippings related to the same incident are found in the Scovel papers.
6. Autobiographical memo, SS.
7. Statement of T. F. Millard, Shafter file, SS.
8. Scovel's letter of thanks to McKinley, dated Dec. 22, 1898, is in the McKinley Papers, Library of Congress.
9. Sylvester Scovel to the *World*, n.d. but Feb. 1899, SS.
10. Scovel to Chadwick, Mar. 19, 1900, SS.
11. Rutherford Corbin to Sylvester Scovel, July 29, 1900, SS.
12. Pérez, *Cuba Between Empires*, p. 368.
13. Scovel to Frances, Sept. 17, 1902, SS.

Postscript   Still Filibustering and Revoluting

1. Gray, "The Early Arthur Brisbane," n.d., AB.
2. Thomas Alva Edison to Arthur Brisbane, Apr. 20, 1925, AB.

3. Quoted in Langford, *The Richard Harding Davis Years,* p. 274.
4. George Rea to Frances Saportas, Mar. 26, 1934, SS.
5. Ibid.
6. Frances Saportas to John Berryman, n.d., JB.
7. Ibid.

Bibliography

IN THE COURSE of my research I consulted the following manuscript collections: American Committee for the Statue of Liberty, New York Public Library; John Berryman Papers, Wilson Library, University of Minnesota; Brisbane Papers, George Arents Research Library, Syracuse University; Crane Collection, Rare Book and Manuscript Library, Columbia University; Richard Harding Davis Collection, Alderman Library, University of Virginia; William McKinley Papers, Library of Congress; Pulitzer Papers, Columbia University; Sylvester Scovel Papers, Missouri Historical Society; Don Seitz Papers, New York Public Library; and New York *World* Collection, Columbia University.

I perused back files of the New York *World*, the *Journal* (morning and evening editions) and the New York *Herald* from May 1895 to January 1899, as well as the relevant issues of *Harper's Weekly, Leslie's Illustrated Weekly* and *Scribner's*. Individual articles from the latter publications are not listed individually in the bibliography unless they are of exceptional importance.

Also consulted were the Atlanta *Constitution*, Brooklyn *Eagle*, Chicago *Tribune*, Jacksonville *Times-Union*, London *Daily Mail*, St. Louis *Post-Dispatch*, and *Stephen Crane Newsletter*, vols. 2–5.

Only the most important periodical articles consulted are included in the bibliography.

Abbot, Willis J. *Watching the World Go By*. Boston, 1933.

Atkins, Edwin F. *Sixty Years in Cuba*, Cambridge, Mass., 1926.

Allen, Douglas, *Frederic Remington and the Spanish-American War*. New York, 1971.

Baker, Ray Stannard. "How the News of the War is Reported." *McClure's Magazine* (Sept. 1898).

Barrett, James Wyman. *Joseph Pulitzer and His World*. New York, 1941.

———. *The World, the Flesh and Messrs. Pulitzer*. New York, 1931.

Bassan, Maurice. *Stephen Crane: A Collection of Critical Essays*. Englewood Cliffs, N. J., 1967.

Beals, Carleton. *The Crime of Cuba*. Philadelphia, 1937.

Beer, Thomas. *Stephen Crane*. New York, 1923.

Berton, Pierre. *The Klondike*. New York, 1958.

Berryman, John. *Stephen Crane*. New York, 1950.

Bigelow, John, Jr. *Reminiscences of the Santiago Campaign*. New York, 1899.

Bigelow, Poultney. "The Battle of Cabañas." *Harper's Weekly* (May 28, 1898).

———. "In Camp at Tampa." *Harper's Weekly* (June 4, 1898).

———. *Seventy Summers*. 2 vols. New York, 1925.

Blanchet, Christian, and Bertrand Dard. *Statue of Liberty: The First Hundred Years*. English-language version by Bernard A. Weisberger. Boston, 1985.

Bonsal, Stephen. *The Real Condition of Cuba Today*. New York, 1897.

Brisbane, Arthur. "The Modern Newspaper in Wartime." *Cosmopolitan* (Sept. 1898).

Brown, Charles H. *The Correspondents' War*. New York, 1967.

Bullard, F. Lauriston. *Famous War Correspondents*. Boston, 1914.

Carlson, Oliver. *Brisbane*. New York, 1937.

Carnes, Cecil. *Jimmy Hare, News Photographer*. New York, 1940.

Chadwick, French Ensor. *The Relations of the United States and Spain*. 3 vols. New York, 1909, 1911.

Chaney, Lindsey, and Michelle Cieply. *The Hearsts*. New York, 1981.

Cisneros, Evangelina, and Karl Decker. *The Story of Evangelina Cisneros*. Richmond, Va., 1897.

Cockerill, John A. "Some Phases of Contemporary Journalism," *Cosmopolitan* (Oct. 1982).

Crane, Stephen. *Active Service.* New York, 1899.

———. *Letters.* Edited by R. W. Stallman and Lillian Gilkes. New York, 1960.

———. *Prose and Poetry.* (Library of America Edition). Edited by J. C. Levenson. New York, 1984.

Creelman, James. *On the Great Highway.* Boston, 1901.

———. "The Real Mr. Hearst." *Pearson's Magazine.* (Sept. 1906).

Cuba. Archivo Nacional. *Inventario General del Archivo del Partido Revolucionario Cubano.* Vol. 11. Correspondencia Diplomática. Havana, 1917.

Davis, Charles Belmont. *Adventures and Letters of Richard Harding Davis.* New York, 1917.

Davis, Richard Harding. "The Battle of San Juan." *Scribner's* (Oct. 1898).

———. *Cuba in War Time.* New York, 1897.

———. "The First Bombardment." *Scribner's* (July 1898).

———. "The Landing of the Army." *Scribner's* (August 1898).

———. *The Novels and Stories of Richard Harding Davis.* 12 vols. New York, 1917.

———. *Notes of a War Correspondent.* New York, 1910.

———. *The Cuban and Porto Rican Campaigns.* New York, 1898.

———. "In the Rifle Pits." *Scribner's* (Dec. 1898).

———. "The Rocking Chair Period of the War"; "The Landing of the Army." *Scribner's* (July 1898).

———. "The Rough Riders' Fight at Guásimas." *Scribner's* (Sept. 1898).

———. *Three Gringos in Venezuela and Central America.* New York, 1896.

Downey, Fairfax. *Richard Harding Davis and His Day.* New York, 1933.

Elmendorf, John E., ed. *Memorial Souvenir: The 71st Regiment New York Volunteers in Cuba.* New York, 1899.

Emerson, Edwin, Jr. "Alone in Porto Rico." *Century.* Sept. 1898.

———. Serialized letters. *Leslie's Illustrated Weekly* (May 5, 12, 19; June 9, 23, 30; July 14, 1898).

———. *Pepys' Ghost.* Boston, 1899.

Emery, Edwin. *The Press and America.* 3rd ed. Englewood Cliffs, N. J., 1972.

Foner, Philip S. *Antonio Maceo.* New York, 1977.

———. *The Spanish-Cuban-American War and the Birth of American Imperialism.* 2 vols. New York, 1972.

Flint, Grover. *Marching With Gomez.* New York, 1898.

Friedel, Frank. *The Splendid Little War.* Boston, 1958.

Gilkes, Lillian. *Cora Crane.* Bloomington, Ind., 1960.

Ginger, Ray. *The Age Of Excess: The United States From 1877 to 1914.* 2nd. ed. New York, 1975.

Gompers, Samuel. *Seventy Years of Life and Labor.* New York, 1925.

Goode, W. A. M. *With Sampson Through the War.* New York, 1899.

Guiteras, John. *Free Cuba.* Philadelphia, 1896.

Halstead, Murat. *The Story of Cuba.* Akron, Ohio. 1898.

Hemment, John C. *Cannon and Camera.* New York, 1898.

Hubbard, Elbert. *Message to Garcia.* East Aurora, N. Y., 1899.

Inglis, William. "Celebrities at Home." *Harper's Weekly.* (Jan. 9, 1909).

Irwin, Will. "The Fourth Current." *Collier's.* (Feb. 18, 1911).

Juergens, George. *Joseph Pulitzer and the New York World.* Princeton, N. J., 1966.

Knight, E. F. *Reminiscences.* London, 1923.

Langford, Gerald. *The Richard Harding Davis Years.* New York, 1961.

LaFeber, Walter. *The New Empire: An Interpretation of American Expansion, 1860–1898.* Ithaca, N. Y., 1963.

Leech, Margaret. *In the Days of McKinley.* New York, 1959.

McIntosh, Burr. *The Little I Saw of Cuba.* New York, 1899.

Mañach, Jorge. *Martí, Apostle of Freedom.* Translated by Gabriela Mistral. New York, 1950.

Marshall, Edward. *The Story of the Rough Riders.* New York, 1898.

———. "A Wounded Correspondent's Recollections of Guasimas." *Scribner's* (Sept. 1898).

Martí, José. *Inside the Monster.* Edited by Philip S. Foner. New York, 1975.

———. *Our America.* Edited by Philip S. Foner. New York, 1977.

Mason, Gregory. *Remember the Maine.* New York, 1939.

Meriwether, Walter Scott. "Remembering the Maine." United States Naval Institute Proceedings. May 1948.

Michelson, Charles S. *The Ghost Talks.* New York, 1944.

Miley, John D. *In Cuba With Shafter.* New York, 1899.

Millis, Walter. *The Martial Spirit.* Boston, 1931.

Morison, Elting E., ed. *The Letters of Theodore Roosevelt.* 8 vols. Cambridge, Mass., 1951–54.

Musgrave, George Clarke. *Under Three Flags in Cuba.* Boston, 1899.

Nevins, Allen. *Ordeal of the Union.* Vol. 2, *A House Divided.* New York, 1947.

"Newspaper Correspondents in the War." *Review of Reviews* (Oct. 1898).

"Newspapermen in the War." *Literary Digest* (Oct. 15, 1898).

Older, Mrs. Fremont. *William Randolph Hearst: American*. New York, 1936.

O'Toole, G. J. A. *The Spanish War: An American Epic—1898*. New York, 1984.

Paine, Ralph D. *Roads of Adventure*. Boston, 1925.

Partido Revolucionario Cubano. *La Revolución del '95*. 5 vols. Havana, 1932–37.

Pérez, Louis A., Jr. *Cuba Between Empires*. Pittsburgh, 1983.

———. *Cuba Under the Platt Amendment: 1902–1904*. Pittsburgh, 1986.

Rea, George Bronson. *Facts and Fakes About Cuba*. New York, 1897.

———. "The Night of the Explosion in Havana." *Harper's Weekly*. (March 5, 1898).

Rickover, H. G. *How the Battleship Maine Was Destroyed*. Department of the Navy, Washington, D.C., 1976.

Roosevelt, Theodore. *An Autobiography*. New York, 1913.

———. *The Rough Riders*. New York, 1904.

Rosehault, Charles J. *When Dana Was the Sun*. New York, 1931.

Rowan, A. S., and M. M. Ramsey. *The Island of Cuba*. New York, 1896.

Rubens, Horatio S. *Liberty: The Story of Cuba*. New York, 1932.

Sacks, Oliver. *The Man Who Mistook His Wife for a Hat: And Other Clinical Tales*. New York, 1987.

St. Johns, Adela Rogers. *The Honeycomb*. Garden City, N. Y., 1969.

Seitz, Don Carlos. *The James Gordon Bennetts*. Indianapolis, 1928.

———. *Joseph Pulitzer: His Life and Letters*. New York, 1924.

———. "Stephen Crane: War Correspondent." *Bookman* (Feb. 1933).

The Spanish American War: The Events Described by Eye-Witnesses. Chicago, 1899.

Stallman, Ralph W. *Stephen Crane: A Biography*. New York, 1968.

Stallman, Ralph W., and E. R. Hagemann, eds. *The War Dispatches of Stephen Crane*. New York, 1964.

Steffens, Lincoln. "Hearst, the Man of Mystery." *American Magazine*. (Nov. 1906).

Stone, Candace. *Dana and the Sun*. New York, 1938.

Swanberg, W. A. *Citizen Hearst*. New York, 1961.

———. *Pulitzer*. New York, 1967.

True, Marshall M. "Revolutionaries in Exile: The Cuban Revolutionary Party, 1891–1899." Ph.D. dissertation, University of Virginia, 1965.

Watson, Thomas E. Untitled article on W. R. Hearst. *Watson's Jeffersonian Magazine* (Feb. 1907).

U. S. Congress. Senate. *Cuban Correspondence*. 55th Cong., 2nd sess., S. Doc. 230.

U.S. Navy. *Report of the Naval Court of Inquiry Upon the Destruction of the United States Battleship Maine in Havana Harbor, February 15th, 1898.*

Waugh, Coulton. *The Comics.* New York, 1947.

Wisan, Joseph E. *The Cuban Crisis as Reflected in the New York Press.* New York, 1934.

Young, James Rankin, with J. Hampton Moore. *Reminiscences and Thrilling Stories of the War by Returned Heroes.* Pictorial edition. Philadelphia, 1899.

Index